How the Vote Was Won

How the Vote Was Won

Woman Suffrage in the Western United States, 1868–1914

Rebecca J. Mead

NEW YORK UNIVERSITY PRESS

New York and London

NEW YORK UNIVERSITY PRESS
New York and London
www.nyupress.org

First published in paperback in 2006.

Library of Congress Cataloging-in-Publication Data
Mead, Rebecca J.
How the vote was won : woman suffrage in the
western United States, 1868–1914 / Rebecca J. Mead.
p. cm.
Includes bibliographical references aned index.
ISBN-10: 0–8147–5676–x (cloth : alk. paper)
ISBN-13: 978–0–8147–5676–8 (cloth : alk. paper)
ISBN-10: 0–8147–5722–7 (pbk : alk. paper)
ISBN-13: 978–0–8147–5722–2 (pbk : alk. paper)
1. Women—Suffrage—West (U.S.)—History.   I. Title.
JK1896.M4   2004
324.6'23'0978—dc22   2003017731

New York University Press books are printed on acid-free paper,
and their binding materials are chosen for strength and durability.

Manufactured in the United States of America

c 10 9 8 7 6 5 4 3 2 1
p 10 9 8 7 6 5 4 3 2 1

Contents

Illustrations appear as a group following p. 52

Acknowledgments

Any book project is long and complicated, but finishing it is a bittersweet accomplishment. Certainly one hopes that the work has been worthwhile and that others will find insight and value in the results, yet no creative project ever realizes its initial inspiration. Further, as a human product, by definition it can never be perfect, so inevitably errors and flaws will remain even after careful researching, writing, and editing, and for these I assume full responsibility.

Yet the project would never have been possible at all without the support I have received from innumerable sources. First, I wish to acknowledge my debt to all the local historians, scholars, and graduate students who prepared the many detailed studies over the years that have provided much of the basic information for this project. Even when they lack great analytical depth, I could not have done a broad synthetic regional study without these data. Second, I must thank the friends and colleagues who affectionately pushed and prodded me along. Most significantly, my adviser and friend, Ellen DuBois, has been stalwart in her unflagging support. Other colleagues who have provided both personal and professional assistance include Joyce Appleby, Steve Aron, Jackie Braitman, Karen Brodkin, Kathy Brown, Robert Cherny, William Deverell, John Durham, Susan Englander, Liz Faue, Anibel Ferus-Comelo, Rochelle Gatlin, Gayle Gullett, Darryl Holter, Elizabeth Jameson, Robert Johnston, Sherry Katz, Regina Lark, Dianne Layden, Barbara Loomis, Valerie Matsumoto, Melissa Meyer, Jonathan Nashel, Emily Rader, Jan Reiff, Lisa Rubens, Donna Schuele, Ralph Shaffer, and Jules Tygiel. Over the years, I have also benefited from the comments of members of my various dissertation and discussion groups, including Rumi Yasutake, Anastasia Christman, Jennifer Koslow, Lisa Materson, Allison Sneider, and Daniel Hurewitz. My apologies to anyone I have overlooked.

Third, I must thank the many helpful librarians and archivists who facilitated my research and shared material with me. No historian can do any study without such assistance, but academics often tend to forget this contribution after the acknowledgments have been written. Fourth, this study was made possible by grants from the UCLA History Department, the UCLA Center for the Study of Women, the Huntington Library in San Marino, California, and a decade of 60- to 80-hour work weeks.

I also want to thank the folks who have provided so much personal support, including Linda Bernard, Grace Hawes, Mark and Marie Hoeppner, Greg Kington, Theone Masoner, Ellen Schmeding, and my beloved cats. I also owe a debt to the resurgent Los Angeles labor movement of the 1990s. The basic idea of labor as the overlooked function in the suffrage equation occurred to me long before I had any practical experience, but my own antisweatshop activity gave it substance. As I studied the experiences of suffragists learning to be streetspeakers and activists, I could understand the process precisely because I was going through the same thing, doing my best to combine theory and practice.

Finally, I want to thank my parents, Richard Thomas Mead and Carol McGaughey Mead. Although neither of them lived to see this result, they taught me early and often about the importance of creative imagination, moral integrity, and communicative action. This book is dedicated to them, and to the spirit of adventure and intellectual challenge that they embodied.

Acronyms

AFL   American Federation of Labor
AWSA American Woman Suffrage Association
CESA   California Equal Suffrage Association
CESL   College Equal Suffrage League
CFL   California Federation of Labor
CFWC California Federation of Women's Clubs
CLJ   Citizens League for Justice
CU   Congressional Union
EFL   Equal Franchise League
ESL   Equal Suffrage League
GFWC General Federation of Women's Clubs
HWS   *History of Woman Suffrage*
IWW   Industrial Workers of the World
LWV   League of Women Voters
MWSA Montana Woman Suffrage Association
NAWSA National American Woman Suffrage Association
NCWV National Council of Women Voters
NESA Nevada Equal Suffrage Association
NWP   National Woman's Party
NWSA National Woman Suffrage Association
OESA Oregon Equal Suffrage Association
PCWPA Pacific Coast Women's Press Association
PEL   Political Equality League

SFLC	San Francisco Labor Council
SFWSA	San Francisco Woman Suffrage Association
SUP	Sailors Union of the Pacific
ULP	Union Labor Party
WCTU	Woman's Christian Temperance Union
WESA	Washington Equal Suffrage Association
WESL	Wage Earners Suffrage League
WFM	Western Federation of Miners
WLU	Western Labor Union
WPC	Workingmen's Party of California
WSFL	Washington State Federation of Labor
WSP	Woman Suffrage Party
WTUL	Women's Trade Union League
WULL	Women's Union Label League

How the Vote Was Won

1

The Context of the Western Woman Suffrage Movement

I think civilization is coming Eastward gradually.
—Theodore Roosevelt[1]

By the end of 1914, almost every western state and territory in the United States had enfranchised its female citizens in the greatest innovation in participatory democracy since Reconstruction. These western successes stand in profound contrast to the East, where few women voted until after the ratification of the Nineteenth Amendment (1920), and to the South, where African American men were systematically disfranchised. The regional pattern of early western victories has remained unclear, despite many state studies, and adequate explication requires reevaluation within the contemporary political context.[2] This study establishes western precocity as the result of the unsettled state of regional politics, the complex nature of western race relations, broad alliances between suffragists and farmer-labor-progressive reformers, and sophisticated activism by western women. It recognizes suffrage racism and elitism as major problems deeply embedded in larger cultural and political processes, and places special emphasis on the political adaptability of suffragists. It argues that the last generation of activists, often educated and professional women, employed modern techniques and arguments that invigorated the movement and helped meliorate class tensions. Stressing political and economic justice for women and deemphasizing prohibition persuaded increasing numbers of wary urban voters and weakened the negative influence of large cities. Thus, understanding woman suffrage in the West reintegrates this important region into national suffrage history and helps explain the ultimate success of this radical reform.

The western victories fall clearly into three phases closely related to distinct periods of political instability and reform. The first successes occurred in the fluid "frontier" environment of western states and territories. Experiments in Wyoming Territory (1869), Utah (1870), and Washington Territory (1883) were connected to Reconstruction and territorial politics, as well as to Mormon influence. In the early 1870s, many women's rights leaders felt betrayed by the failure of the Reconstruction amendments to establish universal suffrage as a fundamental citizen's right. In the West, however, discussions of voting-rights issues continued because constitutional questions arose every time a western territory held a convention and applied for statehood. "Pioneer" suffragists took advantage of small territorial legislatures, the statehood process, third-party challenges, and reform politics to pursue a broad women's rights agenda. Populist energy achieved suffrage in Colorado (1893) and Idaho (1896), but hostility to the People's Party, as well as internal ambivalence, prevented further success in other states. Building on this legacy of radical reform in the West, Progressive momentum finally carried woman suffrage in Washington State (1910), California (1911), Arizona, Alaska, Oregon (1912), Montana, and Nevada (1914).

Western suffragists often supported third-party and reform coalitions in the expectation of reciprocal assistance, helping to create a progressive political environment. These contacts helped western women suffragists develop strategies to overcome urban electoral opposition through trade unions and political parties. Women's rights activists were able to draw attention to gender issues because male reformers of all classes needed female help—whether enfranchised or not—to elect candidates and implement programs. Women's political activity took many forms, given their common exclusion from electoral rights. Some women established influential voluntary associations or lobbied legislators and candidates on behalf of bills. Some participated symbolically and actively in local party events, including boisterous parades, bonfires, and outdoor meetings.[3] Many western suffragists joined the temperance movement and supported the Prohibition Party, while others became Nationalists, Populists, Socialists, and Progressives. Working-class women voted and ran for office within their unions, went on strike, supported labor parties and candidates, and lobbied for legislation.

In the 1890s, suffrage gained respectability as more moderate temperance and clubwomen became involved, frequently radicalized by their experiences in social reform. The western women's club movement expanded rapidly in the 1880s and 1890s, and many clubwomen began to argue that the externalization of many decisions affecting family welfare required female civic participation. When involvement in reform activity quickly revealed the practical limits of indirect influence, women demanded the enforcement power of the vote. Leaving the domestic sphere in order to defend it transformed many women, while mainstream political culture also changed in response to female participation and priorities, including greater support for government social welfare intervention.[4] "Municipal housekeeping," "maternalism," and "nonpartisanship" were all important motivations, but they should not obscure the inherent radicalism of the demand for political rights for independent women citizens.[5]

Understanding the western suffrage movement requires a basic comprehension of the movement in general, including its radical and fundamental challenge to the existing political status of women. Suffrage was radical in several ways. In the dictionary, "radical" primarily means "root," or "fundamental," in an explicitly political sense, and secondarily "extreme," as in challenging the status quo. Both meanings fit the western suffrage movement. First, woman suffrage challenged the legal principle of coverture, which deprived married women of an independent political identity. As one California woman observed, "It was all right enough for a man to eat a meal, but that meal did the woman no good, and so it was with political rights."[6] In the 1840s, states began to pass legislation to protect women's marital property and business interests ("sole trader" laws) from the worst effects of coverture, but they did not challenge the principle as fundamentally as suffrage. These efforts began in the East, but after the Civil War they accelerated in the West, where California, Colorado, and Nevada had passed such laws by 1873. Sometimes attributed to a "frontier effect," roughly defined as a combination of economic need and political experimentalism, winning these legal reforms still required sustained effort by early women's rights activists.[7] Failure to credit women's activism has obscured the radicalism of their goal and methods, limiting many earlier analyses.

Second, woman suffrage cultivated support among radical and third-party critics of the existing political order. In the 1890s, Populist support was responsible for referenda, and in the early 1900s Progressives agreed that woman suffrage was one of several direct democracy measures necessary to reform the political system. In theory, female enfranchisement roughly doubled any given constituency; in reality, no one knew how women would tend to vote until they actually began to do so, making it an inherently radical experiment. With more political options, women could and did threaten to abandon established parties unreceptive to female concerns. Finally, the western woman suffragists utilized radically modern direct-action tactics derived from the labor movement and popular politics. Similar developments were occurring simultaneously in England, but American suffragists never became violent suffragettes. In the West, suffragists refined creative new uses of drama, popular culture, advertising, and modern technology, including cars, telephones, billboards, and slide shows. The 1911 California campaign established the effectiveness of this bold new model, and by the end of 1914, a voting population of 4 million western women confirmed its success.

General suffrage histories have generally neglected the West, or failed to evaluate its significance within the national movement. Even contemporary studies often take a quick western tour, acknowledging the breakthrough victories before returning to the East. Women's own efforts to organize against formidable geographic and demographic obstacles have received little attention aside from criticism for their failure to maintain viable organizations over decades of struggle. Instead, the popular "gift theory" emphasizes male boosterism and desires for women settlers, as well as efforts to strengthen particular constituencies with female voters (e.g., Mormons in Utah). This model favors "gentle tamers," naïve, polite, middle-class women with "municipal housekeeping" and social purity goals. These women were often active suffragists, but they never won a campaign by threatening to "civilize" rowdy western communities.[8] Aside from the obvious fact that men did the voting in legislatures and referenda, they did not "give" the vote easily—women won it only after many long and exhausting legislative lobbying sessions and public campaigns. Beverly Beeton has correctly identified male boosterism, political factionalism, and an experimental political environment as important factors, but ultimately reduces these to matters "of expediency, not ideology."[9] In fact, men often viewed the demand for woman suffrage as politically *in*expedient, even when they conceded its justice.

The West is largely ignored in the leading paradigm of late nineteenth century suffrage, the "justice v. expediency" model proposed by Aileen Kraditor over thirty years ago. Kraditor proposed that fin-de-siècle suffragists retreated from earlier high principles and compromised with racism and nativism to win political gains and elite support.[10] Kraditor's examination of suffrage racism is extremely significant, but her neat dichotomy is falsely reductive. The model conflates racism and nativism based on eastern conditions, and overgeneralizes the experiences of the national, largely eastern leadership. Most importantly, it describes moral declension when the political struggle demanded a constant process of negotiation between "justice" and "expediency." Both aspects have been consistently present within the suffrage movement, often linked rhetorically as complements, not polarized as opposites. In western suffrage debates, it is striking how often *both* of these terms appear together. In fact, the appeal to justice remained fundamental, but the development of *many* rationales for suffrage, including those tailored to specific interests, was a crucial element in the success of modern campaigns.[11] Kraditor defines "expediency" as instrumentalism and identifies a shift toward suffrage as a means to other ends rather than a goal in itself. This study uses the dictionary definition: "what is immediately advantageous independent of ethics or consistent principles."[12]

"Expediency" is an appropriate term to describe suffrage racism. Suffragists were not exempt from contemporary prejudices and political pressures, and they struggled to reconcile noble ideals and practical realities as social attitudes hardened and legal options narrowed. Frequently challenged by white supremacist arguments, suffragists also manipulated white racial fears even though nonwhite western racial-ethnic groups were geographically, culturally, and politically marginalized by the 1890s. African American populations remained small and scattered until the twentieth century.[13] Citizenship for Native Americans was inconsistent until the Immigration Act of 1924 finally granted full rights. Suffragists sometimes idealized Native American culture in search of an idyllic matriarchal past, but they also shared societal prejudices that dismissed indigenous peoples as degraded savages in need of intervention, instruction, or rescue.[14] The Mexican American population of the Southwest theoretically enjoyed full citizenship rights under the Treaty of Guadalupe Hidalgo (1848), but the reality was a lost land base, de facto discrimination, and impoverishment.[15] Particularly in Southern California, the tendency to romanticize both these cultures—once they had been firmly subjugated—helped to elide the reality of Anglo-American conquest and dominance. In the West, the "indispensable enemy" was the Chinese population in America, which suffered from widespread discrimination, hostile labor agitation, and violence. The federal Chinese

Exclusion Act of 1882 declared the Chinese permanently "ineligible for citizenship," and this naturalization ban was extended subsequently to other Asian Americans.[16]

The conflicted nature of western race relations probably strengthened support for woman suffrage among white residents of newly settled agrarian areas. Western politics and race relations fit the pattern of a "herrenvolk democracy," in which an egalitarian code applied, but only to those qualified for inclusion.[17] In fact, the term "franchise" denotes admission to a limited group and enjoyment of the rights and privileges available only to the members of that group, and white western suffragists used contemporary racial stereotypes to establish and monitor the boundaries. They used universalistic arguments for their own inclusion in the polity, but accepted racial differentiations that privileged whiteness. White western women generally avoided direct discussion of "the color question," but they often reminded white western men how female labor promoted settlement and helped maintain white hegemony. To highlight their demands, they manipulated ideas about racial and ethnic "Others," usually reinforcing contemporary racialist and racist attitudes, particularly those linking race, sex, and "civilization."

The trope equating woman suffrage and "civilization" reflects the heavy influence of late nineteenth-century scientific racialist theories, especially Social Darwinism. Maladapted from evolutionary theory, these models conflated biology, race, morality, and culture into a crude biological determinism and ranked distinctions between "inferior" and "superior" peoples accordingly.[18] Progressive evolution, or "civilization," was frequently linked to the status of women, with the white, middle-class, "separate spheres" model defined as the apex of human success. White people considered themselves more "civilized" because they discouraged women's manual labor and emphasized female purity and nurturance. In contrast, people of color were considered "savages" because of their allegedly uncontrolled sexuality and general irresponsibility, demonstrated by female "drudgery" and male sloth. White working-class people used these ideas to assert their white racial superiority, but the growing realities of proletarian economic dependence and a permanent female workforce blurred this distinction.[19]

Evolutionary progress requires sex, reproductive sex requires females, and sex—especially its symbolism and its regulation—is a powerful factor in knowledge/power relations, cultural values, and social institutions. Since racial purity is so tenuous and so easily corrupted by unauthorized

intercourse, female sexual behavior is controlled by powerful gender pre-
scriptions mediated by family, society, science, and the law. The political
metaphor of "family," rooted in shared blood, soil, and resources, is a
common theme in nationalist and imperialist rhetoric. The root word
"familus" means "servant" or "slave," however, reflecting the status of
the traditional patriarch as the only independent member of his household, as well as the economic nature of many family and kinship arrangements. Although they remain powerful, patriarchal metaphors that cast
all authority figures as "fathers" and classified all women as perpetual de-
pendents became anachronistic with the consolidation of industrial capitalism. Men found it increasingly difficult to fulfill these roles, and more
women began to demand equal rights.[20]

The use of "civilization" rhetoric compromised woman suffrage when
it encouraged racism. In 1903, Susan B. Anthony and other National
American Woman Suffrage Association (NAWSA) officials publicly assured southerners that the race question was irrelevant to their purposes
and adopted a "separate but equal" membership policy. As part of their
questionable "southern strategy," the national leadership accepted a series of compromises hoping to gain southern support. This approach created serious internal dissension and never really satisfied the "states'
rights" southern suffragists, who impeded efforts to revive a federal strategy well into the 1910s. Nor did it persuade southern legislators, who understood full well that African American women hoped to use this
weapon to oppose racial discrimination and male disfranchisement.[21]
The prominent black intellectual and suffragist W. E. B. Du Bois repeatedly warned elite white women that this position "represents a climbing
of one class on the misery of another," but his words had little effect.[22]
Unwilling or unable to resist contemporary racist attitudes, white suffragists thus helped to reinforce them.

White suffragists who segregated, manipulated, or avoided race issues
received little encouragement within the black community, but African
American women organized their own clubs and suffrage organizations
nationwide. They wanted the ballot to defend and "uplift" their communities, demanding both "rights" and "expedients," in the sense of real so-
lutions to oppressive conditions.[23] In the West, African American suffragists sometimes organized with white women, but they established
their own groups in communities with sufficiently large black populations. Prominent western African American women suffragists included
Elizabeth Piper Ensley, Sarah Overton, and Naomi Anderson. Ensley was

a founding member of the Colorado Equal Suffrage Association and the Colorado Association of Colored Women's Clubs (1904). Overton, the second vice-president of the San Jose Suffrage Amendment League, was also involved in school desegregation activities. Anderson lived in the Midwest until moving to Sacramento, California, around 1895. She was a Woman's Christian Temperance Union (WCTU) organizer in the 1880s, and campaigned for suffrage in Kansas in 1894. Her work in California in 1896 drew praise from both Elizabeth Cady Stanton and Susan B. Anthony, but nothing more is known about her later life.[24]

The campaigns of the 1890s taught western suffragists that they needed the support of at least a solid minority of urban working-class voters to win a referendum. Once no constituency was considered too small or insignificant to insult freely or dismiss safely, white supremacist arguments diminished (at least in public), and cooperative efforts increased. Some eastern suffragists shared this insight and also began developing racial-ethnic and working-class coalitions, but the conservative NAWSA leadership preferred an elite strategy. The idea of developing working-class support, particularly among wage-earning women, was not new. Early republican, labor, and utopian socialist ideologies offered support for women's rights.[25] Anthony and Stanton sought trade union allies in the 1860s, hoping to connect labor and suffrage activists in a new political reform movement, but conflicting loyalties disrupted their brief cooperation.[26] By the 1890s, the presence of women in the workforce was a recognized if contested phenomenon. A terrible economic depression drew public attention to their problems and stimulated interest in measures for their relief, including the ballot and protective legislation.

The connection between economic rights and political equality helped link suffragists of different classes, but there were tensions, especially during labor conflicts. All could agree on equal rights, equal pay for equal work, and access to workplace opportunities, but wage earners tended to prioritize economic issues over suffrage. For wage-earning women, a job can mean greater autonomy, control over separate property or earnings, and perhaps a release from unremunerated domestic labor, but most women were (and are) overworked and underpaid. Middle-class women often failed to appreciate their own educational and vocational advantages or the distinction between a "job" and a "career." Middle-class suffragists expressed concern for working women, but they were often quite patronizing. Marginalized labor and socialist suffragists tended to work independently of mainstream clubwomen suffragists. The situation improved after the establishment of the Women's Trade Union League (WTUL) in 1903, because suffragists began to push for better cooperation with labor.[27]

In the past, historians neglected working-class support for woman suffrage because middle-class suffragists perpetuated the false assumption that urban, immigrant populations were consistently hostile. All successful state campaigns ultimately depended upon convincing some segment of this key constituency. Large cities usually rejected woman suffrage measures, but working-class precincts were often among the most supportive. Western cities were heavily populated by foreign-born migrants, but they were long-term residents, relatively "Americanized," who formed stable communities.[28] Working-class families emulated middle-class values and sought respectability, carefully distancing themselves from the young, male, transient workforce. Woman suffrage gained support in these communities when it was perceived as a benefit and not a threat to personal, familial, and ethnocultural interests. As a measure to strengthen and stabilize the working class, many important national, state, and local labor organizations endorsed woman suffrage.[29]

The 1890s was a period of extensive labor organizing and labor conflict in the region and in the nation. Idealists still envisioned the West as a "safety valve," but Gilded Age economic reality was massive development of capital-intensive, extractive resource industries dependent upon rapidly urbanizing metropoles for commercial and support services.[30] The consolidation of industrial capitalism provoked violent reactions by labor, especially in mining areas, and conflict rocked the region for decades. The West attracted new immigrants, but many arrived too late to homestead, or they lacked capital. By the 1890s, the cities of San Francisco, Denver, and Seattle all had substantial working-class populations, communities, and organizations.[31] Urban workers, farmers, and small merchants who feared proletarianization and a concomitant loss of political power catalyzed a series of organized political reform movements, including Nationalism, Populism, Socialism, and Progressivism. Third-party radicals usually supported democratization measures such as the secret ballot, initiative, referendum, recall, and woman suffrage that would help break the political control of large business interests.

The Knights of Labor, which had strong western roots, encouraged organization among women workers and developed broad family-based strategies that required female cooperation. In 1887, 65,000 women Knights, representing 10 percent of the total membership, were organized into more than four hundred locals. Their "labor feminism" combined demands for equal rights, pay, and respect with claims to the moral superiority of the domestic sphere. Women Knights organized to protect the working-class family and community against the ravages of industrial capitalism, and suffrage and temperance were their most important weapons. This culture generated many influential female activists, including Leonora Barry (Lake), Mary Harris ("Mother") Jones, Mary Elizabeth Lease, and Leonora O'Reilly. In 1886, the Knights appointed Barry, a widowed mother and former textile worker, as general investigator for women's work, and she traveled around the country speaking, investigating working conditions, and supporting strikes. Barry retired after her remarriage in 1890, but the Knights sponsored her tour of Colorado during the 1893 campaign.[32]

The American Federation of Labor (AFL) endorsed woman suffrage from its founding in 1886.[33] Many working-class men legitimately feared cheap female economic competition, while socialists often believed that women were essentially conservative class enemies, but the increasing presence of women in the workforce and growing evidence of their ability to organize helped moderate this opposition.[34] Women were union members, voters, officials, and they were also involved in other organizations and clubs, similar to those of middle-class women. Samuel Gompers and other AFL officials occasionally appeared at NAWSA conventions or spoke in favor of suffrage. In 1910, Arthur Holder overlooked labor's persistent gender discrimination to advocate women's equality: "The law is no respecter of persons. Women cannot shirk their responsibility because they are women; neither should they be longer denied their normal citizenship rights and privileges because they are women."[35] Assurances from labor leaders were significant, but they did not commit trade union resources or guarantee the vote of the working man. Like their middle-class counterparts, labor men endorsed woman suffrage as one of many reform measures during a period of dramatic change, but they had other priorities, and woman suffrage slipped low on the agenda unless pushed by female colleagues.

Populism is often characterized as a protest movement by economically distressed farmers, but the western economy contributed a significant labor component.[36] A broad agenda helped overcome the contradictory material interests of farmers ("free silver, cheap money, and inflation") and urban workers ("cheap food, hard money, and high wages").[37] As writers and publishers as well as organizers, many important Populist women, including Mary Elizabeth Lease, Annie Diggs, and Eva Valesh, tried to bridge this gap, often by identifying urban women wage earners as the city-dwelling daughters of farm families. Most of these leaders were urban women connected to the Knights of Labor, which reinforced their strong sympathies for workers, but they tended to neglect farm women. Like the Knights, the Grange, and the Farmers' Alliance, the Populists sought to develop a family-based, cooperative "movement culture" by actively recruiting and encouraging female participation. Founding People's Party state conventions often included mixed-gender delegations and representatives from local suffrage and temperance organizations as well as labor and agrarian groups. Yet the new emphasis on organized political and electoral activity tended to marginalize all women, especially as the political stakes increased.[38]

Populist antecedents in the Grange, Farmers' Alliance, Greenback Party, Union Labor Party, and the Knights of Labor encouraged support for woman suffrage, but it was a controversial measure, easily sacrificed to political exigencies. Endorsement was not automatic, and largely resulted from internal pressure exerted by western women. Support for woman suffrage weakened in state and national elections when the stakes were high, but it often remained strong at the local level. Tracing the development of the People's Party, the pattern of declining support is clear. In 1889, when members of the Southern and Northern Farmers' Alliances met with the Knights of Labor in St. Louis to discuss the wisdom of forming a separate party, they endorsed woman suffrage. In Ocala, Florida, the following year, they reiterated this support, although still undecided about political action. Continuing the discussion in Cincinnati early in 1891, they began to waver on the suffrage resolution. Prominent women delegates such as Annie Diggs, Mary Elizabeth Lease, Frances Willard, and other women on both the resolutions and organizing committees secured only a weak endorsement: "that the question of woman suffrage be recommended to the favorable consideration of the various states and territories." By 1892, the St. Louis convention in February and the Omaha convention in July both refused to include woman suffrage in the platform, despite increasing numbers of female delegates and the presence of WCTU president Frances Willard and NAWSA president Susan B. Anthony (who was refused permission to speak).[39] Clearly amused by their disappointment, Colorado governor Davis Waite later justified this action by calling woman suffrage a distraction, and "a political platform must not be loaded down with unnecessary issues, no matter how excellent."

Always ambivalent, Waite was soon openly hostile to woman suffrage, blaming newly enfranchised Colorado women voters for his failure to win reelection in 1894.[40]

At the 1896 St. Louis convention, a Colorado woman seconded the nomination of William Jennings Bryan and spoke for woman suffrage, but to no avail. At this point the People's Party appeared to be at the peak of its influence, but it was already internally divided between idealists and fusionists, and the latter strongly resisted woman suffrage as a radical measure that would endanger alignment with the Democrats. In 1896, the defeat of Democratic-Populist presidential candidate Bryan by Republican William McKinley defeated Populist hopes for national power. The party and its influence often persisted on the local level. In the early 1900s, many western Populists became Socialists, Progressives, or insurgents within the regular parties. Through continued agitation, they won many of the reform measures considered too "radical" when proposed by the People's Party in the 1890s. In a familiar pattern, male Progressives generally supported woman suffrage as both an equal rights principle and a political democratization measure, but waffled on official endorsement, prioritized other issues, and left female colleagues to manage suffrage by themselves.

Innovative suffrage ideas and tactics grounded in farmer-labor-progressive politics were particularly effective in the U.S. West for many reasons, but not unique. In many areas, a younger generation of suffragists adopted new, more aggressive techniques from the labor movement, including the British suffragettes.[41] More generally, woman suffrage was a modernist tendency related to progressive reform movements and growing numbers of working women of all classes.[42] In New York and Boston, young college women joined trade unionists, clubwomen activists, and members of the WTUL to energize urban suffrage revivals. Most of the older generation had no idea how to win the crucial cities, but younger leaders recognized the need to dissociate from prohibition and to connect with working-class and racial-ethnic communities through their labor unions, clubs, churches, and settlement houses. In New York and Boston, new tactics included parades, open-air meetings, advertising, and dramatic demonstrations. In New York, Harriot Stanton Blatch, Elizabeth Cady Stanton's daughter, introduced these dynamic new tactics and emphasized the importance of cross-class coalitions. In January 1907, Blatch established the Equality League of Self-Supporting Women, but the league suffered from persistent class tensions. The wage earner members who objected to elite control created their own organization in 1911, explicitly citing the precedent of the San Francisco Wage Earners Suffrage League (WESL), established for similar reasons in 1908. In both cities, working- and middle-class activists were alienated by lingering anger over major strikes, while labor suffragism in New York was stimulated by the Triangle Shirtwaist Fire in March 1911.[43]

These efforts were finally successful in New York in 1917, when woman suffrage received the strongest support in New York City from immigrants, particularly the Jewish and working-class Italian communities. Working-class women employed in highly unionized, politicized occupations were the strongest suffragists, especially in areas where the garment trades were concentrated. NAWSA president Carrie Chapman Catt was aware of these trends but explicitly denied them, probably due to the climate of nativism and repression during World War One.[44]

The militant suffragette movement in Britain had many of the same elements, but the white settler societies of New Zealand and Australia (AustralAsia) provide the closest parallels to the U.S. West. In both areas, white men needed the labor of white women to build and defend their brave new worlds against resentful indigenes. Although the lack of manhood suffrage temporarily blocked woman suffrage in some of these areas, the general tendency was toward liberalization of the franchise for white men, followed by white women, but a contraction of rights for men and women of color. In these areas, race and citizenship issues relating to Aboriginal and Asian peoples complicated the franchise, and official policies resulted in deeply segregated societies. Politicized labor movements allied with other reform groups to win democratization measures like woman suffrage, but they did not protest the disfranchisement of people of color. There was a major difference in national constitutional systems, however. In AustralAsia, legislative approval was sufficient, but the U.S. system required a first phase of intensive legislative lobbying for a referendum followed by an arduous public campaign.[45]

In New Zealand, full male suffrage was established in 1889, and an innovative Liberal-Labour government passed woman suffrage in 1893. Interestingly, the indigenous Maori people were not as systematically disfranchised in New Zealand as similar groups elsewhere because they had more political power as fierce militants, and ironically, as Christians.[46] A year later, South Australia enfranchised women in a similar pattern of cross-class coalitions of woman suffragists, labor-liberal support, and grassroots WCTU involvement. The extensive transnational networks of the WCTU encouraged diversity in outreach, but attention to aboriginal peoples generally emphasized missionary work or "uplift." Western Australia, which enfranchised its female inhabitants in 1889, shared a development pattern common in the U.S. West: a gold strike, followed by rapid growth and demographic shifts that overwhelmed the indigenous population with whites (40 percent female) and migrants from Asia. Worried by the growing power of organized labor in the mines, conservative politicians reversed their positions and endorsed woman suffrage as a stabilizing influence, only to lose the next election. Queensland had a similar history of gold rush, immigration, strong trade unionism, and active labor suffragists, but conservative politicians (no doubt chastened by the example of Western Australia), as well as the lack of full adult male suffrage, delayed implementation until 1908.[47]

In both countries, female enfranchisement in one colony or territory made problematic the process of national federation because representatives often insisted upon the inclusion of women citizens and usually prevailed. Debates in the U.S. Congress revealed fears that admitting new states with woman suffrage would set dangerous precedents. The example of Australia was not reassuring to opponents of woman suffrage. In 1902, the constitution of the new Australian commonwealth enfranchised white women in order to maintain consistency with the states that had already enfranchised them. Soon all the new states complied, pressured by labor-liberal coalitions, facilitated by women activists. To settle the "race question," a "states' rights" provision stipulated that the aboriginal population had to be enfranchised on a state level before receiving national rights, an unlikely possibility.[48]

Abandoning exceptionalism, the current study analyzes the woman suffrage movement in the western United States, introducing important western regional women activists, identifying dominant ideas, and tracing associations with contemporary social and political movements. The first chapters examine the early period of woman suffrage activism in the U.S. West. Chapter 2 focuses on important women's regional publications, organizations, and networks, concluding that women writers, editors, lecturers, and organizers helped coordinate a grassroots movement of "organic intellectuals." These women analyzed and politicized their personal experiences into articulate feminist critiques, which they systematically disseminated to support their demands for equal rights. Chapter 3 examines woman suffrage in the context of Reconstruction and Gilded Age politics, including the "New Departure" strategy, territorial politics, and the statehood process. The earliest successes in Wyoming (1869) and Utah (1870) were achieved by simple votes in territorial legislatures, although each required confirmation when applying for statehood. Utah women were enfranchised in 1870, disfranchised by the U.S. Congress in 1887 as an anti-polygamy measure, and then reenfranchised when admitted as a state in 1896. The women of Washington Territory were also briefly enfranchised by the territorial legislature in 1883, but disfranchised by the territorial Supreme Court in 1888. Other states faced the issue of determining suffrage qualifications as they held conventions, wrote constitutions, and anticipated statehood. Both sides used racial and racist reasoning, but many states' rights advocates compromised themselves (temporarily) by insisting that the federal government intervene to prohibit voting by women, Mormons, or people of color.[49]

Chapters 4 and 5 examine the relationship between woman suffrage and Populism in the Rocky Mountain West in the 1890s. The importance of the People's Party in winning woman suffrage in Colorado in 1893 is well established, although the victory in Idaho in 1896 is less well understood. In 1896, Susan B. Anthony considered the California campaign so crucial that she directed it personally, but the woman suffrage amendment shared the grim fate of the Populists in that critical election year.

The final chapters analyze the successful western woman suffrage referenda of the Progressive period. Chapter 6 traces suffrage in the Pacific Northwest, where suffragists first gained a powerful new weapon in the initiative process. In 1910, woman suffrage won in Washington by a large majority, aided by considerable working-class support, but Oregon did not enfranchise women until 1912. The regional movement was burdened by personality and factional conflicts, but these had the beneficial effect of encouraging local innovation. Chapter 7 focuses on the crucial 1911 California victory, a major breakthrough in a large state with powerful industrial interests and large urban immigrant populations. The cities were still hostile, but support in working-class districts increased significantly between 1896 and 1911, largely due to the efforts of labor suffragists. They converted working-class men by linking female enfranchisement to economic issues, labor's political aspirations, and working-class community concerns. California suffragists applied an amazing array of modern suffrage tactics, cleverly utilizing advertising, technology, and mass culture. The California victory inspired other efforts, and within three years most western women could vote. The momentum shifted back to the East, where similar methods proved critical to success, especially in New York in 1917.

Chapter 8 summarizes the final "frontier" campaigns in Nevada, Arizona, and Montana in 1912 and 1914. In these isolated and sparsely populated regions, a new generation of suffragists—often born, raised, and educated in the West—used women's economic status and actual voting behavior to persuade socialists and workers to support their demand. Enfranchised western women took their responsibilities as voters seriously, aware that they were establishing important precedents, and deserve some of the credit for passing a veritable flood of progressive legislation in the 1910s. The chapter concludes with some tentative conclusions about the western influence on the national movement after 1914, although a full assessment is beyond the scope of this study. Many of the Congressional Union (CU) militants were western veterans, including Maud Younger of California and Anne Martin of Nevada. Their aggressive tactics attracted public attention and began to frighten politicians into serious consideration of the federal amendment.

Woman suffrage was a highly gendered but classically political issue that reflected changing socioeconomic conditions, concepts of citizenship, and gender norms for women. Decades of suffrage agitation stimulated public education and debate involving a constellation of ideas about women's rights, economic roles, class and race relations, and political reform. By 1900, growing numbers of women in the workforce and in public life provided incontrovertible evidence of female abilities and validated their demands for equal political rights. Western suffragists of all classes found a bit of common ground and a connection to larger reform movements by insisting on economic justice and equal political rights as complementary necessities. Winning state campaigns was very difficult, but key western victories between 1890 and 1910 helped reinvigorate the national movement and generate support for the federal amendment. This study is an attempt to document those efforts and to assess their significance within the fluid political climate of the region.

2

Early Western Suffragists as Organic Intellectuals

> Some men say they are not interested in a paper published in the interests of women. How do they suppose we women have survived the papers so many years . . . [with] Woman seldom mentioned unless to point out her sphere for her.
> —Caroline Nichols Churchill[1]

The first generation of white western suffragists was an iconoclastic cohort of self-identified feminists and freethinkers, "free-lovers" and "Communists" to their opponents. Many had histories of involvement in women's rights, abolitionism, Spiritualism, Unitarianism, and other "isms" in the East. More than a few were lecturers, writers, publishers, including Abigail Scott Duniway (Oregon), Clara Colby (Nebraska and Oregon), Laura DeForce Gordon and Emily Pitts-Stevens (California), Caroline Nichols Churchill (Colorado), and Emmeline B. Wells (Utah). Often divorced or widowed and usually self-supporting, these "organic intellectuals" used their personal experiences to analyze and to articulate feminist issues, protesting the economic disabilities of women in connection with their disfranchised political status.[2] Creating their own niches in a public sphere that largely excluded or marginalized women, their communicative activities stimulated public debate and connected isolated activists.[3] By the end of the century, however, these individualistic radicals clashed with more conservative temperance activists and mainstream clubwomen as the suffrage movement broadened its base and gained respectability.

Early western suffragists often referred to "frontier" egalitarianism and "chivalry," but this was an ethnocentric conclusion that privileged white women. Native Americans and Mexican Americans frequently experienced disruption and dislocation as a result of European American settlement, so they had no interest in reinforcing the political power of white women. Nor is there consensus on the effects of the western settlement process on European American women because their experiences varied so greatly. For some, the western environment offered economic and educational possibilities, while others hated their bare, lonely, and difficult lives and re-created familiar forms of eastern domesticity as quickly as possible.[4] Modern scholars caution against facile acceptance of Turnerian "frontier democracy" theories due to these differences, and because they obscure the "legacy of conquest" involved in securing the region for the United States.[5]

Western women of many groups did earn respect within their families and communities for their resiliency and hard work. The strong support for woman suffrage in agrarian areas reflected the reciprocal dependence of men and women on homesteads, farms, and small businesses. The informal and wage economies controverted Victorian ideals of sheltered domesticity, but they could be highly remunerative. Women provided personal services (e.g., food, lodging, or laundry) or migrated to the cities to work in manufacturing and service jobs.[6] Access to education was also an important factor in determining employment opportunities. The Morrill Land Grant Act of 1862 established land grant colleges with provisions for women's programs. By the turn of the century, western universities were graduating women Ph.D.s. In 1900, fewer western women were wage earners (14.5 percent) than nationally (18.8 percent), but 15.2 percent were engaged in professional occupations, compared to 8.1 percent nationally.[7] Professional women were often vigorous suffragists and frequently leaders who contributed their expertise to the movement. They had usually experienced discrimination in their careers and understood very well the connection between political rights and economic opportunities for women.

Printing and publishing especially offered significant opportunities for women, despite the bias and hostility of male colleagues and labor unions. Many nineteenth-century newspapers were small-town family businesses that provided training, income, and an intellectual outlet for women journalists. One result was a considerable number of periodicals run by women, including many that explicitly addressed feminist issues. The first western women's rights journal was the *Pioneer*, published by Emily Pitts-Stevens in San Francisco from 1869 to 1873. Most of these papers were relatively short lived, but some continued for many years:

Abigail Scott Duniway published the *New Northwest* for sixteen years (1871–1887); Clara Colby issued the *Woman's Tribune* for twenty-six years (1883–1909); and Mormon women, primarily Emmeline Wells, published the *Woman's Exponent* for forty-two years (1872–1914). Technically, Caroline Churchill of Colorado published her *Queen Bee* from 1879 to 1895, but according to an obituary she was still out selling copies a few months before her death in 1926.[8] There were women journalists in the East, too, but in the West they filled an important niche by providing isolated communities with education and entertainment. In order to attract a diverse audience and stay solvent, these papers covered a range of issues in addition to women's rights. By the 1900s, a new generation of professional newspaperwomen in the West was so effective in using the mainstream press that separate women's journals became virtually obsolete.

Experienced lecturers, journalists, radicals, and freethinkers formed the core of the early women's rights activism in California, concentrated in the San Francisco Bay Area. The oldest generation of these "brave and adventurous argonauts," included Elizabeth T. Schenck, Clarina Howard Nichols, and Eliza Farnham.[9] Often including veteran abolitionists, Quakers, Unitarians, and Spiritualists, they brought experience and connections to the regional movement. Younger women included the dynamic Laura DeForce Gordon, who arrived in San Francisco in February 1868 and catalyzed local suffrage organization with a public speech entitled "The Elective Franchise—Who Shall Vote?" Largely self-educated, Gordon moved West just after the Civil War, settling briefly with her husband in White Plains, Nevada, then permanently in Lodi, California, in the early 1870s. As Gordon lectured and organized in the area, she rapidly developed extensive connections among women activists, journalists, Spiritualists, Democratic politicians, and local radicals.[10] Reviewing her West Coast debut in 1868, the *San Francisco Examiner* reported that Gordon was "a pleasing speaker, but her doctrines don't suit these orthodox times just yet. Her sentences are too prolix and complex."[11] The *Chronicle* criticized her identification with Spiritualism, as Gordon had been a noted Spiritualist trance speaker in her youth. In 1905, two years before her death, Gordon identified herself as an agnostic, "with leanings toward Theosophy."[12]

Many early suffragists were sympathetic to Spiritualism, because it was an individualistic form of transcendentalism with a radical feminist critique of organized religion. Women trance mediums made experienced and effective speakers, and several other early California suffragists shared this background, including Addie Ballou, Amanda Slocum Reed, Elizabeth Kingsbury, and Elizabeth Watson. Ballou, an artist, was actively involved with the Nationalists, Socialists, and the Republican Party. Kingsbury was active in Southern California during the 1880s, while Watson was still going strong in 1911 as president of the state suffrage association. Reed and her husband published a series of Spiritualist suffragist papers in Santa Cruz and San Jose. When these failed in the mid-1870s, they blamed factionalism and opposition within the radical left due to Spiritualism's anticlerical and "free love" associations.[13]

The Bay Area intellectual milieu encouraged local feminists, including editors, writers, printers, and publishers. Lisle Lester, who published the *Pacific Monthly* briefly in 1863, rejected the women's rights label, but she frequently addressed the problems of working women and criticized gender discrimination by the printers union. In 1864, she joined Schenck, a previous editor of the *Pacific Monthly,* and several other women to form the Female Typographical Union.[14] In 1868, San Francisco printer Agnes Peterson had trouble finding work because she was not in the union, which contemptuously rebuffed her application. In response, Peterson helped establish the Women's Cooperative Printing Union, which continued under different partners until 1901.[15] Emily Pitts-Stevens, one of the earliest suffrage leaders in California, was a former printer and teacher who moved to San Francisco in 1865. After briefly managing the Woman's Cooperative Printing Union, she transformed a local paper into the West's first explicitly feminist journal, *The Pioneer.* Pitts-Stevens stressed the dignity of female labor, insisting that "women must learn to evolve pleasure from remunerative occupations, to take the same pride in being producers of material wealth as men do. Labor is health. Labor is wealth. The idle aimless woman is the most wretched of all mortals, just as she should be."[16]

Although working-class women activists did not always prioritize suffrage, they publicly supported and promoted women's equality within these groups, while early labor and socialist organizations sometime supported women's rights. Anna (Mrs. Burnett) Haskell, Anna Ferry Smith, and Kate Kennedy were active trade unionists, socialists, and suffragists. Anna Haskell was married to a famous local radical, contributed to the local socialist press, and published a short-lived paper of her own entitled *Truth in Small Doses.* Smith was involved with the Workingmen's Party of California in the 1870s, the Nationalists and the Populists in the

1890s, and in 1902 she became a founding member of Eugene Debs's new organization, the Socialist Party, USA. Kennedy, an Irish immigrant, was a member of the International Workingman's Association, the Knights of Labor, and the Union Labor Party (ULP). She was instrumental in winning laws allowing women to serve as school board officials in 1874 and mandating equal pay for teachers in 1875.[17] Despite so many other commitments, these women were suffragists precisely because they understood how their subservient political status undermined their economic opportunities.

Thus, the California suffrage movement encompassed very diverse individuals from the beginning, and it suffered badly from chronic factional conflicts as a result. Suffragists often differed over tactics, including partisanship, nonpartisanship, support for radical or third-party challenges, and the formation of separatist women's parties.[18] Some of the early difficulties related to the split in the national women's rights movement between supporters of the American Woman Suffrage Association (AWSA) and the National Woman Suffrage Association (NWSA). Many westerners preferred the more radical NWSA, but as transplanted easterners they also had ties to prominent AWSA leaders like Lucy Stone and Henry Brown Blackwell. One big difference between the two organizations was that the NWSA did not admit men. As Susan Anthony explained to Gordon, "Women are too easily made tools of by the men . . . & everyman of them wants all of us women to follow his lead. . . . We know that women must lead our movement or we go directly into politicians['] hands."[19] In the 1870s, gender conflicts over leadership were often masked by charges of radicalism and "free love."

The San Francisco Woman Suffrage Association (SFWSA) was formed in July 1869. Almira Eddy recalled that she "heard there was a paper in the city edited by a woman," so she went with a friend to meet Pitts-Stevens. Then Eddy and Pitts-Stevens "went to see Mrs. Schenck, who had been appointed Vice President for California of the National Association," and urged her to form a local suffrage organization.[20] Schenck immediately met opposition from an AWSA faction led by the Reverend Charles G. Ames, his wife Fanny, John Collins, the "president of the Society of Progressive Spiritualists," and Collins's wife. In the early 1870s, these long-winded gentlemen (described in the local press as "gas-pipes") tried to dominate the state suffrage organization. Anthony and Stanton encouraged Schenck to persevere, but she soon resigned the presidency. Her successor was Marietta Stow, who also quickly resigned, protesting criticism of her management. Stow remained a colorful San Francisco character for many years, but she never rejoined the organized state suffrage movement. From 1881 to 1885, she published the *Women's Herald of Industry and Social Science Cooperator*, but never mentioned local suffrage activity.[21]

Laura DeForce Gordon confronted the Ames-Collins faction at the state suffrage convention in January 1870. She was warmly applauded when she encouraged the women to speak up and "not sit like mummies," but her opponents packed the executive board with allies, and Gordon withdrew. She claimed to be "hugely amused at the muddle these men had got into," and decided "to decline acting under the auspices of any & all organized Societies for the present."[22] Gordon joined a delegation in an appearance before a special committee of the state Senate in March, and spoke in San Francisco in April, but she considered herself "an outsider" at the Pacific Slope suffrage convention in May.[23] When California suffragists returned to the state legislature in 1872, members of the Assembly "were not inclined to give much notice of the wailings of the he-hens and female roosters," yet appointed a committee to consider woman suffrage. Advocates also pursued other women's rights bills in the 1870s. For example, Nettie C. Tator, who had recently lost a legal challenge to allow her to practice law, "read a printed address upon the subject of equal pay for the same labor, and the consequences to women of the infringement of this right." Tator was unable to achieve remedial legislation, but a few years later Laura Gordon and Clara Foltz would be more successful.[24]

Pitts-Stevens was a skillful suffrage politician, but perhaps also a "weak vessel" (as Gordon once described her) dependent upon male allies. In 1871 she condemned the formation of "rings" but sided with Collins and became president of the local Woman Suffrage Association in 1872. She also headed a newly organized Pacific Slope Suffrage Association, which resolved to form a "Woman Suffrage Party of the Pacific Coast," dedicated to "work for the election of any worthy candidate, of whatever party, who will work with us, and we will vigorously oppose any candidate . . . who is opposed." A delegation attended the state Democratic convention, but the organization did not last. Nevertheless, it demonstrated an early realization that political means would be necessary to achieve an essentially political goal.[25]

In the spring of 1873, the Collins faction tried to oust Pitts-Stevens based on "free-love" charges. The anti-suffrage *San Francisco Chronicle* joined in, identifying Pitts-Stevens as a member of the Radical Club, an institution "composed exclusively of Socialists, Spiritualists, Free Lovers, Woman Suffragists and all who by reason of their sentiments are ostracized from the society which they so much condemn." Pitts-Stevens denied the charge that she was "an instrument" of the "Woodhull phase of the woman suffrage movement," a likely reference to her Women's Party activities the previous year. She warned against discussing "free-love or anything of the kind; but to talk of the ballot, and the best way to get it." She attributed the charges to her leadership struggle with "a *certain* Masculine Member, whose ambition is to rule all creation."[26]

At the next suffrage convention, "Field Marshal" Collins attempted to adjourn prematurely, then walked out with his friends, the association's records, and all its funds. Pitts-Stevens received support from many prominent local woman suffragists, including Laura Gordon, but soon sold the *Pioneer,* citing ill health. Pitts-Stevens dominated the suffrage organization for the next several years, working closely with James J. Owen, the editor of the *San Jose Weekly Mercury,* a Spiritualist and former state legislator. In 1878, Owen was elected president of the state society. In the 1880s, Pitts-Stevens remained an active suffragist, but she concentrated on temperance while Laura Gordon resumed her position as the movement's dominant leader.[27]

A very active and generous group of woman suffragists lived in the south Bay Area, including Sarah Wallis (Mrs. Judge Joseph S. Wallace) and Sarah Knox-Goodrich. Wallis was the only other woman on the platform at Gordon's first San Francisco suffrage speech, and the two women collaborated on efforts to reform married women's property acts in the 1870s and early 1880s. Knox-Goodrich, the former widow of a state legislator, was also an experienced lobbyist who helped win an 1874 bill allowing women to run for (but not vote for) local school boards. She nominated herself for the Assembly in 1877.[28] The previous year, Knox-Goodrich "determined to make a manifestation" on the Fourth of July, covered her house with banners, filled her carriage with prominent friends, and joined the holiday procession. Their signs read: "We are the disfranchised Class," "We are Taxed without being Represented," and "We are governed without our Consent." Many comments were sympathetic: "Good for Mrs. Knox"; "She is right"; "If I were in her place I would never pay a tax"; "I guess one of the strong-minded lives here." When embarrassed officials placed them in the front of the parade, Knox-Goodrich was annoyed. She had requested "a place in the procession *next*

to the negroes as we wished to let our legal protectors have a practical il-
lustration of the position occupied by their mothers, wives, sisters and
daughters in this boasted republic." She "*did* want to go in, however,
ahead of the Chinamen, as we considered our position at present to be between the two."[29] This casual manipulation of race illustrates the privileged assumptions of white suffragists even as they used the egalitarian
symbolism of the holiday to challenge their own categorization as inferior
political persons.

In the 1870s, Laura Gordon was the state's most active lecturer and organizer, and she resumed leadership of the organized California suffrage
movement in the mid-1880s. Funds were not available to send her to help
during the 1877 Colorado campaign, but Sarah Knox-Goodrich and
Ellen Clark Sargent paid for her trip to Washington Territory in 1889.[30]
During this time, Gordon was also a Democratic journalist and speaker,
although she encountered much gender antagonism and resistance within
the party. She was an exception to the general pattern of women journalists because she produced Democratic Party papers, not women's rights
journals, from 1873 to 1878. She also worked as a legislative correspondent for the *Sacramento Bee* and the *San Francisco Post* (edited by Henry
George). In 1878 she gave up "this hateful work," complaining of the financial drain, lukewarm Democratic Party support, and gender bias.[31]
She switched to studying law, moved to the Bay Area, and filed for divorce. Expressing her sense of vanguard radical feminism, Gordon once
told an interviewer that she felt like "Joan of Arc, Zenobia, Maid of
Saragossa, Charlotte Corday."[32]

Laura Gordon and Clara Shortridge Foltz, a recent widow with five
children, had similar ambitions to practice law, so they decided to challenge the California law restricting the legal profession to white males.
Foltz drafted a Woman Lawyer's Bill, Assemblyman Grove Johnson
pushed it through the legislature at the last minute, and Gordon used her
partisan influence to pressure the Democratic governor to sign it. Foltz
and Gordon also began attending classes at the new Hastings Law
School, part of the University of California, but within days they were rejected as ineligible for admission. The women filed suit and made an impressive showing in court. They won their case on the basis of the new
Woman Lawyer's bill, the university's coeducational policy, and two
equal employment and education clauses in the new 1879 California state
constitution—inclusions for which Gordon and Foltz were also largely
responsible. Neither woman could afford to wait out an appeal, however,

so both returned to private legal training and practice. Foltz became the first woman admitted to the bar in California; Gordon was the second woman (after Belva Lockwood) admitted to practice before the U.S. Supreme Court. Following their lead, the first woman graduate of Hastings Law School, Mary McHenry Keith, was a very important leader of the next generation of California suffrage leaders.[33]

During the 1880s, Foltz and Gordon concentrated on their professional legal careers but remained active in party politics as well as the suffrage movement. Foltz was president of the state suffrage association in the early 1880s, then Gordon assumed control in 1884. Yet both women had problems cooperating with their colleagues and were operating independently by the late 1890s. Neither woman was in close touch with the growing trend of organization among women in clubs and other voluntary organizations. Democratic hostility to woman suffrage also probably limited Gordon's effectiveness. In 1887, Gordon declined the ULP nomination for state attorney general, but published a Democratic newsletter and spoke for the Democratic Party in 1888, 1890, and 1892.[34]

Foltz was an active Republican most of her life but worked for the Democrats in 1886–1888 and for the Populists in the early 1890s. In 1892 she ran for San Francisco city district attorney as a Populist. Between 1887 and 1890, Foltz practiced law in San Diego and edited a daily newspaper, the *San Diego Bee*. She then bounced between San Francisco and New York City, until finally settling permanently in Los Angeles in 1906. She continued to practice law, agitated for suffrage, briefly published another women's journal, and remained active in Republican Party politics, seeking the party's gubernatorial nomination in 1930 at the age of eighty-one.[35] Gordon was less fortunate: declining health and family responsibilities forced her to abandon legal practice in 1901, and she died suddenly in 1907. Although they had their differences, Foltz insisted that Gordon had always taken "the most radical and progressive stand on all public matters, and it was this that made her always an effective, practical and impressive speaker. Her hearers might not believe as she did, but they knew that she had studied these matters and had profound personal conviction upon them."[36]

In the Pacific Northwest, the most prominent suffragist was Abigail Scott Duniway, another controversial individualist. One of the early white inhabitants of Oregon, Duniway trekked across the continent in 1852, burying her mother and infant brother en route, and she was very proud of her "pioneer" status. Due to Mr. Duniway's lack of business acumen and later disability, Mrs. Duniway supported her large family, but still found time to become involved in a local suffrage organization. She used purchasing trips to California for her millinery store to connect with Laura Gordon, Emily Pitts-Stevens, and others. Pitts-Stevens appointed Duniway as the Oregon editor of *The Pioneer,* but Duniway wanted her own women's rights journal. In the spring of 1871, family obligations forced her to cancel a trip to the Pacific Coast suffrage convention in San Francisco and a subsequent lecture tour. Duniway returned home, sold the store, relocated to Portland, opened a new store, and began publishing the *New Northwest.*[37]

Duniway's paper was "not a Woman's Rights, but a Human Rights organ" a voice for "we toiling and tax-paying, but reading and reasoning women." Like other women journalists, Duniway drew upon her personal experiences to articulate female disillusionment with marriage, the importance of productive work, and the connections between economic and political rights. She rejected "the long-exploded nonsense that 'women are supported and protected by men,'" and stressed the hardships of both wage work and agrarian life for women. In 1875, "The wonder is, not that so few women display business tact and thrift, but that so many succeed in earning for themselves an honest living, as . . . they must make their way against prejudice, custom, inexperience, ridicule, apathy, and indifference."[38] Unlike many inhabitants of the West Coast at this time, Duniway was relatively indifferent toward the Chinese, convinced that the "coolie question" would "peacefully settle itself in less than a single month" if everyone followed her example and refused to hire Chinese labor. She tentatively supported the Knights of Labor and flirted with the Greenback, Prohibition, and Populist parties, but her sympathies were fundamentally Republican, which probably aggravated her difficulties in a predominantly Democratic state.[39]

Duniway confirmed her status as an important suffrage leader when she toured the Pacific Northwest with Susan B. Anthony in 1871. That summer, Elizabeth Cady Stanton and Susan B. Anthony traveled west to see how suffrage worked in the territories of Wyoming and Utah, which had just enfranchised women. Embroiled nationally with Victoria Woodhull and the "free love" scandal, they created an uproar in San Francisco by sympathizing with Laura Fair, imprisoned for killing her duplicitous lover. The San Francisco press commended Stanton's speeches, but panned Anthony's presentation as "dry and disappointing," and recommended "Mrs. Stanton should be permitted to make the campaign alone."[40]

Anthony was hurt by the bad reviews, so after a trip with Stanton to Yosemite, she gladly accepted Duniway's invitation to lecture in the Pacific Northwest. On this tour, they crossed paths with Laura Gordon. In fact, Gordon later recalled how Duniway "made her first woman suffrage speech" extemporaneously while introducing Gordon at a meeting. She "became so enthused . . . as to become most eloquent and astonished herself, as much as she delighted me, to feel that another strong-souled, eloquent voiced woman was added to the ranks of woman suffrage workers." Although she made a very favorable impression, Gordon canceled her speaking tour and returned to California in September to accept the Independent Party's nomination for state senate. Gordon campaigned vigorously, won several hundred votes, and considered her experience a valuable educational opportunity.[41]

In the meantime, Duniway and Anthony continued on their Pacific Northwest trip, but it was a difficult journey. The two women traveled approximately 2,000 miles through the Willamette Valley of Oregon, the Puget Sound, and British Columbia before finally returning to Portland. They gave sixty speeches, including Anthony's address to the Washington territorial legislature in November. They worked with Mary Olney Brown, well known in Washington Territory for her attempts to vote, Abby H. H. Stuart, the founder of the regional women's club movement, John Miller Murphy, the Democratic editor of the [Olympia] *Washington Standard,* and others to establish suffrage clubs in Seattle, Olympia, and Portland. Although these early groups were small and unstable, Anthony was actively recruiting grassroots leadership and teaching basic organizing techniques. Although Duniway was very conscious of this debt, she later included Anthony in her criticism of "outside organizers."[42] Anthony was pleased with the financial proceeds from the Northwest tour and glad of the chance to emerge from Stanton's broad shadow. Although she missed Stanton, "I can not but enjoy the feeling that the people call on *me,* and the fact that I have an opportunity to sharpen my wits a little . . . instead of merely sitting . . . and listening to the brilliant scintillations as they emanate from her."[43]

Anthony generated controversy on this trip but considered it mild compared to her hostile reception in San Francisco. She accepted a sip of wine from the son of an old friend who kept a saloon in a tiny backwoods town, then spoke in dance halls after indignant churches closed their doors in protest. With the notable exception of Murphy, the largely Democratic press was hostile. Martin Van Buren Brown, editor of the Albany *Democrat,* considered the suffragists "enemies to Christian civilization," associated with "Mormonism, Oneida Communism, Freeloveism," and the violence of the recent Paris Commune. In Washington, the *Territorial Dispatch* insisted that "it is a mistake to call Miss Anthony a Reformer, or the movement in which she is engaged as a reform; she is a Revolutionist, aiming at nothing less than the breaking up of the very foundations of society and overthrow of every social institution. . . . The whole plan is coarse, sensual and agrarian, the worst phase of French infidelity and communism."[44]

Duniway responded to harsh comments and scandalous rumors with angry insults that did not improve her popularity, nor did her growing hostility to the Women's Christian Temperance Union (WCTU). After being pelted with eggs and burned in effigy in the southern Oregon town of Jacksonville in 1879, Duniway identified "its would-be leading men" as "old miners or refugees from the bushwhacking district whence they were driven by the civil war. The taint of slavery is yet upon them and the methods of border-ruffians are their hearts' delight."[45] The mutual antagonism between Duniway and temperance advocates was particularly destructive. Duniway initially supported temperance, but eventually rejected its connection to suffrage because it diverted female organizational energy from women's rights, antagonized too many voters, and mobilized the powerful opposition of the "liquor interests." Duniway actively opposed several successful municipal reform and local option campaigns in Washington Territory in the 1880s, infuriating local WCTU activists. Duniway's astute awareness of this problematic connection escalated into an obsession with the liquor opposition, which damaged her ability to lead effectively. Other suffragists shared her insight but never became so alienated from the temperance movement, a vital if conservative component of the suffrage coalition.[46]

Duniway ruined her chances for national influence when she loudly criticized her colleagues and denigrated Anthony's method of publicly cultivating press, party, and labor support as a "hurrah campaign." In contrast, Duniway's "still hunt" method stressed careful lobbying during the legislative phase followed by a discreet campaign to avoid waking the "sleeping dragon" of the opposition. During the legislative phase, Duniway's tactics worked well, but they were of little use in mobilizing volunteers or persuading voters. Duniway's autocratic management style discouraged organizational expansion, alienated younger activists, and encouraged factionalism. She intentionally decided "to give up organizing suffrage societies, as I had learned that lecturing, [and] writing . . . afforded a more rational means of spreading the light."[47]

Without preliminary organization, inexperienced local suffragists solicited national advice and assistance, exacerbating Duniway's jealousy and hostility. In the 1900s, national suffrage officials blamed Duniway for repeated referenda losses and dismissed her as a cranky provincial. She blasted them as insensitive and interfering "outsiders" who drained local funds with hefty lecture fees and losing public ("hurrah") campaigns. Duniway particularly disliked the Reverend Anna Howard Shaw, a prohibitionist, but in the late 1890s, Carrie Chapman Catt eclipsed them both as a national leader.[48]

Colorado's women's rights journalist and lecturer was Caroline Nichols Churchill, who published the *Queen Bee* (initially *The Antelope*), from 1879 to 1895 (and sporadically thereafter). For many years, Churchill was an important educational and inspirational influence as she traveled extensively throughout the region promoting her paper, lecturing, and establishing local suffrage societies. Never constrained by false modesty, Churchill often proclaimed the "wonderful work" she performed "under most difficult circumstances."[49] Churchill's sense of mission resulted from painful personal experiences, but she used her problems to analyze structural gender inequities. Her autobiography, *Active Footsteps* (oddly written in a distant third-person voice), reveals an unhappy childhood and first marriage: "A husband was selected, and, however inappropriate, the girl was expected to conform to the condition."[50] When Churchill's husband died unlamented in the early 1860s, she cited ill health, sent her daughter to live with her sister (eventually a permanent arrangement), and began traveling to market her writings. Living in California from 1870 to 1876, she became acquainted with West Coast suffragists, but she preferred the climate in Denver and settled there permanently in 1879. Her memoir does not mention the second husband or the two additional children identified in a 1926 obituary.[51]

Churchill was a well-rounded nonconformist: "The politics of this paper are as follows: We are a Democratic-Republican, a Greenback-Know-Nothing, Pro-China-Woman Suffragist." She was also intensely anti-Catholic and anti-Mormon.[52] A mild sex radical, Churchill published sex information and advertised special medical services for women (often euphemistic references to birth control). She defended a regular columnist, Elmina Slenker, when the latter was prosecuted and acquitted under the Comstock anti-obscenity law.[53] Drawing from her painful personal experiences, Churchill insisted "children are not the necessary outcome of marriage partnership" and denied "that because a woman chooses to marry she should be compelled by law and custom to become a mother." She wrote that a couple "had by far better live as lovers do. Live in love and friendly companionship, with no more thought of procreation being desirable or even possible."[54] Churchill's "free love" position was consistent with her general heterodoxy, but it probably shocked mainstream women and possibly contributed to her alienation from the organized suffrage movement in Colorado.

Like Duniway, Churchill's estrangement coincided with her growing disillusionment with temperance. Initially, she thought "any agitation is better than stagnation," but she grew suspicious of this conservative influence: "The Temperance people set woman at work in this line in order to divert her attention from citizenship for a quarter of a century." Like many other women's rights activists, Churchill was attacked personally, but she usually countered with sharp wit or dry sarcasm. In reply to accusations of drinking, she insisted, "I never go in a saloon as a matter of taste, or for entertainment, it is a matter of business." Her radicalism and rejection of temperance seriously offended WCTU traditionalists. In 1881, one of Churchill's new suffrage recruits wrote to report that the local WCTU treasurer had told her that "'the leaders of the Equal Suffrage movement were all prostitutes'—her very words."[55] Churchill was Colorado's most flamboyant suffragist, but in the 1880s she was marginalized by the emergence of a more moderate movement concerned about its respectability.

Churchill's fundamental principles were economic autonomy and political equality for women. She boosted the West as a land of opportunity for women able to work hard, although she understood the reality of poorly paid wage labor and rejected escapist fantasies about marriage. She used the "woman as slave" metaphor to refute the idea that men protected women, warning of the systematic exploitation of female property and labor by a "class of human animals calling themselves men." Disfranchised women lacked control over their own property, labor, and wages, and "unless a woman is a voter she will never get equal pay for equal work, and legislatures composed of men will legislate her out of occupations."[56] As an advocate of female entrepreneurial enterprise, she printed numerous stories about successful business and professional women, often the female proprietors of hotels, restaurants, and stores she met in her travels. Noting their capacity for hard work, Churchill dismissed as "largely arbitrary . . . the conventional division of 'spheres,'" suggesting "these things can safely be left to be settled by natural aptitudes and the 'survival of the fittest.'"[57]

This Social Darwinist phrase, ubiquitous in Gilded Age discourse, signaled strong racial-ethnic prejudices and fears. Churchill repeatedly recommended woman suffrage as a way to uplift the entire "race" as well as guarantee economic and political justice for women. Unlike most of her contemporaries, however, Churchill was unperturbed by the idea of interracial sex and mixed-race offspring.[58] Yet her attitudes toward her racial-ethnic neighbors were often ambivalent. Like many westerners, she was hostile toward the Native Americans while they posed a real threat, but condescending once native resistance had been suppressed. She supported violent measures against the Utes in 1880, suggesting that the men be executed "and the rest of the tribe sent over into Utah. They are already accustomed to polygamy and all they need is to be baptized . . . to make first-class Mormons."[59] Churchill shared the widespread belief that the Native Americans were doomed to extinction, and she was not sorry to see them go. She expressed "a sad kind of pleasure in watching these waning phases of primitive humanity. . . . Savage life it seems must also succumb to the great law of eternal change."[60] The ideology of evolutionary racism was particularly useful in the western United States, where it helped justify the conquest of the region and its native inhabitants, and local intellectuals like Churchill contributed to this rationalization process.

Churchill's gendered economic analysis led to a controversial pro-Chinese position. Her interest was essentially utilitarian because Chinese men relieved white women of heavy housework that white men refused to do. Laundry was a particularly sore subject: "The business of washing could all be taken out of the hands of the Chinaman if the working white man so willed it. Instead of doing this he sits back upon his dignity and refuse [*sic*] to do what his prejudices consider work fit only for women, when in reality no woman should ever perform such labor, especially when bearing children."[61] As western white labor seethed with anti-Chinese sentiment, she commended Chinese industriousness. She advised "the American laborer" to stop blaming the Chinese and the Indians, "let whiskey alone, [and] attend strictly to business." She criticized the Chinese Exclusion Act as a "bungling piece of work" and opposed its renewal in 1892.[62] She observed that white society criticized the Chinese for not wanting to assimilate but rejected them as too alien when they tried. In her travelogues, Churchill described a number of courteous and hard-working Chinese people, especially women and children. In Idaho City, Churchill envied the Chinese women their comfortable clothing and noted how parents "raise up their little black-eyed babies as other folks do," but she did wonder if the absence of girls in one family indicated infanticide.[63]

Churchill's tolerance vanished completely when ethnicity intersected with religion. She claimed to have no prejudice against the Mexicans, or the Irish, or "any particular priest or layman," but she had no patience for subservient religiosity of any creed. She had noticed, "This degradation [*sic*] of the human race by the church is much like the subjection of woman." Mexican Americans could be "ingenious, tasteful, and naturally cleanly" or "very ragged, very dirty, and very much of a Roman Catholic."[64] She defended her prejudices: "An individual who is weak enough to be priest-ridden with such a mangy old institution as Roman Catholicism (or Mormonism)" deserved to be ridiculed.[65] Her contempt for the "great hordes" of "wild, Roman Catholic savages"—a large proportion of the western working class—led to some ugly personal encounters with hostile servants, waitresses, and boardinghouse keepers. Churchill usually dismissed such women as ignorant and slatternly, yet they also embodied the characteristics of female independence she admired, so she explained their hostility "on exactly the same principle that a dog would defend her master and his goods. No one has a right to judge what woman could do if free, by her work as a partial slave."[66] Churchill considered herself "a friend of the workingmen the world over," but her elitism, anti-Catholicism, and pro-Chinese position strained her relations with organized labor. She endorsed the Knights of Labor due to their progressive policies toward women, but she distrusted the national leader, Terence Powderly, probably because he was a Catholic.[67] Churchill shifted her support from the Prohibition Party to the Populists in 1892, but little is known about her life after the *Queen Bee* ceased regular publication in 1895.

Churchill began to clash with the organized woman suffrage movement as it broadened its base within more conservative women's clubs and voluntary associations. By one estimate, there were approximately one hundred women's clubs in Denver before 1900, primarily middle-class literary and educational groups.[68] The clubs were slow to officially endorse woman suffrage, but the political agitation of the late 1880s and 1890s energized and politicized them. Churchill helped organize a suffrage convention in 1881, but she criticized the proceedings as too much "speechifying" and was excluded from office in the resulting organization. She blamed "the city women," although she admitted that she had been trying "to show off." After being told "young persons should be seen more and heard less," Churchill "very sensibly declined to accept office because of her extreme youth [forty-eight years] and ignorance of Parliamentary usages."[69] Churchill supported an unsuccessful municipal suffrage bill in the Colorado legislature that year, but did not lobby the legislature.[70] Like many other regional suffragists, Churchill also had conflicts with the national leadership. According to Churchill, Susan B. Anthony commended the "sprightly little sheet," but the relationship soon soured. Apparently Churchill had rebuffed the business importuning of an Anthony relation, but she also suggested that Anthony was afraid "that there was younger blood in the field and . . . her laurels [were] in danger." Similarly, "Lucy Stone exchanged papers [*The Woman's Journal*] with Mrs. Churchill for fourteen years," but "never had a good word for her work."[71] Alienated from most of her colleagues, Churchill withdrew from organized suffrage work. She was largely absent during the successful 1893 Colorado campaign, busily touring nearby states.

The longest-running woman suffrage publication in the nation was the *Woman's Exponent,* published by Mormon women in Salt Lake City for forty-two years. The periodical began in 1872, after Utah's women gained the vote, and it continued to provide them with an important voice and organizational base as proposals to punish polygamy through disfranchisement gained strength and eventually passed the U.S. Congress. After Emmeline Woodward Wells took over in 1877, woman suffrage became an increasingly important theme. Wells was a plural wife at a young age who later separated from her husband, but she remained loyal to the church. Like many suffrage journalists, Wells relied upon her paper for her livelihood, so she also emphasized emotional and economic self-reliance for women. She reconciled these convictions with her pro-polygamy position by claiming that plural marriage was a positive innovation that "makes woman more the companion and much less the subordinate than any other form of marriage." She received some support from Elizabeth Cady Stanton, who believed that while Mormon women operated under religious delusions, so did traditional women in conventional monogamous marriages. Anthony was less tolerant of polygamy on principle, but together the NWSA leaders protested efforts to punish polygamous Mormons through disfranchisement. As the loyal supporter of a patriarchal religious order, Wells may not seem very radical, but she defended an alternative form of marriage, provided a public voice for Mormon women, and was an activist Republican at a time when most Mormons were Democrats.[72]

In summary, these early women's rights activists and intellectuals were significant because they articulated the concerns of many (white) western women about their lack of political and economic rights. They provided geographically isolated populations with information, advice, and motivation, stimulating organization. They established regional networks and national connections, although they frequently questioned whether eastern suffragists adequately represented "national" leadership. They lived challenging lives as individual examples of courage and commitment to a basic justice, undaunted by criticism and slander. While more conservative suffragists eventually rejected these early radical leaders as contentious, autocratic, legalistic, or old-fashioned, few failed to acknowledge the trailblazing contributions of this first generation of "pioneers."

3

Reconstruction, Woman Suffrage, and Territorial Politics in the West

> If we once establish the false principle, that United States citizen-
> ship does not carry with it the right to vote in every state in this
> Union, there is no end to the petty freaks and cunning devices that
> will be resorted to, to exclude one and another class of citizens
> from the right of suffrage.   —Susan B. Anthony[1]

There is a tendency to dismiss the early enfranchisement of women in Wyoming (1869) and in Utah (1870) as isolated western anomalies, but these events acquire greater significance when examined within the context of Reconstruction, territorial, and statehood politics. The Reconstruction amendments restructured American citizenship, but tensions and conflicting interpretations over national and state identity persisted. Within this transformed political environment, suffragists tried to define the ballot as a fundamental right of citizenship, but the U.S. Supreme Court squashed this "New Departure" strategy in the mid-1870s. Several important decisions at that time indicated increasing judicial tolerance for narrow interpretations of the constitutional guarantees of the Reconstruction amendments.

Nevertheless, woman suffrage continued to stimulate discussions of citizenship and nationalism as part of a larger process of national civic definition in the late nineteenth century. Several scholars have described a shift in suffrage logic from *natural* rights to *national* rights, "from antebellum arguments for women's ballots based on the abstract rights of individuals to post-bellum arguments based on the rights of citizens." As citizenship rights became increasingly racialized and restricted, the tension within the suffrage movement between the dynamic interaction between natural rights and political pragmatism was also acute. Some suffragists made racist political compromises, while others established alliances with social justice and participatory democracy movements.[2]

In the territories, the statehood process kept issues of federal control over the ballot and voter qualifications alive from Reconstruction until the early twentieth century, and suffragists took advantage of those opportunities. The tiny territorial legislatures could and sometimes did enfranchise women, but Congress could and did disfranchise some of them. States gained the power to determine the composition of their electorates, so woman suffragists pushed for inclusion in territorial constitutional conventions. These debates frequently used racialist arguments and proposed literacy or property requirements to disfranchise nonwhite voters. Paradoxically, woman suffrage was discussed as both a basic citizenship right and a strategy to maintain white supremacy. Ultimately, most delegates preferred to restrict rather than to extend the franchise, and to sacrifice woman suffrage to statehood.

The larger context of Reconstruction in the West has not been well studied, despite the antebellum conflicts over the expansion of slavery into the region. After the Civil War, western congressional representatives were strongly Republican, accustomed to federal administration, and pushing for extensive economic development. Actively complaining of regional neglect, they demanded federally funded projects and pressed for an end to southern Reconstruction. On the West Coast, with the largest populations of Democrats and former southerners as well as Chinese, the Democrats revived their party with free labor and anti-Chinese rhetoric. Oregon and California both rejected the Fifteenth Amendment, helping the Democrats regain political control in these states. Westerners defeated African American suffrage in most territorial referenda votes, often due to concerns about the effects of civil rights legislation on local racial-ethnic groups. African American efforts to block or repeal discriminatory legislation were largely unsuccessful until the passage of the Territorial Suffrage Act in 1867. Largely overlooked as a Reconstruction act, this legislation resulted when African Americans in Colorado lobbied Congress *against* statehood unless and until proposed state constitutions included voting rights guarantees—at least for men.[3]

Suffragists were angry about the failure of the Reconstruction amendments to grant universal suffrage explicitly, but they developed a judicial argument to gain the vote. The "New Departure" strategy asserted that the Fourteenth Amendment established national citizenship, with the vote as a basic right guaranteed by the Fifteenth Amendment. The strength of this interpretation, which is now generally accepted, encouraged Susan B. Anthony. Early in 1871, she wrote enthusiastically to Laura DeForce Gordon exclaiming "I have new life, new hope that our battle is to be short, sharp and decisive under this 14th & 15th Amendment clause—it is unanswerable."[4] Different individuals developed this idea, but it was most clearly articulated by Francis and Virginia Minor in 1869 and by Victoria Woodhull in her 1871 presentation to Congress. Stanton, Anthony, and the Minors advocated direct grassroots action, urging women to attempt to vote. In 1872, Anthony was arrested and tried for voting, but her famous case was not unique. A series of adverse U.S. Supreme Court rulings ended these experiments by the mid-1870s. The 1873 *Bradwell* and *Slaughterhouse* decisions both rejected the argument that the Fourteenth Amendment had created new rights or established the supremacy of national over state citizenship. The case of *Minor v. Happersett* (1875) decided that the Constitution did not automatically grant the right of suffrage as a condition of U.S. citizenship. Anthony was not alone in realizing that these decisions set dangerous precedents, which the Court immediately began citing to allow limits on the suffrage of African American freedmen. [5]

As Stanton and Anthony traveled west in 1871, they urged suffragists to implement the New Departure voting strategy and encountered women who had already tried. In July, Stanton encouraged San Francisco women to register to vote on the "no taxation without representation" principle; in August, nine women, including Emily Pitts-Stevens, made an attempt, but the county clerk dismissed the case.[6] In Santa Cruz, Stanton and Anthony met Ellen Van Valkenburg, a wealthy widow who had filed a lawsuit when her registration was refused. Reportedly inspired by the enfranchisement of Wyoming women, the local suffrage society had set up this test case with the county clerk, Albert Brown, a suffragist ally. When Brown formally rejected Van Valkenberg's registration, she went to the state Supreme Court, and then considered an appeal to the U.S. Supreme Court.[7] In a letter to Laura Gordon, she reported that the judge who had ruled against her was sympathetic, urging the women "to press forward for a 16th Amendment." Despite its failure, Van Valkenburg concluded that her challenge had gained significant attention and support, and she was encouraged "that Mrs. Stanton and Miss Anthony think we have been doing a good work for the enfranchisement of our sex."[8]

After the New Departure strategy failed, Stanton and Anthony focused on a federal woman suffrage amendment. Initially proposed as the Sixteenth Amendment, ultimately passed as the Nineteenth Amendment, and often known as the "Anthony Amendment," it is quite simple: "The right of citizens to vote shall not be denied or abridged by the United States or by any State on account of sex." California Senator Aaron A. Sargent, a good friend of Susan B. Anthony, formally introduced the measure in the U.S. Congress in 1878. Anthony, Sargent, and Mrs. Ellen Clark Sargent became well acquainted in the winter of 1872 during a long snowbound train trip east. Luckily Ellen Sargent brought a big bag of crackers.[9] Senator Sargent was a stalwart Republican closely identified with the Southern Pacific Railroad machine, so his support for woman suffrage was politically contradictory but quite firm. In 1871, a nervous Ellen Sargent asked Laura Gordon to excuse her husband from public statements of support, but at the next suffrage convention he delivered "a radical speech . . . taking the most advanced views." Upon concluding, Sargent remarked to a friend: "They have my views now, and can make the most of them. I would not conceal them to be senator."[10] Ellen Sargent became a stalwart of the California movement after they relocated from Nevada to San Francisco, and she continued to file tax suits long after the courts had rejected this strategy. By the end of her life, Sargent declared herself "a homemade anarchist and this Gov. [*sic*] has made me so." When she died during the 1911 suffrage referendum campaign, the flags of San Francisco flew at half-mast for the first time in honor of a woman.[11]

As a consistent supporter of women's rights, Aaron Sargent introduced woman suffrage into congressional debates whenever possible, and he used every argument he could muster.[12] In 1871 and 1876, he tried to attach it to District of Columbia government bills. In a territorial debate in 1874, Sargent tried to include "sex" as a protected suffrage category. He acknowledged the dedicated activists, numerous petitions, and "large and popular conventions . . . making strong efforts," and warned, "There is as much agitation on this point as there was for the abolition of slavery before the war broke out." Sargent discussed the Reconstruction amendments, the example of Wyoming, "good government" issues, and he also included an "appeal" for "the great class of laboring women in the country." He reiterated the New Departure claim that large classes of people should not be excluded from the vote under the Reconstruction Amendments, but this was the weak spot in his argument. When an opponent observed that California included a very large class of disfranchised "Asiatics," Sargent was unable to resolve the contradiction between his support for female enfranchisement and Chinese exclusion and dropped the point. Four years later, however, he formally introduced the federal woman suffrage amendment in the Senate, although that august body did not vote on the matter until 1887.[13]

Sargent's career representing Nevada and California in both Houses of Congress indicates the political volatility of California from its inception. Due to rapid Anglo-American settlement and the Gold Rush, California was never a territory, becoming a state in the Compromise of 1850. Within thirty years, two constitutional conventions had debated women's rights. After the end of the Mexican American War (1849–1850), the first convention addressed incompatibilities in the Hispanic and Anglo-American legal systems relating to the status of women, specifically property rights. In arguing for woman suffrage, future Union general Henry Wager Halleck hoped to attract women to the heavily male state: "I would call upon all the bachelors in this Convention to vote for it. . . . It is the best provision to get us wives that we can introduce."[14] The California constitutional convention of 1879 convened in response to massive working-class agitation, organized as the anti-Chinese, anti-monopolist Workingmen's Party of California (WPC) (also known as "sand-lotters" for their tendency to riot after open-air meetings). Senator Sargent considered the WPC "a violent faction which assailed property rights and demanded extreme concessions to labor." Their "unfortunate" timing resulted in "a constitution extraordinary in some of its features, but which was adopted by the people after a fierce contest."[15]

The WPC was not supportive of woman suffrage, and the new constitution did not enfranchise California women, but it did contain equal education and employment clauses, largely due to the ability of women's rights activists to take advantage of anti-Chinese prejudice.[16] Some convention delegates accepted woman suffrage, usually on the presumption of white female superiority, and saw no contradiction in supporting equal rights for white women and Chinese exclusion simultaneously. One man observed that "a woman who has to pay her taxes has as good a right to vote as a man. If we give negroes, and Chinamen, and everything else, a right to vote . . . why in the name of God don't you give them equal rights. The woman is just as intelligent. . . ." At this point, another delegate interrupted, "Are you going over to that doctrine of the universal brotherhood of man?" and the first responded, "In regard to women, I am."[17] Countering ominous predictions that 25,000 Chinese voters "would always be masters at the polls, and us," enfranchising white women would be "a legal and constitutional way to prevent the Chinese power in this state." Obviously, "if you allow ten or fifteen thousand women to vote, will they not overbalance the Chinese power and give us the majority?"[18] Even when supportive of women, white labor's implacable hostility to the Chinese undermined otherwise egalitarian tendencies and goals and helped reinforce exclusionary democracy.

White western women's attitudes toward the Chinese varied, usually due to their class position. In 1871, Susan B. Anthony identified the Chinese as scapegoats, but angrily rejected being stuck in the same legal category of inferior and dependent persons. She condemned exclusionary proposals as a "pretense . . . matched only by their denial of citizenship to the women of the entire nation." Abigail Duniway was less enthusiastic about the Chinese than Caroline Churchill, but both feminist journalists noted how frequently Chinese workers relieved white western women of the heaviest burdens of housework, especially laundry.[19] Replacing Chinese workers was difficult because white working-class women disliked domestic work and tried to limit their employment in this area, creating a putative "servant problem." Commenting from the working woman's point of view, San Francisco socialist Anna Haskell cited the disrespectful treatment of domestic workers received as a major reason "that women teach and clerk and sew and do anything or everything except housework."

Some working-class suffragists shared the anti-Asian prejudice and hostile gendered imagery of the labor movement, while others understood their common oppression within the secondary labor market. Sue Ross Kennan, a Portland boardinghouse keeper, trade unionist, and suffragist, often stressed the displacement of white women and children workers. She fumed that "as a mother she had worked hard to raise her family and wanted her children to have a chance to make an honest living 'by the sweat of their brow.'"[20] In Seattle, Mary Kentworthy was president of the King County Equal Suffrage League in 1883, and part of an anti-vice coalition in 1884, but in 1885 and 1886 she was a leading anti-Chinese agitator. In 1886, she was one of a group that was later indicted, tried, and acquitted under anti-KKK statutes for advocating the forceful expulsion of the Chinese. Kentworthy organized a women's group that investigated Chinese living and working conditions, warned the Chinese out of town, and visited Seattle women to convince them to fire Chinese servants. Laura Hall Peters, a labor activist, utopian socialist, Populist, and state suffrage official, assisted Kentworthy in these activities and raised money for her legal defense. The strong turnout of working-class women in the 1886 municipal elections and their public presence at anti-Chinese rallies and disturbances upset the "law and order" group, including many of the progressive men who otherwise supported woman suffrage. Clarence Bagley later suggested that this alienation undermined their enthusiasm for the experiment and limited their protests to disfranchisement in 1888.[21]

California's most prominent female anti-Chinese agitator was Anna Ferry Smith, an early labor radical and suffragist, later a Nationalist, Populist, and Socialist. Significantly, Smith seems to have reversed her position in the late 1870s, perhaps the price of acceptance into organized radical politics. In 1880, she supported expulsion, hoping "to see every Chinaman—*white or yellow*—thrown out of this state" (a likely reference to class divisions within the Chinese community). Yet Smith had been very supportive of the Chinese four years earlier while testifying at hearings of the Congressional Joint Special Committee to Investigate Chinese Immigration in San Francisco (1876). Questioned by Senator Aaron Sargent, Smith reported that she had operated a laundry in Colorado, employed Chinese workers, and "found them honest, truthful, fair, and straightforward in their dealings with me at all times." She stated that Chinese men were no worse, and possibly better servants than whites. Smith could not maintain this attitude in contradiction to the antagonistic position of western organized labor at this time.

Laura DeForce Gordon was also a labor activist and a Democrat who supported the party's anti-Chinese line out of conviction or political expediency. Gordon attended the 1879 constitutional convention as a newspaper correspondent and suffrage lobbyist, and she took advantage of the political climate to win two important women's rights clauses. Article 2, Section 18 stated, "No person shall be debarred admission to any of the collegiate departments of the State University on account of sex." (This provision later helped Laura Gordon and Clara Foltz win their case against Hastings Law School.) Gordon worked closely with two prominent delegates who moved to delete a poorly designed anti-Chinese clause, substituting an anti-employment discrimination clause. Article 20, Section 18, passed without comment: "No person shall, on account of sex, be disqualified from entering upon or pursuing any lawful business, vocation or profession." One important ally, Democrat Charles Ringgold, informed Gordon, "The agony is over—the child is born, but is a bastard." Nevertheless, "Your section, presented by me, is preserved, thanks to the ignorance of many whom [*sic*] supported it not knowing the privileges it extends."[22] These unusual provisions did not grant the right to vote, however, and the state constitutional moment had passed by the 1880s.

Unlike California, most territories went through an established process for statehood based on the 1787 Northwest Ordinance. When the population reached 60,000, residents could ask Congress to authorize a constitutional convention, then review the document and vote on admission.[23] In general, representatives were unwilling to jeopardize statehood with radical provisions, but sometimes they were willing to experiment. Wyoming, Utah, and Washington territories all had exceptional histories of early female enfranchisement. The reasons for passage of woman suffrage in Wyoming in 1869 are not completely clear, partly because there was surprisingly little initial discussion. William H. Bright introduced the measure in the territorial legislature, influenced by his wife, several other local women (including Esther Morris), and by the territorial secretary, Edward M. Lee, the probable author of the bill.[24] Mrs. Bright later reported that her husband, a southerner, decided that since Negroes could vote, so should his own wife and mother. In a letter to the *Denver Tribune,* however, Bright gave different reasons: "I knew it was a new issue, and a live one and with a strong feeling that it was just, I determined to use all my influence."

The leader of the opposition indicated that the law was passed as a joke before his colleagues could reconsider their action. Some supported a "big noise" designed to advertise the territory and encourage immigration, while others hoped that white women would offset the growing number of African American voters in Wyoming. One unidentified member reportedly remarked, "Damn it, if you are going to let the niggers and pigtails vote, we will ring in the women, too." Perhaps the Democratic territorial legislature hoped to embarrass the Republican governor, John Campbell, who did not support woman suffrage, but he surprised everyone and quickly signed the bill. Apparently Mrs. Campbell exerted significant influence, but she insisted that "the spirit of justice to women and their intelligence" ultimately persuaded her husband to approve the measure.[25] As they began to vote, Wyoming women apparently favored the Republican Party, disrupting the Democratic monopoly of the legislature in 1871. The Democrats retaliated by attempting to repeal the woman suffrage law during the next session, but they could not override the governor's veto.

There was little organized suffrage activity prior to enfranchisement, and not much afterward until Wyoming applied for statehood. In 1873, a group of about sixty women called a mass meeting to form their own Woman's Party and nominate female legislative candidates, but they received little support and the organization died.[26] In 1889, the possibility of statehood mobilized Wyoming women to elect delegates sympathetic to a permanent woman suffrage provision. At the 1889 constitutional convention, an effort to require a popular referendum on woman suffrage was soundly defeated. When Wyoming applied for statehood, the largely Democratic opposition in the U.S. Congress resisted the admission of another Republican state by attempting to block the woman suffrage clause. This opposition put some congressional Democrats in the very awkward position of arguing *against* their states' rights principle that every state (or potential state, i.e., territory) should determine the qualifications of its voters. Wyoming delegates stated forcefully that they would become a state with their women voters or not at all, and the measure passed by a close vote in 1890.[27]

Congressional Republicans were also inconsistent when they supported the admission of Wyoming but opposed the entry of Democratic Utah as a woman suffrage state. Statehood for Utah presented some unique issues, particularly the continuing Mormon practice of polygamy, linked by Republicans with slavery as the "twin relics of barbarism." Congress began efforts to reform polygamous Mormons during Reconstruction. Some early non-Mormon proposals to enfranchise Utah women assumed that they would vote to reject polygamy. The Mormon elders knew differently and approved the passage of woman suffrage legislation in 1870. In the 1880s, Congress passed increasingly harsh anti-polygamy legislation, beginning with the Edmunds Act (1882), which authorized anti-polygamy sanctions that included disfranchisement. In 1887, two major pieces of legislation firmly established federal control over territorial as well as Native American voting rights. The Dawes Act included provisions for Native citizenship after renunciation of tribal affiliation, while the Edmunds-Tucker Act disfranchised Mormons, male and female. To be consistent, states' rights advocates opposed the Edmunds-Tucker Act and reluctantly supported woman suffrage in Utah, but others ignored this principle and helped pass the bill even though it strengthened federal control over voting rights. In 1890, the Mormon leadership capitulated and rejected plural marriage in the Woodruff Manifesto. In 1893, the men of Utah were refranchised, but not the women, who had to wait until statehood in 1896.[28]

The Utah Woman Suffrage Association formed early in 1889, stimulated by the constitutional process and encouraged by suffrage journalist and NWSA organizer Clara Colby. The "Mormon question" further disrupted a divided woman suffrage movement, however, as members of the American Woman Suffrage Association (AWSA) were dedicated to the elimination of polygamy at any cost. Stanton, Anthony, and other leaders of the National Woman Suffrage Association (NWSA) also disapproved of polygamy but rejected any effort to disfranchise women. In 1871, Stanton and Anthony stopped and spoke in Salt Lake City, and they subsequently maintained contact with Utah suffragists. This connection was uncomfortable and controversial, but NWSA leaders consistently defended woman suffrage in Utah and protested punitive legislation.[29]

The abolition of polygamy helped ease these tensions and Utah moved toward statehood. As the 1895 constitutional convention approached, Susan B. Anthony issued her standard warning to avoid being "deluded by any specious reasoning," and to resist any proposals that woman suffrage be submitted to a separate vote. She advised them to "demand justice now. Once ignored in your constitution—you'll be as powerless to secure recognition as are we in the older states."[30] In preparation for the convention, Utah suffragists obtained endorsements from both major parties and identified sympathetic delegates. Emmeline Wells, publisher of the *Women's Exponent* and president of the state suffrage association, led a delegation to the convention session when their petition for refranchisement was presented.[31] Expecting quick success, the suffragists were surprised when the issue became controversial and consumed two weeks of debate. As Anthony had predicted, opponents proposed the separate submission of a woman suffrage amendment in the ratification election (where it might be defeated), and they also attempted to separate delegates from their party platform pledges. These efforts were unsuccessful, and Utah became the third woman suffrage state in 1896 (after Colorado in 1893).[32]

The cases of Wyoming and Utah are familiar, but woman suffrage in Washington Territory also had an unusual history of early enfranchisement and disfranchisement closely related to statehood aspirations. The territorial legislature approved the measure in 1883, but the territorial Supreme Court invalidated the law in 1888. In 1910, Washington women regained the right to vote in a vanguard state victory. Despite regional similarities, there were important political differences between Oregon, which became a state in 1859, and Washington, which remained a territory until 1889. Early white residents in Oregon's Willamette Valley were often transplanted Southern Democrats or former anti-slavery residents of the border regions (like Abigail Scott Duniway). Even in Portland, with a larger population of Republican New Englanders, Democratic machines traditionally controlled party politics.[33] In contrast, the area north of the Columbia River was predominantly Republican during the territorial period.[34] In Washington Territory, a woman suffrage proposal came within one vote of passage in 1854. In 1867, an effort to disfranchise former Confederate soldiers resulted in a new law that could be interpreted as allowing white women to vote. In the fall of 1868, a pro-suffrage legislator, Edward Eldridge, wrote a series of articles presenting an early version of the "New Departure" strategy and arguing that women could vote under the new Reconstruction laws.

In 1869, Mary Olney Brown decided to test these ideas by attempting to vote in Washington Territory. An Iowa native who had lost two children while moving west in 1846, Brown was an active suffrage writer and lobbyist until her death in 1886.[35] Unable to convince other women to join her, Brown went to the polls with her husband, daughter, and son-in-law. When she demanded to vote, election officials informed Brown that she was not an American citizen. She started to read the Fourteenth Amendment, but was told "the laws of congress don't extend over Washington territory." Brown argued "that the . . . emancipation of the Southern slaves threw upon the country a class of people, who, like the women of the nation, owed allegiance to the government, but whose citizenship was not recognized. To settle this question, the fourteenth amendment was adopted." Brown recalled how "an Irishman called out, 'It would be more sensible to let an intelligent white woman vote than an ignorant nigger.' Cries of 'Good for you, Pat! good for you, Pat!' indicated the impression that had been made." One election official conceded the principle but rejected her ballot out of concern that it would invalidate the entire precinct vote. The following year, Olympia officials simply ignored Brown's challenge, but her sister organized women in another town, and they voted by hosting a picnic dinner for the election officials right before making their demand. Quickly informed and inspired by this success, another local group of women went out and cast their ballots, too.[36] In the fall of 1871, the Washington legislature passed a new law explicitly prohibiting women from voting, despite a personal plea from Susan B. Anthony.[37]

Throughout the 1870s, Abigail Duniway and other suffrage activists assiduously lobbied the Oregon state and Washington territorial legislatures and constitutional conventions.[38] When one Oregon legislator who claimed that no respectable woman in his county wanted to vote received a petition headed by the name of his own wife, he became so upset that he provoked a reprimand from the chair. Duniway noted that "the ladies of his district have successfully defeated his candidacies for office ever since."[39] Suffragists made some partial gains, as full suffrage received large votes in the Oregon state legislature in 1871, 1873, and 1875, and women's school voting and office-holding measures passed in 1877. An early Washington constitutional convention in 1878 rejected a woman suffrage measure by only one vote (8 to 7). As a compromise, delegates placed woman suffrage and prohibition amendments on the referendum ballot, but both lost. Paired referenda elections, which reinforced the linkage between these two controversial issues, always lost.[40]

As in other areas, proponents and opponents of woman suffrage both consistently employed racial rhetoric within the context of Reconstruction-era politics. Republican Cyrus Reed, an early ally, was the only man who could be convinced to join Duniway and "Mrs. Beatty (colored)" on the platform at the first meeting of a new Oregon state association in February 1873.[41] In 1881, William H. White, "a Democrat of the old ['states rights'] school," assisted the suffragists in the Washington territorial legislature. In debate, White "based his plea for woman suffrage upon the enfranchisement of the colored men, urging it strongly as a means of Democratic retaliation." After the bill passed the lower chamber, it was narrowly defeated by the upper territorial council. At a subsequent public meeting, White charged "saloon-keepers" with using alcohol to influence council members to oppose the measure, a charge none of the officials present bothered to deny. Washington suffragists were encouraged by the passage of a strong married women's property act, however, and correctly anticipated success in the next territorial legislative session.[42]

Duniway claimed that there was little suffrage activity in the fall of 1883 when she arrived in Olympia to lobby the Washington territorial legislature. She reported that local women had been intimidated by criticism that such behavior was unfeminine, or lulled into thinking that it was unnecessary.[43] She was not particularly welcome, either, by those who resented her ego, her tactics, or her interference. The woman suffrage measure was introduced by a Republican member as a novelty, but others agreed that this was "as a good time to try to experiment—if experiment it was—and if it proved a failure, it could be corrected when we become a state." The bill carried both houses with bipartisan support.[44] Some editors scolded: "Every legislature seems to try to do something greater or more absurd than its predecessors, so our present one has achieved notoriety by passing the woman suffrage bill."[45] Others expected much from new women voters: "purity, progress, and reform" and "intelligence, temperance and good morals." A sympathetic reform editor, Charles Bagley, described the victory as "a triumph of justice," but he warned that woman suffrage was "now on trial" in Washington Territory.[46]

As in Wyoming, the woman suffrage experiment in Washington was heavily scrutinized. As voters, Washington women received new attention and respect. One Port Townsend resident, recently relocated from New Orleans, stated that she had never received such "respectful consideration," although she was "accustomed from babyhood to the deferential gallantry of the men of the South." Many observers reported high turnouts among women, more orderly elections, and cleaner candidates. Duniway published stories about Washington women serving on grand juries, participating in political meetings, and voting for reform candidates. In 1884, both the Democratic and Republican conventions endorsed the innovation, and it was generally "conceded that ethics had become a factor in politics." The *Seattle Post-Intelligencer* observed that women "display as much interest as the men, and, if anything, more . . . a warning to that undesirable class of the community . . . that disregard of law and the decencies of civilization will not be tolerated."[47]

Yet they also provoked hostility and backlash, especially with reform projects like prohibition. In 1884, Seattle women immediately became involved in political housekeeping, supporting an anti-vice campaign and a municipal reform slate in large numbers. In 1886, Seattle politicians courted female votes, but prohibitionist and suffragist women split over a local option liquor-control campaign as well as anti-Chinese tension.[48]

Duniway was concerned that antagonizing powerful vice and liquor interests would encourage challenges to suffrage, and her accommodation of the opposition and criticism of prohibitionists infuriated temperance supporters. When an Oregon woman suffrage referendum lost badly in 1884, Duniway denounced both the vice interests and the "ignorant rabble" stirred up by prohibitionists.[49] In Washington in 1886, she actively campaigned against local option, arguing that it was a decoy by the liquor interests to discredit women. Indeed, they were blamed by all parties for sponsoring such a divisive issue.[50] Duniway's contentious behavior convinced many suffragists that she had become a liability. Another energetic organizer and former president of the Oregon suffrage association, Hannah Loughary, and others convinced Duniway to withdraw from active suffrage work. Depressed by her daughter's death, she conceded that "maybe these ladies are right; maybe, if I should get out of their way the work would be more successful." Duniway lived on an Idaho ranch from 1886 to 1894, and did not resume serious suffrage activity until after the death of her invalid husband in 1896.[51]

As Duniway anticipated, these activities did awaken the powerful oppositional interests that ultimately destroyed the woman suffrage experiment in Washington Territory. Opponents claimed that woman suffrage endangered statehood, especially after congressional debates in 1886 included an unsuccessful proposal to disfranchise women voters (the Eustis Amendment). Senator Eustis and other Southern Democrats articulated explicitly racial rationales and reminded western senators that allowing territorial legislatures to determine their own voting requirements could enfranchise "Chinamen," who were otherwise "ineligible for citizenship" under the 1882 Chinese Exclusion Act.[52] Other Democrats opposed woman suffrage, but rejected this effort because it contravened states' rights principles and privileged federal control over voting rights.

As Washington planned another constitutional convention in the summer of 1889, opponents moved quickly to eliminate women from the statehood process and the electorate. Early in 1887, Jeff Harland, a member of a Tacoma gambling ring, appealed his conviction by a mixed jury on the grounds that women were not legal voters and thus ineligible for jury service. The Washington territorial court dismissed the woman suffrage law on a technicality, but the next legislature passed a revised version early in 1888.[53] In April 1886, Mrs. Nevada Bloomer, a dancehall girl, "the wife of a saloon-keeper and herself an avowed opponent of woman suffrage," filed a more serious challenge to the law's constitutionality. In mid-August, two newly appointed territorial Supreme Court justices decided "a Territorial Legislature had no right to enfranchise women." Chief Justice Roger S. Greene dissented, as did Justice John P. Hoyt, but the latter was disqualified because he had heard the case in a lower court. The decision, which ignored the precedents of Wyoming and Utah, as well as explicit provisions in the organic act, was widely attributed to Democratic judicial manipulation.[54] Many people believed that Washington women had been cheated out of their votes by a Democratic political maneuver. In Congress the following spring, Senator George Hoar (R-MA) proposed that they should be eligible to elect and serve as constitutional convention delegates, and he was supported by a number of distinguished colleagues, including Henry Blair (R-NH), Henry Dawes (R-MA), and Leland Stanford (R-CA).[55]

Angry disfranchised Washington women began organizing for the upcoming constitutional convention. Laura Peters recalled: "I was paralyzed when I saw . . . that the rights had been taken from us, and I have hardly got over my paralytic shock yet. . . . I believe we should go into the war and fight against the war on women."[56] In March 1889, they established the Equal Suffrage League under the leadership of Zerelda McCoy and initiated a statewide leafleting and petitioning effort intended to place a woman suffrage article into the new state constitution. Clara Colby and Mrs. E. L. Saxon began organizing in April, and labor suffragist Matilda Hindman of Pennsylvania made an extensive speaking tour during the summer. The Seattle Equal Suffrage League invited Laura DeForce Gordon, president of the California state association, who was funded by Sarah Knox-Goodrich and Ellen Sargent. Colby used the *Woman's Tribune* to appeal for help in "this struggle against machine politics and the allied forces of vice and corruption." Colby, McCoy, and others recommended rejecting any constitution that lacked an equal suffrage clause, even if it meant delaying statehood.[57]

When the constitutional convention assembled in Olympia in July 1889, the suffragists met concurrently and resolved that "any Constitution which does not recognize and embody" woman suffrage "is not republican in form, and is repugnant to the principles of the Declaration of Independence."[58] Advocates at the constitutional convention included longtime ally Edward Eldridge, Henry B. Blackwell, the venerable Eastern suffragist, and Justice Hoyt, who almost lost the convention presidency because of his suffrage sympathies. They could not win full or partial suffrage from delegates who were convinced that such a radical proposal would defeat the new constitution, but the convention did authorize separate suffrage and prohibition amendments on the November ratification ballot.[59] Organizers had little time to prepare for an election in two months, so the Equal Suffrage League proposed a radical strategy: women should attempt to vote in the ratification election. If the U.S. Supreme Court later overturned the recent territorial court decision, the women's ballots would be counted and certainly carry the woman suffrage amendment. The very negative referendum vote (35,527 to 16,613) scuttled this plan, and the establishment of state government ended the territorial experiment. As in other states, Washington suffragists now faced the laborious two-stage process of winning legislative authorization *and* a popular referendum. In 1890, the legislature granted Washington women school suffrage, but it was poor consolation. Despite Populist agitation and continuing WCTU activism, full refranchisement would have to wait another twenty years.[60]

After 1888, a number of territories made plans for statehood. Montana held a constitutional convention in 1889 that granted partial school and taxpaying suffrage. Throughout the 1890s, suffragists unsuccessfully lobbied the legislature for a referendum bill, but even with Populist support they failed to obtain the necessary two-thirds majority. Ella Knowles Haskell, a Montana attorney and prominent Populist, was an important early leader, but she died in 1911.[61] In the early 1900s, the Populists continued to support woman suffrage, and the NAWSA continued to send top organizers. For example, Carrie Catt, Laura Gregg, and Gail Laughlin all visited in 1902. They held mass meetings, targeted clubs and labor unions, and organized suffrage clubs. Laughlin stayed to lobby the 1903 legislature because the governor seemed supportive, but these efforts were frustrated and the movement languished until it was reinvigorated by a new leader, Jeannette Rankin. In 1911, Rankin addressed the state legislature, then spent the next three years organizing, lobbying politicians, and winning a popular referendum in November 1914. In 1916, Rankin became the first woman elected to the House of Representatives, where she became famous for her pacifist opposition to both world wars. [62]

The statehood process extended Reconstruction-era controversies over race, citizenship, and the composition of the electorate into the twentieth century. Most of the remaining western "frontiers" were incorporated into the nation by the end of 1912. In Oklahoma, increased activism by WCTU members, Populists, and NAWSA organizers pushed woman suffrage bills through the state House in 1897 and 1899, only to be killed by Southern Democrats in the Senate. Agitation revived after the federal Hamilton bill (1904) authorized the admission of Oklahoma, Indian Territory, Arizona, and New Mexico territories. Nationally, suffragists protested this bill because it allowed the abridgment of voting rights by "sex," and they succeeded in eliminating the offending clause.[63] As Oklahoma prepared for a constitutional convention in 1906, Susan B. Anthony repeated her warning that if woman suffrage were excluded at this stage, "it will take a long time and a great deal of hard work to convert over one-half of the men to vote for it." At the convention, a strong farmer-labor-socialist coalition included woman suffrage on its agenda, but the Southern Democratic majority blocked the measure with racist and red-baiting rhetoric.[64] Oklahoma became a state in 1907, but did not approve woman suffrage until 1912. The *Woman's Tribune* commended the "women of Oklahoma who have done as much to build up that Territory as the men have done," and advised them to resist separate submission. Colby believed "it would be wiser to stand for their rights at every step of the way," although she proposed a compromise, "a simple clause making women voters for members of the constitutional convention."[65]

In Arizona, early activists included Josephine Brawley Hughes, a teacher and the wife of the territorial governor from 1893 to 1896. Hughes founded the *Arizona Weekly Star* in 1877 as a Democratic, pro-labor, temperance paper, and in 1895, the paper and the governor supported an unsuccessful suffrage measure. In 1899, NAWSA organizer Carrie Catt spent a month lobbying the legislature, and in the early 1900s, a small group of suffragists, including Lida Robinson and Frances Munds, continued this work.[66] In 1903, they won the requisite two-thirds votes, but the governor vetoed the measure. In 1905, the NAWSA sent Mary Bradford of Denver to help, but the political situation seemed hopeless. Robinson moved away, and the effort languished until NAWSA organizer Laura Clay arrived in 1909 and began working with Munds to create a territorial suffrage organization. Anticipating statehood in 1912, suffragists won pledges of support from one-third of the constitutional convention delegates, but despite their strong labor and progressive sympathies, Munds accurately described the convention as "far too timid to put anything so 'radical' as woman suffrage in the constitution." Progressives did implement the initiative process, however, which allowed suffragists to bypass the legislature and place the issue directly on the ballot. In 1912, Munds and Hughes led a quiet campaign, assisted by

NAWSA organizers Laura Gregg and Laura Johns, as well as Alice Park of California. The measure passed easily (13,442 to 6,202) with heavy labor and socialist support.[67]

New Mexico also became a state in 1912, but woman suffrage was delayed until passage of the federal amendment by an impossibly difficult constitutional amendment process ironically intended to protect Hispanic voting rights. In 1909, New Mexico women's clubs formed a state federation and successfully requested partial suffrage in the 1910 state constitution, but full woman suffrage was virtually impossible to achieve.[68] In 1912, when Alaska applied to Congress for organization as a territory, a Wyoming congressman added an amendment giving the territorial legislature explicit authority to enfranchise women, which it did unanimously the following year (1913). The Alaska bill had to consider the roughly 10 percent of women who were Native American, so it contained special provisions. Indian women could vote if married to voting white men, married to an Indian who had "severed tribal relations," or were unmarried and "severed."[69]

Thus the vigorous debate over definitions of citizenship, the limits of the franchise, and the composition of the polity that characterized the Reconstruction West persisted into the twentieth century. Suffragists used the constitutional process required for statehood to protest the political exclusion of women and to petition for the franchise. Once the territorial constitutional moments passed, however, the new state systems posed many obstacles to winning legislative authorizations and public elections. This important goal was first achieved in Colorado in 1893, when economic misfortune encouraged radical political experimentation.

Colorado women voted regularly after their enfranchisement in 1893. (Courtesy of the Denver Public Library, Western History Collection.)

Susan B. Anthony in Yosemite in 1895. After attending the 1895 Women's Congress in San Francisco, Anthony toured the state in preparation for the 1896 campaign. She is accompanied in the photograph by Anna Howard Shaw, Hester Harland, and others. (Reproduced by permission of the Huntington Library, San Marino, California.)

Suffrage leaders during the 1896 California campaign. The photograph is uncaptioned, but the individuals have been tentatively identified. From left to right, the front row consists of Lucy Anthony, Anna Howard Shaw, Susan B. Anthony, Ellen Sargent, and Mary Hays. Standing in the back, from left to right, are Ida Husted Harper, Selina Solomons, Carrie Chapman Catt, and Annie Bidwell. (Courtesy of the California Historical Society; FN-24015.)

Washington suffragists placing posters during the 1910 campaign. (Photograph by Asahel Curtis, #19943. Courtesy of the Washington State Historical Society.)

This poster by Bertha Boyé was the winner of the poster contest sponsored by the San Francisco College Equal Suffrage League during the 1911 California campaign. (Courtesy of the Schlesinger Library, Radcliffe Institute, Harvard University.)

The support of labor, and especially labor suffragists, was critical to western suffrage success, and one tactic was to join Labor Day parades. In this photograph, members of the Los Angeles Wage Earners Suffrage League, organized by Frances Noel in 1911, and their wagon. (Reproduced by permission of the Huntington Library, San Marino, California.)

Several activist Chinese women received the honor of being the first of their racial-ethnic group to register and vote, but the identity of this individual has not been firmly established. (Reproduced by permission of the Huntington Library, San Marino, California.)

4

Suffrage and Populism in the Silver State of Colorado

The vote is an indefinable something that makes you part of the plan of the world. It means the same to women that it does to men. You never ask a boy, "Have you closed the saloons, have you purified politics and driven all the political tricksters out of the state?" No, you put your hand on his shoulder and you say, "To-day, my boy, you are an American citizen," and that is what you say to your daughter.
—Sarah Platt Decker[1]

In 1893, Colorado became the first state to enfranchise women in a popular referendum after a vigorous campaign. The victory was radical because it was directly linked to third-party politics in a climate of financial panic and economic despair. This unexpected success demonstrated the importance of reform alliances, party endorsements, and politicized urban clubwomen. It also established the reputation of Carrie Chapman Catt as the NAWSA's top organizer, facilitating her elevation to the presidency in 1900. Catt stressed centralized control of affiliate organizations, systematic precinct canvassing, endorsements from all political parties, and elite leadership. The goal of her "society plan" was to enhance the respectability of the suffrage movement, but she first developed this strategy among radical Denver clubwomen. Avoiding partisanship but not politics, Colorado suffragists enlisted farmer-labor support, advocated "free silver" just like everyone else in the "Silver State," and defined woman suffrage as a vital social and economic reform. This success stimulated other Populist-inspired referenda in other states in the 1890s, but the unusual circumstances were difficult to replicate, and most of these failed, with the exception of Idaho in 1896.[2]

Colorado was one of several western territories considering the enfranchisement of women after the Civil War. Beginning in 1868, the territorial legislature discussed the issue periodically, especially after neighboring Wyoming women received the ballot in 1869. Early in 1870, Governor Edward McCook, a recent Republican appointee, and his
"gracefully aggressive" wife joined other prominent residents who lobbied for a woman suffrage bill, submitted petitions, and attended legislative sessions. When Elizabeth Cady Stanton and Susan B. Anthony passed
through Denver in 1871, they stayed with the McCook family, made well-
received speeches, and received considerable attention from a sympathetic local press. In 1870, Democratic legislators also supported the measure, perhaps to embarrass McCook. As typical during Reconstruction-
era debates, race figured prominently on both sides of the argument.
Some members of the heavily Democratic legislature protested the un-
fairness of excluding white women from suffrage when black men could
vote. Others resisted enfranchisement because they feared African American or Chinese women voters. One representative asked bluntly: "Are
the supporters of this measure aware that . . . they confer upon Negro
wenches the right to vote?" The legislature effectively killed this bill
through postponement.[3]

Interest in woman suffrage revived in 1876 as Colorado planned a cen-
tennial-year application for statehood. In preparation for the requisite
constitutional convention, the American Woman Suffrage Association
(AWSA) sent Margaret and John Campbell to Colorado late in 1875.[4] Albina Washburn recalled the excitement among "a few of us waiting ones
. . . then scattered" when the Campbells arrived. After a brief organizing
tour, the Campbells planned a suffrage convention in Denver in January
1876, carefully notifying constitutional convention delegates of the proceedings.[5] Dr. Alida C. Avery, a prominent physician well connected to
eastern suffragists, was elected the first president of the new Colorado
Woman Suffrage Association (CWSA). Another early leader, Mary
Shields, made her first public speech at this convention. Margaret Campbell concluded that it was the "intelligent and leading ladies of the city . . .
who first ranged themselves on the side of equal rights."[6] She was less encouraged by visits to Denver editors and ministers. One journalist agreed:
"Yes, I will publish that; I believe in human rights," but, "In another office the men looked at us as if we were lunatics, and said, 'No such thing
had ever been done in Denver.' Well, I answered, there must always be a
beginning. Some of us can remember when there was no such city as Den-

ver; even it had a beginning." Due to these efforts, the convention was well attended and judged a success.[7]

Soon a CWSA delegation confronted the state constitutional convention. Campbell, Shields, Washburn, and Ione (Mrs. John) Hanna, the wife of a prominent Denver banker, each spoke briefly at a meeting of the suffrage committee. Campbell stressed the basic theme of "no taxation without representation," which Shields reinforced with the example of taxpaying women in her hometown of Colorado Springs. From her experience in the Grange, Washburn testified that female voting worked well in practice. Hanna described herself as a recent convert, fully supported by her husband, who "represented a much larger class of women than either of the other ladies; the great class of women who are uninformed upon political questions," but who "believe it is our right and duty to vote."[8] Later the suffragists waited all morning for the full convention debate, then were informed that the session would adjourn without discussion of their question because "'the man who intended to make a speech against you, and who is one of the ablest debators, is drunk.' 'Drunk, is he?' I [Campbell] said, 'that is the kind of man we expect to oppose our cause, always and everywhere. If he is a suitable man to sit here to help make a constitution for us to live under, we ought to be glad to hear him, drunk or sober.'" Disregarding these objections, "the Convention adjourned and ate peanuts and smoked cigars, the remainder of the day."[9]

Fearful that any radical action might endanger statehood, the convention rejected full woman suffrage, but powerful allies helped broker a compromise. Henry H. R. Bromwell, a prominent Republican and a member of the suffrage committee, denounced his colleagues as "savages" and suggested that perhaps Colorado was not ready for statehood. Presented with legitimate petitions, "we cooly fling the request aside as though it came from the Cheyenne Indians." Bromwell and his colleague, Agapita Vigil, coauthored an influential and strongly supportive minority report.[10] Bromwell was a former congressman from Illinois with known feminist sympathies, but Vigil was a rancher from southern Colorado who spoke no English and represented a constituency presumed hostile to woman suffrage. Vigil, who conferred with suffragist Mary Shields through an interpreter, resisted considerable political pressure to change his position because he said he knew it was right. Both men were also involved in the subsequent campaign: Bromwell gave numerous speeches, and Vigil served on the state suffrage association executive board.[11]

The minority report strongly supported equal rights: "We are a human race, part of *us* are men, part of *us* are women—both equal—each superior and each inferior—each is part and parcel of the same humanity. If either is to tread on the other, why must Woman be the victim?" It denounced the disfranchisement of half the population as a significant problem in a republic, where "the right of Suffrage is part of being a shareholder in the government." Practical considerations included "more than three millions of children who are dependent on the support of their mothers or sisters." School suffrage, a suggested compromise, was "right as far as it goes, [but] it is not a magnanimous movement; for it appears to recognize a right without the determination to establish it."[12] Ultimately, the convention granted women the right to hold school office and to vote in school board elections, and instructed the first session of the new state legislature to schedule a popular vote on full woman suffrage.[13]

In 1877, few suffragists had experience organizing a popular referendum campaign, so Colorado activists sought help from national leaders. In the fall of 1876, Albina Washburn left her isolated dairy farm to attend the AWSA suffrage convention and solicit financial support. Washburn reported, "We have only skirmished a little, and the main battle, or a series of battles rather, are before us," and she requested "reinforcements: cavalry, artillery, infantry,—troops by land and sea; in short, the sinews of war in any shape or manner."[14] Margaret Campbell also made an East Coast fundraising trip, returning in June 1877.[15] In January 1877, a second state suffrage convention packed the hall on a bitterly cold evening and reelected Dr. Avery as president. She warned that "we are too far away . . . and too poor to make the longed for eastern aid possible to any great extent; we must depend on ourselves." In fact, Avery used her personal connections to attract a number of volunteers, including eastern suffrage luminaries Lucy Stone, Henry B. Blackwell, and Susan B. Anthony.[16]

Colorado suffragists developed experience and innovative tactics suited to a mass-based campaign. Press coverage expanded and became more respectful, especially as more elite women became involved. Campbell reported that woman suffrage was "the most prominent theme of public discussion" everywhere she went: "Miners discussed it around their campfires, and 'freighters' on their long slow journeys over the mountain trails argued pro and con, whether they should 'let' women have the ballot."[17] Mary Shields was particularly effective, with an "element of 'motherliness' it was, which gained her the respectful attention of an audience of the roughest and most ignorant Cornish miners in Caribou, who would listen to no other woman speaking upon the subject."[18] According to a Trinidad newspaper "Mrs. Shields lays no claims to oratorical powers, but she has a modest and unassuming manner of presenting her subject which carries force with it." After her first address in that town, "several influential Spanish-speaking citizens" asked Shields to delay her departure and speak again (through a translator) to a meeting of "over one hundred Spanish people . . . who gave the lecture close attention and showed considerable interest in the subject."[19] Shields had the unusual ability to communicate with diverse and potentially hostile constituencies, a valuable skill in a political campaign.

Basically the only way to contact voters in this isolated region was to get out and find them. The Campbells made two extensive tours during the summer, traveling over 1,250 miles in their horse and buggy.[20] The geography presented a formidable challenge: "To reach the voters in the little mining towns a hundred miles apart, over mountains such as these, involves hardships that only those who have made the journeys can understand."[21] Their adventures included a precipitous 30-mile burro ride over a 12,500-foot summit one afternoon. In California Gulch, the local schoolhouse "was filled, inside and outside, mostly with miners, some of whom had had too much to drink, and were not inclined to be quiet at first. They asked questions, which I answered as well as I was able, and at last they became interested, and were quite respectful to me. The saloon-keeper took up the collection." "In one of the little hamlets" they met "the since famous U.S. Senator Tabor [who] was keeping a little store" and the first Mrs. Tabor, "working hard to earn a living." Deep in the San Juan Mountains, "inhabited by civilized men less than three years," people had access to magazine and papers, including "one copy of the *Woman's Journal* [that] crossed that range every week, and was read by many persons." The Campbells were respectfully but coolly received in the southern part of the state and gladly "concluded to leave the Mexicans to vote as their priests advised, rather than cultivate their friendship at the ballot-box through the use of money and whiskey."[22]

By late summer, "the immortals of the East," Susan Anthony, Lucy Stone, and Henry Blackwell, were busy in Colorado.[23] Anthony concentrated on the southern part of the state, mostly mining camps and Latino communities considered hopeless by most organizers. There were no railroads, few hotels, and rarely did anyone meet her or make prior arrangements. Speaking in the open air, or in smoky saloons to rough crowds,

Anthony sometimes encountered hostility, sometimes respectful attention.[24] After one speech, an observer described how "an acre of bronzed-
face miners set up a shout of applause." In El Moro, Lucy Stone and
Henry Blackwell shared the platform with state representative Casimiro
Barela, who "addressed the Mexican portion of the audience in Spanish,
explaining the action of the constitutional convention and of the legislature in submitting the question, and expressing his hearty approval of
their action in doing so." Other reports confirmed that these visits stimulated discussion among men who had never seriously considered the
issue before. Large public meetings also improved voter outreach and education, especially the closing campaign rally, when Anthony spoke on
women, work, and the ballot.[25]

On election day, Colorado women made a public showing at the polls,
talking to voters, distributing ballots, answering questions, and staffing
"flower-covered tables to debate the doubters." Lucy Stone got into a
heated verbal exchange with a hostile Presbyterian minister, but otherwise the day was quiet.[26] Such public political behavior by women was
very controversial, and they received both criticism and praise. From
Georgetown, Mrs. H. L. Mendenhall reported "many women avoided
this duty," but she had gone to the polls and had "not been on the ground
half an hour when I knew it was the best thing to do, and, from that time
on, felt myself entirely in place." Despite these efforts, the measure lost
(14,053 to 6,612). Analyzing the results, Mendenhall distinguished between the older, "reliable class of [married] working men" who "gave us
our largest support," and younger men, including "the loafers, who
"were mainly against us."[27]

Most suffragists blamed Mexicans, miners, African Americans, Germans, former southerners, and the "saloon element," but this rhetoric
was too harsh. Visiting suffragists aggravated local hostility by failing to
understand the effects of their prejudices upon local populations. In Denver, African Americans organized a Colored Woman's Suffrage Association and held church meetings.[28] Although the predominantly Latino
counties of southern Colorado generally had the lowest rates of support,
the measure did relatively well in two of them, La Plata (48 percent), and
San Juan (40 percent).[29] The extreme opposition of the bishop of Colorado, Joseph Machebeuf, undoubtedly influenced many, but not all
Catholics. Mendenhall reported that the Roman Catholics in Georgetown "were not all against us, some of the prominent members of that
church working and voting for woman suffrage."[30]

Some suffragists dissented from the racial-ethnic bashing. Margaret Campbell identified "Some of our warmest friends . . . among the intelligent Germans who have been citizens for many years," while Lucy Stone reported a pro-suffrage action by an African American woman. When an African American man protested, "We want the women at home cooking our dinners," this "shrewd colored woman" promptly "asked whether they had provided any dinner to cook, and added that most of the colored women there had to earn their dinner as well as cook it." Identifying "the immaturity of women" as a more fundamental obstacle to suffrage, Campbell advocated education and mobilization and concluded privately: "The temperance question must be ignored and political parties forgotten."[31] Henry Blackwell attributed the defeat to poor support or actual opposition from politicians, and insisted the "Lesson of Colorado" was: "*Woman Suffrage can never be carried by a popular vote, without a political party behind it*"[32] (original emphasis). As the national organizers returned east to ponder these lessons, local editors were glad to be rid of the "men in petticoats and women in pantaloons," "all of the crowing hens and clucking cocks" who "were collected, brought west, and let loose like a flock of magpies upon the people of our State." Adios to "[Grandma] Jimmy Blackwell, known in Southern Colorado as the carpet bag carrier of Grandma Stone," and his comrades: "Good bye girls."[33]

After the 1877 loss, the legislature refused to authorize another popular referendum for fifteen years. Suffrage agitation continued within the WCTU, women's clubs, voluntary associations, and the farm-labor movement, but many women turned to other projects as they awaited another political opening. During the 1880s, many temperance activists supported suffrage but focused their energies on social welfare projects. For example, the Denver WCTU established a Women's Exchange, a kindergarten, a home for unwed mothers, and a lunchroom for working women.[34] Mary Shields and Albina Washburn established the Colorado WCTU, the largest and most active women's organization in the state, in April 1880, with the explicit goal of building support for woman suffrage. Shields became the first president, dominated the organization, and took advantage of shared resources to direct "franchise work so effectively that a separate suffrage organization was not deemed necessary."[35] The broad vision of the WCTU encouraged the politicization of more moderate members: "Many a woman who felt a few years ago that she could not go [to] the ballot box is now not only *willing*, but anxiously waiting to use this 'home protection' weapon."[36] Half of the Denver WCTU membership came from the working-class community, often women who lived in saloon-infested neighborhoods or suffered domestic abuse under an alcoholic regime.[37] Some Denver trade unionists also supported temperance as part of a strong communitarian trade union culture. In particular, the Knights of Labor hoped to reorient working-class communities around the labor movement, rather than saloons or ethnic associations, by stressing family participation in educational and leisure activities.[38]

By the late 1870s, Denver was a well-established regional center providing financial services and a limited manufacturing base for the railroad, smelting, and mining industries. In the late 1880s, the Denver working class consisted largely of four immigrant groups—Germans, Irish, British, and Scandinavians—as well as African Americans (3,923) and Chinese (325). The population increased from fewer than 5,000 to 130,000 inhabitants between 1860 and 1900, but larger size and urbanity led to social stratification, growing poverty, and labor tension, especially during the hard decade of the 1890s.[39] The city's labor movement, which grew from one union in 1870 to a membership of 15,789 in 1892, quickly earned a reputation for radicalism. In the 1890s, economic depression, strikes, and violence pushed Colorado labor further toward a syndicalist vision of industrial unionism. The Western Federation of Miners (WFM) was established in May 1894, and in 1905, the WFM led in the formation of the anarcho-syndicalist Industrial Workers of the World (IWW). In 1896, skilled Denver crafts unionists and socialists helped establish the Colorado State Federation of Labor (CFL) and affiliated with a new western regional federation, the Western Labor Union (WLU).[40]

Women became integrated into the Denver labor movement in the 1880s due to increasing numbers and the broad program of the Knights of Labor, but their influence declined in the 1890s as the movement narrowed its focus to the industrial workplace. Like Abigail Duniway, Denver feminist Caroline Churchill supported the Knights of Labor because "that great and powerful organization—recognizes the equality of woman with men, [and] is certainly going to force the principle of equal rights irrespective of sex into practical operation."[41] In the mid-1880s, Denver women formed their own Hope Assembly and established a boardinghouse and an employment agency for women workers, who worked mostly in domestic service or the sweated trades. Women leaders of the garment workers union local were active in both city and state labor organizations, sending the lone female delegate to the first state labor convention in 1896. In 1897–1898, women bindery, textile, and garment workers all went on strike. Trade unionists supported equal rights in theory and universal suffrage in practice when women voted and ran for office in union elections.[42] Thus, Denver's working women gained training and experience in the labor movement at the same time middle-class women were becoming politicized through their clubs. They linked the two movements and targeted the working class by focusing on the importance of the ballot to women wage earners.

Women who were active in Denver's labor and socialist politics in the 1880s often became urban Populists in the 1890s. Early in 1886, the editor of the *Labor Enquirer,* Joseph R. Buchanan, created the socialist Rocky Mountain Social League. Buchanan was also active in the Union Labor Party (ULP), established in 1887 by Denver trade unionists and an important part of the emerging Populist coalition. In 1887, the league became the center of trade union organizing when Burnett Haskell, a famous radical agitator from San Francisco, arrived to edit the paper. His wife, Anna, was also a radical journalist and she contributed a regular column.[43] Neither the league nor the paper lasted long after the Haskells left in September, although Albina Washburn took over the women's column for a while. In 1887 the new labor party unsuccessfully sponsored Miss L. E. McCarthy, a local businesswoman, for superintendent of schools, but Anna Haskell was skeptical. Although women were "speaking and helping along . . . the cause of man. . . . nothing [is] said of women voting." She warned, "Men are not going to 'emancipate' women; we must stand on our own rights." Given that "taxation without representation is tyranny," she suggested that women "raise a little kick on our own account."[44]

Populist women like Albina Washburn and Emma Ghent Curtis, editor of the Canon City *Royal Gorge,* were ready to do some kicking when they helped establish the Colorado People's Party in September 1891. Populism was strongest in the western and northern areas of Colorado, recently settled by native-born farmers, but it also appealed to miners, including immigrant Catholic Democrats who did not otherwise share Populism's agrarian and sometimes prohibitionist goals. The common bond in this major silver-producing state was "free silver." All parties endorsed the remonetization of silver, and this consensus essentially depoliticized the issue locally. Nationally, the currency controversy split both Republicans and Democrats, briefly favoring the Populists. In 1892, the Populist presidential candidate, James Weaver, carried Colorado, while the state party won twenty-seven of sixty-five seats in the legislature and elected a labor newspaper editor, Davis Waite, as governor.[45] Colorado Populists gained largely at Democratic expense, however, and the Republicans in the legislature proved quite capable of impeding Populist reform proposals. A series of embarrassing confrontations and controversies during Waite's administration led to Republican "redemption" in 1894, although the Democrats recaptured the governor's office in 1896. Thus, Populist legislative success was limited, represented largely by the woman suffrage victory, but the party's influence persisted in a strong Democratic Party and economically activist state governments.[46]

Women were integral to Populism in the early years when it was a broad grassroots reform movement, and Colorado women Populists were very vigorous, but they lost influence as the political stakes grew higher. For example, Emma Ghent Curtis was a delegate to the Cincinnati meeting in 1891 and to both 1892 conventions in St. Louis and Omaha.[47] Curtis recalled "open war" over the suffrage question in May, when the Populists met to elect delegates to the Omaha convention. Representing a group "very largely of Knights of Labor and members of the Farmers Alliance," Curtis and her husband encountered another group "very largely of organized working men. These almost without exception declared themselves in favor of equal suffrage, but favored delay in openly advocating it." Curtis and her delegation "had its orders" and "acted up to them so well that, after a bitter fight of three hours," equal suffrage was approved."[48]

Women Populists also achieved more women delegates (including Curtis) to the upcoming Omaha national convention and more women officers at the state and county levels. Some women remained unsatisfied, however, especially after exclusion of woman suffrage from the Omaha platform.[49] Washburn warned that "you men folks are not to 'get there' first and say—'Come on sisters, we will give you this or that.' We are going right along with you. When you 'get there,' we women folks will be there, too, at your side."[50] Washburn was reminding her male colleagues of women's political significance within the Populist Party even as she affirmed their loyalty.

Middle-class Colorado clubwomen also became politicized in the fluid political environment of the 1890s, and many joined the suffrage movement. In October 1889, Caroline Churchill excitedly announced "a meeting in Denver at last," and early in 1890 an ad hoc group formed to assist the campaign in neighboring South Dakota. (Unfortunately, Churchill became alienated from the organized movement and was absent from the state during most of the 1893 campaign.)[51] Soon the Colorado Equal Suffrage Association was officially organized by six prominent Denver women, including newspaperwomen Ellis Meredith (Stansbury) and Minnie Reynolds, teacher Martha Pease, physician Mary B. Bates, and African American club leader Elizabeth P. Ensley.[52] They were assisted by Louise Tyler, an AWSA organizer sent by Lucy Stone, who quickly became president of the group as well as the head of the WCTU franchise department.[53] Early in 1893, the organization changed its name to the Non-Partisan Equal Suffrage Association of Colorado. Vice-President Ellis Meredith explained that "in the word 'equal' there is an appeal to justice which does not seem to exist in the word woman," but suffragists also hoped to avoid political controversy as a nonpartisan organization.[54]

Managed by Louise Tyler, the state legislative lobby was "treated with . . . scant courtesy" in 1891, but the 1892 Populist victories created a more promising situation in 1893.[55] In his inaugural speech, Governor Waite endorsed municipal suffrage, a limited measure, but the rapid introduction of five different suffrage bills in the 1893 legislature indicates a broad base of interest in full suffrage. In addition to the suffrage lobby, the state Farmers' Alliance and the Knights of Labor established committees for "the careful watching" of the bill through the legislature. Populists were pledged to support the measure, but Republicans were in a position to block it. The Senate waited for the lower House to pass the bill, which was initially reported out of committee with a negative recommendation. The speaker of the House forced through the minority report instead, and the bill finally passed. In both Houses, most Populists, approximately one-third of Republicans, and only one Democrat supported the measure authorizing a popular referendum.[56]

Once again, Colorado suffragists faced a long public campaign with few resources. They had fewer than one hundred official members and less than twenty-five dollars in the treasury, but the organization sponsored Ione Hanna as a candidate for the Denver school board to demonstrate its interest in suffrage. In May, Denver women lined up at the polls to elect Hanna against hard opposition.[57] Inexperienced and overwhelmed, they also appealed to outsiders for help. Ellis Meredith attended the annual NAWSA convention at the great Chicago Columbian Exposition in June, but found national suffrage leaders preoccupied with state referenda in New York and Nebraska (both failed). Lucy Stone asked "Why did you introduce a bill now?" Recalling her own experiences in Colorado in 1877, Susan B. Anthony "looked over her spectacles and asked with kindly skepticism, 'Have you converted all those Mexicans?'"[58] Meredith emphasized several positive new elements, including the secret ballot, support from the WCTU, labor unions, and especially the Populists, but the deteriorating economic situation limited the chances of financial assistance to Colorado. Meredith did offer a further insight in a letter to Anthony, noting how "a 'greaser' Senator" had told her "that all the women down there had sat up nights to discuss our bill, and threatened to run him out of the county for voting against it."[59]

Anthony and Catt were involved in other campaigns and so were ambivalent about going to Colorado. With a "guilty conscience smitten for not going," Anthony offered to "hold herself ready" in the fall, but ultimately decided against it on the grounds that she was not needed. Carrie Chapman Catt, the NAWSA's best organizer, did not plan to go to Colorado initially, but she offered advice to Ellis Meredith: "Don't get men or women who are simply suffragists. . . . They must know about politics and how to work a campaign."[60] Convinced by midsummer that the opportunity was too good to miss, Catt changed her mind and received three hundred dollars from Lucy Stone and Henry Blackwell to fund her trip west. Stone asked Ione Hanna to introduce Catt in Denver, seeking to expand contacts between the largely middle-class suffragists and sympathetic society women. Encouraged by Catt, Hanna and Eliza (Mrs. Gov. John) Routt established the Denver Equal Suffrage League to mobilize local clubwomen, while other new groups included the Young Women's League and various neighborhood leagues. By the end of the campaign, outreach efforts had resulted in a statewide coalition of fifty affiliated organizations.[61]

Catt arrived in Denver on Labor Day, but it was a bad time for the city's wage earners. The deepening depression left approximately one-third of Denver's adult men unemployed by August.[62] Their funds were frozen temporarily in the initial financial panic, but suffragists "caught our breath again," and ran the campaign on a shoestring budget (total cost: $1,900).[63] They found the "silver lining" in "the dark financial cloud" by linking the vote to the free silver controversy, the depression, and economic reform. Even middle-class clubwomen sympathized with the Populists and employed radical rhetoric: "The merciless power of plutocracy that crushes you crushes us also. Without a vote you would be powerless; without a vote we are powerless. . . . Is it possible for any man who believes in the free and unlimited coinage of silver to cast a ballot to exclude 50,000 voters for the white metal from the polls?"[64] They recognized the "thousands of mothers in the mining States [who] are to-day without bread for their children," and urged "every true daughter of Colorado to come to the rescue. Charity can never do it. Philanthropy can never do it. Only right laws rightly executed can reform social conditions." Elite ladies recognized a "duty to aid . . . less fortunate sisters. . . . Think of 126,000 self-supporting women in Colorado."[65] Catt and Meredith carried this message into the working-class community, including the city's slums. These appeals increased popular appreciation for suffrage as a social welfare measure even if struggling to survive probably diverted some working-class activists from the suffrage campaign.[66] Encouraging a sense of common misfortune in shared hardship resulted in a "marked and outspoken interest in our cause among the masses."[67]

The Denver suffragists were largely middle class, but working-class women were involved, too.[68] The second Mrs. Tabor, Elizabeth B. ("Baby Doe") Tabor, convinced her husband to donate rooms in his grand opera house for the state association headquarters, staffed by professional women, while working-class women contributed much of the basic labor. According to Meredith, "most of this service was given freely, but some of the women who devoted all their time received moderate salaries, for most of the workers belonged to the wage-earning class." Helen Reynolds was hired as secretary, while Meredith and Minnie Reynolds, both Denver newspaperwomen, constituted the press committee. Minnie Reynolds polled all the newspapers in the state, received very positive replies, and kept editors steadily supplied with copy throughout the campaign. She later observed that the involvement of Denver's "best people" had "a most marked result . . . not one paper in Denver said a word of ridicule or even mild amusement concerning suffragists."[69]

An indefatigable organizer, Catt galvanized the Colorado suffragists, rapidly proving "better than silver or gold" as an asset to the campaign.[70] With considerable irony, given her own preference for society elites, this Populist-inspired, mass-based campaign established Catt's reputation as a leader. She kicked off the campaign with a big Labor Day rally, and was encouraged by strong trade union support and the lack of urban opposition. She reported that "most of the issues of the national parties here are forgotten in the fight for free silver," and Populist Party leaders "everywhere tell me that the woman suffrage question will carry the State." In one town, "a saloon keeper, also the mayor met me at the train and escorted me to my hotel. The Populists told him he must do it, and he did. Verily the world moves!"[71] Touring the state, Catt traveled over one thousand miles and had many adventures. Once she missed her train and boarded a handcar before she realized how dangerous it was: "Liable to jump the track any minute," her guide informed her. Catt flew down the mountain, perched precariously on the side of a cliff, losing hat and hairpins along the way. She arrived safely for her next meeting, but "shaken to the marrow," she vowed, "I'd never ride down a mountain on a hand car again if Congress were waiting to hear me."[72]

Catt usually emphasized small, private meetings to attract elite support and to avoid alerting the opposition, but for maximum impact a few large public rallies with prominent speakers opened and closed the campaign. Few local women emerged as speakers, so experienced volunteers helped. Catt vetoed a visit by the controversial Kansas Populist Mary Elizabeth Lease and recommended Emma DeVoe, a young South Dakota woman and NAWSA organizer working under Catt's supervision. Catt believed that DeVoe would "be especially good to send to the miners and Populists," because DeVoe either was a Populist, or "she can talk that way when necessity requires."[73] DeVoe later used her experience to good advantage as the president of the Washington state suffrage association during the successful 1910 campaign. The Knights of Labor sponsored a speaking tour by Leonora Barry Lake, formerly the union's general investigator for women's work. After the victory, Emma Ghent Curtis commended Barry Lake, whose work sometimes required "mounting upon a bootblack stand in the open air and addressing hundreds of miners when the crowd proved too large for any building in the vicinity. Her influence in the mining camps was very great."[74] Thus Populist and labor suffragists generated crucial working-class, trade union, and socialist support.

The WCTU also appointed two organizers who worked quietly and independently, but there were conflicts between suffragists and prohibitionists. Helen Reynolds later told Emma DeVoe, "Nothing in the way of language could ever make you understand the meanness of the W.C.T.U. during that campaign."[75] When Catt later depreciated the WCTU contribution, offended state officials published a reply politely rejecting the superior claims of newcomers, "who, with fresh steeds and burnished trapping, rode gallantly 'in at the death.'" They affirmed the organization's consistent support: "For nearly two decades the 'white ribbon' women of Colorado have been earnestly and untiringly hammering at the adamantine wall of prejudice."[76] Catt acknowledged these efforts, but continued to emphasize the "new elements" of the Colorado victory, specifically all-party endorsements and "the Knights of Labor and Labor Unions, which by their own efforts carried a number of large mining camps where there was no W.C.T.U. and no Suffrage Association."[77] Catt was surprised by the degree of labor support: "I believe we have never recognized the influence of the labor organizations in this direction half so kindly and graciously as they have recognized us."[78]

Another important element of the campaign strategy was obtaining political endorsements and platform planks from all the state party conventions. Ideally, this "all-party" strategy helped bind political support and removed the issue from partisan struggles. In Colorado, the Republican State Central Committee was "the first to notice" and the first to endorse woman suffrage, but both the Republican and Populist parties donated funds and advice.[79] Anthony and Catt both warned of the dangers of partisan alliances, and Meredith assured the latter, "We entirely agree with you, and are pushing our claims for suffrage simply and solely on the grounds of right and justice." She repeated the advice of Populist Emma Curtis, who believed that "we can win suffrage if we ask for it on the ground of right and justice, and don't talk temperance." Meredith confided that some Populists were "trying to get us to come out for them, [but] . . . we will not hear of it," although "individually many of us are with them" (including herself). She assured Anthony "we have made many friends by sticking closely to a non-partisan basis of action."[80] With endorsements from all the parties and agreement on free silver, they avoided the debilitating partisan conflicts that disrupted Kansas suffragists the following year.[81]

On election day, some women volunteers worked at the polls to help distribute 65,000 instructional leaflets explaining the new secret ballot, an innovation designed to reduce fraud.[82] Public political activity was still controversial behavior for women, and suffragists were criticized both for being at the polls—a "gauntlet of women"—and for failing to be everywhere. Activists concluded that "the men appreciated our earnest efforts" when the measure passed by an ample margin (35,798 to 29,451). Counties that voted Populist in 1892 approved woman suffrage in 1893, a few with more than 70 percent support. Most of the mining towns "supported the cause by a generous vote. Denver, under the influence of the saloons, gave a small adverse majority." The predominantly Mexican American southern counties defeated the measure, but all of these reported at least a 25 percent favorable minority, usually a considerable improvement since 1877. For example, 34.6 percent of male voters in Conejos County supported woman suffrage in 1893, up from only 0.7 percent in 1877.[83]

Woman suffrage passed in Colorado in 1893 due to economic crisis, consensus on silver in an off-year election, the participation of middle-class clubwomen, the positive example of neighboring Wyoming, and the weak mobilization of the opposition. Distracted by the depression and the Populists, overconfident that male voters would reject the measure, opposition forces organized slowly. Eventually they established headquarters at a local brewery, hired an anti-suffrage organizer, distributed leaflets (usually anonymously), and held public meetings. Although hardly a Populist, Catt observed with some satisfaction that "the great English brewers of Denver" were "about the only 'gold bugs' in Colorado," which made them very unpopular. Catt attributed success to the "break in party control," "the fine condition of organized labor," and the Farmers' Alliance and the People's Party. Impressed, Catt was "afraid you will not think I am in earnest, but I am 'Go West, Young Women.'"[84] Populist editor and suffragist Emma Ghent Curtis considered this acknowledgment insufficient, and reiterated the importance of the Knights, the Farmers' Alliance, and the Populists. Particularly concerned that the contributions of labor suffragists had been slighted, Curtis praised the work of Leonora Barry Lake, and stressed how women union members had done much of the canvassing during the campaign. In fact, "So many of the women who have won laurels in this cause are members of labor organizations that it seems difficult to consider the two forces separately."[85]

Catt always preferred to court the elites rather than the masses, but the essential irony of her "society plan" was its initial development and success within a radical western political context among "free silver" clubwomen. Under Catt's authority as NAWSA head organizer, experienced suffragists applied the insights gained in Colorado to other western referenda during the Populist period, but with minimal success. Emma DeVoe campaigned in Idaho, Montana, and Nevada in 1895 and 1896, while Denver clubwomen Helen Reynolds and Mary C. C. Bradford also visited Idaho and Montana. Under less stressful economic conditions, Catt and her assistants were often frustrated by the apathy of small-town society women. Reynolds was skeptical and confided to DeVoe, "As for society I have very little hope from it." She proposed: "What we want to enlist, is the brain, professional and self supporting women. They are the ones for whom men have respect and are willing to help, and it is from them that the appeal for suffrage will come the most successfully."[86] In 1910, Denver journalist Minnie Reynolds worked in Washington State, initially solicited by Catt's genteel protégé, Emma DeVoe, but eventually hired by DeVoe's gaudy rival, May Arkwright Hutton.[87]

Success in Colorado was due to an odd combination of unusual political and economic conditions, but it established important precedents as the first state referendum victory. After 1893, the political behavior of Colorado women attracted close attention and much comment. A variety of positive and negative consequences were attributed to the state's new female voters. As late as 1916, one anti-suffragist remarked that "I have heard the State of Colorado held up so persistently as an example on both sides of the fence that I could think it must be showing signs of fatigue, if not actual wear."[88]

In general, anti-suffragists manipulated fears that partisan politics would coarsen and corrupt women even as they represented the interests that exploited them. For example, a sensational story connecting woman suffrage, vice, and female degradation in Denver was reprinted in the *San Francisco Examiner* just days before the 1896 California referendum vote. A "girl" reporter, Winifred Black ("Annie Laurie"), toured Denver on election day focusing on corruption and indifference among women voters at all social levels. Escorted through the "tough wards" by "Bat" Masterson, a ward boss, pugilist, and "noted gambler," she described a steady stream of "disreputable men and pitiful revolting women" with "dyed hair" who "walked with a swagger" and trailed "sickening perfumes." In the "working-women's ward," "dozens of self-relying women" seemed disappointed: "We're acting just like the men, and it just doubles the ballot, and what is the use?" In more affluent districts, wealthy women supposedly voted as their husbands dictated, then instructed their servants. Suffrage was declared a failure because "we women have found out that our politics are just as corrupt as men's politics, and they are just a little bit trickier if anything." When Anthony visited in Denver on her way home after the California campaign, she found local clubwomen "incensed" by this story.[89]

Over the next two decades, Colorado women were often blamed for turmoil in state politics. They were criticized for their failing to eliminate prostitution, but Denver clubwomen and the "sisters of darkness" generally left each other alone. An unusual exception occurred in 1895, when a delegation from the demimonde asked the Denver Woman's Republican

Club to help prevent their compulsory registration and forced voting. Three prominent Republican women visited municipal officials and received assurances (subsequently ignored) that the sex workers would not be bothered. Progressive women voters took more interest in social welfare reform measures. They noted with pride how easily they passed a state home for dependent children in the first equal suffrage legislature, while a similar measure cost Illinois women nine years of work. They also helped endorse, elect, and retain progressive candidates like Judge Ben B. Lindsey, a prominent ally noted for his reforms of the juvenile court system.[90]

Estimates from different sources indicate that approximately 40 to 51 percent of eligible Colorado women cast their new ballots in the first years of enfranchisement.[91] Writing from a small mining town on the New Mexico border, one correspondent reported to the *Woman's Tribune* that "all the women, even the Mexicans, go to vote and are very enthusiastic."[92] Initially the parties courted these new voters by establishing equal representation on state and county committees and including women in party delegations, but these efforts declined in the early 1900s when no consistent "women's bloc" emerged.[93] Women immediately organized political clubs, including the Women's Populist League and the Colorado Women's Democratic Club, which reported 10,000 members in 1900.[94] In that year, a new Women's Republican League of Colorado was established, but it was captured by the state party chair and his female allies in 1902. Denver also had an active Colored Woman's Republican Club, as well as Italian, Swedish, and German women's clubs.[95]

After the 1893 victory, most local editors warned women against running for office prematurely, preferably never, citing negative stereotypes about the "female politician." Predictably, Caroline Churchill disagreed, insisting that "women should be represented in the legislature of the State at the earliest possible moment."[96] In the late 1890s, all the parties—Republicans, Silver Republicans, Democrats, and Populists—ran and elected women candidates. They were generally modest and efficient public officials with different levels of commitment to progressive reform.[97] In the 1910s, State Senator Helen Ring Robinson, a former teacher, helped pass "a women's minimum wage law, pure food legislation, juvenile courts, joint guardianship and child labor laws." These were "only the little things by means of which we strive to make our cities and our states better places for our children and other women's children to live in. Only the little things."[98] In 1911, four women legislators confronted a colleague who suggested that Colorado rescind women's voting rights and proposed disfranchising men. He quickly claimed that he was "just kidding."[99]

Supporters of woman suffrage widely cited these achievements as beneficial consequences of woman suffrage, while opponents readily blamed female voters for the state's political troubles. One of the most damaging critics was Populist former governor Davis Waite, who blamed his 1894 loss upon newly enfranchised women voters, Denver laborites, and political corruption rather than his own controversial behavior and anti-fusion position. Waite was erratic, widely disliked, and rejected by important elements of his own party, but he insisted that the women—"good" and "bad"—had defeated him. He accused the "15,000 gamblers and lewd women in Denver" as well as "at least 30,000 ignorant hired girls, whose votes are purchaseable [*sic*] and at the disposal of the wealthy classes who have hired their services." Waite hoped that "Female suffrage . . . will hereafter be opposed by all Populists." Prominent colleagues such as Eugene Debs and Ignatius Donnelly vainly counseled Waite to keep quiet. With good reason, Donnelly feared that Waite's denunciations "ended woman's suffrage in the People's Party."[100]

Carrie Catt had similar concerns: "The miner and other organized labor vote may not be as enthusiastic as they would have been had the Colorado women voted Populist." She complained that Populists "have treated the Colorado election as though the women had been enfranchised by the Populists only and then proved traitors to the party that had befriended them. All this will have its influence against us."[101] In 1894, Henry Blackwell alienated Populists by approving a Republican national convention resolution congratulating Colorado women on their enfranchisement and "cordially invited their cooperation in the work of rescuing the country from Democratic and Populist misrule." Even when chided, Blackwell only grudgingly acknowledged Populist support in Colorado, and they resented his attitude.[102]

Republican indifference in 1894 infuriated Anthony, especially during the disastrous Kansas campaign. The Kansas Populists endorsed woman suffrage, but the Republicans refused, then used the measure as an anti-Populist political weapon. Obliged by her "all-partisan" strategy to support the party that endorsed woman suffrage, she campaigned for the Populists in Kansas, infuriating the Republicans, and precipitating deep partisan divisions among suffragists.[103] Teased by a newspaper reporter about converting, Anthony quickly corrected him. No, "I didn't go over to the Populists by doing what I did in Kansas. . . . I have been like a drowning man for a long time, and have been waiting for someone to throw a plank at me. The Republicans of Kansas refused . . . but the Populists . . . threw an excellent plank in my direction, and I stepped on it. I didn't step on the whole platform, but just on the woman suffrage plank." The Colorado victory raised suffragist hopes that Populist strength was sufficient to enfranchise women, but Kansas proved otherwise. By 1896, the Populist movement was at the height of its influence, and the California referendum campaign offered Susan B. Anthony another chance for victory.

5

California, Woman Suffrage, and the Critical Election of 1896

> All that women should or do claim is the right to compete with men, in any position to which their inclination or capacity may call them, on equal terms, without fear or favor. And if men are indisposed to grant them this, it argues that they are either tyrannical or else that they fear the outcome of the contest.   —"Tara"[1]

In 1888, "Tara" was a Los Angeles workingman who supported a variety of radical causes, including women's rights. In 1896, Tara probably voted for the Democratic-Populist presidential candidate, William Jennings Bryan, and for woman suffrage, lamenting when both lost statewide. As a western, urban "knight" of labor, Tara was surprised by the response of a young woman who rejected his condescending gallantry. Like Tara, the Populists confidently challenged established politics in the early 1890s, but the "critical election" of 1896 ended their hopes nationally.[2] During the decade, Populist pressure broke legislative logjams to authorize a number of state woman suffrage referenda, but only Colorado and Idaho passed the measure.[3] Susan B. Anthony tried to take advantage of these political opportunities in Kansas in 1894, although her participation was very controversial, and she used the same general strategy in California in 1896. Many California suffragists venerated the elderly "Aunt Susan," but this arrogation of authority generated considerable resentment against "Autocrat" Anthony (her term). While unsuccessful, the 1896 campaign was an important educational experience. It confirmed the importance of farmer-labor-reformer reform alliances as well as mobilizing clubwomen, who gave suffrage mainstream respectability at the same time the radical Populists gave it a chance at the polls. After Populism waned, suffrage agitation continued in the early 1900s, becoming an early element of the Progressive reform movement.

Female mobilization within the women's club movement during a period of political instability and reform raised hopes for woman suffrage in the 1890s. The women's club movement flourished in California, especially in the more homogeneous Anglo American Protestant environment of Southern California.[4] The first clubs were established in San Francisco, including the elite Century Club, the Pacific Association of Collegiate Alumnae, and the Pacific Coast Women's Press Association (PCWPA). In 1890, the PCWPA was organized by Charlotte Perkins (Stetson) Gilman and others to encourage female writers and to challenge professional discrimination, but the "advancement of their professional interests" was restricted to white women. In 1891, the PCWPA denied membership to a black woman, Mrs. R. M. Lockett, after half the membership threatened to quit if Lockett were admitted. The PCWPA rejected Lockett as not "suitable," ignored her protests, and denied public charges of discrimination. What role Gilman played in this controversy, if any, remains unclear—certainly her published autobiography does not mention this episode.[5]

In Southern California, experienced veterans of eastern social movements included "Madame" Caroline M. Severance, the venerable "Mother of Clubs," a founding member of the New England Women's Club (1868) and the American Woman Suffrage Association (1869). Severance, a former abolitionist and professed Christian socialist, moved with her husband to California in 1875 to grow oranges but soon became active in establishing churches, kindergartens, women's clubs, suffrage organizations, and other groups. Despite her age, Severance was a dedicated suffragist in the 1880s, cofounding the Los Angeles Woman Suffrage Association with Elizabeth Kingsbury in 1885.[6] She also established the Los Angeles Woman's Club (1878), the prestigious Friday Morning Club (1891), and the Women's Parliament Association of Southern California (1892). In 1900, the extensive club network was formalized in the California Federation of Women's Clubs, a branch of the General Federation of Women's Clubs (GFWC), under the leadership of Clara (Mrs. Robert) Burdette.[7]

The Woman's Christian Temperance Union (WCTU), the largest and most influential women's organization in California, was established in 1883 after an organizing tour by Laura DeForce Gordon and Frances Willard.[8] There were eventually two organizations, ostensibly due to the size of the state, but another factor might have been the greater radical-ism of the northern leaders. For example, Mary Garbutt and Beaumelle Sturtevant-Peet, president of the northern union for seventeen years, were both socialists who built farmer-labor and third-party support for woman suffrage, prohibition, and other reforms. Peet was a tremendous organizer who boosted WCTU membership, collected thousands of sig-natures on suffrage petitions, and maintained a constant legislative vigil. The organization's outreach and educational programs targeted many racial-ethnic and working-class groups, with African American, Swedish, and German unions in San Francisco, as well as Chinese and Japanese missions.[9]

In the 1890s, many middle- as well as working-class California women became involved in radical labor and reform movements. Based on Ed-ward Bellamy's book, *Looking Backward* (1888), Nationalism was ex-tremely popular in California, where it helped urban labor radicals de-velop a strong farmer-labor coalition.[10] Women were attracted by Na-tionalism's promise to emancipate labor and women "with equal rights and equal compensation." Anna Ferry Smith, Laura Gordon, Clara Foltz, Anna Haskell, Mary Garbutt, and many other California suffragists were active Nationalist Party officers, delegates, lecturers, and organizers. Smith stated, "We do not claim to be better than men, but we have the same inborn rights that they have—the right to think, to act, to produce and to have the results of our labor."[11] The California Nationalist move-ment also attracted Charlotte Perkins (Stetson) Gilman, who lived in the state from 1888 to 1895. Gilman later described California as "a seed-bed of all manner of cults and theories, taken up, and dropped, with equal speed," but she received much material and moral support from Nationalists, socialists, and the labor movement at a difficult time in her life.[12] For example, she presented her first paid lectures as a Nationalist speaker in 1890. Gilman's "early humanitarian kind" of socialism sought "not revolution, but an evolution," and rejected "the narrow and rigid 'economic determinism' of Marx, with its 'class consciousness' and 'class struggle.'"[13]

By early 1891, Gilman had relocated permanently from Pasadena to Oakland, where she continued to speak and write prolifically. She was closely associated with the PCWPA, becoming president in 1893. In 1894, she inaugurated the *Impress* as an organizational journal, but it soon failed due to public hostility relating to her divorce. Despite her no-toriety, Gilman helped organize two very successful women's congresses in 1894 and 1895. These meetings helped reinvigorate the state suffrage movement and helped launch Gilman's national career. Encouraged by Susan B. Anthony and Jane Addams, she left California after the 1895 women's congress and headed for Hull House.[14]

When Gilman published *Women and Economics* in 1898, she entered the vigorous debate over women's proper roles in modern society. Her arguments challenged many assumptions about gender but relied heavily upon prevailing racialist paradigms. Gilman did not challenge contemporary discourses about "civilization" and "race suicide." Instead, she modified and reinforced these ideas for feminist purposes, helping to reinscribe nativist and racist prejudices in the public mind. Gilman rejected the idea of female sexual and economic dependence as a sign of progress. She insisted that weak and fluffy (white) women perpetuated inferior genes and became the inadequate mothers of puny children, debilitating "the [human? white?] race." In 1891, Gilman told the Los Angeles Woman's Club: "Some of you will say again that it is part of the male function in the human race to provide for the family . . . and the female function merely to serve the family. . . . But it is a lie! . . . The dominant soul—the clear strong accurate brain, the perfect service of a healthy body—these do not belong to *sex*—but to *race*!" (emphasis in original).[15] Sexual equality and female economic autonomy were necessary to rectify this imbalance and to assure continued progress toward evolutionary perfection, which invariably naturalized white ideals.[16]

These ideas were very much in evidence at the women's congresses Gilman helped organize, and she surely benefited from the many discussions of gender, race, civilization, and progress. These meetings grew popular after a national Woman's Congress gathered at the great 1893 Chicago Columbian Exposition. At large public celebrations and expositions, women sometimes sponsored exhibits, buildings, and events, but male executive boards imposed many constraints.[17] In contrast, women's congresses were autonomous assemblies that allowed greater flexibility, demonstrated female organizational skills, and catalyzed suffrage activism. Inspired by the recent Colorado woman suffrage victory, California women began to plan a woman's congress in conjunction with the 1894 Midwinter International Exposition in San Francisco. The program, broadly entitled "The Relation of Women to the Affairs of the World," drew together women "who have achieved distinction in any and every line of work."[18] The meeting produced the Woman's Congress

Association of the Pacific Coast, a permanent statewide organization which authorized the *Impress* as its official organ.

Suffragists routinely scheduled their conventions to coincide with women's congresses, which shared many common themes and attracted a lot of positive publicity. The June 1894 suffrage convention displayed a popular contemporary image: "The face of an intelligent American woman . . . surrounded by those of an Indian, a lunatic, a convict, and an idiot. Under the whole is the legend, 'The American Woman and Her Political Peers.'"[19] In her address, state president Gordon eschewed nativist arguments (at least temporarily) to discuss growing reform sentiment. She warned, "you men have made an Augean stable of the halls of legislation[;] we are coming in to have a housecleaning, and don't you forget it." Candidates "will vote for woman suffrage, [or] we'll put a ticket in the field ourselves, and we'll agitate with women orators in every ward. We'll have the liveliest campaign that has ever been seen in San Francisco."[20] Gordon's rhetoric reflects her continued commitment to the Democratic Party and farmer-labor causes, particularly Nationalism and Populism, even though her political influence was limited. It is also possible that these associations affected her leadership position within the suffrage movement as it began to incorporate more conservative women.

At this convention, young women affiliated with the newly formed San Francisco Equal Rights League successfully challenged Gordon for the state suffrage association presidency. They won control of the state executive board and replaced Gordon with Nellie Holbrook Blinn, a young Republican activist. The insurgents were impatient with Gordon's musty classical rhetoric, idiosyncratic leadership, and legalistic approach, all of which discouraged grassroots mobilization. They complained "we never had any chance to work. She would talk and talk and talk, and there was never anything in it."[21] Initially Gordon seemed to accept her rejection, but she became bitter and dismissed the younger women as "kindergarteners." Despite Gordon's decades of association with national suffragists, Anthony and the national association supported the Blinn faction, as did Gordon's old colleague, Clara Foltz. Gordon dismissed Foltz as "a bluejay . . . [who] never did take any interest in the cause," but Foltz brushed off the insult.[22] Once again, Gordon was alienated from the organized movement, although she continued to actively lobby the legislature.

California suffragists were encouraged as the People's (Populist) Party emerged from Nationalism, the Grange, and the Farmers' Alliance. In addition to Foltz, other important activists included Margaret Longley, Anna Ferry Smith, Addie Ballou, and Kate Squires Nevins. In California, Populists were more labor oriented, less interested in silver, and more resistant to fusion than in other western states. As a result, woman suffrage enjoyed considerable internal support, and Populist suffragists were more likely to protest the national party's disregard.[23] Margaret Longley reported how the California People's Party had "invited the cooperation of . . . woman's clubs and societies" to the Los Angeles organizational convention in October 1891. These delegates "were received kindly and heartily, and a woman suffrage resolution was incorporated into the platform of the new party."[24] The state convention in Stockton in June 1892 endorsed woman suffrage and named Mrs. Thomas V. Cator, the wife of a prominent state leader, and another woman as delegates to the upcoming Omaha convention.[25]

In 1892, Longley and many other California Populists protested the omission of a woman suffrage plank in the national Omaha platform, insisting that the decision "disturbed and discouraged the women here who have affiliated with the movement." In a conciliatory response, the editor of the *People's Party Press* acknowledged that others (including himself) shared Longley's objections, but the paper was committed to the official platform. Thus woman suffrage "is not an issue in this campaign. . . . This battle is to be fought on money, land and transportation." His acknowledgment that "certainly four-fifths of the voters in the People's Party are heartily in favor of woman's enfranchisement" earned a "scorching review" from Longley, who replied sarcastically that this would seem to be a definitive majority.[26] In 1894, Longley served as vice chair of the state convention, where she helped win a woman suffrage plank in the state platform. In contrast, angry Colorado Populists generally refrained from actions that might seem disruptive or disloyal. In California, their persistence reflected the broader agenda and relative isolation of the state party.[27]

Serious third-party challenges gave suffragists a valuable bargaining chip with the major parties. In 1894, California Republicans also included a woman suffrage plank, theoretically because "taxation without representation is against the principles of the Government we favor," but also due to political pressure.[28] At a Southern California Republican party meeting, Alice McComas, of the Los Angeles Woman Suffrage As-

sociation, alluded to these political options in noting how "two other parties have been very generously inclined toward us." McComas was a
writer who moved to Los Angeles in 1887, contributed to the *Los Angeles Evening Express,* and served on numerous local boards and committees, including the Woman's Industrial Union. Although a loyal Republican, McComas cautioned: "Some of us have been wavering lately, a few
on the fence, and many just ready to spring over [to the Populists] in case
the State Convention again ignored the plea for equal rights women have
been making so long in this State." Endorsement relieved her concerns:
"You have done right at last . . . now all is forgiven . . . and we pledge you
loyal support in the coming campaign.[29]

The suffrage lobby had little success until the Populists made significant gains in the legislature in 1894, while the new governor, James Budd,
was a sympathetic Democrat. Early in 1891, Gordon, Sturtevant-Peet,
Pitts-Stevens, and others won a Senate bill authorizing legislative enfranchisement of women, but it died in the Assembly. Early in 1895, the suffrage lobby returned to Sacramento to take advantage of Populist
strength and support, but factional hostility lingered.[30] Specifically, the
older veterans distrusted the exuberant inexperience of their younger and
greener colleagues. Sarah Severance, franchise coordinator for the
WCTU, hoped that Beaumelle Peet and Louise Sorbier could outmaneu-
ver "the lunatics." She was "sorry that the two suffrage societies are so
inharmonious, a disgrace to the few who bring discredit and all suffer the
consequences."[31] Peet was concerned that Gordon, "the noblest Spartan
of them all," might "retreat from the field" after her recent rejection, but
she appeared with a full suffrage bill.[32] It was hard for Gordon to lobby
in Sacramento and maintain a law practice in San Francisco, so she
sought assistance from Louise Sorbier and wondered if "dear Mrs. Sargent could be induced to come up here for a little time?" Chiefly she
feared her upstart rivals: "I tremble for the success of our efforts this session if [they] . . . come charging up here."[33]

Severance was also distressed because the "WCTU did not wish this
amendment" in the first place. WCTU lobbyists had prepared partial
school and municipal suffrage bills, but Gordon and Blinn preempted
these with full suffrage proposals. Severance urged solidarity, but de-
ferred reluctantly, worried because supporters included "some of our bit-
terest foes." She was not alone in suspecting that some opponents pre-
tended to support full suffrage in order to defeat it, 'to throw us to the
dogs,' as they expressively term it."[34] She was unable to "see aught but

defeat sure, if we work for Constitutional Amendments." If Kansas, "after having school and municipal suffrage for years, and the women having local political power, votes down a Constitutional Amendment by a large majority . . . what hope for this state ruled by liquor and dives? We should be snowed under hopelessly." Nevertheless, "we must work" and "make all we can of it," partly to prove they wanted the vote, even "if we *do* work we shall lose."[35]

Early in January 1895, Gordon "drew up the bill today and gave it to Judge [Ephraim V.] Spencer," and she worked closely with Mrs. Philenda Spencer in lobbying members of the legislature and their wives.[36] In early February, suffragists held two large meetings in the assembly chamber, heavily attended by women, and the "hearty applause of the speakers' strong words went a long way to disprove the assertions . . . that the women did not ask for the right of suffrage." Speakers included Gordon, Spencer, Sturtevant-Peet, Annie (Mrs. John) Bidwell, and Blinn. Spencer reported that her husband had presented over 20,000 signatures on suffrage petitions to support his bill, but complained: "When we bring petitions we are told that it is not ladylike, and if we do not, then it is said that it is proof positive that the women do not want the vote." They also presented data demonstrating significant female property ownership and tax liability.[37]

Party obligations added a new dimension to the debate. Republican and Populist women expected their representatives to redeem their pro-suffrage pledges, while Gordon vainly urged "my dear Democratic brethren," to "stand shoulder to shoulder and not let the Republicans get away with all the glory." Judge Spencer reminded wavering colleagues that "the question was not one of sentiment, but of party policy." It was "the duty of every Republican to vote as his platform had promised," because "we cannot afford to allow our Democratic friends to say we do not keep our promises." This time the legislature refused to directly enfranchise women but agreed to authorize a popular referendum for the 1896 ballot.[38]

With a Populist referendum on the election calendar, the mood at the 1895 Woman's Congress in San Francisco was ecstatic. Populist reform mayor Adolph Sutro opened the assembly with a strong statement of support that emphasized the familiar themes of civilization and evolutionary progress. He considered "it a part of evolution that women . . . should be permitted to cast their ballots in favor of a purified and improved administration which will cause us to rise higher and higher in civilization."

The broad theme of "Woman and the Home" included many sessions on women and politics. Participants analyzed the home as a political institution, examined the concept of "municipal housekeeping," and concluded that the vote would help overcome the debilitating effects of female dependency and encourage a greater sense of civic responsibility. The presence of Susan B. Anthony, Anna Howard Shaw, and other prominent leaders, the timeliness of the issues, and the participation of respected and affluent women filled the Woman's Congress daily.[39] The growing respectability of the movement gained public support and generally favorable publicity. City reporters expressed surprise "that the women of San Francisco cared for aught except their gowns, their teas and their babies." Even the unsympathetic *San Francisco Chronicle* admitted that "five thousand people waiting on the steps of the Temple Emanu-El for the purpose of hearing [Shaw] does not look as if her position were uncertain."[40]

California suffragists had overcome the legislative hurdle, but they now faced a difficult electoral struggle with a fractured organization and few resources. After a post-congress meeting to discuss preliminary campaign plans, Anthony and Shaw toured the state, including a visit to Yosemite National Park. Along the way, California women expressed their gratitude for Anthony's "kindly words [which] . . . have lifted the fog, . . . leaving us a clearer view of our duty not only to humanity but to ourselves. You have left a trail of light." Returning to San Francisco, the national suffrage leaders rode in the Fourth of July parade in "the very next carriage to that of the mayor [Sutro] . . . and the rousing cheers of the people along the whole line of march showed their appreciation."[41]

The state suffrage convention elected Ellen Sargent chair of the state association, and Sarah Cooper became nominal chair of the joint campaign committee, although it was dominated by Anthony and her assistants.[42] Sargent, Cooper, and many California women appreciated Anthony's leadership, but many resented her involvement. Gordon was still upset that Anthony "had taken sides with the Blinn faction" the previous year. She complained that "Aunt Susan has fairly or actually taken everything into her own hands and proposes to run it herself, with those *she* prefers." Anthony "gave me to understand that *I* was to yield to a superior power which she possessed" and "keep in the background." Angrily she told Emily Pitts-Stevens, "I never took a back seat in woman suffrage work in all my life and shall not begin now." Gordon planned to rest, then to "go into the campaign, heart and soul and work . . . in my own way." She claimed to have a plan to convert thousands of working men, but her activities during the campaign, if any, remain unclear.[43]

The NAWSA's head organizer, Carrie Catt, was frustrated, too. She was invited to California, but annoyed because local women resisted outside advice and volunteers. She wanted to send her lieutenant, Emma DeVoe, but the California women "will employ no one." She also planned to "send Mrs. Bradford for six weeks, with the help of Colorado," but "that is all the speaker they will have." "Like everybody else," they "don't want any outside help and think they can carry a campaign without organization."[44] Catt also objected to Anthony and Shaw's "old fashioned scheme" of lectures which paid famous speakers "a good price" but left little behind in campaign funds or permanent organization. Catt could "get Miss Anthony and Miss Shaw to see the modern way of getting money and organization just so long as I am talking but no longer."[45] Publicly, Shaw's 1895 visit was a great success, and she was warmly praised when she returned to San Francisco for the 1896 woman's Congress, but Catt had accurately anticipated some of the negative repercussions. In 1896, the first state organizer, Hester Harland, also criticized Shaw for accepting hefty lecture fees from the state suffrage treasury. Sargent and Cooper fired her, and Anthony took control of this important campaign.[46]

In March 1896, Anthony returned to California to face local resentment, tremendous logistical problems, and a tense political and economic environment, but she was optimistic. Her strategy emphasized political party endorsements, grassroots organizing, and dissociation from prohibition. She planned a bold public campaign based upon party endorsements, good media coverage, voter outreach through churches, clubs, unions, systematic canvassing, and disengagement from prohibition. She knew that an open public campaign provoked the opposition, but concluded that those groups already enjoyed the advantage of covert action, while mass education required overt appeals. Anthony donated her time, paid her secretary, and enlisted two experienced eastern organizers, Harriet May Mills and Mary G. Hay. In less than three months, Mills and Hay planned almost two hundred local suffrage conventions, timed to coordinate with local party conventions and to culminate with the next Woman's Congress in late May. The two women traveled extensively. In rural Humboldt County that summer, they noticed "even the cowboys whom we met driving their cattle had tied yellow bows at their horses' bridles."[47] In an appeal for aid, Mills suggested "California people are . . . more ready for new thought than the majority of one's audiences in the East," and stressed the national significance of winning this large and complex western state.[48]

California suffragists included a number of wealthy women, including Phoebe Hearst, Sarah Knox-Goodridge, Ellen Sargent, and Mary Sperry. Some contributed large sums to the campaign (approximate cost: $19,000), while others donated goods and services. Senator Sargent's old office served as headquarters until the Emporium department store provided a larger space. Susan Anthony met Jane (Mrs. Leland) Stanford on the train in Utah, Phoebe Hearst on the San Francisco ferry. As the widow of one of the Southern Pacific Railroad's cofounders, Stanford obtained a few valuable railroad passes, but she was upset when these were granted grudgingly. She wrote Anthony: "You do not wonder that I am for woman suffrage, do you? Were I Mr. Stanford, I would not be obliged to ask but could make out as many passes as I pleased." She knew "could I vote and wear *trousers* I might enjoy more rights."[49] Most of the contributions were small, however. Ida Harper recalled: "Often when there was not enough money on hand at headquarters to buy a postage stamp, there would come a knock at the door and a poorly dressed woman would enter with a quarter or half-dollar." Most of the work was done by volunteers, including one woman "who worked hard ten hours a day to earn her bread, [and] would come to headquarters and carry home a great armload of circulars to fold and address [night] after night."[50]

Anthony's "all-partisan" strategy had backfired in Kansas in 1894, and she did not wish to repeat the experience in California, but she did not alter her approach. Despite the Kansas disaster, Anthony remained dedicated to her "pet theory," convinced that endorsements from *all* parties were necessary to neutralize partisan advantage and protect woman suffrage from partisan attack. The California campaign demonstrated that endorsements were necessary but insufficient to guarantee genuine party support. In theory, platform commitments would bind "each and every party orator and editor . . . to advocate the amendment or keep silent at least, for it will not be good policy to denounce a measure that is in the party's platform."[51] Anthony and the California suffragists obtained endorsements from the Republicans, the Populists, and Prohibitionists and interpreted the support of one quarter of the state Democratic convention as progress. In reality, however, all the California parties ignored the issue during the campaign regardless of their platform positions, distracted by many other controversial issues in that critical election year.

The suffragists visited all the state party conventions and were generally well received. In Sacramento in May, Republican delegates "flocked" to suffrage headquarters, heard speeches by Anthony and Shaw, and accepted the plank with little dissension. Suffragists celebrated (prematurely) "the first time that the Republican party of any State . . . has endorsed a pending Constitutional Amendment enfranchising women."[52] Nevertheless, California Republicans ignored woman suffrage during the election, while the national Republican Party remained unresponsive. The state Populist convention warmly greeted the suffrage delegation and quickly adopted a strong plank with three cheers, "as woman suffrage was one of the fundamental principles of their party." Yet fusion with the Democrats in 1896 restricted the Populist agenda and female participation to the detriment of controversial issues like woman suffrage. The only woman delegate, Mrs. Cator, thought woman suffrage was just, but she was preoccupied with free silver.[53]

Publicly the relations between suffragists and Populists appeared cordial, but there were deep tensions. The Populists remembered the ambivalent comments of Henry Blackwell and Susan B. Anthony in 1894, and especially the former's reluctance to give them any credit for the 1893 Colorado victory. In addition, ex-Governor Waite's damaging criticisms were a major problem, so Anthony asked another former Colorado governor, John Routt, for a positive testimonial, while Ida Harper published a refutation of Waite's charges.[54] The suffragists were determined to stay focused on their single goal, while the Populists expected more support for their broader agenda, and Populist suffragists were stuck in the middle.

Prominent male Populists were upset by suffragist political neutrality partly because they felt that their supportive efforts went unappreciated. Writing to Thomas Cator, John Dore described how many Fresno suffragists were Populists trying to inject much of the latter program into the former. He thought the single-goal strategy was a miscalculation because it was too easy for the regular parties to dismiss, whereas politicians had to take suffrage more seriously as part of a broader reform movement. A founding party member and steadfast suffragist, Dore was angry because he felt that consistent Populist support had generated major shifts in public opinion, and the suffragists knew it, but that many of them "absolutely ignore our existence and work." He asked, "Why can't they do us & themselves simple justice? Is it indifference or policy?"[55] Apparently it was a little of both, as suffragists and Populists courted each other opportunistically.

After the Prohibition Party convention endorsed the measure, only the Democrats remained. At the state Democratic convention in June, few delegates called upon the suffrage lobby, "too well subjugated by the political bosses even to pay a visit of courtesy."[56] Mary McHenry Keith, a young Democratic lawyer just starting her career as a major California suffragist, attended her first political convention in the hopes that she could help get the plank into the platform. She thought she perceived "quite a change of prevailing sentiment; in favor of the women," and anticipated "a lively fight" over the platform committee's minority report.[57]

Before the platform committee, the women presented a petition with 40,000 signatures, and Sarah Cooper, Ellen Sargent, Ida Harper, Anna Howard Shaw and Susan B. Anthony all spoke, as did Mrs. Carrie Murray, an anti-suffrage representative.[58] The committee tabled the suffrage resolution without a vote, but one of the authors of the minority report, Charles Wesley Reed of San Francisco, protested this suppression. The hour was late, with the chair pressing for a vote, when an anti-suffrage San Francisco delegate, John P. Irish, suggested that Anthony be allowed to speak. Given the opportunity, she roundly rebuked the assembly "for treating the women of the State in this unjust and undemocratic manner." Anna Howard Shaw then soothed the Democrats with oratory, and soon "half the convention were on their feet demanding the report." Reed and other supporters forced a floor vote, which lost, but Anthony was thankful for "even a fourth of a promise not to oppose us."[59] Encouraged by these results, Anthony warmly praised the Democrats and the Populists, but she was most encouraged by the Republican endorsement.

Prominent male allies were members of all parties. Speakers at a suffrage rally included Democrat James Maguire and Populist T. V. Cator. Maguire regretted "that he was not authorized to speak for the Democracy," but promised that "there will be a large body of Democrats who will do their duty in November."[60] At another large meeting in September, Assemblyman Reed teased Anthony by alleging that the infamous Democratic municipal ring headed by Christopher Buckley had "put a suffrage plank in its platform. . . . [because] I heard that Miss Anthony had dinner with him." Amid laughter, Miss Anthony admitted she had seen Buckley, who "told me he had been a woman suffragist ever since he could remember."[61] On this occasion, at least, "Blind Boss" Buckley did not fit the stereotype of an anti-suffrage, urban machine politician.

The exclusive emphasis on suffrage allowed activists to approach all parties equally, but Mary Keith complained that each party wanted political support that would alienate the others. She lamented, "Women suffragists are almost in despair at the seeming impossibility of bringing the men of all parties to realize that if this amendment is going to be carried it must be by the votes of men from all parties." When Republicans reproached the suffragists for attending Populist meetings but refused to allow them to speak at Republican meetings, Keith warned, "So don't be jealous gentlemen, if you hear of your Republican women talking to the Buckleyites or of your Democratic women 'sitting on' Republican platforms, or of your Populist women sitting on the side of the road. They're not coquetting; they're only talking woman suffrage."[62]

The single focus on suffrage also helped activists avoid internal partisan conflict, although not always completely. The failure of the all-partisan strategy in Kansas had divided suffragists according to their partisan allegiances and created tremendous internal conflict. Determined to avoid a repetition of these events in California in 1896, Anthony railed against the formation of partisan suffrage groups. She insisted "all-partisan" meant that California suffragists should refrain from party issues until the vote was won. Eventually there would be "time enough for the women of California to enroll themselves as Republicans, Democrats, Populists, etc.," but until then, women were "disfranchised citizens—outlaws— shut out of the 'body politic,' humble suppliants, veriest beggars at the feet of all men of all parties, alike."[63] She became concerned because important suffragists began to line up in support of their respective parties. For example, Nellie Blinn became a hired Republican speaker, while Laura Gordon committed to the Democrats.[64] In Southern California, Alice McComas, the Republican president of the Los Angeles Woman Suffrage Association, apparently broke with the northern suffragists because she wanted to work on a more partisan basis.[65]

Anthony prioritized politics, but she understood the importance of publicity and outreach. Large meetings, public concerts, and other events attracted mass audiences, complimented by numerous small gatherings in private homes. The "young, talented and handsome" Carrie Chapman Catt arrived in September to speak at the huge mass rally that opened the fall campaign. Anthony spoke anywhere and everywhere, "in the most elegant homes; and in pool-rooms where there was printed on the black-board, 'Welcome to Susan B. Anthony.'" She was proud of her endurance: "I would like to see the man of my years who could pass the week I have just passed and still be anxious and ready for more work."[66] Local women tackled the tedious jobs of leafleting and canvassing by precinct. While no one liked surveying voters or fund-raising, suffragists encountered little overt hostility, and by the end of September, 150 San Francisco clubs had members walking the city's precincts.[67] Anna Haskell became captain of the South Park District club in July, and subsequently canvassed, leafleted local industries, and sold tickets to suffrage events. Haskell was pessimistic by election day, however, sensitive to growing conservatism and apprehensive about the fate of William Jennings Bryan, free silver, and woman suffrage in California.[68]

Newspaperwoman and NAWSA official Ida Husted Harper was in charge of press work. With the important exceptions of the *San Francisco Chronicle*, the *Sacramento Record-Union* and the *Los Angeles Times*, most papers were supportive or at least receptive to suffrage material, printing regular columns by Anthony and others. Harper and Anthony were courteously received by the editors of all the major San Francisco papers, and reassured of "respect, . . . no ridiculing, no cartooning and no attempt to create a sentiment in opposition."[69] The *San Francisco Chronicle* broke that promise right before the election with a "vituperative frenzy of hostility," including hostile editorials and lantern slide caricatures projected outdoors on a cloth screen.[70] Another Republican paper, the *San Francisco Call*, edited by Clara Foltz's brother, Charles Shortridge, prominently endorsed woman suffrage at first, but his editorial enthusiasm diminished as party interest waned.[71] Anthony wrote to *Examiner* publisher William Randolph Hearst, Jr., to solicit his support, "for the love of your noble mother, . . . California . . . [and] for the Democratic party of your State." The paper remained editorially neutral, although it published two thousand pro-suffrage leaflets for distribution at the state Democratic convention.[72] The *Los Angeles Times* and its publisher, Harrison Gray Otis, were implacably hostile. The paper, which had ridiculed Anthony and Shaw as "two mischievous old maids" in 1895, published negative editorials and cartoons and gave anti-suffrage activities prominent coverage.[73]

Recognizing the need for active outreach to new groups of urban voters, suffragists contacted foreign-born and racial-ethnic groups through their neighborhoods, associations, churches, publications, and trade unions. Harper recorded positive notices in working-class, African American, Spanish, French, Italian, Jewish, "the temperance, the A.P.A. [American Protective Association] and the Socialist organs," often finding progressive editors in these communities. For example, the publishers of *L'Italia*, "a staunch Republican paper," endorsed the amendment and spoke at suffrage meetings, while the "revolutionist" Italians also "were said to be solidly in our favor."[74] Tentative and awkward in 1896, these new methods were key to building urban working-class support for woman suffrage and they provided important experience.[75] Catt and Shaw delivered noontime speeches at "factories, foundries, and mills," while Anthony and others spoke to the Socialist Labor Party on "How the Ballot Will Lift Women Workers." Challenged by Socialists as to "why the woman suffragists did not ally themselves to the labor cause," Anthony replied that "a woman was a cook and baker and always had been, and [she] was in sympathy with their cause, but she could only be of use to them and their brother workers when she had the ballot."[76] Harper published labor appeals that highlighted endorsements by union leaders and stressed the hardships of working women. Labor's political strength would double with the inclusion of wage-earning women, as well as "many more women whose sympathies and whose work in the charities and reforms has brought them in touch with the working people." Indeed, "There is no one class of men so vitally concerned in giving a vote to women as are the wage-earners."[77]

The influential Catholic publication, *The Monitor*, edited by Father Peter Yorke, was initially supportive and published full front-page endorsements. Yorke stressed the need for "an infusion of new blood into the electorate" to achieve political reform, and rejected the idea "that there is anything in Catholic discipline . . . which should forbid the enfranchisement of women." He argued that "it is not fair to deprive the whole sex of a voice in politics because of the loud-mouthedness of a few." Although suffragists were "assured . . . of his full sympathy," Yorke suddenly stopped publishing their material. Anthony tried to call upon him several times to find out what was wrong, but Yorke refused to see her.[78] Possibly, Yorke was reacting to alleged associations between the suffrage movement and the virulently anti-Catholic APA, or to rumors that Anthony had criticized Yorke at the Prohibition Party convention. Anthony denied these reports and refused "to think that Father Yorke felt unfriendly toward the movement," but the incident suggests how nativist and anti-Catholic prejudices compromised suffrage appeals to urban, immigrant, working-class populations.[79]

Due to their moral influence and local contacts, churches provided important opportunities for suffragists, and this was especially true in the African American community. Western blacks generally supported equal suffrage in theory and editorially, but they disliked the unexamined assumptions of privilege white suffragists frequently displayed.[80] Anthony addressed black churches in the Bay Area, drawing immense crowds, and she praised the work of Naomi Anderson, an experienced African American suffrage organizer from Sacramento. "The negro alone was set free," Anderson told one San Francisco Baptist congregation, but "the negress was very little better off now than during the days of slavery." She reminded "all men who had been in bondage" to remember and help liberate women "from their latter day slavery." She appealed to the interests of the entire community when she observed that "the black laws on California's statute books would never be canceled until women had their rights and cast their votes."[81] The subsequent vote of "the immense audience was unanimous in its favor." At a meeting of the Los Angeles Afro-American League, Anderson requested and received a pro-suffrage resolution over some opposition.[82] Mary Keith described Anderson as a "wonderful orator." She assessed the impact of Anderson's work in Oakland by quoting the Reverend J. E. Edwards, a local African Methodist Episcopal Church pastor (and a suffragist), who was "astonished to observe the interest and enthusiasm which the woman suffrage campaign has stirred up among the colored people across the bay." The Reverend Edwards reported that Anderson was "a powerful orator" who won a unanimous endorsement from his congregation. He concluded, "It looks as though the cause could rely upon Oakland's colored vote." Oakland's African American women quickly formed several precinct clubs and held at least one rally described as "enthusiastic."[83]

The few native-born Chinese men eligible to vote in 1896 generated concerns totally out of proportion to their actual numbers. The few whites familiar with the Chinese community were Protestant missionaries and WCTU activists. The WCTU "delegated a woman, long in Chinese mission work, to visit . . . our new native Chinese voters in the interest of our Amendment," and she reported, "All the men in the Chinese churches are in favor of woman suffrage." The unconverted, especially "the Asiatic people of mature age," were more skeptical, as "they do not take kindly to the gospel of universal brotherhood, which we preach but do not practice."[84] Commenting on the recent Supreme Court case of Wong Kim Ark, WCTU franchise coordinator Sarah Severance acknowledged, "The Chinese have been shamefully abused in California," but she still distrusted them. Severance warned that unless they were "more grateful to the women who have befriended them in danger, and taught them . . . English . . . [then] it is adding 2,000 new voters with heathen ideas about women."[85]

In order to win a popular referendum, suffragists had to find less insulting ways to convince crucial urban swing voters to support woman suffrage, and they used every argument they could muster. They employed conservative maternalist and "home protection" arguments, but they emphatically dissociated themselves from the controversial issue of prohibition. Susan Anthony and Frances Willard agreed that "the two movements cannot successfully unite to win for either cause," but Anthony offended the state WCTU when she convinced Willard to change the venue of the national convention, scheduled for San Francisco just before the election. Irate California WCTU leaders resisted, but Willard forced them to accept her decision to cancel the convention.[86] Frustrated, Sarah Severance later discussed the issue of cooperation with Louise Sorbier, pledging unity but explaining that the WCTU women were "puzzled and cannot understand why we have no voice in the management, why in so many cases our guns are silent."[87] Disappointed WCTU suffragists kept a low profile but worked vigorously during the campaign, hiring many speakers primarily "for the benefit of the laboring men."[88]

Prohibition and woman suffrage remained strongly connected in the public mind, and the open campaign did alert the opposition. Just before election day, the Liquor Dealers' League circularized saloon keepers, hotel proprietors, druggists, and grocers, urging them to defeat the measure.[89] Suffragists heard rumors that politicians and liquor dealers had arranged "to get all the bad women in Oakland . . . to act loudly and boisterously, and so disgust men, who might believe they represented the suffrage cause," and they repudiated such behavior. "Bad women," real or imagined, evoked earlier "free love" accusations used to discredit woman suffrage as radical and immoral. On election day, some "irregulars" may or may not have "climbed up on the telegraph poles and waved yellow handkerchiefs and cried 'Vote for the sixth amend!' In some places they threw their arms around the men's necks and asked them to vote for suffrage."[90] Hindered by their concerns for feminine propriety, suffragists did not campaign at the polls on election day in 1896, but they carefully watched the count at over three hundred Bay Area precincts. Suffragists anticipated foul play, and their fears were heightened when the amendment was renumbered and moved to the end of the ballot at the last minute.[91]

The woman suffrage amendment lost in California (137,099 to 110,355), with a 44.6 percent positive vote statewide. The greatest support was in small towns, rural areas, and stable working-class urban districts. In a familiar pattern, all but one of the thirty-one counties voting Populist in 1892 supported the amendment, whereas Republican and Democratic counties were evenly split.[92] San Francisco supported McKinley, while Los Angeles voted for Bryan, but many presidential voters passed on woman suffrage, suggesting distraction and uncertainty on this issue. Woman suffrage prevailed in Southern California, and the mining regions of the Sierra Nevada mountains also provided strong pockets of support. Some suffragists realized that the opposition clustered at both the extreme ends of the social scale, suggesting that powerful political and economic factors, not immigrant voters per se, thwarted suffrage progress. For example, Ida Harper was careful not to blame "the liquor dealers, or to the densely ignorant, or to the foreigners" because "in the wealthiest and most aristocratic wards . . . the proportion of votes against the amendment was just as great as it was in the slum wards of the two cities."[93] Others missed or ignored this evidence and continued to blame the usual suspects: immigrant urbanites, political machines, and liquor and vice interests.[94]

Ignorance and racial prejudice encouraged many suffragists to exaggerate the significance of the few native-born Chinese voters. Vastly overestimating their numbers, Carrie Catt described "Chinese voters, in 'pigtails' and sandals, at the polling booths. . . . rarely informed enough to mark more than one item on the ballot, in which case their vote was invariably marked against the amendment." She concluded that Chinese voters had retaliated with "their votes to deny self-government to American women" due to Pacific Coast anti-Chinese sentiment." Reviewing previous failed referenda, she cited the "saloon's hour [of victory] in Washington" in 1889, declared that Indians and "illiterate Russians" had wrecked the 1890 South Dakota campaign, and now California "was the hour of the Chinese!" In short, "There had been hours for the Indian, the Russian, the German, the Chinese, the foreigner, the saloon, hours when each had decided the limits of woman's sphere, but no woman's hour had come."[95] Again missionaries and WCTU activists refuted these charges.

An investigation discovered only twenty-two Chinese registered in San Francisco and two in Oakland, and "these were very intelligent young men, quite as likely to vote 'for' as 'against.'"[96]

Susan B. Anthony attributed the loss to bad timing during a controversial election, perfunctory support from the political parties and insufficient attention to organizing rural districts.[97] She had already predicted Bryan's defeat, "but whatever the issue, protection, free trade, gold or silver, women will get nothing out of it."[98] She was right: desperate to carry this important state, most Republicans and Populists ignored their platform commitments. Fusion put negative pressure on the Populists "since the Democrats, as a party, were opposed to woman suffrage, and there they were!"[99] After the election, women from across the political spectrum accused the Republicans with corruption and collusion, "of slavish adherence to the liquor men." Sarah Severance stated bluntly: "We were sold out. That is the truth of the matter. We got more votes from Democrats than we did from Republicans." The experience of having been "traded for McKinley . . . ought to teach women better than to put faith in politicians." Yet "far from 'settling it,' they have only aroused good men and women to much greater zeal and enthusiasm, and the women are to keep up all the organizations and go on fighting."[100] Socialist Anna Haskell concurred: "The Republicans have proved themselves lowdown liars! . . . The whisky ring got in its work well."[101]

California suffragists rallied at the next state suffrage convention, liquidated the remaining campaign debts, and resolved to "enter at once on a vigorous campaign which will end only when the ballot is placed in the hands of California women." Anthony constantly pressed for resubmission, preferably during an off-year election, and California suffragists returned to Sacramento in 1897 with 30,000 signatures on petitions. Despite continuing efforts, the Republican-dominated legislature refused to authorize another referendum until 1911.[102] In 1899, a WCTU-sponsored school suffrage bill passed the legislature almost unanimously, but the governor vetoed it. Severance characteristically blamed the liquor interests and political corruption, yet "we are no worse off than before, [and] all agitation helps." A similar effort failed in 1901. Complementing the steady work of the WCTU, the state suffrage association persisted but made little headway until the Progressive insurgency disrupted conservative Republican dominance of state politics.[103]

As the old century waned, many of the California "Generation of 1896" remained active despite advancing age. In San Francisco, Ellen Sargent, Mary Swift, Mary Sperry, and others formed the Susan B. Anthony club "to hold together some of those who had shared in the toil and the disappointment."[104] In 1900, Sperry succeeded Swift as president of the state association, serving until 1907. Anthony approved of Sperry, who "links the old people to the new," and instructed her younger California protégés to "sustain her right loyally."[105] Sperry and Swift also tried to improve ties with Southern California suffragists. In 1900, Swift helped Caroline Severance reorganize the Los Angeles Equal Suffrage Society, which reaffiliated with the northern association in 1903. In 1904, the annual state convention met in Los Angeles for the first time and voted to rename the organization as the California Equal Suffrage Association (CESA) in order to attract a broader audience, including men who would not otherwise join a "woman's club."[106]

The failure of the 1896 California campaign was a bitter blow to these suffragists, who had hoped the Populist momentum would help them sweep the West, but they were consoled by the Idaho victory in that same year. Populism, labor, and Idaho's significant Mormon population were all important factors, but there was very little public suffrage activity by women before the bill passed the legislature. Discussions in the early 1870s died for fear that woman suffrage would fortify the power of Mormon Democrats. Catt planned to send Emma DeVoe and Laura Johns of Kansas to Idaho in 1895, but there was "a little stumbling block which I must tell you about," that is, Abigail Scott Duniway.[107] The veteran suffragist had lived in Idaho for the past decade concentrating on her family and only occasionally becoming involved in politics. One important exception was the 1889 constitutional convention. True to form, Duniway alienated many local activists when she opposed the linkage of suffrage and prohibition amendments.

Duniway did not establish any permanent suffrage contacts in Idaho prior to 1895, when she organized a group in Boise with William Balderston, the editor of the *Boise Statesman*. Duniway claimed that the local people had asked for and needed her help because the "WCTU is spoiling everything," but she might have been justifying her intervention at this point.[108] Carrie Catt later reported that the "suffrage Association . . . says she talks all the time, and is always making out that she is neglected."[109] Catt was impressed with Duniway initially, and the two women seemed to reach an understanding, but Duniway reneged and persuaded the local leadership to reject NAWSA advice and organizers. From that point, Catt considered Duniway as untrustworthy and corrupted by

personal ambition, "a jealous minded and dangerous woman."[110] Catt
circumvented Duniway by asking Balderston to identify influential local
women, then she enlisted Denver clubwomen to write to their Idaho
counterparts, and this society connection eased the way for DeVoe and
Johns when they came in the summer.[111] The national organizers held
conventions and tried to create permanent suffrage organizations. Sensitive to criticism about "outsiders," Catt insisted "after we have given
them that much help we will clear out and let them paddle their own ca-
noes."[112] DeVoe arranged a series of meetings and raised $900 (the total
campaign cost was $2,500). Catt considered DeVoe's work "splendid in
every particular," especially in Boise, where she linked "the society people and Suffrage." Catt understood the importance of "political endorsement. . . . We never won without it anywhere," but she worried about the
weaknesses in the "all-partisan" approach. She was confident of support
from Idaho Populists, but concerned because the Republican convention
met first, and she had "reason to believe that the Populists will not endorse unless the Republicans do before them." Ultimately all of the state
parties (including the Democrats) endorsed woman suffrage, and the
measure passed easily (12,126 to 6,282).[113]

Similar circumstances helped woman suffrage pass in Colorado and
Idaho, but these proved difficult to generalize or to sustain in the profound political shift of 1896. As head of NAWSA's organizing committee,
Catt did her best to take advantage of the western momentum. Part of her
strategy involved soliciting testimonials and participation from prominent men and public officials in western equal suffrage states, including
former Colorado governor John Routt and Denver judge Ben Lindsey.
Most western politicians obliged, affirming the benefits and refuting negative reports. For example, Idaho governor Frank Steunenberg commended female turnout in 1898, when three women (a Democrat, a Populist, and a Republican) won seats in the legislature. They "made most
acceptable public officers, serving with ability and success," proving that
"the only vital question at the polls were those of merit and party."[114]
Idaho was an isolated and thinly populated rural state, however, and the
clear challenge for suffragists was winning urban voters. Suffragists
waited fourteen years for the next state victory, leading some observers to
describe this period as "the doldrums." In fact, it was a period of considerable activity, as a younger generation of suffragists helped develop
successful modern methods of persuasion. Additional suffrage victories
also depended upon a resurgence of reform energy to open the windows

of political opportunity, provided by the Progressives in the early 1900s. After the People's Party faded, reformers regrouped as Socialists, trade unionists, and Progressives, and continued suffrage agitation helped find allies, build networks, and create new political options.[115] By 1911, California activists realized that "there were earnest suffragists in every kind of association in the State . . . the Socialist party, the State Grange and the ever-growing Labor Unions," and they "determined to make a strenuous effort to get into touch with every progressive element."[116] In the new century, suffragists would assist progressive candidates, broaden their coalition, and gain leverage within the established parties. As reformers, they would help create the farmer-labor-progressive political climate of the 1910s that eventually approved woman suffrage as a direct democracy measure. These new developments were often local and subtle, so it was quite a surprise to most people when Washington State passed woman suffrage quite easily in 1910. The California victory the following year made it clear that Washington had not been a fluke, and confirmed that the suffrage movement had entered a new and more dynamic period in the twentieth century.

6

Woman Suffrage and Progressivism in the Pacific Northwest

Eastward the star of woman's empire takes its way. . . . It is to the strong, courageous and progressive men of the Western States that the women of this whole country are looking for deliverance. . . . It is these men who must start this movement and give it such momentum that it will roll irresistibly on to the very shores of the Atlantic Ocean.   —Ida Husted Harper[1]

In 1910, Washington State approved the first woman suffrage amendment in fourteen years by a generous margin. By this time, many frustrated suffragists had almost given up on state campaigns as impossibly difficult to win, so this surprise victory needs explanation.[2] The most important factors were the political opportunity created by the Progressive movement, the active support of farmer-labor allies, strong leadership, and the innovative tactics developed by a new generation of suffragists. In addition, the growing women's club movement and a strong WCTU sustained interest in suffrage through the years of disfranchisement and provided much of the organization, resources, and personnel for the 1910 campaign. Washington women lost the vote in 1888 through political manipulation, but regained it as part of Progressive reform efforts to end such machinations. In general, people on the West Coast considered themselves the Progressive vanguard. This attitude was due to early passage of the initiative and referendum, the continuity of Populist farmer-labor agitation into the 1900s, and more than a little western exceptionalism.

As suffrage became synonymous with progress, activity in all the Pacific Coast states increased dramatically. As with the Populists, however, the support of male reformers was never automatic or guaranteed. Suffragists had to work at the creation of strategic alliances and they had to develop arguments that emphasized their goal as a democratic reform for the general benefit. Thus, woman suffrage needs to be understood as an integral part of Progressive political reform, rather than as a separate issue. Success in Washington gave new impetus to other campaigns and new ideas to try, resulting in victories in California in 1911, Oregon in 1912, and most of the other western states by the end of 1914. These developments encouraged national suffrage leaders, who always predicted that the next breakthroughs would come from the West, but they never expected to wait so long.

This faith in the progressive West led the NAWSA to become intensely involved in the 1906 Oregon campaign, and bitter over its failure, which was widely attributed to fraud. As in other states, this participation often alienated local suffragists, especially those who aspired to national leadership, because they considered themselves more progressive and more effective than easterners who had yet to win a single state campaign. As a result, suffragists in Washington, California, and Oregon largely rejected NAWSA "interference" during their final campaigns, an indication of their growing organizational maturity.

Several talented and experienced suffragists provided strong leadership for the movement in the Pacific Northwest, but this was a mixed blessing because it precipitated ugly factional struggles in both states. The suffrage histories Washington and Oregon reveal serious women politicians with their own ideas, ambitions, constituencies, and conflicts. In Oregon, Abigail Duniway reasserted her dominance in the early 1900s, still devoted to her outdated "still hunt" methods. Duniway's contemporaries blamed her intransigence for repeated campaign failures, while her denunciations of the NAWSA as well as the WCTU became almost pathological. In Washington, the feud between Emma Smith DeVoe and May Arkwright Hutton split the state, but each was able to do effective work in her own region. Despite factionalism, these victories resulted from strong farmer-labor support and the selective adoption of modern campaign tactics.

Factionalism and personality conflicts among ambitious women politicians hindered the movement, but fragmentation and decentralization stimulated independent organization and facilitated outreach to many different constituencies. Nationally as well as regionally, the suffrage movement was in transition as older leaders resisted or selectively adopted public, mass-based techniques under pressure from an impatient younger generation. The 1910 Washington campaign was a hybrid of older, conservative educational tactics and newer, modern ideas, while the latter predominated in California the following year. Together these victories established a new model for state campaigns and helped reinvigorate the national movement.

After disfranchisement in 1888, many Washington women refocused their energies on the women's club movement, the WCTU, and reform politics, often using these networks as the basis for continued suffrage agitation. When Abby Stuart started the first Washington women's club in Olympia, her explicit goal was to "give women who oppose the Suffrage Movement (or think they do) an opportunity to divest themselves of their prejudices." In the 1890s, the regional movement blossomed, and the Washington State Federation of Women's Clubs was formed in 1896. By 1904, it represented eighty-five organizations and a total membership of about two thousand. In June 1896, the Portland activists held a woman's congress attended by NAWSA leaders Susan B. Anthony and Anna Howard Shaw, and it was a great success. A second congress in 1898 confirmed the growing organizational sophistication of northwestern clubwomen.[3]

The political reform energy of the 1890s encouraged suffrage alignments with Populists, the Grange, the Farmers' Alliance, and the Knights of Labor, but this did not happen automatically. As in other areas, Washington Populists tended to support woman suffrage in the abstract, but it was vulnerable to fusion pressures. In 1896, fusion involved *three* parties—the Populists, the Democrats, and the Silver Republicans—and this combined strength elected Populist John Rogers governor. The Populists were still strong in 1898, but in decline by 1900, when Rogers was reelected, but as a Democrat.[4] Strong Populist sentiment persisted in Washington after this point, but the organized party never regained its earlier strength.

This instability and political maneuvering encouraged Washington Populists to avoid a divisive issue like woman suffrage unless prodded by female colleagues like Laura Hall Peters. The 1896 state Populist convention passed a strong suffrage plank, largely due to her efforts.[5] In accordance with Anthony's "all-partisan" plan, Peters urged all female partisans to introduce the issue at their respective party conventions. When the regular Republicans were not receptive, at least one frustrated suffragist threatened to support the People's Party. Republican suffragists were angry with their party for its lukewarm and insincere position on both the state and national levels. In 1898, female delegates pushed the state Populists and Silver Republicans for a woman suffrage plank, but Democratic opposition eliminated it from the fusion platform. Enraged, Peters charged publicly that the Populist Party had abandoned the measure.[6]

In 1896, Washington Populists carried the state for William Jennings Bryan, elected Rogers governor, and made significant gains in the state legislature. Early in 1897, a Silver Republican prohibitionist representative introduced a suffrage amendment in the House, and the Populists helped pass it despite their discomfort with the inclusion of an English literacy clause. State Senator Joseph Hill, an Irish-born Populist, was an important supporter who used both equal rights and good government arguments in debate. The Senate eliminated the literacy requirement, approved the bill, and returned it to the House for reconciliation.[7] Peters led the small suffrage lobby, and her political connections proved crucial at key moments. For example, when an observant senator noticed a last-minute effort to substitute a fraudulent version of the bill, Peters personally carried the correct version to Governor Rogers and witnessed his signature.[8]

The legislative maneuvering to win an authorization bill had been successful, but Washington suffragists still faced the challenge of a public referendum. Unfortunately, they delayed the beginning of the 1898 campaign for nine months, one likely reason for their defeat. Realistically, inexperienced local suffragists were not prepared for the logistical demands of a campaign, but even at the time, the leadership was criticized as timid, old-fashioned, and excessively focused on prohibition and moral reform.[9] The link between suffrage and prohibition was highly problematic. During the campaign, the WCTU sponsored a state organizer and otherwise lent "a helping hand judiciously," but the presence of a prohibition amendment on the same ballot inevitably advertised their relationship.[10] Saloons posted signs reading, "Vote against woman suffrage. With the WCTU as leaders in the movement, it means prohibition." The Washington Equal Suffrage Association (WESA) did try to reach many audiences, but the small size and decentralized structure of the organization necessitated heavy reliance on literature distribution, press work, and organizational endorsements. They approached political parties, trade unions, and other voluntary associations to facilitate outreach, especially among urban immigrants alienated by middle-class elitism, nativism, and racism.

WESA state president Carrie Hill, a Seattle clubwoman, reported support from the Prohibition, Social Democratic, and Socialist Labor parties, the Western Central Labor Union of Seattle, the *Freemen's Labor Journal* of Spokane, "Single Taxers," and the State Grange. Hill remarked, "Many of the most self-sacrificing workers came from the liberal and free-thought societies, which are generally favorable to equal rights."[11] Governor Rogers was supportive, but the pressures of maintaining the fusion alliance and the anti-suffrage tirades of former Colorado governor Waite probably dampened his enthusiasm. After the 1898 referendum failed, he wrote to Hill, reminding her that he had spoken for it, and "voted for it, although I had expressed to you some fear that if women were given the right to vote the fusion party would not profit thereby."[12] The heavy negative vote on the amendment (30,540 to 20,658), suggests the damaging effects of these issues on Populist support.[13]

After 1898, reform momentum continued in the Pacific Northwest despite distractions such as the Alaska Gold Rush, the Spanish-American War, and the dispersion of Populists into other parties. In Oregon in 1899, members of the Grange, Knights of Labor, the Union Labor and Prohibition parties formed a "Union Party," and their agitation helped place a suffrage referendum on the ballot in June 1900.[14] Although it lost, the vote was very close (28,402 to 26,265), indicative of lingering support in a waning reform environment. Suspicious and jealous of national organizers, Duniway retained tight organizational control and accepted no outside funding or assistance except two visiting speakers with Socialist and Populist credentials, Lena Morrow of Illinois and Ida Crouch Hazlett of Colorado, who toured the Oregon backcountry. When the measure was defeated, Anthony held Duniway and her "still-hunt" methods responsible, but Duniway blamed prohibitionists and the *Oregonian* (edited by her brother), which "stirred up and called out" the "slum vote of Portland and Astoria."[15] In 1902 Oregon voters passed an Initiative and Referendum Act, which allowed advocates to put suffrage measures directly on the ballot every two years until it finally passed in 1912.

Within the suffrage movement, frustration with Duniway generated escalating factional conflict and debilitating leadership struggles. A prominent Portland clubwoman, Sarah A. Evans, described the cause in Oregon in 1901 as "almost becalmed upon a sea of indifference. With an ultra conservative population, defeats in five previous campaigns, the existence of bitter prejudices and an utter lack of cooperation among the suffragists themselves, the outlook was almost hopeless." Between 1901 and 1904, Duniway and her allies dominated the state association, no conventions were held, and frustrations mounted. In 1905, Evans joined forces with Clara Colby, the publisher of the *Woman's Tribune,* to plan a coup.[16]

Colby and Duniway had much in common as women's rights journalists, ambitious regional leaders, and poor organizers. Colby began publishing the *Woman's Tribune* in 1883 in Nebraska, where she served as president of the state suffrage association from 1885 to 1898. She moved the paper to Washington, D.C., when her husband took a position in the Benjamin Harrison administration (1889–1904). After her divorce, she moved to Portland in 1904, correctly predicting the next wave of suffrage success in this area.[17] Aspiring to national leadership, Colby hoped the *Woman's Tribune* would become the official publication of the NWSA. It started well, but steadily declined due to poor management, multiple relocations, and controversial topics, and finally ceased publication in 1909, just a year before the successful 1910 Washington referendum campaign. Colby never realized her national ambitions, but she was prescient about the significance of the region for the success of woman suffrage. Having given up the *New Northwest* in 1884, Duniway was initially congenial and complimentary of the *Woman's Tribune,* but her attitude changed when Colby tried to establish a leadership position within the Oregon suffrage movement. She held her grudge against this "arch-pretender" for a long time.[18]

Facing another campaign in 1906, Duniway feared "the irrepressible ambition" of outside organizers, but authorized the OESA to invite the NAWSA to hold its 1905 convention in Portland in conjunction with the Lewis and Clark Exposition. If Duniway expected to play a starring role at the meeting, she was terribly disappointed. After a token tribute to her pioneer status, everyone essentially ignored her to focus on younger activists and modern issues.[19] Important reformers, including Florence Kelley and Portland physician Marie Equi, stressed the problems of wage-earning women and children.[20] May Arkwright Hutton of Idaho, a key figure in the 1910 Washington campaign, represented the equal suffrage states. Hutton recalled how a young lawyer, future president William McKinley, once spent the night at her grandfather's house in Ohio. After a lively discussion of women's rights, McKinley turned to May, and "patting my head he said: 'I believe when this lassie grows up she will be a voter.'" He was right, although Hutton became a steadfast Democrat and a friend of William Jennings Bryan.[21]

Speeches and resolutions at the convention reveal the national significance suffragists attributed to this particular campaign, the progressive reform environment, and the West generally. Ida Husted Harper shamelessly appealed to state pride and boosterism: "Today the eyes of the whole country are on this beautiful and progressive state. . . . Would it not add the crowning glory . . . if the free men of Oregon should decree that this shall be . . . the land also of free women?" Local notable Charles E. S. Wood claimed to know little about suffrage (although he later became the long-term partner of suffragist Sara Bard Field), but "it seemed to him that what was back of it all was justice." One of the most important Progressive politicians in Washington, William S. U'Ren, spoke on "The Initiative and Referendum and What It Seeks to Accomplish." His presentation "acknowledged the help the women had given in obtaining this law," and firmly rejected "the 'still hunt' in carrying reform measures." Clara Colby followed up with a resolution in support of "the initiative and referendum as a needed reform and as a potent factor in the progress of true democracy." Duniway immediately tried to suppress it, fearful of alerting the opposition to the upcoming Oregon campaign, but the majority adopted the resolution. Observers described the adoption of several other resolutions "only indirectly connected with woman suffrage," indicating "a marked change in the attitude of the association," which had previously rejected such resolutions.[22]

As Duniway feared, NAWSA organizers remained after the convention "to take charge" of the 1906 Oregon campaign. To Duniway's horror, they applied Anthony's public "hurrah" approach, with the death of "Aunt Susan" in the spring adding a poignant memorial element. Bypassed and annoyed, Duniway stepped aside into an honorary position in favor of her associate, Viola M. Coe, who became the local leader under the direction of national organizer Laura Gregg (Cannon) of Kansas. The NAWSA spent approximately $20,000 and sent some of its best organizers, including Gregg and Laura Clay of Kentucky. They arrived in September and immediately began circulating suffrage initiative petitions and speaking to many local groups, including the Women's Union Label League (WULL) and the Grange.[23]

Displaced from active leadership, Duniway did not attend the fall suffrage convention, where speakers included Clay, Colby, and Colorado attorney Gail Laughlin. Clay reported that "nearly every man she meets is a suffragist and she is having a delightful experience." She "had found men of all classes very friendly, and especially a large proportion of voters of foreign birth."[24] Laughlin based her arguments on modern economic conditions, although "at bottom it is not an economic but a moral question." "Women are laboring under the double handicap of sex and unjust laws," she stated, and as a "permanent economic factor in our national life, they should be considered in our national policy." Later that fall, Laughlin prepared a five-page text explaining the measure that was distributed to every voter by the state as part of the initiative process. Then Laughlin moved on to California, where her efforts doubled the size of the state organization in 1906.

During the last months of the campaign, more outsiders arrived, including Emma Smith DeVoe, Mary Bradford of Colorado, Alice Stone Blackwell, and NAWSA president Anna Howard Shaw, who articulated NAWSA frustrations and hopes. Shaw recalled how "year after year, in State after State," male politicians "have played shuttle cock and battledore with our measure . . . in a hypocritical desire to appear favorable and inspire us with hope, that they might retain our friendship and the small amount of political influence they think we already possess." Now that adoption of the initiative and referendum had altered the political landscape, "Our hope lies in the power of the people to compel action." Bradford was especially welcome because "not only can she fix the lies and the liars that are throwing mud at the women of Colorado, but then she is so sweet and womanly herself that it really is quite encouraging to the rest of us."[25] Mary Sperry, president of the California Equal Suffrage Association (CESA), contributed her services and $1000 donated by San Francisco suffragists convinced "that Oregon's cause is California's."[26]

Organizers courted working-class support, apparently with considerable success. Laughlin and Gregg spoke to workers "in their halls, at industrial plants and on the streets," and to labor and socialist organizations, including the state Socialist Party convention, where they "gave their assent by a rising vote."[27] The previous year, the state secretary of the Socialist Party had attended an Oregon Equal Suffrage Association (OESA) meeting, where he joined the society and volunteered to aid its work in every way possible. The Socialists, he said, were all in favor of woman suffrage, and he himself had seen its good results in New Zealand, where it had been carried by the Socialists. He received warm applause, but "at the same time the absolute non-partisan attitude of the Society was re-affirmed. Just let the Republicans and Democrats send us their representatives bearing the same message of good will, and they will be received as gratefully."[28]

Much of this work built on the foundation prepared by Luema Johnson, secretary of the OESA, who was also active in the Portland WULL. Johnson told the WULL that "the ballot is the mightiest prayer of the workingman, and will be for working women."[29] At a spring suffrage conference, she "appealed for the ballot for the protection of women wage-earners" and insisted, "Our hope for suffrage lies with the working people." She read a letter from American Federation of Labor (AFL) president Gompers, "urging the labor forces to stand for this amendment," while Laughlin presented a long communication from the state federation of labor.[30] Trade unionists expected great things from female enfranchisement: "better government, happier homes and a more contented people. . . . less 'sweatshop' miseries, fewer children in the mills and mines and a higher code of morals in the social, political and economic affairs of our country." They believed "it is going to succeed because it is a mission of equity, and it is destined to become one of the strongest factors in the solution of the economic struggle of the common people against plutocratic expression." Sensible suffragists rarely made such grand claims, but they appreciated such enthusiastic support.[31]

Despite all the optimistic projections, the measure lost in the June election by more than 10,000 votes. The results did not contradict growing suffragist faith in working-class voters, however, because they were convinced that they had been cheated. Clara Colby's experience at the polls seemed to justify this conclusion. Volunteering at her local precinct in the evening, she observed "what the workers found everywhere, the young men giving out the Anti-card . . . and working hard to earn the extra dollar they were to have if the amendment was defeated." Oregon anti-suffragists had employed their own organizer, and the Brewer's and Wholesale Liquor Dealers' Association of Oregon mobilized its membership.[32] Assigned to monitor the vote, Colby complained that the judges made it as hard as possible to see, but she insisted "sweetly and firmly . . . and I did see every one." The results from this precinct were rather odd: "The votes from the top of the box were nearly two to one in favor of woman suffrage, showing that the workmen of the longer hours who had come home latest were largely with us." Underneath was a "layer of votes against us more than 2 to one," which she attributed to purchased votes. Nevertheless, the final result was a tie. While this sample is too small to support reliable generalizations, Colby's cursory analysis indicated that

42 percent of Democrats and Republicans (by far the largest block) supported the measure, as did 71 percent of the few Socialists and Prohibitionists.[33] It is interesting that the level of support was about equal within the major parties, while prohibitionists were apparently no more committed to woman suffrage than socialists. As a result of this experience, suffragists everywhere became vigilant poll watchers and vote counters, regardless of concerns about appropriate female behavior.

The failure of this campaign allowed Abigail Duniway to regain control of the official state suffrage organization in 1906 despite a coup attempt by Colby and Evans. At the fall convention, Colby introduced a motion to "retire" an active president after two terms, which removed the current president, Duniway's protégé Viola Coe. This action precipitated a full-scale battle between the Duniway/Coe and the Colby/Evans factions, but the latter did not have a strong replacement to offer and Duniway ultimately triumphed. At the convention and in the *Woman's Tribune,* Colby professed her loyalty and justified her actions. Citing Elizabeth Cady Stanton's criticism of the "still hunt," she openly blamed Duniway's methods, including her objections to building a large movement, as "the reason suffrage has been defeated three times in Oregon." She asserted that many Oregon women felt that "if the suffrage work is to proceed in the State, it must be thoroughly organized, which Mrs. D. does not believe in." Furthermore, "Something must be done to let the State know that Mrs. Duniway's attitude of antagonism to the WCTU and to the NAWSA for coming to Oregon to help in the campaign . . . does not represent the sentiment of the suffrage organization." Even Colby grudgingly admired the political skill Duniway displayed as she printed up and distributed her "ticket," packed the meeting with brand-new members, then pushed her people into office. Colby insisted that while "the election of Mrs. Duniway . . . was an endorsement by the majority of those present," it was "by no means . . . the sentiment of the majority of those who have done the work for suffrage in Oregon."[34] The national leadership supported the Colby/Evans challenge, ended all financial support to the OESA, hinting about possible misappropriations of funds, and channeled the money to a committee of the Portland Woman's Club headed by Evans and Colby.[35]

After the 1906 defeat, Duniway routinely denounced her WCTU and NAWSA rivals and the "hurrah" campaign, especially Shaw and Colby (the "arch-pretender"), but under her leadership the situation steadily deteriorated.[36] Duniway controlled the OESA until 1912, refused to organize, and stuck to the "still hunt" in several increasingly unsuccessful campaigns. In 1910, she supported limited taxpayer suffrage, which even conservatives rejected because of its obvious offense to the working-class and the labor movement.[37] Predictably, this approach alienated "many of . . . the staunchest suffragists, who openly opposed it," and the amendment "was bitterly fought by labor and fraternal organizations." The result was a loss in Oregon by 22,000 votes in the same year that neighboring Washington adopted woman suffrage by roughly the same margin![38] The Duniway faction was clearly bereft of effective new ideas, and would have to be dislodged somehow before victory could be achieved.

The Washington State suffrage movement revived in 1906, energized by the excitement in Oregon and by new leadership, Emma Smith DeVoe and May Arkwright Hutton, who moved to the state around this time.[39] Both women were key figures in the successful 1910 campaign, but their personality conflicts and power struggles generated intense hostility and factionalism. Ironically, their methods differed little, but DeVoe considered Hutton vulgar, while Hutton became convinced that DeVoe was a hypocrite who was protecting her salaried position as a NAWSA organizer. With her experience as president of the South Dakota association and as a national organizer in the 1890s, DeVoe quickly became president of the Washington state suffrage organization, but her rapid rise to power, combined with her autocratic management style, upset some Washington activists.[40] In addition, she continued to receive her controversial subsidy of one hundred dollars per month until the NAWSA cut her off in 1909.

In contrast to the genteel DeVoe, May Hutton was a loud and brassy character. After her encounter with McKinley as a child, Hutton migrated to Idaho and worked as a cook in a mining camp, where she married Levi (Al) Hutton, a locomotive engineer. The Huttons were involuntarily caught up in the violent labor struggles in the Coeur d'Alene mining district in the early 1890s. A stint for Al in the "bull pen" radicalized May, who wrote a book about their experiences. Hutton was never militant, but she supported industrial unionism and felt that labor people generally supported equal rights for women. In 1901, the Huttons struck it rich as partial owners of a fabulous mine, the result of assisting a steady stream of hard-luck miners over the years.[41] Now a woman of unlimited means in an equal suffrage state, May became a writer and politician. In 1904, she ran for the Idaho state legislature as a Democrat. She electioneered "just like any man. I gave away cigars—and hustled," but she credited her near-victory to newly enfranchised Idaho women.[42] Also active in national Democratic politics, Hutton became frustrated by the equivocation of both national parties on the issue of woman suffrage. In 1912, she described herself as "nearly" a Socialist, and warned "unless progressive ideas prevail and progressive laws are enforced we'll have socialism in this country. It's evolute or resolute."[43] Extremely class conscious, Hutton always identified with working women, the "laundry worker, the shop girl, the stenographer, the teacher, the working woman of every type, whose home and fireside and bread are earned by their own efforts."[44] Refuting arguments against women sitting on juries, she observed "women who stand behind counters, or in factories, at the cook stove, wash tub, ironing table, dish sink, and baby crib, would be mighty glad to sit on almost anything for a rest."[45] By early 1907, the Huttons had moved a few miles over the mountains to Spokane, Washington, the regional metropole. Although May Hutton gave up her right to vote, they both gained a larger scope for their activities.

Initially Hutton and DeVoe cooperated effectively, but problems developed during the 1909 legislative session. In 1908, they jointly organized a Spokane suffrage club, and Hutton paid the annual rent for the state headquarters.[46] In 1909 they were optimistic because a 1907 direct primary law had helped loosen Republican control of the state legislature.[47] Under DeVoe's direction, suffragists did not debate the merits of woman suffrage, but requested only the submission of the measure to the voters. DeVoe stated, "We haven't attempted to convert a single legislator to our cause, save to appeal to his sense of fairness."[48] The implied threat was obvious, however, because if disappointed, women could "easily combine with the reform forces and see to it that only those legislative candidates are nominated who will be favorable to woman's suffrage at the next session."[49] A rotating corps of attractive young lobbyists were trained, "never bore a legislator by too much insistence," but supporters and opponents alike received coordinated volleys of letters, telegrams, and visits. When a reporter suggested that this tactic took "rather an unfair advantage . . . of defenseless legislators," Katherine (Mrs. George A.) Smith, a young clubwoman from Seattle, answered, "It is a little like politics, isn't it?" Smith, who "sort of got in the habit of voting in Colorado," thought "it would be just as good a habit to acquire in Washington." The press described these "cultured women" as "a constant won-

der to the legislators . . . [who] had expected another type [and] arguments."[50]

DeVoe established broad legislative support. In the Senate, allies included Democrat George F. Cotterill (a pro-labor "dry" who became
mayor of Seattle in 1911), and George U. Piper, the former editor of the
Seattle Post-Intelligencer. Although "a friend of the liquor interests,"
Piper acted "in honor of his dead mother, who had been ardently in favor
of woman suffrage."[51] Trouble began after the House passed the bill at
the end of January and DeVoe and Hutton disagreed on the next step.
DeVoe favored delaying the Senate vote until success was certain, but
Hutton pushed ahead independently, concerned that postponement signaled weakness and defeat. Piper later criticized "Mrs. Hutton [who]
greatly injured the cause . . . by continually interfering with the people
who were doing the work. It became necessary to ignore her entirely . . .
[which] made her very angry."[52] In late February, Piper guided the measure through the Senate while opponents were distracted by anti-race-
track gambling, local option, and women's eight-hour-day bills.[53] When
the vote was announced, the state senators "burst into applause and were
rapped to order by the president," while jubilant suffragists gently flut-
tered their handkerchiefs. [54]

Once the Washington legislature had authorized a referendum, national organizers took interest, but they soon became embroiled in the
ugly factional struggle. Once again taking advantage of the attendant
publicity, the 1909 NAWSA annual convention met in Seattle in the summer of 1909 in conjunction with the Alaska-Yukon-Pacific Exposition. At
the fair, suffragists hosted a permanent exhibit, a suffrage day, and even
a "dirigible balloon . . . [with] a large silken banner inscribed Votes for
Women."[55] As in Oregon in 1905, national officials hoped to boost the
upcoming campaign, and they were livid when called upon to referee the
internal conflict. It was more than a personality clash with Hutton, however, as DeVoe's micromanagement style irritated many busy modern
women who protested that she wasted their time and ignored their opinions. Devoe appreciated the energy and enthusiasm of the new generation
of suffragists, who did things like planting suffrage banners on Pacific
Coast mountain peaks, but she also wanted to keep them under control.[56]
For example, when the College Equal Suffrage League formed in 1907,
she tried to subordinate the group to the WESA. Even her young allies expressed a desire for more independence. One wrote to ask whether it

would "be all right for me to break away from the old club here & form a young peoples club, or working girls club, and let the older women paddle their own canoe."[57]

In the weeks before the 1909 state suffrage convention, mediation efforts ended in failure.[58] The dissidents were determined to replace DeVoe but could not find a good alternative candidate. Efforts to recruit former WESA president and Seattle clubwoman Carrie Hill were unsuccessful. Hill rejected secession and tried to mediate, but the situation went from bad to worse, and during the campaign she also led an independent group of dissident clubwomen, the Seattle Suffrage Club.[59] Hutton later formed the Spokane Political Equality League (PEL), and accepted the presidency reluctantly after she was unable to convince anyone else to take the job. Referring to DeVoe's suspected conflict of interest as a NAWSA organizer, Hutton proposed "that the present incumbent be retained" as a salaried employee, "under the control of an executive body who would be absolutely just and fair minded, and whose interest for ultimate success would be unquestioned."[60] Insurgents also demanded a revised constitution, more financial audits, and a bonded treasurer, clearly expressing a vote of "no confidence" in DeVoe and her loyal ally, WESA treasurer Dr. Cora Smith Eaton. Eaton feared close scrutiny because she had been generous with DeVoe's allowances and lax about bookkeeping, so she hoped for an insurgent walk out, rather than a direct challenge for control of the state association.[61]

Trying to pack the state convention, DeVoe and Hutton both used questionable tactics, but DeVoe and Eaton also attacked Hutton personally. Hutton increased the Spokane delegation by offering trips to the exposition as recruiting incentives and by purchasing memberships for friends and relatives. Eaton objected to these tactics, but she went much further and made a libelous accusation with DeVoe's approval, even after being advised that this action looked like blackmail.[62] The crisis exploded when Hutton sent Eaton $100 representing the dues of four hundred members, including several new clubs like the Spokane Stenographers Equal Suffrage Club. She had collected this money from working women because "it is difficult for them to attend to these matters outside of their working hours."[63] Eaton returned the funds, then informed Hutton (a life member and officer of the state association) that she was "ineligible to membership" on moral grounds. Eaton alleged that Hutton was "Bootleg Mary," who had operated "a bad house, kept for immoral purposes," in the political service of Idaho senator Clark. Eaton also complained of

Hutton's bad language and aggressive behavior during the 1909 lobbying effort, including an alleged attempt to bribe state legislators. Eaton urged Hutton to retreat with the implied threat of exposure if she did not.[64] She later stated, "It was a terribly hard thing to do, but . . . it was a surgical operation—an amputation, following the opening of a very foul abscess."[65] Although Eaton claimed to have seen "pictures and other evidence," and later insisted to Carrie Catt "every word of it was true, & capable of proof," a messenger sent to Idaho was unable to corroborate this story. Neither she nor DeVoe ever recanted or apologized. Hutton turned the matter over to her lawyer and notified Eaton that she would read the letter publicly at the convention. She was dissuaded by her attorney, but Hutton did show it to the members of the NAWSA Executive Board and many others.[66]

The NAWSA officers were furious when they arrived for the national convention and found the state association embroiled in a public scandal. One angry national leader, Harriet Taylor Upton, concluded that Hutton "was not the only prostitute who was in Seattle during the summer nor was she the only one who had her reputation soiled who was attached to the association."[67] Well aware that the Hutton faction planned a challenge to her presidency, DeVoe tried to use her NAWSA connections to shut them out of the national proceedings, and then she manipulated the state convention to quash the insurgents.[68] Unable to prevent the rebels from attending, DeVoe made sure the Spokane delegation was isolated, stalled by the credentials committee, and finally ejected without a hearing.

The insurgents withdrew and appealed to the NAWSA executive board for assistance. Presenting their case, former Colorado Lt. Gov. David C. Coates, now a Spokane labor official and one of Hutton's most valuable allies, angrily asserted their rights. He asked, "Are these women to be sacrificed that the political aspirations of our state president may be satisfied?"[69] DeVoe's only response was "I have no excuses to offer, believing that what we did was perfectly just and proper." Many of her supporters were amazed and upset that DeVoe offered only the "lamest of excuses" and did nothing to avert the conflict. Instead, she aggravated the situation by criticizing the NAWSA intercession. In a solution that satisfied no one, the NAWSA executive board decided to seat both Washington delegations, neither with voting privileges. In addition, they terminated DeVoe's NAWSA stipend and withheld all funds from the WESA.[70] DeVoe wrote to Catt, her former mentor, asking for an endorsement "because we have done no wrong our conscience is clear," but Catt wisely avoided the controversy and replied with her standard five hundred dollar campaign donation.[71] Thus Emma Smith DeVoe, one of the NAWSA's best organizers in the 1890s, became another bitter regional leader critical of interfering outsiders. She retained control of the WESA, however, and was now free to campaign in her own way.[72]

DeVoe used a transitional approach, "partly speech making and partly still hunting," that reflected her training with Catt and the influence of Duniway. She emphasized feminine respectability but used maternalist and civil housekeeping arguments very carefully, never promising specific reforms. She stressed good publicity, key endorsements, and systematic canvassing, but prioritized the "personal intensive work." The Washington Equal Suffrage Association (WESA) established a press bureau, managed by attorney and teacher Adella Parker, and they received good coverage in the newspapers. The Colorado Equal Suffrage Association contributed one hundred dollars to support Minnie Reynolds (Mrs. Scalabrino), a former Denver newspaper writer, suffragist, and publicist who was eventually hired by Hutton. In addition to advertisements, posters, and billboards, suffragists distributed over one million pieces of literature, issued a monthly newsletter, and published a suffrage cookbook.[73] DeVoe spurned NAWSA assistance, but accepted several out-of-state western volunteers, including Duniway, Colby, and Jeannette Rankin of Montana, who got her suffrage start in this campaign. Aside from the personal contributions of individual members, the NAWSA provided no official financial support to any Washington organization during the campaign. The WESA, other suffrage clubs, and many individuals shared the total cost of approximately $17,000.[74] The WESA eschewed large demonstrations or parades, but attended regular meetings of granges, farmers' unions, labor unions, churches, and other organizations. Catholic suffragists approached the church hierarchy, which pronounced the matter an individual decision, allowing several priests to support suffrage publicly. The editor of the *Catholic Northwest Progress,* the state diocesan organ, firmly identified herself as a suffragist.[75]

Once again, progressive-farmer-labor support was key to the success of woman suffrage in a referendum election. For some time, suffragists had carefully cultivated relationships with farmer-labor organizations and vice versa.[76] The state Grange and the Washington State Federation of Labor (WSFL) were both pro-active in the campaign, and each donated $500 to the WESL in addition to supporting their own organizing initiatives.[77] Both these groups were members of the Direct Legislation League, and they perceived woman suffrage as part of the progressive reform program. The Grange had a strong tradition of female participation and consistently supported woman suffrage. In 1909, state leader C. B. Kegley urged Grange women to become more involved in the upcoming campaign, but his wife, Augusta Kegley, was busy with Grange activities and housework, although "willing to have my name used in any honorable way."[78] In 1910, the Eastern Washington Grange employed a male organizer—a Granger, Populist, and good-government reformer—to work among rural and transient workers in twenty counties.[79]

State labor officials supported woman suffrage generally as part of the progressive agenda and specifically as a means to help pass a pending women's eight-hour-day bill. This was a major goal of Washington trade union women, absorbing much of their energy, and they provided the bridge between the labor and suffrage movements. Seattle labor suffragists included Grace (Mrs. Frank C.) Cotterill, Blanche Mason, a state factory inspector, and Alice Lord, the dynamic head of the Seattle Waitresses Union.[80] Some, like Lord, remained committed primarily to the eight-hour bill, but they appreciated the support of Washington women's clubs and they recognized how woman suffrage could help this cause.

These contacts began early, when the Seattle Women's Card and Label League sent a delegate to the 1906 state suffrage convention. In 1908, suffragists spoke before the state labor convention.[81] The growing labor interest is noticeable in the *Seattle Union Record* after George McNamara became editor in 1908, and his wife, Phillipina, started writing a women's column late in 1910.[82] McNamara's arguments were practical and emphasized how female enfranchisement would amplify working-class voting strength. In any case, "there is not the remotest possibility of their ever ceasing their agitation until it is secured."[83]

Apparently at the suggestion of WSFL president Charles R. Case, the WESA appointed a special Superintendent for Labor Unions, Dr. Luema G. Johnson, an active member of the WULL first in Portland, and now in Tacoma.[84] In 1909 and 1910, she won pro-suffrage resolutions from the state labor convention without any dissent. For Labor Day in 1910, Johnson urged members to join the parades to show "our appreciation of what the laboring men have done, are doing and still expect to do for us in our campaign." Women did participate in a few towns, usually in decorated cars or wagons. Labor officials publicly predicted high levels of support among working men, but reminded DeVoe that "we must win over a part of our membership by argument and by showing that your movement means a strong help to our own."[85] During the campaign, Johnson worked closely with local unions as well as the state labor federation.[86] In 1910, Case identified the amendment as a priority item and insisted, "We must do more than resolute favorably at this convention."[87]

State labor officials often included suffrage literature with their own mailings, and they also conducted a straw poll. Of forty-two locals reporting, only nine were opposed, and five of those represented bartenders, other culinary workers, and brewery workers—men who felt particularly threatened by female job competition or by women reformers. Suffragists tallied "40,000 votes in the labor unions, some 16,000 in the grange and 10,000 in the farmer's union. . . . Allowing for unfriendly individual and failure to vote . . . a solid block of 35,000 or 40,000 voters for our amendment from these three organizations."[88] In November, the WESA made a final appeal to labor "to come out strong next Tuesday for justice and self-interest by voting [to] . . . give women the right to vote."[89]

Suffragists were even more closely linked to the labor establishment in eastern Washington. One of Hutton's key advisers, David C. Coates, was a prominent socialist labor official in Spokane. His wife, Sadie Coates, was secretary of the Equal Suffrage Association of Spokane, and Mrs. Harry Jarvis, the wife of the president of the Spokane Central Labor Council, was also a labor suffragist.[90] Rose Bassett Moore (Ascherman), provided a crucial link as the head of the Spokane Union Label League and a former organizer for the Spokane Trades Council. She later became a prominent labor official in Seattle.[91] Moore and another Spokane clubwoman, Mrs. Philip Stalford, systematically visited the city's union locals. They approached the beer drivers "in such a businesslike way and . . . in so pretty a manner for next November, . . . that the unionists sat up and took notice." The women "talked about 'class consciousness,' 'solidarity of union,' 'economic determinism' and other 'isms' and explained how the ballot for women is in the end a matter of dollars and cents and raising wage scales."[92] During the summer, Stalford and Moore spent weeks traveling and addressing union locals in the major towns, returning well pleased with the results.[93]

On Labor Day, the Spokane women produced an elaborate float, probably designed and financed by Hutton. The tableau featured convicts and idiots literally chained to working women, personified by Sadie Coates and Mrs. A. W. Swenson, the wife of the editor of the *Labor World*. Hutton stood in the center holding a sign: "Brothers unshackle us from the criminal and idiot," while the front of the float carried a ten-foot banner reading "Woman's Status Before the Law: Idiots, criminals and women do not vote." Hutton observed, "This startling announcement brought forth a storm of protest. One prominent union man declared that it was a mistake—that a lot of idiots do vote."[94]

Hutton was friendly to labor, but she rejected militance as a suffrage tactic. Direct action was a sensitive subject generally in Spokane, the site of a sensational free speech fight by the Industrial Workers of the World (IWW) the previous year.[95] Yet Hutton found it difficult to restrain "young people who are bubling [*sic*] over with enthusiasm and an inordinate desire for approbation and newspaper notoriety . . . especially when they pay their own expenses." When the new Spokane College League began holding open-air meetings in the fall, Hutton succeeded "in putting the kibosh on any more street or park meetings."[96] She did appreciate the value of free media coverage, however, so she obtained a weekly column in the *Spokane Spokesman-Review* and hired former Denver newspaper reporter Minnie Reynolds (Scalabrino), "a western woman and voter, . . . [who] understands western men and western ways."[97] Using her language skills (she met Mr. Scalabrino in Italian class), Reynolds held several encouraging meetings in Italian, and designed appeals to other ethnic constituencies. At an Irish nationalist lecture, Political Equality League (PEL) members handed out cards with the phrase "Home Rule for Women," stressing similarities in their struggles for political self-determination. A reporter observed that "as the words were softly spoken with a smile, each Irishman, with the exception of a few, took the proffered card, first with a puzzled expression, and then a knowing look and smile, and an appreciation of the clever idea that the women had conceived."[98] Clever, direct, but low-key tactics like this were typical of the Washington campaign.

Washington suffragists used many different arguments to appeal to different groups, but they studiously avoided prohibition and rarely claimed special power in women's ballots, aside from the general effects of improving the quality of candidates and the conduct of elections. Former residents of neighboring equal suffrage states readily confirmed that woman suffrage did not mean the end (or the beginning) of civilization. Women who had voted in equal suffrage states—including Washington Territory between 1883 and 1888—highlighted the injustice of disfranchisement. The connections between economic and political rights resonated with women of all classes.[99] Suffragists and prohibition-ists agreed, "in order not to antagonize the 'whisky' vote, the temperance women would submerge their hard-earned honors and let the work of their unions go unheralded." This compromise allowed the suffragists to take advantage of the extensive organizational network of the WCTU while distancing themselves from the controversial issue of prohibition. No organized opposition emerged during the campaign other than an in-effective organizer sent by the National Association Opposed to Woman Suffrage and some last-minute circulars. Perhaps overwhelmed by the progressive surge, the Brewer's Association was preoccupied with the Anti-Saloon League and local option campaigns.[100]

As the election approached, many observers praised suffragists for "a vigorous, intelligent, and dignified campaign." They "stuck valiantly to the point at issue, and appealed to reason rather than to sentiment and prejudice."[101] On election day, male and female volunteers distributed suffrage literature in the rain and carefully watched the precinct tallies, anxious to prevent fraud. In an off-year election with low voter turnout, the measure passed by a surprisingly large margin: 52,299 (63.8%) to 29,676 (36.2%), winning every county and city. The newspapers re-ported, sometimes sarcastically, that the "WOMEN OF STATE GET THE BALLOT BY GIFT OF MEN." Olive Bruce of Bellingham protested, "It didn't 'happen'—we earned it!" Working independently, Bruce had pub-lished her own literature and "found a way to getting right to the mill men here in town." She concluded, "After all it is the personal work that counts."[102] Typically, prohibition sentiment correlated with support for woman suffrage, but even "wet" areas reported an average of 60 percent in favor. Success in urban areas was undoubtedly due to the strong labor presence in the campaign. Suffragists believed that they had convinced or-dinary men that their cause was "just and reasonable and everywhere when tried has been found expedient." Neither an accident nor a gift, the victory resulted from the concentrated efforts of suffragists, clubwomen, restrained WCTU activists, progressive farmers, and urban trade union-ists loosely coordinated (at best) in an extensive network.[103]

The 1911 Seattle municipal elections presented the first major test of female refranchisement. During the campaign, suffragists had dissociated themselves from efforts to recall Mayor Hiram Gill "for tolerating graft." Now nearly seven hundred Seattle women registered to vote, signed the recall petition, endorsed the reform candidate, George W. Dilling, and held several mass meetings.[104] These new voters were "*getting into poli-*

tics . . . . it is such a new and wonderful feeling that we really can *do something* in cleaning up this city" (italics in original).[105] The same spring, Tacoma women also helped remove their mayor for being too soft on vice.[106] In Spokane, Hutton helped register "8,000 of my fellow town women," and elect three new city commissioners (including Coates), proving that suffragists "know how to take care of their friends."[107] Female candidates were more controversial, but Washington already had some experience with women school officials. The first two women elected to the state legislature were both "very busy . . . very dignified, and mind their own business, & you don't see any homes broken up because they are in the legislature as was predicted."[108] Many other women hoped "to be a decided force in politics from now on," especially in support of social welfare legislation, so they formed a State Legislative Federation, which represented 140 different groups and over 50,000 women, and maintained a lobby at the state capitol.[109] In 1911, Hutton and other suffragists returned the support of labor by lobbying the state legislature in support of the women's eight-hour-day bill. This time it passed, and the difference was woman suffrage.[110]

DeVoe had ambitious post-suffrage plans to establish a new national suffrage organization based on the voting strength of western women. Well aware of the "tremendous power we have now," she "promised to use it conservatively and avoid radicalism." DeVoe realized that women's organizations "are tremendous machines. They can be for good if the right women are in control."[111] For some time, she had envisioned "a strong centralized organization" which would educate women voters, work for social welfare legislation in equal suffrage states and "aid in the further extension of woman suffrage."[112] Hutton and others supported this idea in theory, but not surprisingly they rejected DeVoe's leadership. They suspected "the conspirators hope to make the National Council of Women Voters (NCWV) the paramount factor in the equal suffrage states, as well as in the Union."[113] They were not far wrong: alienated from many of her former colleagues, DeVoe refused to defer to easterners who had never won a campaign, and concluded that western women should take the national initiative under her guidance.

The contentious founding of the NCWV confirmed these suspicions and prolonged conflict among Washington women activists. Once again, DeVoe arranged an orchestrated conference with handpicked delegates, secret meetings, and forced motions. Dissenters stood on the steps of the building in the snow to protest these "star chamber" tactics, followed by a published exposé. The governor was flooded with complaints, clubs and labor organizations passed condemnatory resolutions, but Eaton dismissed this widespread opposition as insanity, "a madness of desire for publicity & for place of honor. . . . It is pitiful."[114] The NCWV never flourished, but it set an important precedent for both the insurgent National Woman's Party (NWP) and the League of Women Voters (LWV). Carrie Catt and Anna Shaw undermined this rival organization by dissuading prominent western women from participation in the NCWV. After the passage of the national suffrage amendment, Catt happily absorbed the NCWV into her League of Women Voters.[115]

Suffragists throughout the country took new inspiration and valuable lessons from the Washington victory, and in 1912 Oregon finally approved woman suffrage. Abigail Duniway fell ill early in the campaign, allowing Viola Coe, Marie Equi, and others to implement the new model. Released from Duniway's "still hunt" dictum, they even held a parade. The NAWSA stayed well away, but several Californians traveled north to help. At least Duniway enjoyed the satisfaction of seeing the measure pass and becoming the first woman registered to vote in Oregon.[116] The new methods were transitional in Washington in 1910, but California suffragists expanded them into an aggressive new modern campaign model in 1911. Washington veterans assisted in California, possibly including Hutton and DeVoe. Hutton wanted to work with the laboring population of San Francisco, optimistic because "southern California is a hot-bed of socialism . . . and all socialists are suffragists."[117] CESA officials were especially apprehensive about DeVoe, given the controversy surrounding her in Washington. Given their absence in local sources and the hostility of Californians to outsiders, probably neither of them made it to California in 1911. Yet the attraction was real, because the 1911 California victory was a watershed event that confirmed the effectiveness of the western model in a large, complex state.

7

The Western Zephyr and the
1911 California Campaign

The eyes of all the world are on California today, because it is the
most conservative, the richest and the most powerful of all the Pacific coast states. If political enfranchisement is given to women in
this state, the other states will not be long in following suit.

—E. J. Dupuy[1]

The 1910 victory in Washington established woman suffrage
as a Progressive direct democracy reform measure, and success in California in 1911 confirmed the efficacy of the new modern model. Washington suffragists won with moderate public tactics, but Californians
went further with a full-scale mass campaign. Although they faced many
obstacles in this large and complex state, a new generation of suffragists
enjoyed the challenge. They began to adopt assertive direct action methods adopted from the labor movement (rallies, parades, and street speaking), as well as public relations techniques derived from consumer culture
and advertising. Many of the new suffragists were college alumnae, professional women, social workers, and reformers with labor sympathies
and connections, and they helped bridge the class gap and persuade a
large minority of urban working-class voters in California, providing a
crucial margin of victory. There were deep class and other tensions within
the suffrage movement, however. As in Washington, California suffragists were loosely coordinated in a diverse coalition, united only by the
basic argument for justice. This decentralization was often problematic,
but it stimulated grassroots activism and encouraged creative innovation
and outreach to many different populations of voters. After a brilliant
campaign, the amendment squeaked to victory, bringing renewed hope to

suffragists across the country and stimulating referenda in many other states.[2]

The demoralizing defeat of 1896 had provided valuable insights and experience. Politics became the key as suffragists realized that established political systems, not immigrant voters per se, thwarted their progress. Suffragists now recognized that opposition clustered at both ends of the social scale, although the difficulties of seeking upper-class support as well as labor and working-class acceptance generated perennial tension. Susan B. Anthony continually urged renewed effort: "Our trouble is, we don't *stick to it*. I have always felt that if *we had stuck to it* after the campaign of 1896 . . . we should have succeeded it getting it resubmitted then, but we *lack sticktoitiveness*." She believed that the people would approve woman suffrage in another referendum, "if you could only get it past the politicians," but the Republican-dominated legislature repeatedly refused to authorize another popular referendum until 1911.[3] In the interim, California suffragists rebuilt organizationally through better statewide integration and contacts with women's clubs and progressive organizations.

In the early 1900s, the suffrage movement broadened to include more moderate participants, especially clubwomen radicalized and politicized by their growing involvement in reform politics. Many of them employed "maternalist" or "social housekeeping" arguments in addition to basic demands for equal rights. Women like Los Angeles suffrage leader Grace Simons, future president of the California Federation of Women's Clubs (CFWC), began to argue that they had to leave the domestic sphere in order to defend it: "The mother . . . is only fulfilling her responsibility as a mother when she takes a part in making the world a fit place for her children to live in."[4] Mainstream political culture also changed in response to female participation and priorities, including greater support for government social welfare intervention. The suffrage debate within the CFWC reflects this process. In 1902, the organization's first president, Clara Burdette, cautioned "by all that is womanly," to "keep out of politics," but she added that women, as the "supreme creators and moulders [*sic*] of public opinion," bore special responsibilities for public welfare and morals.[5] Simons and other energetic younger clubwomen kept up the pressure on the organization, and in 1911 the annual CFWC convention passed a woman suffrage endorsement by an overwhelming majority. This action by a moderate women's group was significant because it proved "beyond all doubt that the women of the State do want the ballot," and encouraged a membership of 25,000 women to participate in the 1911 campaign.[6]

Suffragists achieved respectability at considerable cost, however, as they grew less likely to take controversial positions on other issues such as race relations. In fact, under Burdette's leadership, the California federation played a key role in establishing the "states' rights" precedent adopted by many white women's organizations in the 1900s and usually attributed to southern suffragists. Within the General Federation of Women's Clubs (GFWC) a dilemma developed over the seating of a black delegate at the 1900 national convention. White southern members pushed for an exclusionary policy, which was intensely debated throughout 1901 and scheduled for resolution at the 1902 convention. Burdette was eager to become president of the national federation, and when Los Angeles was chosen as the site of the 1902 convention, she moved quickly to calm the racial crisis. At a special meeting in February, the national board followed Burdette's recommendations of tolerance for the southern position. In May the national convention accepted a compromise that allowed constituent state clubs to set their own standards, discriminatory or otherwise, thus tacitly acquiescing to segregation. Although many clubwomen complained about Burdette's tactics, few protested this decision, Jane Addams being the notable exception. In New Orleans the following year, the NAWSA made a similar accommodation as part of its questionable "southern strategy."[7]

Perhaps the CFWC agreement was related to the political ambitions of its president, but no less a local personage than Madame Caroline Severance, a former abolitionist and nationally recognized reformer, concurred in this decision. At the convention, Severance commended the GFWC for "its calm and just treatment of the 'color question,' which was dealt with in the spirit of the Golden Rule and under the honest conviction that, with political freedom not even yet securely gained for our Afro-American citizens, their social equality can only come through 'the slow process of the suns.'" Furthermore, she claimed to be "influenced by the impartial opinion of the acknowledged leaders of that race," including Booker T. Washington. In fact, Washington had written that he "resolutely and determinedly refused to be drawn into any discussion of the matters now disturbing the Federation of Women's Clubs."[8]

Criticized for this position by her daughter among others, Severance was anxious not to be thought a "backslider from my past position on the question of the freedom of the slave." She subsequently insisted that she only intended to endorse the admission policy, and not a harsher proposal "to engraft the word 'white' upon the constitution of our National Federation." She justified her position as a moderate compromise: "I thought then, as I surely think now, that the forcing of colored clubs upon the south . . . would be as unfair and as unwise for the southern clubs to force the word 'white' into our constitution." Somehow she rationalized, "In holding these opinions . . . I do not abate a jot my early desire for the political freedom of the race—as of all races."[9] Mabel Craft (Deering), an important young activist, was one of the few to oppose racial exclusion during preliminary debates in the San Francisco women's clubs. She wondered how "many ladies who are intellectual, sympathetic and lovable have an inherent prejudice against the negro. I can't reconcile this prejudice with twentieth century logic or our boasted progress in civilization." Although she threatened to resign over the issue, apparently she did not.[10]

In Northern California, the women's clubs and the suffrage movement contained many of the "New Suffragists," including Deering, Mary McHenry Keith, Charlotte Anita Whitney, Mary Roberts Coolidge, Maud Younger, and Alice Park. Keith was the first woman to benefit from the Foltz-Gordon challenge of the 1870s and graduate from Hastings Law School, although her short legal career ended when she married a well-known artist. Keith helped establish the College Equal Suffrage League (CESL) and the Berkeley Political Equality League (PEL), and she heavily subsidized the state association.[11] Coolidge was a Stanford University graduate and Mills College sociology professor who published an important and sympathetic study of the Chinese "problem" in California in 1909. Alice Park, chair of the 1911 state publicity committee, was the founder of the Palo Alto Women's Club. The wife of a mining engineer, Park had a wide range of reform, labor, and socialist interests and experiences. In 1912 she tried to join the Industrial Workers of the World (IWW), but "I was voted out again as not a wage worker."[12] Charlotte Whitney, a member of a distinguished local family, became a social worker, a socialist, a pacifist, a lukewarm communist, and finally a convict in the 1920s under California's draconian criminal syndicalism law.[13]

Maud Younger, San Francisco's colorful "millionaire waitress," went from high society to settlement house work to labor organizing. Younger was very conscious of her role as "the bridge that connects working women with their wealthy sisters."[14] Keith was one of the first middle-class California suffragists to appreciate the importance of this connection. In 1906 she and Younger won key endorsements from the Union Labor Party (ULP) and the California Federation of Labor (CFL), the latter passing with only one dissenting vote, then they integrated this material into a suffrage leaflet targeted toward labor. As these elite women developed skills, confidence, and insights, they often became radicalized. Park recalled how Younger read her first suffrage speech "from typewritten pages and her hands shook and her voice trembled." Within a year, Younger was a self-identified socialist giving confident newspaper interviews. These women stressed the importance of organization within the working-class community, and they worked with labor suffragists to establish links to the predominantly middle-class suffrage movement.[15]

These efforts were necessary because there were major class tensions within the suffrage movement as well as major gender tensions within the labor movement. The situation was complicated by dramatic political events and labor conflicts that strained class relations in California in the early 1900s. By this time, labor and socialist groups regularly endorsed woman suffrage, and powerful labor officials appeared at suffrage conventions to pledge their support, like San Francisco Labor Council (SFLC) president G. W. Benham in 1903.[16] In 1907 the state association announced a "new line of work," emphasizing "Widening the scope of the suffrage movement by enlisting in its service the tremendous force of the women who work for wages and bring to bear the pressure which organized labor can exert."[17] This belated initiative failed to prevent the defection of the labor suffragists, however, and in May 1908, shortly before the state suffrage convention, the dissidents seceded. Protesting a lack of sympathy with their middle-class colleagues, they established the independent Wage Earners Suffrage League (WESL). Eventually there were chapters in several Bay Area cities, and socialist Frances Noel established a Los Angeles WESL in 1911.[18]

As an organization exclusively composed of working women suffragists, the WESL was a new phenomenon in the United States. Similar groups elsewhere tended to fall under the domination of middle-class leaders, often generating fissures like those in the California movement.[19] At the state suffrage convention, WESL president Minna O'Donnell, a former printer and a columnist for the *Labor Clarion*, claimed middle-class suffragists "had no conception of the meaning of the word 'wage earning.'" They believed "the league was not in sympathy with them and . . . merely wished to gain their added strength of members." O'Donnell insisted, "We want the ballot for very different reasons. . . . Our idea is self-protection; you want to use it for some one else." She stated it was "out of the question" to "join hands with yours." Maud Younger explained: "It is merely a question of sex" with middle-class suffragists, "but with us—and I am a union woman myself—it is a question of the things that affect men and women alike." She reported fears that "certain members of the suffrage league . . . are using the unions as tools only."[20]

At the 1909 national Women's Trade Union League (WTUL) convention in Chicago, San Francisco waitress union official Louise LaRue recalled that they "got along fine" until the violent 1907 streetcar strike and boycott in San Francisco. The WTUL audience understood why "of course we [labor women] had to walk," but apparently many middle-class San Francisco women did not. When they crossed the picket line and continued to ride the streetcars, the lack of labor solidarity undermined cross-class sisterhood. LaRue explained, "You can just imagine how we felt about it. . . . We had to pull out. . . . We felt that we did not get on together—that the working women and women like that cannot mix, and the only thing to do is to separate and try to be as pleasant as we can and let outsiders think we are harmonious."[21]

Some of the putative class differences among suffragists were spurious, however. For example, clubwomen and suffrage lobbyists Lillian Coffin and Katherine Edson reportedly "do not care to discard their womanly ways, button-hole Senators and Assemblymen and make a genuine political fight for what they believe to be their rights. Instead they prefer to be properly introduced . . . and then . . . discuss quietly and with dignity the subject that is uppermost in their thoughts." In contrast, Younger and LaRue "went together . . . and one by one took the members of the Legislature aside and poured into their ears the arguments of the 'votes for women' cause."[22] In fact, all these women were skillful lobbyists who employed modern political tactics, and they sometimes managed to work together. Coffin and LaRue were together at the California Federation of Labor convention in January 1908, where a suffrage resolution passed easily just a few months before the organizational split.

Labor women convinced labor men with sensible arguments about the needs of women workers in particular and the working class as a whole. At the 1908 state labor convention, Anna M. Culberson, a San Francisco garment union delegate, debated Brother Ellison of the Sailors Union of the Pacific (SUP), who "insisted that women did not possess enough political knowledge to warrant their voting." Like many socialists, Ellison believed that women were inherently too conservative or too inexperienced in political and industrial affairs to vote in the interests of the masses. Heavily outvoted in 1908, Ellison was stubborn. In 1911 he argued that woman suffrage "will lead to a war between the sexes and ultimately to the destruction of our civilization and our race."[23] Although he acknowledged that he was almost "alone in open opposition," the influential president of the SUP, Andrew Furuseth, shared this view. It was dangerous to enfranchise so many women with opposing class interests, Furuseth argued, fearful of "the great mass of women who are not our sisters, who do not understand this movement." He added, "If I were a rich man I should vote for woman suffrage . . . and feel assured that with it my wealth would be secure, my special privileges safe, for another hundred years."[24]

By 1911 this was a minority position within the San Francisco labor movement, probably reflecting the influence of a vigorous state socialist women's movement. Frances Noel, Mary Garbutt, Mary Fairbrother, Mila Tupper Maynard, and other California woman socialists established separate organizations and enjoyed considerable party respect. California socialists confirmed the general pattern of western socialists, with stronger ties to the women's movement and to grassroots organizing than the eastern, urban wing of the Socialist Party. Yet ambivalence persisted about "giving strength to the purely suffrage clubs which, if the vote be won, may be turned into political clubs of a different turn from that we favor." Socialist women continued to join middle-class clubs, where they emphasized issues of economic equity and political justice common to working women of all classes, and they often rose to leadership positions within these mainstream groups.[25]

Socialists and labor activists were crucial components of the California Progressive movement, but class tensions disrupted the larger coalition just as they did the suffrage subset. In Northern California, Progressives originated as a good-government movement in opposition to the San Francisco Union Labor Party and eagerly prosecuted corrupt ULP officials during a series of graft trials from 1906 to 1909. Suffragists became involved on both sides, as male politicians turned to women allies and to symbolic female moral authority for support.[26] Working-class women generally supported and defended the ULP. LaRue and other working women assisted ULP candidate Patrick H. McCarthy in his 1907 and 1909 mayoral campaigns, and he won in 1909 with a promise to discontinue the trials. Indifferent to assumptions linking waitresses, vice, and political corruption, LaRue stated, "Now when we want anything we go right to a politician and get it. We have everything we want. Yes, we are politicians."[27] WESL president O'Donnell formed the Women's Municipal League in 1909, objecting to the continued use of public funds for the prosecutions.

On the other side, many middle-class women aggressively defended the prosecution of former ULP officials. In June 1908, a group of prominent middle-class professional men formed the Citizen's League for Justice (CLJ), but when they had no time to sit in court and monitor the trials, local clubwomen volunteered. Criticized as well as praised for this unorthodox public female behavior, they established the Women's Branch of the CLJ. Prominent suffragist members included Ellen Sargent, Mary Sperry, Lillian Harris Coffin, and Alice Park. As the graft prosecutions wound down with very few convictions, the Women's Branch of the CLJ became the California Women's Heney Club in an unsuccessful effort to elect the chief prosecutor, Francis Heney, as San Francisco city district attorney.[28]

Statewide, California Progressives faced tremendous opposition from the powerful financial and industrial interests. In particular, the Southern Pacific Railroad (the "Octopus") had controlled state politics for years.[29] Women activists helped build Progressivism by supporting reform politicians and candidates sympathetic to suffrage, while powerful establishment politicians resisted the inclusion of large numbers of reform-minded women as voters. Progressive direct democracy measures, especially the initiative, helped bypass obstructive legislatures, and suffragists defined female enfranchisement as a similar structural political reform. In one sense, the great San Andreas earthquake in April 1906 aided the reformers by disrupting the state's demographic and political balance. The new NAWSA president, Anna Howard Shaw, wondered whether "it would be a good thing now to go to California and try it again since San Francisco, the great city that defeated us[,] is no longer a voting power." Shaw assumed that recovery would impede suffrage activity, but within a month Bay Area women regrouped and resumed plans to lobby the summer party conventions.[30] San Francisco clubwoman Lillian Coffin became California Equal Suffrage Association (CESA) central committee chair and its chief legislative lobbyist in 1906. Coffin stated repeatedly the "CESA must be a political organization pure and simple. . . . It takes a politician to catch a politician." She encouraged suffragists to learn "the tricks of politicians" in order to begin "turning against them their own weapons." Coffin's contentious personality and her overt Republican partisanship strategy drew controversy and criticism. Many questioned her motives, ambitions, and loyalties, but Alice Park thought Coffin was troublesome because she "was younger than the old suffragists and tried to wake up the movement."[31]

In 1907 the state suffrage association established a new committee on direct legislation, supported progressive alliances, and endorsed the initiative, referendum, and recall.[32] This emphasis on politics was a more assertive variation of Anthony's "all-partisan" strategy and the result of recent political experiences. Since 1896, suffragists had continued to pester state political conventions for endorsements and support. In 1906, the Democrats listened respectfully to a speech by Laura DeForce Gordon and endorsed the measure, but they were not particularly welcome at the state Republican convention in Santa Cruz, an infamously corrupt event. Suffragists condemned the proceedings, but used the opportunity to lobby the delegates, and they were courted in return. According to Coffin, future governor James N. Gillette approached them on the beach, introduced himself, and said: "I believe in your cause and I want to say that if I am elected governor of California I will do all in my power to help you in your movement." After Gillette was elected, the women expected him to fulfill his promise and were furious when he reneged.[33]

During the 1907 legislative session, members were under great pressure from suffragists and from their opponents, including powerful leaders of both parties. Mary Keith encountered a "prominent State Senator from San Francisco" who told her: "Mrs. K., I believe as you do. I think you are right and I should like to vote for woman suffrage." As he spoke, however, he pulled "from his desk a number of red slips of cardboard printed with the words 'Yes' and 'No'. On the card bearing the words 'woman suffrage' was printed 'No!' . . . 'Now,' said he, 'if you will go to every saloonkeeper in my district, every hotel and restaurant keeper, liquor dealer, etc., and get them to tell me to vote for woman suffrage I will gladly do it.'"[34]

The women decided to play their "trump card"—Governor Gillette—but he received them discourteously, repudiated his promise, and laughed at their credulity. Gillette asserted, "The place for you women is home where you belong," and vowed, "As long as I am in the governor's chair, a woman's suffrage bill shall never become law." When Coffin reminded him of his unsolicited promise, Gillette replied that he was "only joshing." Coffin retorted: "You may call it joshing, governor, but some people would designate it by another word." After Coffin told this story at the 1909 state suffrage convention, Governor Gillette denied the episode despite corroborating testimony. He insisted, "The statements of this woman are ridiculous," and he claimed, "I have no recollection of ever meeting her and do not know who she is." Gillette stated, "I have always expressed myself as opposed to the woman suffrage movement, and certainly have not promised support to a movement I am not in favor of."[35] After the woman suffrage referendum bill failed by two votes in the 1907 California legislature, the venerable eastern suffragist, Henry Blackwell, gently reminded Alice Park that it is best to get the promises of politicians in writing.[36]

Suffrage delegations to state party conventions in the summer of 1908 resulted in one of the earliest suffrage parades. In Oakland, Lillian Coffin led two hundred women on a march of several blocks—"yellow ribbons flying bravely"—but they received a very cool response from the Republicans. Several women, including Coffin and Agnes Pease, president of the Women's Republican Club of Utah, presented a range of arguments before the resolutions committee. Pease insisted that equal suffrage worked well in Utah and did not interfere with domestic duties: "I can roll out the biscuits and do the family washing as well as vote." Minna O'Donnell used maternalist arguments, but her fellow labor suffragist, Louise LaRue, who was deeply involved in the concurrent effort to pass an eight-hour work-day law for women, knew "where women vote we [women workers] get better laws."[37] The rude response of establishment Republicans shocked the suffragists into deeper sympathy with the insurgents. At one point, Assemblyman Grove Johnson interrupted a colleague to ask, "Why should a woman vote? She's a woman." At the close of the convention, the chairman thanked the women for their "grace and beauty," but Peace was frustrated by these "platitudes and trite poetical similes." Seated in the front row, she quickly "rose and answered that the women were not there for bouquets but for justice and declined their thanks," as the audience broke into applause.[38]

In contrast, the 1908 Democratic convention welcomed the suffragists and postponed the adoption of an immediate suffrage plank only because a separate delegation "of San Francisco working women . . . wished to submit a different version."[39] This support might seem unusual, but many Democrats, especially former Populists, were sincerely progressive reformers, while pragmatists appreciated the opportunity to disrupt Republican political hegemony. Lillian Coffin was an active Republican, but she urged all-partisan cooperation with Democratic and "good government" candidates alike: "*Work the reform men.*"[40] Progressive women like Katherine Edson urged the Republican insurgents of the Lincoln-Roosevelt League to adopt a woman suffrage plank in their founding platform in 1907, despite some opposition.

Support for woman suffrage varied among male Progressives, but in the summer of 1910, the Santa Clara and Los Angeles County delegations wedged a woman suffrage plank firmly into the state Republican Party platform. John Braly, a Los Angeles businessman with a mystical devotion to the cause, was instrumental in this effort. Prominent Southern California Progressive Marshall Stimson recorded that he and Progressive gubernatorial candidate Hiram Johnson were opposed to woman suffrage, while Meyer Lissner, John R. Haynes, and Braly supported it. Other prominent supporters included Lieutenant Governor Albert J. Wallace, Secretary of State Frank Jordan, and both U.S. senators.[41] Lissner recalled with awkward humor that "there were a lot of bothersome women who were all the time crying for the right to vote, and we observed that they began to impress some pretty good men with what they were talking about, and we thought we had better nip that particular trouble in the bud, so we put a plan for woman suffrage in the platform." Lissner later advised suffragists that they would have to manage the campaign by themselves in order to prove they wanted to vote, because men were "too busy with the distinctly masculine concerns of government to take up arms in the cause of woman suffrage."[42]

Other Progressive politicians were more appreciative of their female colleagues, generally appreciated civic "mothers" as well as "fathers," liberally employed civic housekeeping rhetoric, and endorsed woman suffrage as a direct democracy reform. Guido H. Marx, a mechanical engineer and social reformer at Stanford University, did not "cherish any expectation of the immediate arrival of a political millennium" with female enfranchisement. . . . But in a real democracy there should be genuine equality of opportunity for all, unhampered by consideration of race or sex.[43] Herbert C. Jones, a San Jose lawyer and later state senator, defined woman suffrage as one of the "new instruments of democracy" instituted by the Progressives.[44]

Hiram Johnson was particularly difficult, and he avoided discussing the suffrage amendment throughout the campaign. Mary Keith described a typical reaction when suffragists asked Johnson whether he was "with them." He replied, "'This is where the army retreats.'—Looking around at the same time as though seeking some means of escape." He was warned: "Governor Johnson, this Army *never* retreats!"[45] Nevertheless, once his party endorsed the measure, Johnson demanded strict adherence to the platform, including this controversial plank. Afterwards he confided privately, "The more I think of the situation with regard to woman's suffrage, the more I think you gentlemen in the south have given us something that will inevitably destroy us." Perhaps Johnson worried that female voters would demand radical reform measures that would generate a backlash against the Progressives. He was friendlier later when he wanted the help of women voters, especially during his 1914 reelection campaign.[46]

In 1909, Progressives made significant legislative gains, including a direct primary law that helped them sweep the 1910 elections. During the 1909 legislative session, suffragists received assistance from many labor and Progressive allies, including John I. Nolan, lobbyist for the California Federation of Labor, but once again the referendum bill was outmaneuvered and defeated.[47] In response, Lillian Coffin, the head of the suffrage lobby, became even more politically aggressive. She told the story about Governor Gillette publicly for the first time, and toured the state speaking for progressive reform measures. She advised women to sponsor meetings and gather signatures for sympathetic candidates of both parties, and soon "men are coming now and asking us to do this work for them."[48] Partisan activities could be disruptive, however. For example, Coffin and other CLJ members pushed a pro-Heney resolution at the 1909 state suffrage convention, which was firmly rejected. Undeterred, Coffin asserted "we are for reform," and added "the men are doing fairly well in politics, but are not accomplishing as much as we believe is possible even at this day. We want clean government and are doing a great deal to accomplish it."[49]

At the same convention, Coffin, Keith, and other young activists challenged the traditional leadership of the state association, although they ultimately agreed to support Elizabeth Lowe Watson, a dignified elderly liberal.[50] Angered by the rejection of their own compromise candidate, Elizabeth Gerberding, the conservative faction "determined to get Mrs. Coffin out altogether" as chair of the state central committee. They forced a special vote, which Coffin won easily, and the dissenters seemed satisfied. Problems continued, however, and by January 1911, Gerberding was president of the new Independent Suffrage League, later the Woman Suffrage Party (WSP), emulating the New York model established by Carrie Catt in 1909. During the campaign, Coffin also had her own group, the Equal Franchise League. Watson recognized the advantages of decentralization, but she grew tired of mediating internal conflicts. She was ready to retire by 1910, but a generally acceptable replacement could not be found, and she led the organization throughout the successful 1911 campaign.[51]

Despite these differences, suffragists eagerly anticipated the 1910 elections and supported pro-suffrage Progressive candidates. The election of 1910 was a great Progressive victory, and it quickly led to many new reforms, including woman suffrage. Important sympathizers in the 1911 legislature included the new speaker of the house, the president *pro tem* of the Senate, and the entire Los Angeles delegation. While the hostile municipal machines, manufacturers, "liquor interests," and the Southern Pacific Railroad were still very powerful, Elizabeth Watson was reassured because "many opponents of years' standing, feeling the pressure of popularity, were prepared to capitulate." She hoped to "squeeze through on the back of the Insurgent promises."[52] In Sacramento, Coffin, Gerberding, Younger, and LaRue joined Katherine Edson and Josepha Tolhurst from Los Angeles. Although Younger and LaRue were "here & doing good work," Edson sought additional advice from her socialist colleague, Frances Noel, about winning "the labor vote."[53] By now, most of the arguments were familiar, but one anti-suffrage senator offered "a new definition of a suffragette . . . '*a woman who wants to raise Hell, but no children.*'" Suffragists promptly rebutted with "a suffragette is a woman who wants to raise children, but not in hell!"[54] When the California legislature finally authorized a woman suffrage amendment vote for the October 1911 special election, it was a major victory, but only the first step, leaving little time to organize a mass campaign.

Based on the results of the 1896 referendum, California suffragists relied on strong rural support, especially in Southern California, to balance urban opposition in the north. With the major exception of WCTU activism, there had been little systematic suffrage organizing in the territory "south of Tehachapi" since that time. Southern California suffragists started slowly but eventually organized many meetings and rallies with overflow audiences.[55] Most Los Angeles suffragists were white, middle-class Protestants typical of recent arrivals to the area, and many were politically active clubwomen affiliated with "good government" progressives. Some were old veterans like Los Angeles attorney Clara Foltz, who presided over the Votes for Women club and toured the state at her own expense in 1911, convinced that "California can never win suffrage without C. Foltz." Bitterly contemptuous of the old guard, "a few relics of defunct spouses . . . and mediocrities . . . who . . . had no appreciation whatever of my efforts," Foltz dismissed the state association leadership as "incompetent." Like Coffin, Foltz was convinced "the suffrage cause cannot be won until leaders of ability are chosen—women and men who can and will discuss the question from the constitutional and political points of view."[56]

The Political Equality League was the most influential suffrage group in Los Angeles. The PEL began in 1910 when founder John Braly decided to enlist prominent men, but the irony of an all-male women's rights group soon led to reorganization, and clubwoman Grace Simons replaced the elderly Braly as president.[57] Braly remained active during the 1911 campaign, contributing an automobile and sponsoring speakers. In fact, Braly created a fuss when he wanted to invite NAWSA president Anna Howard Shaw, because so many California women rejected her ponderous leadership.[58]

There were actually *two* PELs in Los Angeles, but Braly declared the first league "discouraged and dispirited" when he appropriated the name. Founding president Ella Giles Ruddy disagreed, but assured Madame Severance, "There seems little danger of the two . . . getting mixed up in the public mind," because "one League gets after the 'way-up' voters, and the other after the stragglers and loafers in the parks." Her group "planned only out-of-door work during the campaign," because "many new workers . . . have been enthused by the idea of what may turn out to be useful 'slumming.'" They promised to behave, and "not be militant like our English sisters, but I trust very dignified in soft persuasiveness among the laborers resting for their noonday luncheons, and the loafers in certain country groceries etc."[59] The residual elitism conveyed in such attitudes probably limited the group's effectiveness even as they enthusiastically employed modern mass campaign tactics.

In both major cities, class tension was high, due to important mayoral elections, continuing labor strife, and violence, including the *Los Angeles Times* bombing and subsequent trial. The California labor movement was at war with the publisher of the *Times,* Harrison Gray Otis, who wanted to break the unions and impose "open shop" conditions. During a 1910 ironworkers strike, an explosion ripped through the *Times* building, killing more than twenty people, and a year later, two trade unionists, the McNamara brothers, were on trial for the crime. Clubwoman

Josepha Tolhurst cautioned audiences to stay calm and "not be misled by any talk of labor and capital in this suffrage question," because "all this talk is being used by the real enemy of the suffrage cause . . . the machine."[60]

On several occasions, suffragists used their imaginations and privileged positions to evade controlled speech ordinances intended to stifle labor protest. In July, Frances Noel and the Los Angeles WESL organized a picnic rally in a local park, but since the law prohibited public speeches, they sang protest songs, sold lemonade, and handed out doughnuts with "Votes for Women" ribbons. For this radical activity, Noel was "promptly ranked with the 'Twietmoe-Johannsen Gang of Dynamyters [*sic*]'" by the *Los Angeles Times*.[61] At another celebration, Katherine Edson and Clara Foltz ascended in a balloon and threw "yellow literature out onto the wind. Thousands of people in the park and adjoining baseball park cheered at the flocks of yellow paper . . . like a golden snow."[62]

In an Oakland park, prominent clubwoman Sadie Cornwall intercepted a police officer, "asked him if he did not wish to wear a button," and began reading a leaflet, pretending not to hear him as he tried to explain that she was breaking the law. Immobilized, the officer "finally sat down and listened to the speech," then asked "in a very meek voice if they would not please get a permit before they came again, as it was certainly against the law. Mrs. Cornwall promised that she would." By this action, Cornwall was able to complete her own presentation and to protect another speaker elsewhere in the park.[63] In an interview, Cornwall explained that her enthusiasm for suffrage was in compensation for being such a recent convert. Now she was proud to be "one of the band of progressive women who know what they are about."[64]

In the San Francisco Bay Area, the most active organization was the College Equal Suffrage League, under the leadership of Charlotte Anita Whitney.[65] Chapters of the CESL were established at Stanford and Berkeley early in 1908 as part of a national organizing effort by Maud Wood Park. This organization catalyzed the 1911 campaign in the Bay Area. Another group of young business and professional women in San Francisco formed a Votes for Women club in January 1910. Apparently unaware of the Wage Earners Suffrage League, this was an effort to reach "that large class of self-supporting women . . . heretofore hardly approached." The organization successfully appealed to working women with special programs and a popular downtown lunchroom splendidly decorated in official suffrage yellow.[66] Other San Francisco groups included Gerberding's Equal Suffrage League (ESL) and Coffin's Equal Franchise League (EFL), both consisting largely of clubwomen.

Like many western suffragists, California women generally rejected assistance from the NAWSA, confident of the superiority of their new methods. Despite this "somewhat churlish attitude," the NAWSA provided some funding and experienced speakers like Gail Laughlin, who "figured as the star refuter of Colorado lies," and Jeannette Rankin, "a favorite with every one." These were usually attorneys, social workers, and labor organizers, "women who had earned their living . . . knew how to appeal to men's sense of justice."[67] There was some discussion of inviting Harriot Stanton Blatch, Elizabeth Cady Stanton's daughter, who had formed her own labor suffrage group in New York. Some considered Blatch the "ideal woman," and she volunteered to come if her expenses were paid. Maud Younger replied that funds were insufficient, and "there is a lingering prejudice . . . against the 'Easterners' which you understand without comment from me." Then Blatch offered to come at her own expense, and the California suffragists discussed it but were unable to agree, so Blatch did not go to California.[68] Ultimately, local activists, "the women who lived right here," were the most convincing speakers.[69]

As the campaign got organized, suffrage mini-headquarters opened in various locations to support precinct canvassing and to encourage drop-in visitors and volunteers. One woman, "a mother of a family . . . said that the only time she could serve was from 6 to 7 o'clock in the morning, before her family was up, and she offered that time, which was accepted gladly." Neighborhood women did most of the local voter canvassing that was so basic to grassroots organizing, but this was exhausting and sometimes unpleasant work, especially if coupled with the solicitation of funds. By late spring, however, the volunteers were busy at their "tramping act."[70]

Automobile touring and public speaking were particularly effective methods for reaching urban working-class audiences and isolated rural communities. While traditionalists condemned this behavior as improper for women, many people appreciated the novelty, or the necessity, for these actions. When one young man remarked that a suffrage speaker should be at home with her children, his female companion responded, "She has to do that. She can't make you men listen any other way."[71] Middle-class women began timidly, but soon "all caught fire with this form of propaganda," gained confidence, and enjoyed the "directness" of the experience. They "had a message to deliver, and . . . faith in our men, their sense of justice and of fair play."[72] Frequently quizzed on issues such as "Socialism, Trade-Unionism, Single Tax, Separation of Church and State, Divorce and half a dozen other problems," they resolved, "the only safe plan is a strict adherence to the one subject, 'Votes for Women.'"[73] Confronted with such diversity, California suffragists agreed that enfranchisement was the key to independent political citizenship for women, the sine qua non of their various reform goals.

In 1911, modern California suffragists produced an ambitious mass campaign utilizing popular culture, consumer psychology, and advertising. They placed posters, billboards, electric and other signs everywhere, including store and office windows, ballparks, the ferry dock, and duck blinds in the San Francisco Bay. Entrepreneurial suffragists convinced merchants and event concessionaires to advertise suffrage in their displays and products, and sometimes peddled commodities themselves, usually common items such as tea or seeds.[74] The millions of banners, posters, stickers, postcards, leaflets, stationery, and other campaign items required simple yet striking designs, colors, and text. Some women objected to yellow, the suffrage color standard in the United States, because of the "vague suggestion of smallpox flags and yellow journalism." They retained the color theme for the sake of solidarity, but transformed it into the orange gold of California poppies.[75]

Seeking images to represent progressive western feminism, the college women sponsored a poster contest, but they were disappointed by the cold symbolism of many of the submissions, especially the ubiquitous figure of "Justice." The winning design was a western version of the "New Woman" archetype that manipulated romanticized indigenous and Hispanic imagery. It depicted "a woman of the California-Spanish type, clad in Indian draperies, standing against the Golden Gate as a background with the setting sun forming a halo around her head."[76] The posters were widely admired and displayed but also sold to cover costs.

Suffragists worked with a local artist, Ida Diserenz, to create a popular stereopticon presentation after they rejected motion pictures as too costly. Intended for mass, semiliterate, or non-English-speaking audiences, slides were easily projected onto screens or buildings. Sympathetic theater proprietors also allowed presentations between the moving pictures in the popular nickelodeons. The clustered sets of images strongly emphasized the many forms of women's work and responsibility, including family welfare and municipal housekeeping. The text of the final cartoon, "Blind Justice," was simple and basic:

> For the long work day,
> For the laws we obey,
> For the taxes we pay,
> We want something to say.
> Give the women a Square Deal on Oct 10.

By mid-September, twenty sets of forty slides were in circulation, and the women were very pleased with the results.[77]

Favorable and extensive press coverage was essential. By this time the mainstream press had largely displaced independent feminist journalism, but a new generation of professional newspaperwomen helped turn the newspapers into an important source of free publicity. With the significant exceptions of the *San Francisco Chronicle* and the *Los Angeles Times,* most of the state's large newspapers were supportive and willing to publish good quality suffrage material. In 1906, Mabel Craft Deering resumed the systematic presswork initiated in California by Ida Husted Harper during the 1896 campaign. Another early graduate of Hastings Law School, Deering worked as a reporter for the *San Francisco Chronicle* in the late 1890s, then married a prominent lawyer. Isolated after the 1906 earthquake, she became state press chair, contacted seven hundred newspapers statewide, and received many encouraging responses. By 1911, she had press contacts throughout California.[78] Deering proudly observed, "Even old-time and hard-headed politicians tell us that they have never seen press work handled better than ours, and naturally we are very proud of it."[79] State publicity chair Alice Park also generated press material, then recycled it into leaflets, posters, signs, billboards, and other formats. The most popular items were testimonials and endorsements by national leaders such as Jane Addams, prominent residents of western equal suffrage states, labor leaders, and Catholic priests. Park's own pamphlet, "Women under the Laws of California," became an influential model for similar publications in other states.

All propaganda was carefully tailored to fit the target populations and designed to be visually appealing while conveying the many arguments for woman suffrage. The demand for basic justice remained the most fundamental.[80] All classes understood the linkage between political status and economic rights: "no taxation without representation."[81] One businesswoman, "until a few months ago an active opponent," now campaigned "to atone for past error." She "came to realize that while my business and my work were those of a man I did not have the right to protect my interests nor express my opinions through the ballot."[82] Suffragists also used maternalist and civic housekeeping and arguments, and advocated many reforms, but they promised no miracles. Citing the apparent failures of men in the public sphere, they refused to be held to a differential standard of civic behavior and spoke of "city mothers and fathers" in equal terms.[83]

All suffragists linked economic equity to political rights for women, while labor suffragists described the vote as both a self-defense mechanism and a key component of working-class political reform. Frances Williamson observed, "A disfranchised class is always underpaid. In the world's work, woman is an economic factor and needs the ballot to protect her interests." Bluntly, "With the ballot women will be given power, and power always commands respect."[84] Cora C. Miller suggested, "Some civic responsibility and less drudgery would have an amazing psychological benefit on the wage earning woman herself, leaving out all talk of how much we are going to 'purify politics.'"[85] Miller observed how "the chivalrous fear . . . lest women should have too much 'responsibility' looks ill timed to the great army of women workers who have been allowed to toil unmolested, working out their economic freedom as best they might."[86] Frances Noel spoke for working-class mothers, who raise children "with care and sacrifice . . . only to see corporation greed and power grind their health and life blood into dollars." They "need to have a voice in making these [work] places safe and sanitary." Noel asked her fellow Socialists "if it is not wiser to win the women of the working class for your political strength, rather than allow them to be an indifferent or competing element against your interests at the polls."[87]

By 1911, suffragists knew that victory depended upon winning a solid minority of urban working-class and racial-ethnic voters, so they made vigorous efforts to reach different groups through the foreign language press, churches, social organizations, and trade unions. Members of the college league often served as translators, speakers, and writers of articles in "Greek, Portuguese, French, German, Swedish, and half a dozen other languages. . . . Even the Chinese papers."[88] By the early 1900s, animosity against the Chinese persisted in the rhetoric of labor suffragists, but middle-class women were more tolerant. Maud Younger still complained that a woman not only had to compete with "Asiatics" for work, but "the native-born Chinese . . . can vote for the law-makers who govern her, and she cannot." Employing a western variation on the theme of white female supremacy, she protested, "In California every adult may vote excepting only Mongolians, Indians, idiots, insane, criminals, and women." A year later, Mary Roberts Coolidge published her sympathetic study, *Chinese Immigration,* which rejected notions of any inherently Chinese defects or vices, and stated boldly that the Chinese became Americanized as rapidly as other ethnic groups when allowed to do so.[89]

Sympathetic Chinese were usually progressive supporters of Dr. Sun Yat-sen, who also saw woman suffrage as an important democratic reform. Reportedly, "a good many of the younger Chinamen stood with us because they said when the Chinese Republic was established they wanted to enfranchise their own women who would help them in their fight for freedom."[90] One local editor (perhaps Presbyterian minister and editor of *Chung Sai Yat Po,* Ng Poon Chew) was an "outspoken friend."[91] San Francisco clubwomen made overtures to affluent, Christianized Chinese American merchants at a Chinatown luncheon, also attended by "pretty little missionary girls who had heard of woman suffrage in school and wanted to know more." When the suffragists noticed the interest of the Chinese waitresses, they encouraged cross-class organization among the young Chinese women. Eventually they persuaded ten prominent merchants sign the petition.[92] According to one post-election estimate, half of the approximately eight hundred voting Chinese in San Francisco approved the referendum, a more favorable proportion than in the city population at large.[93]

Local activists were crucial to success in many communities. In the large Italian community of North Beach, the college league and the members of the local Vittora Colonna club held several successful parlor gatherings. Emboldened, they planned an ambitious mass meeting, encouraged by the sympathetic editors of *L'Italia.* Warned that they might encounter antagonism, the college suffragists wisely allowed community women to organize the meeting as "best to appeal to the Latin mind." "The largest political gathering ever held in the district," the rally was an "unqualified success."[94] Most of the state's Latino population was clustered in the southern part of the state, where María López, a local high school Spanish teacher, spoke in Ventura County and at a mass rally in the Los Angeles plaza in October. In addition, the PEL and the Los Angeles College Equal Suffrage League published and distributed approximately 50,000 leaflets in Spanish.[95]

The historically deep but troubled political ties between suffragists and African Americans were further affected by the indifference of white suffragists to the trend of African American disfranchisement. Nevertheless, there was a solid base of support within this community, especially among clubwomen.[96] They formed independent suffrage groups in large cities with sufficient populations, such as Oakland and Los Angeles, and in smaller communities at least some joined white organizations.[97] For example, Sarah Overton, a member of the San Jose PEL and Suffrage Amendment League, traveled at her own expense to organize in other African American communities.[98] Other African American organizers reported "the Negroes generally supported the suffrage movement."[99]

Suffragists received support from many churches and prominent religious leaders. In San Francisco, the charismatic minister Charles F. Aked became a regular suffrage speaker. Rabbi Martin Meyer insisted that "he will continue to love his neighbor as himself, in other words, to preach 'radicalism'" when criticized for preaching suffrage to "little girls in confirmation class." Rabbi Myers of Los Angeles was also a strong advocate.[100] Catholic suffragists targeted the heavily Catholic working class by leafleting all thirty-six Catholic churches in San Francisco.[101] Coordinated by Rhoda and Mary E. Ringrose, they were "at the doors of the churches at the early mass—six o'clock in the morning—and at all others, standing for hours with their literature, many of the business girls giving up their entire Sunday to this work." When suffragists solicited endorsements from local clergy, Archbishop Riordan promised "that each priest would use his own individual opinion as a man." While seemingly noncommittal, this reply thrilled the suffragists because it liberated priests to make pro-suffrage statements, and several of these were later published as popular leaflets. Visiting Catholic priests in Southern California, Clara Foltz found they "agreed that the movement has gained such proportions that no church of which women are a part can longer refrain from becoming a supporter of what is conceded to be for the good of humanity."[102]

Churches had great influence with many working-class men, but their own mothers, wives, daughters, and sisters had more. Many labor suffragists were well-known women trade unionists or wives of important labor leaders.[103] Labor suffragists were the key to working-class support.

Members of the WESL contacted all the union locals in San Francisco, where they appealed to male pride and union solidarity, highlighted female trade unionism, and discussed progressive reform, especially the recent woman's eight-hour-day bill. They were "your own women who are asking you to do this for us. Every member of our league is a union woman."[104] They won hearty, often unanimous endorsements, most crucially from the brewers' union, probably because of the local's high socialist content. Due to the prohibition issue, "it was thought [the local] would refuse to listen to the speakers of the league," and as Younger and LaRue nervously waited to be introduced, they could hear laughter behind the closed doors. Nevertheless, "the members of that union invited the speakers in, listened attentively, and with but few preliminaries expressed themselves as favorable to the amendment."[105] This episode indicates some success in the effort to decouple suffrage from prohibition, a crucial element in gaining working-class support.

Many prominent trade unionists actively supported woman suffrage, including Walter Macarthur of the Coast Seamen's Union, Andrew Gallagher, the president of the Labor Council (and future president of the San Francisco Board of Supervisors), Edward Nolan, another city supervisor, Will J. French, the editor of the *Labor Clarion,* and John I. Nolan, the state labor commissioner and a future U.S. congressman. Mrs. French and both Mrs. Nolans were strong labor suffragists.[106] These leaders assured suffragists "there was not a doubt but that the amendment would go through."[107] Due to French's influence, the labor press was very supportive of woman suffrage. The *Labor Clarion* editor stated, "In her struggle for the ballot, woman is not asking for a favor or for something to which she is not entitled. She is asking for justice, to which she had as clear a right as has man." French cautioned, "If you want the woman to be a free citizen you must give her this power of expression, otherwise she is not free, even though some of them believe they are."[108] As working-class men debated whether women lacked sufficient experience or wisdom, some asked, "How can we expect them to understand the economic conditions they have been apart from? But if we give them the ballot they will begin to think; they will begin to educate themselves along these lines."[109] An Oakland union official confirmed, "We labor people to a man are in favor of suffrage because we believe that women can and will aid the many problems which confront the world and in which we are interested. Woman are born reformers, and in the conditions as they are today there is a great deal of need for reform."[110] While generally positive, these statements also reveal male assumptions about female loyalty to labor and its progressive agenda.[111]

The San Francisco Labor Council granted the WESL official auxiliary status and permission to enter a float in the Labor Day parade, one of the city's biggest yearly events. Younger soon realized that the working women of the WESL had neither the time nor the resources to finish the float, so she enlisted the college league. Parading in the street was still considered provocative female behavior, but the CESL women realized, "This opportunity to visualize before tens of thousands of people the need of the working-woman for the vote, was one not to be let slip." As a team of prize-winning black horses wearing yellow livery pulled the float down Market Street, large banners announcing the suffrage message floated from each corner. There were two tableaux: on a higher, smaller platform there were two allegorical female figures representing "California asking Justice for the ballot," while the lower level consisted of real working women engaged in their representative tasks. Shop clerks, a typist, sewing and cannery workers, a nurse, and a professional woman (in cap and gown) joined a mother surrounded by young children. The float bore the slogan, "These women need the ballot," while the children held a sign that read, "Give our mother a vote."[112]

The college women were pleased with the effect, which they carefully attributed to the "working-women, in plain working-clothes, [who] gave up their holiday to endure the severe fatigue of being jolted through the streets for hours." Mingling with the crowd they saw "the sincerity of the appeal," and how "the plain tired faces of some of the women reached men who know what it is to work for wages, and what it is to ask for a withheld right." When the parade ended and they started to dismantle the float, "the crowd closed in about the platform cheering and clamoring for flowers and bits of ribbon, calling, 'Speech! Speech!'" Awake since dawn but always alert to an opportunity, they "once more, to hundreds of quieted men, spoke of what political equality means to working-women. And once more came the quick understanding response of the man on the street to the woman in earnest."[113] American Federation of Labor (AFL) president Samuel Gompers, in town for the festivities and the national convention, identified himself as "one of those who believe that union labor will never reach its best until we give the franchise to women. 'Equal wage for equal work—equal voting voice with men!'" All these activities helped persuade urban populations of working men despite continuing class tensions.[114]

Suffragists considered Sacramento a tough case, given its large population of working men, including six thousand employees of the Southern Pacific Railroad yards. Railroad management refused suffragists permission to speak "because of their rule against allowing labor agitators to speak there," but suggested meeting the workers at the gates instead. Timid at first, the women soon found that they "were most cordially treated. As they took the yellow circulars the men remarked "'All right, lady. I'll vote for you!' . . . You bet!' and other rough but cordial phrases." Organizer Mary Coolidge reported, "We did not say anything to them unless they spoke to us, as a rule, but after the first hundred went by we began to enjoy it." The secretary of the Sacramento labor council asserted that "almost every Union man there was for suffrage" and allowed the distribution of leaflets at a speech by Gompers. At the meeting, "Now and then they joshed us a little as they passed but often they would add: 'My wife's fixed me—I've got to vote for you!'"[115] On strike against the railroad by the time of the October election, many of these men were observed wearing yellow ribbons, escorting women poll workers, and discussing the benefits of woman suffrage with policemen.[116] When Sacramento became the only Northern California city to return a small majority on the amendment, Coolidge attributed this result to "the favorable Union Labor vote" particularly "men who are . . . used to making women partners in their affairs and to seeing them work hard for the family welfare. They understand, therefore, women's problems better and have a good deal of sympathy with any struggle for liberty." She concluded, "The best hope of the suffragists is in the comfortable, hardworking American middle class and in the upper organized laboring group."[117]

Connecting suffrage to political reform while dissociating it from social control issues, particularly prohibition, boosted its appeal to working-class and ethnocultural constituencies. Prohibition had become a political liability and a low priority for the cosmopolitan "New Woman," like one suffragist who later recalled a campaign visit to the store "of a cheery old Frenchman." Oh, yes, the proprietor had believed in woman suffrage for years—had heard Susan B. Anthony and Anna Howard Shaw speak—but he hesitated before agreeing to attend the evening meeting. She finally understood his "slightly amused expression" when "my eyes fell upon two great whisky barrels in the back of the store, each with a glass on top, and I realized that I had penetrated a saloon!"[118] In 1910 Coffin and Keith had tried to convince the state executive board to sever any formal connection with the WCTU, claiming it was "unwise to affiliate with any one reform society," but Beaumelle Sturtevant-Peet angrily responded that such a tactless action would alienate a vigorous network of activists.[119] By 1911, most suffragists avoided temperance entanglements as a matter of course, and the WCTU women reluctantly "took off their white ribbon badges . . . to disarm prejudice."[120] However problematic, the WCTU was the largest women's association in the state and its participation was crucial.

As in Washington, the progressive reform environment challenged the "liquor interests" on many fronts and kept them on the defensive. A spokesman for the Royal Arch, the liquor dealers' association, denied any involvement in the woman suffrage campaign. He cited an internal investigation to conclude "that the liquor business has not been hurt the least by the women's vote." He blamed this misconception on prohibitionist threats to vote to abolish the liquor trade: "We heard that statement so often that until recently we believed it."[121] Skeptical suffragists believed that the association continued to fund anti-suffrage activity. They were particularly offended by a leaflet itemizing "the bad effects of female suffrage, especially in encouraging radical and unpatriotic female behavior." Allegedly suffragists entertained "notorious anarchists at dinner," supported Chinese merchants during a boycott, agitated "to have the navy and army reduced," refused to sing the national anthem, and counseled "riot and bloodshed." Mary Keith sent Governor Johnson a copy, complaining, "the suffragists are not fighting the liquor men & it does not seem fair that they should always down us."[122]

Suffragists dismissed all anti-suffragists as puppets or "fronts" for powerful economic interests, which some evidently were, but others were sincerely concerned that political participation would corrupt and coarsen women.[123] Minnie Bronson and several other eastern anti-suffragists lobbied the state legislature and worked among influential anti-suffrage women in the San Francisco Bay Area. Mrs. Benjamin Ide Wheeler, wife of the anti-suffragist president of the University of California, was one prominent founder of the Northern California chapter of the Woman's Association Opposed to Woman Suffrage. The president of the Southern California group, Mary S. Caswell, claimed to represent one thousand women, and the hostile *Los Angeles Times* gave them extensive coverage. The *Times* also announced the formation of a Men's League Opposed to Extension of Suffrage to Women, with a conservative membership heavily tied to the Southern Pacific Railroad.[124]

Sometimes extreme anti-suffrage rhetoric backfired. The Southern California Women's Press Club formally expunged all record of the anti-suffrage speech by a journalist for the *Times*. A rival newspaper reported "it was a new and startling experience for this group of capable and intelligent women, most of whom earn their own living by hard work, to be told that woman is dependent for her place in the world solely on the charm she can exercise over whatever man through the sex function."[125] In San Francisco, anti-suffragists offended at least two important trade unionists. Andrew Gallagher was "set to thinking seriously of the other arguments against woman suffrage by the weakness of the ones he heard." Remarking "women had been voting sensibly in the labor councils for a long time," he "called on the men of labor to . . . give the women their political freedom and see if they could possibly make any worse mistakes than the men have made." Another recent convert, laundry union official Adelaide Walden, challenged the idea that modern women were unable to think and act for themselves.[126]

Concluding that the "best plans were those that advertised themselves," California suffragists made news that even the *Los Angeles Times* had to report. With limited funds, it was "far better to use money in doing things so brilliantly well that their success brings voluntary notice."[127] In March, Bay Area suffragists organized a last-minute speech by British suffragette Sylvia Pankhurst by distributing leaflets for hours in the streets in the rain. Although they were finally "stopped by the awful news that they were violating a city ordinance by giving out handbills on the street," these efforts filled the house. Pankhurst was well received and the free publicity was invaluable.[128] After that point, suffragists frequently turned overflow crowds away from packed houses or addressed extemporaneous outdoor gatherings. In planning mass meetings, they paid close attention to the choice of speakers, advertising, literature distribution, and fundraising, always taking care to reserve good seats for the press and important guests. Public testimonials and endorsements by prominent individuals heightened the effect of large public meetings and open-air rallies.[129]

The college league assumed primary responsibility for the campaign grand finale, a rally at Dreamland, San Francisco's largest auditorium. "Terrified" but excited by the chance to make 2,500 people "give the effect of a great mob," the college women covered the city with announcements and hired a marching band to drum up interest. Everyone was astounded when approximately 10,000 people showed up. The magnitude of the response and the "passionately enthusiastic applause" gave many suffragists "their first suspicion" of impending victory.[130] The program featured Dr. Aked, Rabbi Meyer, Commissioner Nolan, Berkeley's Socialist mayor, J. Stitt Wilson, and several visiting suffragists. Loud cheers greeted the surprise announcement that "Mrs. Phoebe Hearst, philanthropist . . . had, at the eleventh hour, given her endorsement of woman suffrage."[131]

San Francisco suffragists presented another last-minute surprise: Madame Louise Nordica, a famous prima donna, would sing at an open-air meeting in Union Square. The college women later admitted that they "had about decided not to have any public demonstration at all," other than the well-choreographed Dreamland rally. They feared "that some undisciplined enthusiast might at the last moment make a statement that linked 'Rum, Romanism, and Rebellion' [and] would turn the tide against us."[132] Good luck and suffrage press connections made the event possible. In the square that evening, the glamorous star stood in a flower-bedecked automobile and spoke briefly to the huge crowd, appealing to basic fairness in asking for the ballot. Someone shouted: "Sing and we will vote any way you want." Nordica concluded with "The Star Spangled Banner," and as her "glorious voice rang out the very edges of the throng, everyone joined in the chorus."[133]

The campaign was over, but election day presented a different set of challenges. To prevent fraud, the state association had established an election day committee several weeks earlier. It was chaired by attorney Gail Laughlin, who issued detailed instructions.[134] When Bay Area organizers received information "that the enemy had sent emissaries into 22 counties to try to juggle the returns," they quickly telephoned and telegraphed warnings to activists in outlying areas.[135] Mary Coolidge, who supervised election day work in the tough city of Oakland, was subsequently amused by her careful arrangements. Coolidge hired Pinkerton detectives to supplement a corps of volunteer poll watchers: "women over 30 . . . who had earned their own living or were accustomed to meeting working men, such as teachers, and settlement and charity workers." Coolidge recalled how one "young colored woman" had offered the services of her group, the Colored Women's Suffrage League, on election day. When Coolidge promised, "I would take special pains to have my husband protect them," the woman replied "quite calmly that they could take care of themselves and she did not think they would have any trouble." Indeed, the African American women monitored two precincts all day without difficulty.[136] Due to a strict anti-picketing ordinance and police scrutiny, Los Angeles women refrained from conversation at the polls, but they employed a fleet of automobiles for last-minute publicity, voter mobilization, and precinct monitoring. Even the *Los Angeles Times* gave them credit for "a new sort of machine politics. It was automobile politics with smiles as influence. . . . The men who watched the women at work considered that they had done exceptionally well."[137]

In San Francisco, approximately one thousand volunteer poll watchers were at their posts by 6 A.M. on election day, while others circulated by car. At least "one tired waitress volunteered to stand at the polls during the part of the afternoon that is allowed her for rest."[138] Women poll workers were generally well treated: "Grocery men brought out chairs for them to sit upon; bakers brought out cakes and pies for them to eat; election booth officials—who were all saloon appointees and uniformly opposed to suffrage—invited them into booths to see how it was done and to discuss suffrage." Direct contact with voters was controversial female behavior, but suffragists believed that earnest women impressed men who "realized that women do not stand on the street 23 hours a day for fun."[139] One voter was "inspired . . . to dance for the women, if he could not in conscience vote for them" but "right when the dance was at its best" an elderly woman resident passed by, stopped, and chastised all concerned. "'You ought to be ashamed, all of you,' she said. 'Men doing the dancing and women watching the vote.' Things were not so in her young day, that was apparent."[140] There were some discourtesies. A San Francisco schoolteacher scolded a voter who "wished she had something better to do," by explaining "she had been teaching George Washington and Abraham Lincoln to half a hundred children most of the day and that she was engaged even at the moment in expounding some of the principles of government."[141] In the working-class districts, men "voted in large numbers, and one positive citizen replied to the question of whether he had voted, "'I have voted twice.'"[142]

After working at the polls all day, the excited women were dismayed by the negative early returns from urban areas. In contrast, a motley crew gathered downtown to "have a good time" and celebrate the success of the initiative, referendum, and recall and the *failure* of woman suffrage. One sign asked: "'*What is Mrs. Cat* [sic] *Saying Now?*'"[143] On Wednesday, most San Francisco newspapers reported defeat, but the *Call* accurately declared a very narrow victory. Alice Park related a bright episode at suffrage headquarters on that dark day. As "one small daughter, aged seven," sat listening to her mother and the other women, "She heard someone say 'We'll have to start a new campaign and do the work all over again.'" Then "she touched her mother's arm to attract her attention and said 'Shall I fold some more leaflets?'"[144] By Thursday it was apparent that the woman suffrage amendment had carried by a very tiny margin. The final total was 125,037 to 121,450, a margin of only 3,587 votes.[145]

Woman suffrage passed in California in 1911 because urban working-class support combined with the rural vote to overcome the generally negative influence of large cities. As expected, the amendment lost in Oakland and San Francisco, but the few precincts where it passed were predominantly working-class urban neighborhoods.[146] In San Francisco, 40 to 42 percent of the working-class men cast affirmative votes, compared to approximately 37 percent in the professional and middle-class areas. This was an impressive increase in working-class support since 1896, when only 24 to 25 percent of the voters in working-class districts approved of suffrage.[147] In Los Angeles, the amendment passed by an unexpectedly small margin, probably due to the political turmoil in that city as the mayoral runoff election approached. As in San Francisco, the poorer districts of Los Angeles were more supportive than the rich, indicating the influence of labor suffragists and socialists.[148]

Initially some suffragists reflexively blamed immigrant urban voters for their apparent defeat, but others immediately acknowledged the strong support of stable working-class districts. Clara Schelingheyde wrote to her friend, Carrie Catt, about her work "in an awfully tough district, where some of the scum of the earth live like rats, and my booth showed 83 for to 99 against—a remarkable showing for that district. Another booth located across the street showed a majority of 15 for us." She cited two important factors: "There was an able woman stationed at these booths who knew how to approach these men," and "Maud Younger's work in the unions . . . saved us."[149] Thomas V. Cator, a prominent suffragist Populist Democrat and the president of the San Francisco election commission, was offended by the persistent misconceptions of working-class opposition and estimated that "woman's suffrage had gained nearly 100 per cent in this community." He observed that similar increase elsewhere would have resulted in "an overwhelming majority."[150]

Most of the agricultural counties reported a positive vote as expected, and everyone agreed that "the countrymen's vote" had once again "saved the day." Suffragists lauded "the farmers and miners of our great, free western state, . . . our knight-errants," while the *New York Times* corrected its earlier report of defeat with a big headline: "CALIFORNIA FARMERS GIVE VOTE TO WOMEN."[151] Jeannette Rankin explained, "The men of California are used to seeing women do things. The women run fruit ranches; they own and operate mines; they are in all professions and occupations; they are original and efficient." Rankin also acknowledged the support of socialist groups. She subsequently applied these insights as a NAWSA organizer and as the leader of the successful 1914 Montana referendum campaign.[152]

Female voters were immediately an issue in the Los Angeles mayoral run-off race between the favored candidate, Socialist attorney Job Harriman, and the "good government" incumbent, Mayor Alexander.[153] Middle-class Alexander supporters formed the Women's Progressive League (WPL) and held large meetings. They coordinated hundreds of volunteers who visited offices, parks, newspaper offices, women's clubs, and large department stores to register "mothers, housewives, sisters and those who do not work for weekly wages." In support of Harriman, Socialist women also made "Herculean efforts . . . to enroll as many working women as possible."[154] Regardless of their politics, many former suffragists were amused by the anti-suffrage *Times* "on its knees," begging them to turn out and save city, "home and fireside" from "the Reds," which "more than repaid them for all their efforts."[155] As a result, 83,284 Los Angeles women registered to vote in little over a month, and 90 to 95 percent turned out for the December election.[156] The female vote has often been blamed for Harriman's loss, but it is difficult to isolate the gender effect from sensational developments in the *Los Angeles Times* bombing case just days before the election. The sudden confessions of the McNamara brothers stunned the city, discredited the labor movement, and exploded Harriman's candidacy. Katherine Edson was adamant about Progressivism as "the safe middle ground," because "whatever may be said for experiments in socialism, Los Angeles, under existing conditions, was not the place to make one."[157]

After enfranchisement, California women of all classes joined political parties and established women's partisan clubs, but few ran for office. As nonpartisans, they continued to work on reform issues, helping to pass a flurry of progressive laws in the 1910s.[158] Woman suffrage was also credited for protecting the women's eight-hour-day law from constitutional challenge.[159] Late in 1912, approximately sixty women's organizations established the Women's Legislative Council, which prioritized a few measures each year from the many nominated by its constituent members.[160] In 1912, San Francisco trade unionists established the Humane Legislation League (HLL) to enlist women voters in support of labor and protective legislation. Hired to organize the HLL, Frances Noel quickly opened an office, visited local unions, arranged meetings and mass assemblies, and issued literature. She was disappointed with the response from labor unions, but pleased by the several hundred women who answered her mailings. The league did not last long, but working-class women campaigned vigorously in 1914 to reelect Governor Hiram Johnson and to send Labor Commissioner John I. Nolan to Congress.[161]

In conclusion, the 1911 California victory confirmed the significance of modern mass-based methods in a diverse, heavily urbanized state. Grassroots networks and strategic political alliances, combined with sophisticated publicity techniques and mass organizing skills, weakened traditional hostility in the cities. Younger, well-educated suffragists supplied talent, energy, and imagination while the older generation provided resources, connections, and organizational coherence. Women were acutely interested in reform, but they wanted the vote as a fundamental acknowledgment of their rights and responsibilities as productive citizens. The clarity of this goal helped unite women otherwise divided by identities, interests, and prejudices. In California, woman suffrage was a democratizing measure, both a cause and an effect of Progressivism in this key state, and a bold inspiration which catalyzed renewed efforts elsewhere. The California campaign set major organizational precedents and catalyzed a series of suffrage referenda in other states between 1912 and 1914. As the struggle entered its final phase, Californians and other western activists took their innovative ideas to other state campaigns, the Congressional Union (CU), the National Woman's Party (NWP), and the final battle for the federal woman suffrage amendment.

8

The West and the
Modern Suffrage Movement

In Australia they're doing it,
And in Iceland's frigid zone;
Seems that they're voting everywhere,
And comin' closer home.

. . . .

Nevada's not the greatest state,
And if it ever hopes
To be among the best ones, let
The women have their votes.[1]

Inspired by the Pacific Coast victories, all other western states and territories except New Mexico enfranchised their women citizens by the end of 1914. As the Progressive political momentum and bold new tactics allowed a new generation of suffragists to win these state measures, the growing body of western women voters pressured their congressional representatives as part of the revived effort to pass a federal amendment. Within the suffrage movement, the radicalism of modern suffragists challenged the staid leadership of the national movement, resulting in bitter confrontations and the establishment of an alternate national organization, the Congressional Union (CU), later and better known as the National Woman's Party (NWP).[2] Within the NWP, experienced western activists joined British-inspired militants from the East to dispel the "doldrums" with energetic new strategies that were as controversial as they were effective. The last western state campaigns, particularly in Nevada and Montana in 1914, show these new elements in action. Both states had dynamic western-born, college-educated, cosmopolitan young leaders, Anne Martin and Jeannette

Rankin, respectively. Martin was an important early member of the NWP, and Rankin a sympathizer, even as she continued to work within the NAWSA, but both women dominated the movement in their own states. Martin and Rankin effectively energized and mobilized like-minded "New Women" in these final years of the suffrage movement, prodding older colleagues into action and convincing the opposition that they would not behave or rest until their goal was achieved.

On the state level, the young radicals encountered the same perennial challenges to western campaigns. Like their predecessors, modern suffragists endured physical hardships as they canvassed broad and isolated areas in order to reach sympathetic rural voters. For example, in Nevada half the men were transient laborers, leaving only 20,000 eligible voters in a highly scattered population of 80,000 inhabitants. As a result, suffragists continued to cultivate the farmer-labor-socialist coalitions that were so crucial to victory. Since both Rankin and Martin were affluent women with few previous ties to those groups, they tended to hire radicals as organizers, stepping cautiously around western sensitivity to outside interference. Largely indifferent or opposed to prohibition, they struggled to define an appropriate role for the Women's Christian Temperance Union (WCTU). In several states, suffragists faced additional constitutional obstacles, such as the need for two-thirds majorities or multiple legislative approvals. For example, in both Arizona and Nevada any proposed amendment referendum had be authorized by *two* sessions of the legislature, followed by a popular referendum, necessitating a total of *three* suffrage campaigns over the span of four years. This situation repeatedly handicapped Nevada suffragists, but Arizona suffragists overcame the problem with the initiative and referendum provisions of their new state constitution. Obviously one attraction of the federal amendment was that it would obviate the need for these repetitive and often frustrating efforts.[3]

Montana was a suffrage disappointment until 1914, despite agitation at four constitutional conventions. As in many other areas, organized activity first started with the WCTU, encouraged by Frances Willard during her 1883 tour.[4] In 1884, one of the earliest suffrage advocates was Mary Long Alderson, the long-term president of the WCTU, who lobbied without success at the second statehood convention.[5] In 1887, the territorial legislature granted women the vote for school trustees if they were taxpayers in the district. In 1889, Henry Blackwell addressed the fourth constitutional convention with an appeal to justice and to expediency that denied any connection to prohibition. Helena women organized the first suffrage club in January 1890, but it did not prosper.[6]

By 1895, several encouraging signs stimulated renewed efforts. A Populist suffrage measure passed the House (although it lost in the Senate), and several labor unions passed unanimous resolutions. NAWSA organizing committee chair Carrie Chapman Catt sent Emma Smith DeVoe to Montana, where she organized fourteen new clubs and made preparations for a state suffrage convention before continuing to Idaho. Catt attended that meeting, dominated the proceedings, and helped establish the Montana Woman Suffrage Association (MWSA). She organized among the elites, but also spent much time in mining camps and trade union meetings.[7] DeVoe shared Catt's preference for an elite strategy, but she also understood the importance of balance and diversity in the movement. As the Helena club sputtered along, President Sarepta Sanders, a schoolteacher, explained to DeVoe, "We lack workers," and complained, "the women who are capable are the women who are too busy (they think) to assume a new work." Sanders was also pessimistic about "the society woman [who] would not be in sympathy with us, or if she were, would have nothing to add to the interest of the Club." Catt convinced a reluctant Harriet P. (Mrs. Senator Wilbur F.) Sanders, Sarepta's sister-in-law, to accept the state presidency, but no one was ever very satisfied with this choice.[8]

Catt and DeVoe returned in 1896, but the society plan was still not going well. Former Colorado suffragist Helen Reynolds, who was now working for Catt, expressed frustration as she tried to make arrangements for DeVoe's 1896 tour. Reynolds considered Montana (and Idaho) women "about fifty years behind the women of Colorado" and "losing ground" rapidly. Catt also complained that "not one tenth" of their letters to elite Montana women "have met with any response whatever," although she identified future California suffrage publicist Alice Park as "the best worker in the state." To Catt "it seems very ludicrous . . . the way these western people in the small cities assume airs of society. . . . We have tried in vain to win society people to become workers in our cause." Many "announce themselves as suffragists, [but] we have not yet found a real society woman who has amounted to very much as a working force." She was thinking "we will have to organize them into societies by themselves where they will not be expected to do anything but to have their names referred to when they can do any good." Even as the national organizers complained about her, Montana state president Harriet Sanders also lamented the "indifference and thoughtlessness of some of our own sex." DeVoe persevered, established more clubs, and helped organize another state convention, which replaced Sanders with Ella Knowles (Haskell), president of the Helena Business Women's Suffrage Club.[9]

Ella Knowles represented a new generation of suffragists—younger, unmarried, often professional women—and she was also an important Populist.[10] A relative newcomer to Montana, she obtained a special law in 1889 allowing her to become an attorney. In 1892, the Populists unexpectedly nominated her for state attorney general, "by acclamation and with great enthusiasm," and she took her candidacy seriously as an affirmation of women's rights. There was some question whether as a nonvoter she was eligible to run for office, but the incumbent, Attorney General Henri Haskell, approved her candidacy. She traveled many miles and gave at least fifty speeches, mostly related to Populism and free silver, but her Fourth of July address synthesized many dominant ideas about justice, civilization, and progress. Knowles, "The Portia of the People's Party," stated, "Degrade woman, cripple her faculties, hamper her intellectual growth, and the result is a degraded, crippled, or enslaved people." Instead, "Elevate woman, give her full freedom to use the faculties God has given her, not as a matter of favor, but as an act of simple justice." The "result is a people strong and self-reliant, intellectual and valiant," the vanguard of "civilized humanity."[11]

In the election, Ella Knowles placed third, with 11,465 votes, leading some observers to describe her serious candidacy and respectable showing as an indication of Montana progressivism. One editor was less gracious, however, suggesting "that some 'good man' ought to protect her from the shocks of political life by marrying her," which Henri Haskell did the following year after appointing her as his assistant. Ella Knowles Haskell remained an active suffragist, but she also became deeply involved in national Populist politics, serving on the national committee for four years and campaigning for William Jennings Bryan in 1896 and 1900. In 1897 she organized a suffrage petition drive, addressed the Montana legislature, and led the suffrage lobby. The measure won a majority vote, but not the two-thirds needed for a constitutional amendment. A third effort in 1899 met the same fate. After these defeats, Ella Haskell became preoccupied with her career and her marital difficulties, and another professional woman, Dr. Maria M. Dean, was elected president of the state association in 1899. By the early 1900s, Ella Knowles Haskell was divorced and practicing law in Butte, where she died in 1911 at the age of 50.[12]

Montana was changing rapidly in the new century, and the state suffrage movement reflected the demographic, economic, and political shifts. New people were moving into the eastern agricultural regions of the state, while mining in the western areas decreased in relative economic importance. Helena, the state capital, lost population and influence, while Butte became the state's most important city. Younger middle-class and professional women (like Haskell) were moving to Butte or leaving altogether. In the early 1900s, the NAWSA continued to send its best organizers, including Laura Gregg (Cannon) and Gail Laughlin in 1902. Stressing the theme of working women, Laughlin began work among the unions, especially in Butte, where she received the endorsement of the local labor assembly, representing 10,000 men. As in other states, speaking before labor unions usually resulted in endorsements for woman suffrage. Laughlin was invited to the state labor convention, where a pro-suffrage resolution passed with only one dissenting vote. While Gregg coordinated efforts from Helena, Laughlin toured throughout Montana during the summer and fall, organizing thirty new clubs and a state convention. They had high hopes for the 1903 legislative session, encouraged by the support of the governor and many prominent men. Once again, however, the bill passed in the House but lost in the Senate. After another effort in 1905 produced the same result, the suffrage movement lapsed, demoralized by the failure to budge obstructive legislators.[13]

Interest revived in the early 1910s, catalyzed by the Washington and California victories specifically, Progressivism generally, and driven by a new generation of western-born, well-educated women such as Anne Martin and Jeannette Rankin. Rankin came from an affluent family, graduated from college, tried teaching and social work, but had trouble finding a suitable vocation.[14] Although apparently oblivious or indifferent to suffrage activity in Montana during her youth, Rankin found her calling as a suffragist when journalist Minnie Reynolds recruited her into the 1910 Washington campaign. On Reynolds's recommendation, Rankin was hired by prominent New York leader Harriet Laidlaw, who sent her to California in August 1911, and this experience led to a national assignment as a NAWSA organizer. As head of the New York legislative lobby in 1912, she met an indifferent young senator, Franklin Roosevelt. She got the bill out of committee and onto the floor for a vote, but it was narrowly defeated. Later that year she participated in the unsuccessful Ohio and Wisconsin campaigns, then returned to Montana to prepare for the next state legislative session. She did not lead that legislative lobby, however, because in 1913 she accepted a position as NAWSA field secretary. In addition to working on several state campaigns, Rankin supervised and led the Montana delegation (costumed as Indians) in the great March 1913 suffrage parade in Washington, D.C., organized by Alice Paul. The two women became friends, and Rankin joined the struggle for a federal amendment. In the summer she returned to Montana, where the legislature had finally passed an equal suffrage bill, then embarked on a transcontinental automobile tour headed to Washington, D.C., with thousands of names on suffrage petitions addressed to congressional representatives. Thus, in a few short years, Rankin had become a well-established national suffrage leader who helped bring western insights into the eastern movement.[15]

Despite her duties as a peripatetic NAWSA organizer, Rankin remained a key figure in the Montana suffrage movement. Late in 1910, she read in a local newspaper that a state legislator was planning to reintroduce the measure at the 1911 session. (She later discovered that he intended it as a joke.) Rankin formed a new club in Missoula and nominated herself to head the suffrage lobby, then enlisted the support of prominent Helena suffragists like Dr. Dean and Harriet Sanders. Despite initial discouragement, the House committee passed the bill and invited Rankin to speak in its support. She insisted "taxation without representation is tyranny," but the bill failed to win the necessary two-thirds majority. When she returned from her NAWSA duties in the summer of 1912, Rankin became head of a loose state coalition, then chair of a new state organization early in 1913.[16]

In 1912 progressive Democrats swept into office and broke the suffrage stalemate. Rankin obtained endorsements from the Republican, Democratic, and Progressive parties, and the new Democratic governor, Sam Stewart, urged submission as part of his party's reform platform. Suffragists also believed that the politicians were impressed by their efforts to defeat an anti-suffrage representative, James McNally. (They did not succeed, but McNally got the message and voted for the measure in the legislature.)[17] In 1913, Rankin personally interviewed every legislator, and this time the referendum passed easily in both houses with little discussion. For the rest of the year, Montana suffragists prepared for the 1914 campaign by working on internal organization, press work, and endorsements, especially from labor unions.[18]

In 1914, Rankin returned to concentrate on the Montana campaign. She applied the modern model but kept it simple and focused on appeals to working men. Suffragists used the mail to reach country voters, organized by precinct in urban areas, and spoke in the street from automobiles. Experienced women journalists ran several press services and produced a weekly bulletin. A mile-long parade at the state fair in September was headed by Rankin, Dean, NAWSA president Anna Howard Shaw, and a band from Anaconda Copper mines. The procession included horseback riders, automobiles, floats, members of labor unions, and supporters from the Montana State Men's League for Woman Suffrage. One woman portrayed Sacajawea ("the first Montanan suffragist"), while others carried yellow flags representing states with suffrage campaigns in progress, gray for partial suffrage states, and black for nonsuffrage states.[19]

During the campaign, Rankin and other activists traveled extensively trying to reach every mining camp and settlement, and their efforts evidently impressed many men. Some responded: "What would our State have been without the women? You bet you can count on us."[20] Given her national contacts, Rankin was not hostile to "outsiders" and welcomed many volunteers. Margaret Hinchey, an Irish laundry worker from New York, spoke of equal rights for working women: "Isn't your sister and your wife and your daughter a person?" she asked. "And if they are, haven't they the right to be distinguished from the lower animals and nonentities by the possession of the ballot?" The Washington State labor movement sponsored Seattle labor suffragist Grace Cotterill, who spoke to workers as a trade unionist and "as an American mother." She also appealed to nativist and anti-Asian prejudices, insisting, "I deserve as much voice in the government under which I and my children must live as does my Chinese laundryman who has been in this country only a few years, or the Italian laborer, who has just taken out his naturalization papers." Most visitors donated their services or received outside support. In fact, more than half of the nine thousand dollars spent on the campaign came from out-of-state donations.[21]

The temperance connection was more problematic. As in other states, younger suffragists had few if any ties to the temperance movement, and they often upset older colleagues by insisting upon the complete separation of the two issues. WCTU president Mary Long Alderson, a suffragist since the 1880s, denied that prohibition hindered suffrage, calling them "twin sisters." She argued that trying to hide the connection was more harmful than being honest. Tensions reached a peak in September when the WCTU was not allowed to march as a group in the big parade at the fair, although many women joined individually with their county organizations. Alderson commented, "It is laughable to have the suffragists so considerate of the liquor men." Ultimately she acquiesced, convinced that "quiet work counts more than the 'Hurrah.'" Several national anti-suffragists, including Minnie Bronson, organized a state association with some of the "best" women in Montana, but they were embarrassed when news of their collusion with local liquor people leaked out.[22]

On election day, Rankin assigned poll watchers to city precincts, a wise move considering that the measure won by a small margin (52.2 percent) and the final results were suspiciously delayed. In particular, she enlisted local attorneys to watch the vote in Anaconda, a copper company town.[23] In Butte the measure lost by thirty-four votes (49.8 percent), but as in other urban cities, working-class districts were more positive (52.3 percent) than middle-class neighborhoods (46.5 percent), reflecting careful attention to the powerful labor vote.[24] Support was strongest in the northwest area, near the equal suffrage states of Idaho and Washington, where socialist and populist feeling was strong. Most other counties reported small favorable majorities, with the exception of the southwestern region. Like many western suffragists, Rankin sometimes attributed the victory to the "frontier" experience, but she was well aware of the significance of labor and socialist support. After enfranchisement, Montana women were instrumental in the passage of many important social welfare measures, and they helped send Rankin to Congress in 1916. A dedicated pacifist, Rankin lost her seat in part because she was the only representative to oppose U.S. entry into World War I, and many years later she returned to Congress for another term just in time to vote against World War II, too.[25]

A similar pattern occurred in Nevada, which resembled Montana in terms of a sparse and scattered population, an economy based heavily on mining, and strong labor and socialist influences. Nevada differed in its close and sometimes corrupt political and economic connections to California. This proximity brought very early exposure to women's rights, partly due to the work of Laura DeForce Gordon, who lived in Nevada briefly before moving to California. In 1869, the Nevada state legislature passed two measures to amend the state constitution and eliminate the words "male" and "white" from requirements for voting, a clear reflection of the Reconstruction period political context.[26] The woman suffrage proposal excited considerable discussion. One editor suggested, "If suffrage is to be open indiscriminately to negroes, Chinamen, Kanakas and Indians, the intelligent white women of this State should be entitled to as much consideration, at least."[27] In the summer of 1870, Gordon and Emily Pitts-Stevens toured Nevada and coordinated a suffrage convention, which led to the establishment of a state organization with Gordon as president. Gordon lobbied the 1871 legislature and was generally well received, but others resented her involvement and the amendment did not pass. The editor of the *Territorial Enterprise* remarked, "We think the resolution should have been adopted, and would have been, doubtless, but for the over-officiousness of the strong-minded women of the coast."[28] In a familiar pattern, subsequent defeats in the early 1880s encouraged many disappointed activists to redirect their energies to organizing within the WCTU.[29]

Populism helped revive interest in woman suffrage in Nevada in the 1890s. During this decade, the most prominent leader was Frances A. Williamson, the Populist wife of a state senator. In the fall of 1895, she became president of a new state association established with assistance from NAWSA organizer Emma Smith DeVoe. Traveling throughout the state organizing at her own expense, Williamson reported the formation of eleven new suffrage clubs at the next suffrage convention, yet she was unsure about continuing in a leadership position. Discussing the situation with DeVoe, Catt explained that Williamson was concerned "because she was a Catholic, [and] it might draw the attention of the A.P.As. [American Protective Association] toward the suffrage amendment." Recognizing "a mean state of affairs over the A.P.As. and Catholics," Catt nevertheless commended Williamson's work and considered her gesture "very magnanimous . . . but the bigotry of the A.P.As. would hardly appreciate it."[30] Apparently Williamson was persuaded to retain the state presidency and the chair of the legislative committee, and she also began publishing a monthly newspaper, the *Nevada Citizen,* "devoted to the social, civil and industrial advancement of women." This periodical continued until 1899, when the family moved to Oakland, where Williamson continued to write articles and to agitate for suffrage.[31]

Williamson managed the legislative lobby between 1895 and 1899, when suffragists were optimistic that the measure might pass with strong Populist support. Early in 1895, the introduction of a woman suffrage bill was widely anticipated, but as usual partisan politics complicated the situation. For example, the state legislator who promised to introduce the bill reneged, claiming to be "unequivocally in favor of woman suffrage," but supposedly worried that his Republican affiliation might alienate the Populists.[32] As in 1869, the measure did pass, but it was a limited victory because the Nevada constitution required reconfirmation by the next legislature. In 1897 and again in 1899, the bill survived the Senate, but met defeat in the Assembly. Stymied, the Nevada suffrage movement lay dormant for the next decade.[33]

In 1909, Nevada women began to reorganize, initially due to the efforts of Katherine (Mrs. Clarence) Mackay, a wealthy New York socialite suffragist and the daughter-in-law of one of Nevada's original Comstock Lode "Silver Kings." Mackay had established the elite Equal Franchise League in New York, and she contacted Jeanne Elizabeth Wier, a history professor at the University of Nevada, encouraging her to start a branch in Nevada. Wier was busy and initially refused, but a meeting with Mackay in New York changed her mind. Weir returned to Nevada to begin organizing prominent individuals into a Reno chapter, while Mackay displayed no further interest in Nevada suffrage activities. By 1911 the reform climate renewed interest and support, so sympathizers introduced a new bill. In February suffragists formed a new state organization, the Nevada Equal Suffrage Association (NESA), and elected Margaret Stanislawsky as president. Felice Cohn, a Carson City attorney who authored the measure, effectively managed the legislative lobby. Granted a hearing in mid-February, suffragists emphasized party platform commitments and the legal status of Nevada women. The bill passed just before the end of the session, but reconfirmation by the next legislature was necessary in order to authorize a public referendum.[34]

By this time, the driving force of the Nevada movement was Anne Martin, the daughter of a successful businessman and one-term populist state senator. In many ways, Martin and Rankin were very similar and typical members of the new generation of educated western women suffragists, although they eventually differed in their willingness to cooperate with the established suffrage movement. Martin attended Jane Stanford's new coeducational university in California, graduating in 1897 with a master's degree in history, then taught briefly at the University of Nevada. After her father died in 1901, Martin drifted for several years, traveling with her mother in Europe, but in 1907 she became involved in the British suffragette movement. She was first arrested on Black Friday, the memorable day in 1910 when British suffragettes were seriously beaten and bullied by the police during a protest at Parliament. This infamous incident had a radicalizing effect on both sides of the Atlantic Ocean.[35] By the time Martin returned to Reno in 1911, she had a reputation as a "suffragette," although she did not use the term and sometimes downplayed the connection to avoid controversy. Early in 1912, potential conflict within the Nevada suffrage movement was averted when Stanislawsky, the conservative state president, moved to California and Martin was elected unanimously as her replacement.[36]

Internal harmony was short lived, however, because Martin did not delegate authority or tolerate rivals very well, but it lasted long enough to win reconfirmation in the 1913 legislature. With reauthorization pending, Martin surveyed every single candidate in the 1912 election and cautiously concluded that the measure would pass. In January, Governor Tasker Oddie boosted the movement in his annual message, appealing to state pride when he observed "in every Pacific state except Nevada—the right of the franchise is now granted to women. Thus we are entirely surrounded." Oddie based his support on his "own personal convictions of its justice," as well as his practical determination that "sentiment in its favor seems to be overwhelming and participated in by all political parties." The bill passed by the end of the month, once again managed by its author, attorney Felice Cohn.[37]

Martin and Cohn soon clashed, however, and the latter organized a rebellion at the state suffrage convention in February. Martin claimed that Cohn envied her sudden rise to prominence in the movement, while Cohn charged Martin with undemocratic control of the state association. Cohn refused to run for the presidency herself, however, the proposed alternative candidate was easily defeated, and the dissidents withdrew. The name of their new group, the Non-Militant Nevada Suffrage Society, suggests conflicts over tactics as well as personalities, but there were no further challenges to Martin's leadership.[38]

Martin drew upon her western background and her British experience in organizing for the 1914 suffrage referendum campaign. She hoped "to rouse as many women as possible . . . [and] to reach every voter in the State." The establishment of many new local auxiliaries increased membership in the state association to over one thousand by February 1913. She pressured these local women to undertake systematic precinct surveys wherever possible, compiling and submitting their results. Well aware of the need to mobilize isolated rural supporters, Martin used the mail to send them suffrage literature. As Nevada suffragists planned systematic press work and public meetings, they targeted labor unions, women's clubs, and political parties. The state labor federation endorsement was particularly important, establishing a precedent followed by "every union which has discussed the subject, including the Washoe County Building and Trades Council, the Reno Central Trades Council, and the Brotherhood of Locomotive Engineer Firemen." At their state conventions, the Democrats, Progressives, and Socialists endorsed the woman suffrage amendment, but the Republicans did not. To counter the negative influence of powerful business interests, state and local advisory councils of prominent men included judges, state representatives, the governor and lieutenant governor, and both U.S. senators.[39]

Because holding public attention throughout this long process was very difficult, Nevada suffragists constantly sought opportunities for positive publicity and media coverage. Martin developed a press network of forty-five papers and wrote a regular weekly column that was printed by the hostile *Reno Evening Gazette,* the leading Republican journal, as well as the state's supportive Democratic paper, the *Nevada State Journal.*[40] Unlike other states, the Nevada press was not generally sympathetic, largely due to the influence of wealthy businessman and political boss George Wingfield, who dominated the state Republican Party. In fact, there was a special term, "Wingfield cold feet," to describe the condition of hesitancy and caution endemic among individuals connected to the Wingfield machine.[41] For example, J. Holman Buck, editor of the *Western Nevada Miner,* seemed to succumb to this malady. In 1911, Buck was an active suffragist, serving as publicity chair for the state suffrage association, but early in 1914, he abruptly changed his mind and announced that he was now a determined anti-suffragist. He gave little reason, stating merely that it was "a duty I owe to my adopted state," which caused widespread speculation that he had fallen victim to political pressure.[42] Wingfield's influence helps explain why Nevada Democrats actively endorsed woman suffrage in 1912, but the Republicans did not.

Despite western hostility toward "outsiders," Martin also employed traveling organizers, because few local women had comparable experience. Most of the visitors were labor suffragists or socialists, including Charlotte Perkins Gilman, Laura Gregg Cannon, Margaret Foley, Alice Park, and Charlotte Anita Whitney. For example, Boston trade unionist Margaret Foley made her first trip West in 1914 to work among the miners. By the end of the tour, Foley had "talked in the depths of eight mines, attended fifty dances, made one thousand speeches, and worn out three pairs of shoes."[43] These labor and socialist organizers were chosen purposefully to reach the large population of working-class men, and by all accounts they were very effective. Martin was always nervous about their ideological inclinations, however, because independent radicals were not easily contained.[44] They were supposed to focus on suffrage and avoid other controversies, but they rarely complied, honoring picket lines and boycotts as part of their arguments connecting political and economic rights for women.[45] The most disturbing episode occurred in the fall of 1912, when Gilman agreed to speak to Socialists in Tonopah, upsetting the nonpartisan strategy and the local organizer, attorney Bird M. Wilson. When Wilson objected and blocked the speech, Martin supported Gilman, because the famous author was not under an exclusive contract and had waived half of her usual fee. She also noted that Wilson herself had scheduled Gilman for a major Democratic Party meeting in Las Vegas (a major coup), asking why one was "partisan" and not the other? Wilson insisted that Gilman "would *not* . . . speak for Democratic politics, but for Suffrage," but Gilman refused to appear with the Democrats at all, and then experienced a hostile reception when she tried to speak in the streets.[46]

In other cases, Martin tried to repress these impulses. Cannon refused "to keep my personal opinion in abeyance, etc.," arguing that it was precisely her ability to "speak through the psychology of the working class" that made her an effective organizer. Cannon observed that during the 1912 Arizona campaign, she had not been offended when NAWSA president Shaw was well received by local clubwomen, because in the same towns she "had only mild cooperation from these women, but enthusiastic help from the Labor Unions."[47] The little community of Las Vegas presented Cannon with a major challenge, however, due to Wingfield's influence and residual tensions from a recent labor dispute. Timid local women opposed an active campaign, leaving the Socialists to dominate the movement. Although a Socialist herself, Cannon was uncomfortable with the limited base of support, but Martin ordered her to proceed. Apparently Bird Wilson had a similar experience in Tonopah, where "the women . . . who have revived the suffrage society here are all Socialists, and are very capable." She concluded, "Well, better than none, I suppose."[48]

Martin's tendency to micromanage led to misunderstandings and problems with all the organizers she hired.[49] Martin arranged itineraries with little allowance for transportation problems, fatigue or illness, un-expected opportunities for organizing, or unanticipated expenses, complicating the logistical challenges presented by these tours. Martin was quite wealthy, but trade union or socialist women usually were not, and more than one out-of-state worker left feeling angry and shortchanged. In Cannon's case, the conflict led to a confrontation with NAWSA president Shaw. Cannon came to Nevada as a NAWSA organizer, but Shaw expected Martin to cover expenses. When Martin balked, Shaw chastised her. Shaw was "pretty tired of your constant quibbling over financial methods when the National has done so much more for you than it has . . . done for some of the other campaign states." If Martin did not want Cannon's services, Shaw would send her to work with Jeannette Rankin on the Montana campaign.[50] Beyond financial issues, Shaw was sensitive to criticisms about interfering "outsiders" and fearful of youthful militance, but still she berated Martin, who would soon become a powerful force within the Congressional Union (CU).[51]

Martin became involved with the CU when she attended the 1913 annual NAWSA convention in Washington, D.C., seeking NAWSA support. Shaw was quite cool, but Martin convinced Eastern contributors to donate $3,000 of the $5,000 she estimated was necessary for the final campaign (ultimately it cost $7,000). She also received many pledges of assistance, especially from Californians. Gail Laughlin volunteered her services, Seattle labor suffragist Grace Cotterill extended her tour to include Nevada, and the venerable Jane Addams agreed to a short visit. Charlotte Whitney, Maud Younger, and Harriet and James Laidlaw of New York were independently wealthy, while others received external subsidies. The Progressive editor of the *San Francisco Bulletin*, Fremont Older, gave his reporter, Bessie Beatty, time off and paid her expenses so she could direct publicity work in Nevada.[52] Most significantly, Martin secured the services of a CU organizer, Mabel Vernon, for the 1914 campaign.[53]

The Congressional Union was a new initiative in support of the federal amendment that attracted young radicals and upset the staid national leadership. NAWSA president Shaw and her successor, Carrie Chapman Catt, successfully broadened the movement by appealing to elites, thus achieving better funding, bureaucratic centralization, and social respectability, but younger, more militant activists became frustrated and alienated, motivating the establishment of rival organizations like the CU. Influenced by their experiences with the British suffragettes, Paul and her associates invigorated the movement with direct actions and colorful demonstrations. Eventually they succeeded in pushing western legislators to reintroduce the Anthony Amendment, ultimately the Nineteenth Amendment, into the U.S. Congress for the first time in decades.[54] At first they worked within the NAWSA, reviving the moribund Congressional Committee. There was so much work, however, that the CU was established in March 1913 as a NAWSA affiliate responsible for its own organizing and fund-raising. Horrified by the idea of British-inspired militancy in the United States and fearful of whole-scale defections of younger women from their organization, NAWSA leaders tried unsuccessfully to control the radicals.[55] At the fall 1913 national convention, Catt charged the CU with insubordination and financial irregularities, although she later admitted that none of the NAWSA officers ever really believed these accusations. To justify repressive measures, Catt alleged that there was "a dark conspiracy to capture the entire 'National' for the militant enterprise."[56] After a series of charges, resolutions, and nonproductive discussions, the NAWSA ejected the CU and Paul resigned her NAWSA position in order to work independently.[57]

The NAWSA leaders felt threatened by the young radicals, but in addition their ostensible commitment to the federal amendment was compromised by the organization's "southern strategy," which tacitly accepted the principle of states' rights. Southerners did not want to reopen voting rights issues so soon after institutionalizing Jim Crow segregation and African American disfranchisement in their own region, and many westerners shared similar racial prejudices. In Congress, woman suffrage enjoyed some support among western representatives, including Democrats, but hostile southerners routinely outvoted them. Attempting to resolve this conflict, the NAWSA blundered into accepting the Shafroth-Palmer amendment, a complicated proposal for suffrage initiatives and referenda. Suggested by Senator John Shafroth, a former Colorado governor, this plan would have been innovative a decade earlier, but by 1914 it was a weak compromise that elicited widespread criticism from suffragists. Paul's replacement as chair of the NAWSA Congressional Committee, Ruth Hanna McCormick, endorsed the proposal without consulting Shaw or any other national suffrage leader, and the resulting internal turmoil led to Shaw's resignation and replacement by Catt. Catt centralized control of the organization, solidified its financial base with affluent supporters, and quietly dropped the Shafroth-Palmer

Amendment in favor of the federal amendment. In continued negotiations with Paul, both women were unyielding and they parted antagonistically. Despite the damage caused by this controversy, the Shafroth-Palmer Amendment was a sign that congressional opposition was weakening. It indicated that the argument had shifted from *whether* women should vote to *how* they should be enfranchised—and *which ones should be included.*[58]

In the summer of 1914, when the amendment was stalled in the House Rules Committee, Paul decided to implement another controversial element of the British program, an active political campaign against the party in power (i.e., the Democrats) as punishment for their failure to enfranchise women. During the 1914 off-year election, she sent two CU organizers to each of the nine western equal suffrage states to campaign against Democratic candidates. With the exception of Mabel Vernon, who was working with Martin on the Nevada state campaign, these CU teams worked tirelessly to explain the significance of the federal amendment. They urged women in particular to vote against Democratic candidates, irrespective of their individual positions on suffrage, "as a matter of honor on behalf of those not yet franchised."[59]

The effort to target women voters, a western strategy by definition, was extremely controversial. Republicans were amused, but Democrats were furious, as were the NAWSA regulars who were courting both parties and the new Democratic president, Woodrow Wilson. Democratic politicians who endorsed the federal amendment were especially angry, but CU organizers believed that these individuals were responding to pressure, not acting on principle. They caustically observed how suddenly "every candidate . . . felt it necessary to declare that he had always believed in woman suffrage, that his mother had believed in woman suffrage, and that his grandmother believed in it." Despite rough conditions and hostile audiences, the CU organizers were satisfied with the results of their efforts, and even antagonistic observers were impressed by their persistence.[60]

This approach drew public attention and support as well as condemnation, and helped force the issue in Congress. Not surprisingly, a 1915 NAWSA survey found nothing good to report about the CU's impact. Western voters of both sexes objected to "outside interference" and rejected efforts to defeat Democratic friends for the sake of reactionary Republicans as unfair and unwise. Stalwart western Democratic women like May Hutton were appalled by the activities of the CU. She was sure they "would have about as much effect on Washington women as the pouring water on a duck's back. Men to whom I have talked of the matter think it is a joke."[61] More astute observers realized "this wonderful fight . . . was the result of a very short campaign, by only two women organizers in each state, with very little money," and warned "with two years more . . . the women can absolutely assure a Democratic defeat."[62] Most Democrats dismissed this threat publicly, but they broke the blockade in the House Rules Committee and began worrying privately about CU plans for the 1916 presidential election.

In Nevada, Martin and Vernon agreed to eliminate anti-Democratic campaigning and to downplay the CU connection in order to avoid endangering the state suffrage amendment. Alice Paul sent Vernon to work under Martin's direction "to arouse sympathy for Federal work, as well as aiding in the Nevada campaign," but Vernon focused on the latter assignment.[63] Local newspapers easily identified the CU influence anyway, especially after Martin publicly criticized Senator Key Pittman. When the Anthony Amendment was defeated by one vote in the U.S. Senate in March 1914, one Nevada senator, Francis A. Newlands, voted for it, but Pittman did not. Both claimed to be pro-suffrage, but similar reasons had brought them to different conclusions. Newlands opposed enfranchising nonwhite women, but he could "see no reason why the males of the white race should deny the females of the white race the right to vote." Pittman, the junior senator, was "opposed to the ignorant Negro having the right to vote," and as a former southerner he took a firm states' rights position against the federal amendment.[64]

At first Martin criticized Pittman privately because he was an old acquaintance as well as a good suffragist. She shared his racial prejudices, if not his fears about federal intervention and racial integration, and suggested, "Woman suffrage means the establishment of Anglo Saxon supremacy."[65] When the controversy became public, Pittman defended his pro-suffrage record and condemned the CU attack on Democrats, yet he continued to be a strong suffrage advocate within the national Democratic Party.[66] Anna Shaw considered this attack on a sympathetic politician during an active campaign "political tactlessness which I have never known surpassed." She, too, recognized "the action of the Congressional Union for, if there is any possible way of making a political blunder, the Congressional Union has a facility of finding how to do it."[67]

Martin's imperious manner created problems with everyone, especially the suffrage organizers she hired who were not part of the CU network.

Even the favored Vernon recalled Martin as "very able and quite a perfectionist . . . a rather rigid sort of person to start with." Martin's preference for Vernon led to conflicts with Maud Leonard McCreery, an experienced Wisconsin labor organizer and suffragist, hired as Nevada state organizer and press chair. Initially, McCreery had some interesting experiences in the field, including a successful encounter with Washoe Indians at a U.S. flag presentation ceremony in April. She "was almost afraid to speak after the audience was tired out with a long program," yet "when I spoke the words 'votes for women' the crowd cheered in a happy, cordial spirit, making it evident that there was a great deal of sentiment for suffrage in the valley." At a meeting the next day, the band extended the tribal vote to women.[68] Within a few weeks, however, McCreery soon found herself confined to the office and overshadowed by Vernon. She resigned, citing "conditions that were physically and mentally unbearable." McCreery felt misled and misused, but she tried to leave quietly in order to avoid bad publicity. Martin held a grudge, however, and later tried to prevent McCreery's employment on other campaigns, describing her as "unwilling or incapable of performing," a person "who dangerously subordinated the State work to her own interests." [69]

Vernon, Martin, and other organizers traveled extensively, and they noticed that isolated men really appreciated the attention. Martin realized "our hope lies in these outlying country districts," where "we find the sentiment for suffrage strong . . . among farmers, railroad employees, and miners." They discovered that the example of equal suffrage in neighboring states exerted an important influence on Nevada voters: "Probably three out of every five men interviewed says at once, 'Yes, I'm in favor of woman suffrage. I've lived in Idaho'—or Wyoming, or Colorado, or Oregon, or Arizona, as the case may be."[70] Other methods helped to reach working-class and racial-ethnic voters and to disarm their suspicions about suffrage and prohibition. There were parades on the Fourth of July, including a Reno suffrage float featuring ten young women dressed in white (representing the equal suffrage states) separated from their nonvoting sisters by a locked gate and a male doorkeeper. There was a ruckus at the state fair in September when officials ordered suffrage banners removed because they were "political." Governor Oddie defended the women, and Gail Laughlin used the incident to open the fall 1913 campaign. She observed how men had taken the money of women taxpayers for the state fair, then tried to stifle their freedom of expression.[71] In October, the endorsement of the state federation of women's clubs provided crucial support and indicated increasing suffrage respectability and acceptance.[72]

Mary E. Ringrose came from California to organize among the Catholics, as she had done in San Francisco in 1911. Ringrose sent a letter to every Catholic churchman, and Margaret Foley also made contacts among priests, resulting in at least one clerical endorsement.[73] There was little love lost between the state temperance and suffrage movements, but as an extra precaution, Martin warned local leaders "it would be dangerous for our cause to be linked with prohibition at this juncture."[74] The liquor and vice industries were deeply invested in Nevada, and suffragists did not underestimate the opposition. Minnie Bronson, the general secretary of the National Association of Women Opposed to Suffrage, toured the state in 1913 and 1914, but Shaw reassured Martin: "If Miss Bronson does as good service for you as she did for the California women . . . you may thank your stars that she is in your state."[75] As a veteran temperance activist, Shaw knew that anti-suffrage arguments often backfired.

By this time, all suffragists understood the importance of strenuous vigilance against fraud, so Martin mobilized poll watchers on election day, but the measure passed by a large majority (10,936 to 7,258). As expected, urban communities voted against the measure, but the rural vote was consistently positive, especially in southern mining areas characterized by labor and Socialist strength.[76] In 1915, Nevada women reorganized into civic leagues, which were still dominated by Martin and the CU, and promised to raise a "veritable suffrage cyclone." A women voters' convention held in San Francisco in conjunction with the 1915 Panama Pacific International Exposition included various activities and stunts, including an aerial barrage of suffrage leaflets. The grand finale was the departure of Sara Bard Field on a cross-country automobile trip carrying an enormous suffrage petition to Washington, D.C.[77] Field was concerned about safety, and the car did break down in Kansas, but Paul reassured her: "If that happens I'm sure some good man will come along that'll help you."[78] Impressed by the mammoth petition, Woodrow Wilson told Field that as a Democratic president he was bound to honor the party's commitment to states' rights (and thus its opposition to a federal amendment), but as an individual he was going to vote for suffrage in his home state of New Jersey.[79] In 1916, Martin became the president of the new National Woman's Party (NWP), the CU's successor, and she coordinated the anti–Woodrow Wilson campaign in the fall election.[80] Subsequently she tried to run for national office, but unlike Rankin she was unsuccessful.

The energy and militance of the NWP attracted other western suffrage veterans, including Maud Younger, journalist Vivian Peirce, Elizabeth (Mrs. Congressman William) Kent, and Sara Bard Field, who explained, "A new sort of woman it took . . . a militant type, unemotional and logical and yet fired by a desire for justice."[81] There were conflicts over Alice Paul's absolute control of the NWP, however, leading to the formation of a National Advisory Board (including Phoebe Hearst, Charlotte Gilman, Florence Kelley, Harriot Stanton Blatch, and Helen Keller). Charlotte Whitney soon resigned, protesting that the CU "is an autocratic organization with its controls entirely in the hands of one woman."[82] Martin fit in because she shared this authoritarian attitude as well as the group's single-minded dedication to the federal suffrage amendment.[83]

Disagreement persists about the impact of the NWP, but Catt and the NAWSA seemed sensible and moderate in contrast. In 1916, Catt changed her strategy, and introduced her "Winning Plan," which prioritized the federal amendment drive while supporting key state campaigns. Catt and Paul were both autocratic organizational geniuses, and both deserve credit for the final victory. After 1916, they caught national politicians between the right and left flanks of the suffrage movement, and with the help of western women voters finally forced the passage of the Nineteenth Amendment to the United States Constitution in 1919 and its ratification in 1920.

Reviewing the record in 1916, Catt counted 480 state legislative campaigns, 277 efforts to get endorsements from state party conventions, and 30 national appeals, 19 congressional campaigns, and 41 state referenda, ultimately resulting in 9 western victories.[84] Some analysts have considered this a dismal success rate, indicative of suffragist ineptitude and female apathy, but it is actually remarkable that so many people remained committed and mobilized for so long despite major obstacles and terrible disappointments. In the East, the NAWSA was indeed in "the doldrums" between 1896 and 1910, but in the West this was a period of reorganization and growth as woman suffrage became an important component of the Progressive reform movement. Hard lessons learned in early campaigns clarified the importance of party politics and working-class support, leading to the development of new methods and organizational initiatives.

Thus, reevaluation of this movement within its contemporary political context finally explains why the earliest successes occurred in the western states and territories. In a fluid political environment, Western suffragists developed effective political means to obtain an essentially political goal—the radical demand for full and autonomous female citizenship—linked to broader reform programs. In the 1870s and 1880s, "pioneer" suffragists were often controversial freethinkers who preferred politics to housekeeping, "municipal" or otherwise, and they joined a variety of labor and reform organizations long before they could vote. As skilled lobbyists, western suffragists took advantage of the small size of territorial legislatures, the statehood process, third-party challenges, and reform politics to advance their cause. They achieved better laws for women and some partial suffrage measures, usually school or municipal suffrage.

The limited victories of the 1890s confirmed the disruptive potential of reform politics, encouraging suffragists to continue their support for progressive candidates and reform causes. By the 1910s, woman suffrage was an integral part of the Progressive agenda and woman suffragists described themselves as "politicians" without apology. Realizing that they would have to persuade critical swing groups of urban working-class voters, suffragists struggled to repress elitist, nativist, and racist prejudices and to temper their social control impulses with basic arguments that linked political rights and economic justice for women of all classes. By the early 1900s, a younger generation of suffragists included many college-educated and professional women, who helped bridge the class gap through their connections to social work, reform politics, and the labor movement. In addition, growing numbers of working-class suffragists were usually experienced trade unionists, well acquainted with direct action tactics. They frequently disagreed with middle-class suffragists and had their own ideas about what to do with the vote, but the basic demand for equal justice allowed them to cooperate in loose, tense, but effective coalitions.

In conclusion, the western contribution to the national suffrage movement was of crucial significance, but it has been—and continues to be—obscured by several factors. Most importantly, the conservative NAWSA leadership, particularly Carrie Catt, resisted radicalism and militance, and routinely underemphasized or denied working-class and socialist support even though they were well aware of its importance. For example, Catt was a consummate politician who knew from extensive data collection that these folks were key to victory in New York in 1917, but she explicitly denied this fact in order to promote suffrage respectability at a time of war and anti-radical backlash. Subsequently, historians have relied upon the celebratory and biased accounts of these participants and uncritically accepted this perspective. Recent voting studies consistently demonstrate no correlation between support for suffrage and nativity or literacy, while third-party political activity is a positive correlate. Temperance and prohibition advocacy also correlates strongly with support for woman suffrage. This aspect has often dominated discussions of the movement, yet many modern suffragists explicitly rejected this connection.[85]

Another factor that has contributed to the underestimation of western influence is the shift in public attention from the states to the federal amendment campaign by the mid-1910s, largely stimulated by the activities of the Congressional Union. A good deal of work remains to be done to determine the influence exerted by western women voters on their national representatives, but it is clear that these were the politicians who propelled the amendment through Congress. Nor do we fully understand the effects of western campaign experience upon the eastern suffrage leadership. Women like Carrie Catt—and even Susan B. Anthony to some extent—"earned their spurs" during western campaigns, but there has been no systematic examination of their reactions to these experiences, the lessons they learned, or how they incorporated or adapted these insights to subsequent campaigns. Furthermore, the tensions between eastern and western activists are very evident in the western campaigns, but their internal effects on suffragist cooperation within the movement remain largely unexplored.

Finally, a proper understanding of the western woman suffrage successes will mandate a substantive reanalysis of the long-standing historical question of what women did with the vote after it was won. Previous scholars have concluded that the consequences were minimal for either politics or public policy, but those studies concentrate on the national effects of female enfranchisement, which occurred at the beginning of the very conservative decade of the 1920s. Refocusing on female political activity on the state level during the Progressive movement of the 1910s leads to completely different conclusions. Equal suffrage in the West was both cause and effect of Progressivism and heavily responsible for the avalanche of reform legislation passed during this period.

Very recent research has begun to explore the diversity and efficacy of women's political activity in several different areas: voting behavior, legislative advocacy, participation within political parties, and candidacy for office. Preliminary analysis suggests that approximately 40 to 50 percent of women registered and voted, a rate only slightly lower than that of men. Certainly a number of factors determined their choices, especially race and class allegiances, but collectively women reorganized their suffrage groups into nonpartisan civil leagues and legislative councils to coordinate numerous reform projects, especially social welfare laws to protect women and children. This process did not begin with enfranchisement, but women voters were quite effective in terms of installing sympathetic candidates and passing reform legislation. Perhaps enfranchised women were slow to reorient their nonpartisan, issue-based suffrage organizations to party politics, but in the West women voters quickly established partisan Republican, Democratic, and Populist clubs. They achieved better representation at the grassroots level, but little internal party power, especially once male politicians got over their fears of a "women's bloc." Still, those concerns aided the election of a few women to office, usually as superintendents of schools or state legislators.[86] These trends have been largely overlooked because of the dismissive influence of the dominant paradigm, but clearly the assumption that woman suffrage—or early feminism generally—was a "failure" needs to be revised.[87]

The achievement of equal suffrage for women was a long and complicated process, involving several generations and many different individuals with varying rationales and agendas. Some were idealistic and inclusive, others were opportunistic, many were frankly prejudiced and exclusive, and most were some combination of motives and beliefs. No single factor explains the phenomenon completely, but reintegrating the elements of the western suffrage movement that have been previously neglected, dismissed, or otherwise underanalyzed provides many new insights. Despite tensions and conflicts, the collective achievement of suffragists was a fundamental structural political reform that permanently changed the composition of the polity and the legal status of women. After many long, hard struggles, this was a tremendous accomplishment.

Notes

NOTES TO CHAPTER I

1. "The Uncivilized East," *The Reply* 1 (June 1913), 32, as cited by Billie Barnes Jensen, "'In the Weird and Wooly West': Anti-Suffrage Women, Gender Issues, and Woman Suffrage in the West," *Journal of the West* 33 (July 1993), 50.

2. See the numerous articles by Thomas A. Larson, including "Dolls, Vassals, and Drudges: Pioneer Women in the West," *Western Historical Quarterly* 3 (Jan. 1972), 5–16, and "Woman Suffrage in Western America," *Utah Historical Quarterly* 38 (Winter 1970), 7–19; Beverly Beeton, *Women Vote in the West: The Woman Suffrage Movement, 1869–1896* (New York: Garland, 1986), and Beeton, "How the West Was Won for Woman Suffrage," in Marjorie Spruill Wheeler, ed., *One Woman, One Vote: Rediscovering the Woman Suffrage Movement* (Troutdale, OR: New Sage Press, 1995), 99–116; Alan P. Grimes, *The Puritan Ethic and Woman Suffrage* (New York: Oxford University Press, 1967); Sandra L. Myres, "Suffering for Suffrage: Western Women and the Struggle for Political, Legal, and Economic Rights," in Myres, *Westering Women and the Frontier Experience, 1800–1915* (Albuquerque: University of New Mexico Press, 1982), 213–236; Rebecca Edwards, "Pioneers at the Polls: Woman Suffrage in the West," in Jean H. Baker, ed., *Votes for Women* (New York: Oxford University Press, 2002), 151–174.

3. Paula Baker, "The Domestication of Politics: Women and American Political Society, 1780–1920," *American Historical Review* 89 (June 1984), 620–647; Michael McGerr, "Political Style and Women's Power, 1830–1930," *Journal of American History* 77 (1990), 864–885; and Rebecca Edwards, *Angels in the Machinery: Gender in American Party Politics from the Civil War to the Progressive Era* (New York: Oxford University Press, 1997).

4. Karen J. Blair, *The Clubwoman as Feminist: True Womanhood Redefined, 1868–1914* (New York: Holmes and Meier, 1980); J. C. Croly, *The History of the Women's Club Movement in America* (New York: Henry B. Allen, 1898).

5. Ellen Carol DuBois, "The Radicalism of the Woman Suffrage Movement: Notes toward the Reconstruction of Nineteenth-Century Feminism," in DuBois,

Woman Suffrage and Women's Rights (New York: New York University Press, 1988), 30–42.

6. *San Francisco Call,* 10 May 1896.

7. Norma Basch, "Invisible Women: The Legal Fiction of Marital Unity in Nineteenth-Century America," *Feminist Studies* 5 (Summer 1979), 346–366; Carol Pateman, *The Sexual Contract* (Stanford, CA: Stanford University Press), 1988; Mari J. Matsuda, "The West and the Legal Status of Women: Explanations of Frontier Feminism," *Journal of the West* 14 (Jan. 1985), 47–56; Donna Schuele, "'A Robbery to the Wife': Culture, Gender and Marital Property in California Law and Politics, 1850–1890" (Ph.D. diss., University of California, Berkeley, 1999), and Schuele, "Community Property Law and the Politics of Married Women's Rights in Nineteenth-Century California," *Western Legal History* 7:2 (Summer 1994), 245–281; B. Zorina Kahn, "Married Women's Property Laws and Female Commercial Activity: Evidence from United States Patent Records, 1790–1895," *Journal of Economic History* 56 (June 1996), 360–365. See also Carole Shammas, "Re-assessing the Married Women's Property Acts," *Journal of Women's History* 6 (Spring 1994), 9–30; and Amy Dru Stanley, "Conjugal Bonds and Wage Labor: Rights of Contract in the Age of Emancipation," *Journal of American History* 75 (Sept. 1988), 471–500.

8. See Grimes, *The Puritan Ethic and Woman Suffrage,* and the numerous articles by T. A. Larson.

9. See Beeton, *Women Vote in the West.*

10. Aileen S. Kraditor, *The Ideas of the Woman Suffrage Movement, 1890–1920* (New York: W. W. Norton, 1981).

11. Similar points have been made by Nancy Cott, *The Grounding of Modern Feminism* (New Haven: Yale University Press, 1987), 29–30; Suzanne M. Marilley, *Woman Suffrage and the Origins of Liberal Feminism in the United States, 1820–1920* (Cambridge, MA: Harvard University Press, 1996), 1–2; and Sara Hunter Graham, *Woman Suffrage and the New Democracy* (New Haven: Yale University Press, 1996), 30fn–31.

12. *Webster's Ninth New Collegiate Dictionary* (New York, 1991), 436.

13. Quintard Taylor, *In Search of the Racial Frontier: African Americans in the American West, 1528–1990* (New York: W. W. Norton, 1998); William Loren Katz, *The Black West* (Garden City, NY: Doubleday, 1971).

14. Gail H. Landsman, "The 'Other' as Political Symbol: Images of Indians in the Woman Suffrage Movement," *Ethnohistory* 39:3 (Summer 1992), 247–284; and Wendy Wall, "Gender and the 'Citizen Indian,'" in Elizabeth Jameson and Susan Armitage, eds., *Writing the Range: Race, Class, and Culture in the Women's West* (Norman: University of Oklahoma Press, 1997), 202–229, and Margaret D. Jacobs, "Resistance to Rescue: The Indians of Bahapki and Mrs. Annie E. K. Bidwell," in Jameson and Armitage, eds., *Writing the Range,* 230–251.

15. Leonard Pitt, *The Decline of the Californios: A Social History of the*

Spanish-Speaking Californians, 1846–1890 (Berkeley: University of California Press, 1966); Tómas Almaguer, *Racial Fault Lines: The Historical Origins of White Supremacy in California* (Berkeley: University of California Press, 1994).

16. Alexander Saxton, *The Indispensable Enemy: Labor and the Anti-Chinese Movement in California* (Berkeley: University of California Press, 1971); Roger Daniels, *Asian America: History of Chinese and Japanese in the United States since 1850* (Seattle: University of Washington Press, 1988); Lucy E. Salyer, *Laws Harsh as Tigers: Chinese Immigrants and the Shaping of Modern Immigration Law* (Chapel Hill: University of North Carolina Press, 1995); Sucheng Chan, "The Exclusion of Chinese Women, 1870–1943," in Nancy F. Cott and Elizabeth H. Pleck, eds., *A Heritage of Her Own: Toward a New Social History of American Women* (New York: Simon and Schuster, 1979), 75–125, and Chan, ed., *Entry Denied: Exclusion and the Chinese Community in America, 1882–1943* (Philadelphia: Temple University Press, 1991).

17. Pierre van den Berghe, *Race and Ethnicity* (New York: Basic Books, 1970), and *The Ethnic Phenomenon* (New York: Elsevier Scientific, 1981).

18. George Stocking, *Victorian Anthropology* (New York: Free Press, 1987); Richard Hofstader, *Social Darwinism in American Thought,* rev. ed. (New York: George Braziller, 1959); and many others.

19. Gail Bederman, *Manliness and Civilization: A Cultural History of Gender and Race in the United States, 1880–1917* (Chicago and London: University of Chicago Press, 1995); Louise Michele Newman, *White Women's Rights: The Racial Origins of Feminism in the United States* (New York and Oxford: Oxford University Press, 1999), 132–157; Nancy Leys Stepan, "Race, Gender, Science and Citizenship," *Gender and History* 10 (April 1998), 26–52; Jane Rendall, "Citizenship, Culture and Civilisation: The Languages of British Suffragists, 1866–1874," in Caroline Daley and Melanie Nolan, eds., *Suffrage and Beyond: International Feminist Perspectives* (New York: New York University Press, 1994), 127–150.

20. Tessie Liu, "Teaching the Differences among Women from a Historical Perspective: Rethinking Race and Gender as Social Categories," in Vicki L. Ruiz and Ellen Carol DuBois, eds., *Unequal Sisters: A Multicultural Reader in U.S. Women's History,* 2d ed. (New York: Routledge, 1994), 571–583; Sarah Deutsch, "Landscape of Enclaves: Race Relations in the West, 1865–1990," in William Cronon, George Miles, and Jay Gitlin, eds., *Under an Open Sky: Rethinking America's Western Past* (New York: W. W. Norton, 1992), 110–131; Nancy F. Cott, "Marriage and Women's Citizenship in the United States, 1830–1934," *American Historical Review* 103 (Dec. 1998), 1440–1474; and Peggy Pascoe, "Miscegenation Law, Court Cases, and Ideologies of 'Race' in Twentieth-Century America," *Journal of American History* 83 (June 1996), 44–69. See also Linda K. Kerber, "The Meanings of Citizenship," *Journal of American History* 84 (Dec. 1997), 833–854, and Kerber, *No Constitutional*

Right to Be Ladies: Women and the Obligations of Citizenship (New York: Hill and Wang, 1998); Candice Lewis Bredbenner, *A Nationality of Her Own: Women, Marriage, and the Law of Citizenship* (Berkeley: University of California Press, 1998).

21. Marjorie Spruill Wheeler, *New Women of the New South: The Leaders of the Woman Suffrage Movement in the Southern States* (New York: Oxford University Press, 1993); and Elna C. Green, *Southern Strategies: Southern Women and the Woman Suffrage Question* (Chapel Hill: University of North Carolina Press, 1997).

22. W. E. B. Du Bois, in the *Crisis* (Nov. 1917), as cited by Rosalyn M. Terborg-Penn, "Afro-Americans in the Struggle for Woman Suffrage" (Ph.D. diss., Howard University, 1977), 270; see also Terborg-Penn, *African American Women in the Struggle for the Vote, 1850–1920* (Bloomington: Indiana University Press, 1998).

23. National Association of Colored Women's Clubs (NACWC), *A History of the Club Movement among the Colored Women of the United States of America* (Washington, DC: NACWA, 1902), 83; Lawrence B. deGraaf, "Race, Sex, and Region: Black Women in the American West, 1850–1920," *Pacific Historical Review* 49 (May 1980): 309–311; Susan H. Armitage and Deborah Gallacci Wilbert, "Black Women in the Pacific Northwest: A Survey and Research Prospectus," in Karen J. Blair, ed., *Women in the Pacific Northwest,* 136–145; Ann D. Gordon, ed., *African American Women and the Vote, 1837–1965* (Amherst: University of Massachusetts Press, 1997); Terborg-Penn, *African American Women,* 54–106; Bettina Aptheker, *Woman's Legacy: Essays on Race, Sex, and Class in American History* (Amherst: University of Massachusetts Press, 1982), 63–66.

24. Delilah L. Beasley, *The Negro Trailblazers of California* (1919; reprint, San Francisco: R and E Associates, 1969), 232–235; Lynda F. Dickson, "Lifting as We Climb: African American Women's Clubs of Denver, 1880–1925," in Elizabeth Jameson and Susan Armitage, eds., *Writing the Range: Race, Class, and Culture in the Women's West* (Norman: University of Oklahoma Press, 1997), 372–392; Rosalyn Terborg-Penn, "Naomi Bowman Talbert Anderson," in *Black Women Encyclopedia,* 33–34. In his recent study, Quintard Taylor overlooks these activists, even though he mentions Anderson: "Much like African American political leaders in the rest of the nation, black westerners ought to have the right to vote for black men. Apparently few black western women called for suffrage to be extended to them, and there is little evidence they were active in either black male campaigns or in woman suffrage efforts led by white women." See Taylor, *In Search of the Racial Frontier,* 121fn.

25. Mary Blewett, *We Will Rise in Our Might: Workingwomen's Voices from Nineteenth-Century New England* (Ithaca, NY: Cornell University Press, 1991), 39; Ardis Cameron, *Radicals of the Worst Sort: Laboring Women in Lawrence,*

Massachusetts, 1860–1912 (Urbana: University of Illinois Press, 1993); Christine Stansell, *City of Women: Sex and Class in New York, 1789–1860* (Urbana: University of Illinois Press, 1982).

26. Ellen Carol DuBois, *Feminism and Suffrage: The Emergence of an Independent Women's Movement in America, 1848–1869* (Ithaca, NY: Cornell University Press, 1978), 110–161.

27. Ellen Carol DuBois, *Harriot Stanton Blatch and the Winning of Woman Suffrage* (New Haven: Yale University Press, 1997), and Sharon Hartman Strom, "Leadership and Tactics in the American Woman Suffrage Movement: A New Perspective from Massachusetts," *Journal of American History* 62:2 (Sept. 1975), 296–315; Elinor Lerner, "Immigrant and Working Class Involvement in the New York City Woman Suffrage Movement, 1905–1917: A Study in Progressive Era Politics" (Ph.D. diss., University of California, Berkeley, 1981).

28. Michael Kazin, *Barons of Labor: The San Francisco Building Trades and Union Power in the Progressive Era* (Urbana: University of Illinois Press, 1987); Janice L. Reiff, "Urbanization and the Social Structure: Seattle, Washington, 1852–1910 (Ph.D. diss., University of Washington, 1981); and Carolyn J. Stefanco, "Pathways to Power: Women and Voluntary Associations in Denver, Colorado, 1876–1893" (Ph.D. diss., Duke University, 1987).

29. For examples, see *HWS* 4:334, 446, 448; *HWS* 5:206, 249, 281.

30. Carlos A. Schwantes, "Protest in a Promised Land: Unemployment, Disinheritance, and the Origin of Labor Militancy in the Pacific Northwest, 1885–1886," *Western Historical Quarterly* 13 (1982), 373–390; Schwantes, *Radical Heritage: Labor, Socialism and Reform in Washington and British Columbia, 1885–1917* (Seattle: University of Washington Press, 1979); and Melvin Dubofsky, "The Origins of Western Working Class Radicalism, 1890–1905," *Labor History* 7 (Spring 1966), 131–154.

31. William Issel and Robert Cherny, *San Francisco, 1865–1932: Politics, Power, and Urban Development* (Berkeley: University of California Press, 1986); R. A. Burchell, *The San Francisco Irish, 1848–1880* (Berkeley: University of California Press, 1980); David T. Brundage, *The Making of Western Labor Radicalism: Denver's Organized Workers, 1878–1905* (Urbana: University of Illinois Press, 1994); and David M. Emmons, *The Butte Irish: Class and Ethnicity in an American Mining Town, 1875–1925* (Urbana: University of Illinois Press, 1989).

32. Susan Levine, *Labor's True Woman: Carpet Weavers, Industrialization, and Labor Reform in the Gilded Age* (Philadelphia: Temple University Press, 1984); and Levine, "Labor's True Woman: Domesticity and Equal Rights in the Knights of Labor," *Journal of American History* 70 (Sept. 1983), 323–339.

33. *HWS* 4:334.

34. Mari Jo Buhle, *Women and American Socialism, 1870–1920* (Urbana: University of Illinois Press, 1981), 27, 54–56, 214–245. As in the trade unions, organizational support was usually the result of internal agitation and pressure

by women members; see Sherry J. Katz, "A Politics of Coalition: Socialist Women and the California Suffrage Movement," in Wheeler, ed., *One Woman, One Vote*, 245–262, and Katz, "Dual Commitments: Feminism, Socialism, and Women's Political Activism in California, 1890–1920" (Ph.D. diss., University of California, Los Angeles, 1991), 241–362 (book forthcoming). Katz supports Buhle's conclusion that native-born Socialists tended to be more supportive of women's rights than foreign-born members.

35. *HWS* 5:301.

36. On Populism generally, see Lawrence Goodwyn, *Democratic Promise: The Populist Moment in America* (New York: Oxford University Press, 1976); Peter H. Argersinger, *The Limits of Agrarian Radicalism: Western Populism and American Politics* (Lawrence: University Press of Kansas, 1995); Michael Kazin, *The Populist Persuasion: An American History* (New York: Basic Books, 1995); R. Hal Williams, *Years of Decision* (New York: John Wiley and Sons, 1978), 97–127; James Turner, "Understanding the Populists," *Journal of American History* 67 (Sept. 1980), 354–373; John D. Hicks, *The Populist Revolt: A History of the Farmers' Alliance and the People's Party* (Minneapolis: University of Minnesota Press, 1931); and Richard Hofstadter, *The Age of Reform: From Bryan to F.D.R.* (New York: Vintage Books, 1955).

37. On western Populism, see David Burke Griffiths, "Populism in the Far West, 1890–1900" (Ph.D. diss., University of Washington, 1967); James Edward Wright, *The Politics of Populism: Dissent in Colorado* (New Haven and London: Yale University Press, 1974); Robert W. Larson, "Populism in the Mountain West: A Mainstream Movement," *Western Historical Quarterly* 13 (April 1982), 143–164, and *Populism in the Mountain West* (Albuquerque: University of New Mexico Press, 1986); Michael Rogin, "California Populism and the 'System of 1896,'" *Western Political Quarterly* 22 (March 1969), 179–196; Donald Edgar Walters, "Populism in California, 1889–1900" (Ph.D. diss., University of California, Berkeley, 1952); Harold F. Taggart, "California and the Silver Question in 1895," *Pacific Historical Review* 6:3 (Sept. 1937), 249–269; R. Hal Williams, *The Democratic Party and California Politics, 1880–1896* (Stanford, CA: Stanford University Press, 1973).

38. Maryjo Wagner, "Farms, Families, and Reform: Women in the Farmers' Alliance and Populist Party" (Ph.D. diss., University of Oregon, 1986); Marilyn P. Watkins, *Rural Democracy: Family Farmers and Politics in Western Washington, 1890–1925* (Ithaca, NY: Cornell University Press, 1995); Julie Roy Jeffrey, "Women in the Southern Farmers' Alliance: A Reconsideration of the Role and Status of Women in the Late Nineteenth-Century South," *Feminist Studies* 3 (Fall 1975), 72–91; Michael Lewis Goldberg, *An Army of Women: Gender and Politics in Gilded Age Kansas* (Baltimore: Johns Hopkins University Press, 1997), 130–131, 168–169, 252, and Goldberg, "Non-Partisan and All-Partisan: Rethinking Woman Suffrage and Party Politics in Gilded Age Kansas," *Western*

Historical Quarterly 25 (Spring 1994), 21–44. See also Edwards, *Angels in the Machinery*, 91–110.

39. Wagner, "Farms, Families, and Reform," 221, 227–229, 254–264; Goldberg, *Army of Women*, 191–192.

40. Davis Waite and Lorenzo Crounse, "Woman Suffrage in Practice," *North American Review* 158 (June 1894), 737–744; John R. Morris, "The Women and Governor Waite," *Colorado Magazine* 44 (Winter 1967), 11–19; David B. Griffiths, "Far Western Populist Thought: A Comparative Study of John R. Rogers and Davis H. Waite," *Pacific Northwest Quarterly* 60 (Oct. 1969), 183–192.

41. Jill Liddington and Jill Norris, *One Hand Tied behind Us: The Rise of the Women's Suffrage Movement* (London: Rivers Oram Press, 2000); Sandra Stanley Holton, *Feminism and Democracy: Women's Suffrage and Reform Politics in Britain, 1900–1918* (Cambridge, UK, and New York: Cambridge University Press, 1986).

42. Ellen Carol DuBois, "Woman Suffrage and the Left: An International Socialist-Feminist Perspective," in DuBois, ed., *Woman Suffrage and Women's Rights*, 252–282.

43. Lerner, "Immigrant and Working Class Involvement," 6–7, 82–85; Ellen Carol DuBois, *Harriot Stanton Blatch*, 94–120, 135–136, 158–160; Sharon Hartman Strom, *Political Woman: Florence Luscomb and the Legacy of Radical Reform* (Philadelphia: Temple University Press, 2001), 61–92, and "Leadership and Tactics," 303–304; Susan Englander, *Class Coalition and Class Conflict in the California Woman Suffrage Movement, 1907–1912: The San Francisco Wage Earners' Suffrage League* (Lewiston, NY: Mellen Research University Press, 1992); *New York Times*, 23 April 1912.

44. Lerner, "Immigrant and Working Class Involvement," 10–12, 85–89, 139–173. On Catt, see Robert Booth Fowler, "Carrie Chapman Catt, Strategist," in Marjorie Spruill Wheeler, *One Woman, One Vote: Rediscovering the Woman Suffrage Movement* (Troutdale, OR: New Sage Press, 1995), 295–314; and Sara Hunter Graham, "The Suffrage Renaissance: A New Image for a New Century, 1896–1910," in Wheeler, ed., *One Woman, One Vote*, 162–167.

45. Caroline Daley and Melanie Nolan, eds., *Suffrage and Beyond: International Feminist Perspectives* (New York: New York University Press, 1994); Patricia Grimshaw, "Settler Anxieties, Indigenous Peoples, and Women's Suffrage in the Colonies of Australia, New Zealand, and Hawai'i, 1888–1902," *Pacific Historical Review* 69:4 (Nov. 2000), 553–572; Patricia Grimshaw and Katherine Ellinghaus, "White Women, Aboriginal Women and the Vote in Western Australia," *Studies in Western Australian History* 19 (1999), 1–19; Audrey Oldfield, *Woman Suffrage in Australia: A Gift or a Struggle?* (Cambridge, UK: Cambridge University Press, 1992), 46–65.

46. Patricia Grimshaw, "Women's Suffrage in New Zealand Revisited: Writing from the Margins," in Caroline Daley and Melanie Nolan, eds., *Suffrage and*

Beyond: International Feminist Perspectives (New York: New York University Press, 1994), 25–41; and Grimshaw, "Settler Anxieties," 553–572.

47. Patricia Grimshaw and Katherine Ellinghaus, "White Women," 1–19; Oldfield, *Woman Suffrage in Australia,* 112–126.

48. Grimshaw and Ellinghaus, "White Women," 12–16.

49. Allison Sneider, "Reconstruction, Expansion, and Empire: The U.S. Woman Suffrage Movement and the Re-Making of National Political Community, 1870–1900" (Ph.D. diss., University of California, Los Angeles, 1999); and Sneider, "Woman Suffrage in Congress: American Expansion and the Politics of Federalism, 1870–1890," in Baker, ed., *Votes for Women,* 170–193.

NOTES TO CHAPTER 2

1. *Queen Bee,* 12 Sept. 1888.

2. For the concept of organic intellectuals, see Antonio Gramsci, "The Intellectuals," in Quintin Hoare and Geoffrey Nowell Smith, eds., *Selections from the Prison Notebooks of Antonio Gramsci* (New York: International Publishers, 1989), 3–23.

3. Jürgen Habermas, "Social Action, Purposive Activity, and Communication," in William Outhwaite, ed., *The Habermas Reader* (Cambridge, UK: Polity Press, 1996), 160–169; Mary Ryan, "Gender and Public Access: Women's Politics in Nineteenth-Century America," in Craig Calhoun, ed., *Habermas and the Public Sphere* (Cambridge, MA: MIT Press, 1996), 259–288.

4. On western women generally, see the special theme issues of *Frontiers* 7 (1984), and *Pacific Historical Review* 61 (Nov. 1992); Sandra L. Myres, *Westering Women and the Frontier Experience, 1800–1915* (Albuquerque: University of New Mexico Press, 1982); Susan Armitage and Elizabeth Jameson, eds. *The Women's West* (Norman: University of Oklahoma Pres, 1987); Joan M. Jensen and Darlis A. Miller, "The Gentle Tamers Revisited: New Approaches to the History of Women in the American West," *Pacific Historical Review* 49 (May 1980), 173–213.

5. Frederick Jackson Turner, *The Frontier in American History* (New York: Holt, Rinehart, and Winston, 1920); and Patricia Nelson Limerick, *Legacy of Conquest: The Unbroken Past of the American West* (New York: W. W. Norton, 1988). The literature on this famous thesis is vast.

6. Mary Lou Locke, "Out of the Shadows and into the Western Sun: Working Women of the Late Nineteenth Century Urban Far West," *Journal of Urban History* 16:2 (Feb. 1990), 175–204; Michael Bargo, "Women's Occupations in the West in 1870," *Journal of the West* 32 (Jan. 1993), 30–45.

7. Helen L. Sumner (Woodbury), *Equal Suffrage: The Results of an Investigation in Colorado Made for the Collegiate Equal Suffrage League of New York State* (1909; reprint, New York: Arno Press, 1972), 135.

8. Sherilyn Cox Bennion, *Equal to the Occasion: Women Editors of the Nineteenth-Century West* (Reno and Las Vegas: University of Nevada Press, 1990); Roger Levenson, *Women in Printing: Northern California, 1857–1890* (Santa Barbara, CA: Capra Press, 1994); Nan Yamane, "Women, Power, and the Press: The Case of San Francisco, 1868 to 1896" (Ph.D. diss., University of California, Los Angeles, 1995); Martha M. Solomon, *A Voice of Their Own: The Woman Suffrage Press, 1840–1910* (Tuscaloosa and London: University of Alabama Press, 1991); Ruth Barnes Moynihan, *Rebel for Rights: Abigail Scott Duniway* (New Haven and London: Yale University Press, 1983).

9. *HWS* 3:750–751, 764–765.

10. On Gordon, see *HWS* 3:751–753; Robert McHenry, *Famous American Women* (New York: Dover, 1980), 162–163; "Laura DeForce Gordon," *National Cyclopedia of American Biography*, 235–236; *Woman's Tribune*, 25 May 1907.

11. *San Francisco Examiner*, 19 Feb. 1868; Reda Davis, *Woman's Republic: The Life of Marietta Stow, Cooperator* (n.p.: Pt. Pinos Editions, 1980), 203.

12. Draft Gordon biography, John M. Winterbotham Collection, Wisconsin Historical Society, as cited by Ann Braude, *Radical Spirits: Spiritualism and Women's Rights in Nineteenth-Century America* (Boston: Beacon Press, 1989), 195.

13. Braude, *Radical Spirits*, 193–195; Robert J. Chandler, "In the Van: Spiritualists as Catalysts for the California Women's Suffrage Movement," *California History* 73 (Fall 1994), 189–201; Sandra Sizer Frankiel, *California's Spiritual Frontiers* (Berkeley: University of California Press, 1988); Davis, *Woman's Republic*, 93; Levenson, *Women in Printing*, 137–149.

14. Levenson, *Women in Printing*, 53–68.

15. *Revolution*, 10 Sept. 1868; Lillian Ruth Matthews, *Women in Trade Unions in San Francisco*, University of California Publications in Economics, vol. 3 (Berkeley: University of California Press, 1913), 10, 13–14, 57–58; Levenson, *Women in Printing*, 75–88, 116–124.

16. Bennion, *Equal to the Occasion*, 57–62; Davis, *Woman's Republic*, 91–92.

17. On Smith, see Donald Edgar Walters, "Populism in California, 1889–1900" (Ph.D. diss., University of California, Berkeley, 1952), 18–44; Sherry Jeanne Katz, "Dual Commitments: Feminism, Socialism, and Women's Political Activism in California, 1890–1920" (Ph.D. diss., University of California, Los Angeles, 1991), 47–48, 50–53; Alexander Saxton, *The Indispensable Enemy: Labor and the Anti-Chinese Movement in California* (Berkeley: University of California Press, 1971), 144–146.

18. On Kennedy, see Davis, *Woman's Republic*, 130–134; Yamane, "Women, Power, and the Press," 42–43.

19. Susan B. Anthony to Laura Gordon, 17 Nov. 1876, Gordon Collection, Bancroft Library, University of California, Berkeley (hereafter cited as BL).

20. *San Francisco Alta,* 2 Nov. 1869; *HWS* 3:752.

21. Elizabeth T. Schenck to Gordon (?), 20 July 1871, Georgiana Bruce Kirby (Santa Cruz) to Gordon, [n.d.], Gordon Collection, BL; *San Francisco Alta,* 23 Nov. 1869; Davis, *Woman's Republic,* 164–194; Bennion, *Equal to the Occasion,* 98–104; Levenson, *Women in Printing,* 150–157; Schuele, "Community Property Law," 277–280.

Stow killed the paper in 1884 when she rededicated it to suffrage and to Belva Lockwood's presidential candidacy. As the "Equal Rights Party of the Pacific Slope," Stow nominated various women for president without permission. Her first choice, Abigail Duniway, furiously insisted that her name be withdrawn. Her second, attorney Clara Foltz, refused the honor, but suggested Lockwood, a Washington, D.C., lawyer who had been associated with Victoria Woodhull's 1872 campaign. Stow and Foltz sent Lockwood a telegram notifying Lockwood of her "nomination," then published the news before receiving her reply. Whatever she thought initially, Lockwood decided it would be a good educational opportunity, so she accepted the challenge, published an extensive platform, and actively campaigned in the East. She won a few votes in 1884, and tried again in 1888, but the novelty was gone, and national suffrage leaders repudiated her candidacy.

22. *San Francisco Alta,* 30 Jan. 1870; *San Francisco Chronicle,* 20–30 Jan., 11 March 1870; *HWS* 3:753–754; Emily Pitts-Stevens to Gordon, 30 Jan. 1871; Laura Gordon to Mrs. Ames, Feb. 1870, Gordon Collection, BL.

23. Ellen Sargent to Gordon, 25 Jan. 1871 (?), Gordon Collection, BL; *San Francisco Alta,* 17–20 May 1871.

24. *San Francisco Call,* 14 Feb. 1872; *San Francisco Chronicle,* 14 Jan. 1872; Donald Waller Rodes, "The California Woman Suffrage Campaign of 1911" (M.A. thesis, California State University, Hayward, 1974), 5.

25. *San Francisco Alta,* 14 Feb., 19 June 1872; *San Francisco Chronicle,* 22 June 1872; *San Francisco Call,* 25 June 1872.

26. *San Francisco Chronicle,* 11, 27 April 1873, and "To the Public," *Pioneer,* 8 May 1873.

27. San Francisco *Alta,* 9 April, 7 May 1873; Davis, *Woman's Republic,* 92; Levenson, *Women in Printing,* 101–113; Sherilyn Cox Bennion, "THE PIONEER: The First Voice for Women's Suffrage in the West," *Pacific Historian* 25:4 (Winter 1981), 15–21.

28. Sarah Wallis to Gordon, 25 June, 22 Oct. 1871, Gordon Collection, BL; Davis, *Woman's Republic,* 203–204; Schuele, "Community Property Law," 276.

29. *HWS* 3:765–766.

30. Alida Avery to Gordon, 11 July 1876, 26 March 1877, Sarah Knox-Goodrich to Gordon, n.d., Gordon Collection, BL.

31. *Stockton Daily Evening Leader,* 25 Jan., 2 Feb. 1876; Gordon to her parents, 19 Jan. 1877, Gordon to Laura (?), 16 Feb. 1877, Gordon Collection, BL.

The successful newspaperwoman in the family was Laura's sister, Gertie DeForce Cluff, who published the *Lodi Valley Review.*

32. Davis, *Woman's Republic,* 205.

33. *HWS* 3:758–761; Foltz to Gordon, 2 May, 20 Nov. 1878, Gordon Collection, BL. On Foltz, see Barbara Allen Babcock, "Clara Shortridge Foltz: Constitution-Maker," *Indiana Law Journal* 66:4 (Fall 1991), 849–940; and Babcock, "Clara Shortridge Foltz: 'First Woman,'" *Arizona Law Review* 30 (1988), 686–695.

34. *Woman's Tribune,* 25 May 1907.

35. On Foltz, see Davis, *California Women: A Guide to Their Politics, 1885–1911* (San Francisco: California Scene, 1967), 151–152; McHenry, *Notable American Women,* 136–137; as well as Babcock, "Clara Shortridge Foltz"; and *Woman's Journal,* 31 Dec. 1892.

36. *Woman's Tribune,* 27 April, 25 May 1907; *San Francisco Examiner,* 7 April 1907.

37. Ruth Barnes Moynihan, *Rebel for Rights: Abigail Scott Duniway* (New Haven and London: Yale University Press, 1983), 84–89; *HWS* 3:768–769.

38. Moynihan, *Rebel for Rights,* 90; *New Northwest,* 28 May 1875.

39. *New Northwest,* 8, 29 Oct. 1885; Moynihan, *Rebel for Rights,* 151–153.

40. *San Francisco Alta,* 12, 13, 15 July 1871.

41. *Woman's Tribune,* 22 July 1905.

42. SBA interview in *Portland Herald,* 18 Nov. 1871; G. Thomas Edwards, *Sowing Good Seeds: The Northwest Suffrage Campaigns of Susan B. Anthony* (Portland: Oregon Historical Society Press, 1990); Beverly Beeton and G. Thomas Edwards, "Susan B. Anthony's Woman Suffrage Crusade in the American West," *Journal of the West* 21 (April 1982), 5–15; Moynihan, *Rebel for Rights,* 92–100; Clarence B. Bagley, *History of Seattle from the Earliest Settlement to the Present Time,* vol. 2 (Seattle: Clarke, 1916), 487–488; Ida Husted Harper, *Life and Work of Susan B. Anthony,* 2 vols. (Indianapolis and Kansas City: Bowen-Merrill, 1898), 2:387–408.

43. Harper, *Life and Work,* 2:396.

44. Abigail Scott Duniway, *Path Breaking: An Autobiographical History of the Equal Suffrage Movement in Pacific Coast States,* 2d ed. (1914; reprint, New York: Source Book Press, 1970), 46; Edwards, *Sowing Good Seeds,* 75–76, citing *Albany Democrat,* 13 Oct. 1871, *Portland Bulletin,* 14 Oct. 1871, and p. 101, citing *Washington Territorial Dispatch,* 6 Nov. 1871.

45. *HWS* 3:775; Duniway, *Path Breaking,* 84–85.

46. Duniway, *Path Breaking,* 69; *New Northwest,* 11 Dec. 1884. See also Norman H. Clark, *The Dry Years: Prohibition and Social Change in Washington* (Seattle: University of Washington Press, 1965); John E. Caswell, "The Prohibition Movement in Oregon," *Oregon Historical Quarterly, pt. 1 (1836–1904):* 39

(Sept. 1938), 235–261; *pt. 2 (1904–1915)*: 40 (March 1939), 65–82; and Bagley, *History of Seattle*, 488–489.

47. Duniway, *Path Breaking*, 52–53.

48. See, for example, Duniway to Ryan, 17 Sept. 1913, Reel 7, Carrie Chapman Catt Papers, and Duniway to Catt, 3 June 1916, Congressional Union Folder, Reel 33, both in the NAWSA Microfilm Collection; Ruth Barnes Moynihan, *Rebel for Rights*, 186.

49. Caroline N. Churchill, *Active Footsteps* (1909; reprint, New York: Arno Press, 1980), 80–81. See also Patricia Grimshaw, "Suffragists Representing Race and Gender in the American West: The Case of Colorado," in Patricia Grimshaw and Diane Kirkby, eds., *Dealing with Difference: Essays in Gender, Culture and History* (Melbourne, Australia: History Department, University of Melbourne, 1997), 79–81.

50. Churchill, *Active Footsteps*, 19.

51. Churchill, *Active Footsteps*, 20–21; *Queen Bee*, 7 Nov. 1888; *Colorado Springs Gazette*, 15 Jan. 1926.

52. *Colorado Antelope*, Feb. 1880.

53. *Queen Bee* 10 Aug. 1884.

54. *Queen Bee*, 5 Nov. 1884.

55. *Colorado Antelope*, May 1881; *Queen Bee*, 1 Sept. 1886, 25 July 1888, 12 Oct. 1892.

56. *Queen Bee*, 15 Aug., 26 Sept. 1888, 28 Aug. 1889.

57. *Queen Bee*, 5 Sept. 1888.

58. *Queen Bee*, 28 March 1883.

59. *Colorado Antelope*, Feb. 1880.

60. *Queen Bee*, 2 June 1886.

61. *Queen Bee*, 19 May 1886.

62. *Queen Bee*, 31 May 1893.

63. *Queen Bee*, 28 March, 17 Oct. 1883, 26 March 1884.

64. *Queen Bee*, 4 Feb. 1885.

65. *Queen Bee*, 16 April 1884.

66. *Queen Bee*, 22 Dec. 1886.

67. *Queen Bee*, 3 Nov. 1886, 19 Jan. 1887.

68. Carolyn J. Stefanco, "Pathways to Power: Women and Voluntary Associations in Denver, Colorado, 1876–1893 (Ph.D. diss., Duke University, 1987), 62–63; Lynda F. Dickson, "Lifting as We Climb: African American Women's Clubs of Denver, 1880–1925," in Elizabeth Jameson and Susan Armitage, eds., *Writing the Range: Race, Class, and Culture in the Women's West* (Norman: University of Oklahoma Press, 1997), 372–392.

69. *Colorado Antelope*, Feb. 1881; Churchill, *Active Footsteps*, 211.

70. Ellis Meredith, "Women Citizens of Colorado," *Great Divide* (Feb. 1894), 53.

71. Churchill, *Active Footsteps,* 210–214.

72. HWS 4:936–943; *Woman's Exponent,* 1 Sept. 1877; Sherilyn Cox Bennion, *Equal to the Occasion,* 72–83; and Bennion, "The *New Northwest* and *Woman's Exponent:* Early Voices for Suffrage," in Carol Cornwall Madsen, ed., *Battle for the Ballot: Essays on Woman Suffrage in Utah, 1870–1896* (Logan: Utah State University Press, 1997), 173–185; Joan Iverson, "The Mormon-Suffrage Relationship: Personal and Political Quandries," in Madsen, ed., *Battle for the Ballot,* 150–172.

NOTES TO CHAPTER 3

1. Cited by Ellen Carol DuBois, "Outgrowing the Compact of the Fathers: Equal Rights, Woman Suffrage, and the United States Constitution, 1820–1878," in Ellen Carol DuBois, ed., *Woman Suffrage and Women's Rights* (New York: New York University Press, 1998), 105.

2. Allison Sneider, "Reconstruction, Expansion, and Empire: The U.S. Woman Suffrage Movement and the Re-Making of National Political Community, 1870–1900" (Ph.D. diss., University of California, Los Angeles, 1999), 125; Allison Sneider, "Woman Suffrage in Congress: American Expansion and the Politics of Federalism, 1870–1890," in Jean H. Baker, ed., *Votes for Women: The Struggle for Suffrage Revisited* (New York: Oxford University Press, 2002), 77–89; Philip N. Cohen, "Nationalism and Suffrage: Gender Struggle in Nation-Building America," *Signs* 21:3 (Spring 1996), 716–718. Marjorie Spruill Wheeler's work on the suffragists' "southern strategy" and the southern suffrage movement illuminates these trends and describes how they tried to take advantage of southern state constitutional conventions in the 1890s and early 1900s, which were called for the purpose of African American disfranchisement. See Marjorie Spruill Wheeler, *New Women of the New South: The Leaders of the Woman Suffrage Movement in the Southern States* (New York: Oxford University Press, 1993), and Marjorie Julian Spruill, "Race, Reform, and Reaction at the Turn of the Century: Southern Suffragists, the NAWSA, and the 'Southern Strategy' in Context," in Baker, ed., *Votes for Women,* 102–117.

3. Eugene H. Berwanger, *The West and Reconstruction* (Urbana: University of Illinois Press, 1981); Quintard Taylor, *In Search of the Racial Frontier: African Americans in the American West, 1528–1990* (New York: W. W. Norton, 1998), 103–129; Saxton, *The Indispensable Enemy.*

4. Anthony to Gordon, 9 Feb. 1871, Box 1, Laura DeForce Gordon Collection, BL.

5. Ellen Carol DuBois, "Outgrowing the Compact of the Fathers," and "Taking the Law into Our Own Hands: *Bradwell, Minor,* and Suffrage Militance in the 1870s," in DuBois, *Woman Suffrage and Women's Rights,* 81–138.

6. Ida Husted Harper, *The Life and Work of Susan B. Anthony*, 2 vols. (Indianapolis and Kansas City: Bowen-Merrill, 1898), 2:387–408; *San Francisco Alta*, 12 July 1871.

7. Carolyn Swift and Judith Steen, eds., *Georgiana: Feminist Reformer of the West* (Santa Cruz, CA: Santa Cruz County Historical Trust, 1987), 36–46; *Santa Cruz Sentinel* 5, 12, 26 Aug. 1871.

8. Ellen Van Valkenburg to Laura DeForce Gordon, 13 Oct. 1871, Box 2, Gordon Collection, BL.

9. Harper, *Life and Work*, 2:406–408; "Aaron Augustus Sargent," *Who Was Who* (New York: A. N. Marquis Company, 1967), 534; *HWS* 3:757.

10. Sargent to Gordon, 21 Oct. 1871, Gordon Collection, BL; Harper, *Life and Work*, 2:405; *HWS* 2:483–484.

11. Minutes, 10 Sept. 1910, Keith-McHenry-Pond Collection, BL; *HWS* 3:757, 4:504–505, 6:27; Selina Solomons, *How We Won the Vote in California: A True Story of the Campaign of 1911* (San Francisco: New Woman Publishing, [1912]), 57.

12. Beverly Beeton, "How the West Was Won for Woman Suffrage," in Marjorie Spruill Wheeler, ed., *One Woman, One Vote* (Troutdale, OR: New Sage Press, 1995), 102–103.

13. *HWS* 2:545–555, 564–568; *HWS* 3:8–9, 70–75; Eleanor Flexner, *Century of Struggle*, rev. ed. (Cambridge, MA: Belknap Press, 1975), 176–178.

14. Donna C. Schuele, "Community Property Law and the Politics of Married Women's Rights in California," *Western Legal History* 7:2 (Summer 1994), 245–281; Donald E. Hargis, "Women's Rights: California 1849," *Historical Society of Southern California Quarterly* 37:4 (Dec. 1955), 320–334; J. R. Browne, ed., *Report of the Debates in the Convention of California* (Washington, DC: John T. Towers, 1850), 257–267, as cited by Gordon Morris Bakken and Brenda Farrington, *Learning California History: Essential Skills for the Survey Course and Beyond* (Wheeling, IL: Harlan-Davidson, 1999).

15. *HWS* 3:760–761; Barbara Allen Babcock, "Clara Shortridge Foltz: Constitution Maker," *Indiana Law Journal* 66 (Fall 1991), 849–940.

16. The WPC convention made "quick work" of woman suffrage with ironical cheers, "laughter and 'yahs,'" as well as a slighting reference to labor activist and suffragist Anna Ferry Smith. See the clipping enclosed with the letter from Sarah Knox-Goodrich to Susan B. Anthony, 21 May 1880, Roll 4:39, *The Papers of Elizabeth Cady Stanton and Susan B. Anthony* [microfilm] (Wilmington, DE: Scholarly Resources, 1991).

17. E. B. Willis and P. K. Stockton, *Debates and Proceedings of the Constitutional Convention of the State of California . . . 1878* (Sacramento, 1880), 833.

18. E. B. Willis and P. K. Stockton, *Debates and Proceedings*, 1010.

19. Ida Husted Harper, *Life and Work*, 2:398; *New Northwest*, 18 Dec. 1884; *Labor Enquirer*, 19 March 1887.

20. John Putnam, "The Emergence of a New West: The Politics of Class and Gender in Seattle, Washington, 1880–1917" (Ph.D. diss., University of California, San Diego, 2000), 119–139, 165–183, 317; Margaret K. Holden, "Gender and Protest Ideology: Sue Ross Keenan and the Oregon Anti-Chinese Movement," *Western Legal History* 7 (Summer 1994), 223–243; Clarence B. Bagley, *History of Seattle: From the Earliest Settlement to the Present Time,* vol. 2 (Seattle: Clarke, 1916), 489–490.

21. U.S. Congress, *Report of the Joint Special Committee to Investigate Chinese Immigration* (issued as Senate Doc. 689, 44th Cong., 2d session) (Washington, DC: Government Printing Office, 1877), 879–901; Victor G. and Brett de Bary Nee, *Longtime Californ': A Documentary Study of an American Chinatown* (New York: Pantheon Books, 1972), 53, citing *Alta California,* 27 Feb. 1880.

22. David Terry to Gordon, 20 Nov. 1878, Charles Ringgold to Gordon, 30 Jan., 28 Oct. 1879, Box 2, Gordon Collection, BL; Babcock, "Clara Shortridge Foltz," 888–893; *HWS* 3:760.

23. Sneider, "Reconstruction, Expansion, and Empire," 75.

24. Miriam Gantz Chapman, "The Story of Woman Suffrage in Wyoming, 1869–1890" (M.A. thesis, University of Wyoming, 1952), 8–13.

25. *HWS* 4:994–995; Chapman, "The Story of Woman Suffrage in Wyoming," 51–68.

26. Chapman, "The Story of Woman Suffrage in Wyoming," 70–81; *Woman's Tribune,* 13 July 1889.

27. *HWS* 4:995, 1000–1004; Chapman, "The Story of Woman Suffrage in Wyoming," 96–111.

28. Sneider, "Reconstruction, Expansion, and Empire," 93–97, 101–109; Carol Cornwall Madsen, "Schism in the Sisterhood: Mormon Women and Partisan Politics, 1890–1900," in Carol Cornwall Madsen, ed., *Battle for the Ballot: Essays on Woman Suffrage in Utah, 1870–1896* (Logan: Utah State University Press, 1997), 245–271.

29. Thomas G. Alexander, "An Experiment in Progressive Legislation: The Granting of Woman Suffrage in Utah in 1870," in Madsen, ed., *Battle for the Ballot,* 108–131; Richard Poll, "The Political Reconstruction of Utah Territory, 1866–1890," *Pacific Historical Review* 27 (May 1958), 111–126; Joan Iversen, "The Mormon-Suffrage Relationship: Personal and Political Quandries," in Madsen, ed., *Battle for the Ballot,* 151–161.

30. As cited by Jean B. White, "Woman's Place Is in the Constitution: The Struggle for Equal Rights in Utah in 1895," in Madsen, ed., *Battle for the Ballot,* 222.

31. *HWS* 4: 945–947.

32. White, "Woman's Place Is in the Constitution," 221–243.

33. Marte Jo Sheeran, "The Woman Suffrage Issue in Washington,

1890–1910" (M.A. thesis, University of Washington, 1977); T. A. Larson, "The Woman Suffrage Movement in Washington," *Pacific Northwest Quarterly* 62 (April 1976), 49–62; Stella E. Pearce, "Suffrage in the Pacific Northwest: Old Oregon and Washington," *Washington Historical Quarterly* 3 (April 1912), 106–114.

34. Jan Reiff, "Urbanization and the Social Structure: Seattle, Washington, 1852–1910" (Ph.D. diss., University of Washington, 1981), 3–4, 36; Pearce, "Suffrage in the Pacific Northwest," 106–108.

35. *HWS* 3:780–781; Pearce, "Suffrage in the Pacific Northwest," 110; Larson, "The Woman Suffrage Movement in Washington," 49–50.

36. *HWS* 3:780–786.

37. *New Northwest,* 11, 18, 25 Aug., 14, 21, 28 Oct. 1871; Larson, "The Woman Suffrage Movement in Washington," 50–51.

38. *HWS* 3:774–775; Larson, "The Woman Suffrage Movement in Washington," 52–53; *New Northwest,* 29 Nov. 1883.

39. *HWS* 3:771.

40. *HWS* 3:775; Ruth Barnes Moynihan, *Rebel for Rights: Abigail Scott Duniway* (New Haven and London: Yale University Press, 1983), 178.

41. *HWS* 3:773.

42. *HWS* 3:776–778.

43. *New Northwest,* 18 Oct., 1, 8, 22 Nov. 1883; *Puget Sound Weekly Courier,* 3, 6, 20 Nov. 1883.

44. *Olympia Washington Standard,* Oct. 19, Nov. 16 1883.

45. *Olympia Transcript,* 17 Nov. 1883.

46. *Puget Sound Weekly Courier,* 20 Nov. 1883.

47. *HWS* 4:967–968; *New Northwest,* 24 July (reprint), 2 Oct., 20 Nov., 11 Dec. 1884; Bagley, *History of Seattle,* 488–489.

48. Putnam, "The Emergence of a New West," 59–62.

49. Abigail Scott Duniway, *Path Breaking: An Autobiographical History of the Equal Suffrage Movement in Pacific Coast States,* 2d ed. (1914; reprint, New York: Source Book Press, 1970), 51; Moynihan, *Rebel for Rights,* 174; Larson, "The Woman Suffrage Movement in Washington," 53–54.

50. Duniway, *Path Breaking,* 69; *New Northwest,* 2 July 1875, 11 Dec. 1884.

51. Duniway, *Path Breaking,* 82–83.

52. Sneider, "Reconstruction, Expansion, and Empire," 111–120; *Woman's Tribune,* 1, 8, 15, 22 May 1886.

53. *Jeff Harland v. Washington* in *Territorial Reports,* vol. 3, *Cases Determined in the Supreme Court of the Territory of Washington* (Seattle, 1906), 131–163; Nelson A. Ault, "The Earnest Ladies: The Walla Walla Woman's Club and the Equal Suffrage League of 1886–1889," *Pacific Northwest Quarterly* 42 (April 1951), 130, citing a leaflet by Adella Parker, c. 1891; C. H.

Baily, "How Washington Women Regained the Ballot," *Pacific Monthly* 26 (July 1911), 4–7.

54. *Nevada M. Bloomer v. John Todd et al.*, in *Washington Territorial Reports*, Washington State Archives, Olympia; *HWS* 3:599–623.

55. *Woman's Tribune*, 2, 9 March 1889. See also the statement by Chief Justice Roger Greene, *Woman's Tribune*, 27 Oct. 1906.

56. Putnam, "The Emergence of a New West," citing *Seattle Post-Intelligencer*, 20 Feb. 1887.

57. *Woman's Tribune*, March 16, 20 April, 11 May, 29 June, 13, 27 July, 10 Aug. 1889, 27 May 1907.

58. *Woman's Tribune*, 10, 24 Aug. 1889; Ault, "The Earnest Ladies," 135; Bagley, *History of Seattle*, 491.

59. *HWS* 4:969–970. The minutes of the constitutional convention were never fully transcribed because the legislature neglected to pay the transcribers. Extant material has been gathered into Beverly Paulik Rosenow, ed., *The Journal of the Washington State Constitutional Convention, 1889* (Seattle: Book Publishing Company).

60. *HWS* 4:976–977; Ault, "The Earnest Ladies," 134–137; Clark, *The Dry Years*, 48–49. The prohibition measure also lost badly, but by a smaller margin (19,546 to 31,487).

61. Richard B. Roeder, "Crossing the Gender Line: Ella L. Knowles, Montana's First Woman Lawyer," *Montana* 32:3 (Summer 1982), 64–75.

62. *HWS* 4:796–801, 6:360–363.

63. *Woman's Tribune*, 10 Dec. 1904, 7 Jan. 1905.

64. James R. Wright, Jr., "The Assiduous Wedge: Woman Suffrage and the Oklahoma Constitutional Convention," *Chronicles of Oklahoma* 51:4 (Winter 1973–1974), 421–443.

65. *Woman's Tribune*, 5 Aug. 1905.

66. Sherilyn Cox Bennion, *Equal to the Occasion: Women Editors of the Nineteenth-Century West* (Reno and Las Vegas: University of Nevada Press, 1990), 138–140.

67. *HWS* 6:10–15; *Woman's Journal*, 18 Jan. 1896.

68. *HWS* 4:384–385; 6:434–439; Maurilio E. Vigil, "The Political Development of New Mexico's Hispanas," *Latin Studies Journal* 7:2 (Spring 1996), 3–29.

69. *HWS* 6:713–715.

NOTES TO CHAPTER 4

1. Decker was a Denver clubwoman and president of the General Federation of Women's Clubs (1904–1908), cited by Ellis Meredith, "What It Means to Be an Enfranchised Woman," *Atlantic Monthly* (Aug. 1908), 196–197.

2. Beverly Beeton, *Women Vote in the West: The Woman Suffrage Movement, 1869–1896* (New York: Garland, 1986), 104–115; Billie Barnes Jensen, "Colorado Woman Suffrage Campaigns of the 1870s," *Journal of the West* 12 (April 1973), 254–271; Billie Barnes Jensen, "The Woman Suffrage Movement in Colorado" (M.A. thesis, University of Colorado, 1959), and Billie Barnes Jensen, "Let the Women Vote," *Colorado Magazine* 41 (Winter 1964), 13–25; Carolyn J. Stefanco, "Pathways to Power: Women and Voluntary Associations in Denver, Colorado, 1876–1893" (Ph.D. diss., Duke University, 1987); Stefanco, "Harvest of Discontent: The Depression of 1893 and the Women's Vote," *Colorado Heritage* (Spring 1993), 16–21; and Stefanco, "Networking on the Frontier: The Colorado Women's Suffrage Movement, 1876–1893," in Susan Armitage and Elizabeth Jameson, eds., *The Women's West* (Norman and London: University of Oklahoma Press, 1987), 265–276; Rebecca Edwards, "Pioneers at the Polls: Woman Suffrage in the West," in Jean H. Baker, ed., *Votes for Women: The Struggle for Suffrage Revisited* (Oxford and New York: Oxford University Press, 2002), 90–101; Suzanne M. Marilley, *Woman Suffrage and the Origins of Liberal Feminism in the United States, 1820–1920* (Cambridge, MA: Harvard University Press, 1996), 124–128; Joseph G. Brown, *The History of Equal Suffrage in Colorado* (Denver: News Job Printing, 1898). See also Marcia T. Goldstein and Rebecca A. Hunt, "From Suffrage to Centennial: A Research Guide to Colorado and National Women's Suffrage Sources," *Colorado Heritage* (Spring 1993), 40–45.

3. *HWS* 3:713–715; *Colorado Transcript*, 26 Jan. 1870, as cited by Jensen, "Colorado Woman Suffrage Campaigns of the 1870s," 256–260.

4. *Woman's Journal*, 11 Nov. 1893, 28 July 1894.

5. *HWS* 3:716–317; Stefanco, "Networking," 266–267; "Pathways," 40–41, citing *Denver Daily Tribune*, 16 Jan. 1877; Jensen, "Colorado Woman Suffrage Campaigns of the 1870s," 260–261; *Woman's Journal*, 20 Jan. 1877.

6. *Woman's Journal*, 27 Oct. 1877, 28 July 1894; *HWS* 3:717.

7. *HWS* 3:717; Jensen, "1870s," 263; Stefanco, "Pathways," 40–42.

8. *Woman's Journal*, 22 Jan., 5 Feb. 1876, 20 Jan. 1877; *HWS* 3:717–720.

9. *Woman's Journal*, 27 Oct. 1876.

10. *Woman's Journal*, 19 Feb. 1876; *Denver Times*, 7 November 1903 (full text).

11. *HWS* 3:719; William B. Faherty, "Regional Minorities and the Woman Suffrage Struggle," *Colorado Magazine* 33 (July 1956), 215.

12. *Woman's Journal*, 19 Feb. 1876, 20 Jan. 1877.

13. Stefanco, "Pathways," 43.

14. *Woman's Journal*, 7 Oct. 1876.

15. *Woman's Journal*, 5 Aug. 1876.

16. *Rocky Mountain News,* 16 Jan. 1877, as cited by Stefanco, "Pathways," 44–47.

17. *HWS* 3:718–722.

18. *HWS* 3:719.

19. *Woman's Journal,* 14 April 1877.

20. *Woman's Journal,* 22 Aug. 1894.

21. *HWS* 3:712.

22. *Woman's Journal,* 4 Aug. 1894.

23. *Woman's Journal,* 11 Nov. 1893; *HWS* 3:719.

24. Ida Husted Harper, *Life and Work of Susan B. Anthony* (1898; reprint, Salem, NH: Ayer, 1983), 2:489–493.

25. *Rocky Mountain News,* 11 Sept., 1–2, 10 Oct. 1877; Brown, *The History of Equal Suffrage in Colorado,* 12–16; Jensen, "Colorado Woman Suffrage Campaigns of the 1870s," 267–268; Anthony in *Denver Times,* 11 Oct. 1877.

26. *Denver Times,* 2 Oct. 1877; Jensen, "Colorado Woman Suffrage Campaigns of the 1870s," 268–270. The Rev. Mr. Bliss, who refused debate invitations but slammed woman suffrage in his sermons, apparently went out of his way to meet Lucy Stone. When he introduced himself, Stone withdrew her hand, whereupon Bliss informed her, "You are no lady," initiating a spirited exchange. *Rocky Mountain News,* 9 Oct. 1877.

27. *HWS* 3:724.

28. *Woman's Journal,* 15 Sept., 13 Oct. 1877; Jensen, "Colorado Woman Suffrage Campaigns of the 1870s," 254, 271.

29. Faherty, "Regional Minorities," 212–217; *Woman's Tribune,* 12 Nov. 1904.

30. *HWS* 3:724.

31. Campbell to NAWSA, 8 July 1877, Reel 5, NAWSA Collection; *Rocky Mountain News,* 7 Oct. 1877; *HWS* 3:725.

32. *Woman's Journal,* 20 Oct. 1877.

33. Reprinted in the *Woman's Journal,* 27 Oct. 1877.

34. Stefanco, "Pathways," 113–114, 130–132; Marilley, *Woman Suffrage and the Origins of Liberal Feminism,* 114–120.

35. Untitled typescript, Box 5, Colorado WCTU Papers (CWCTU), Western Historical Collections, University of Colorado, Boulder, as cited by Stefanco, "Pathways," 127.

36. M. F. Gray-Pitman, "Response," *Minutes CWCTU* (Colorado Springs: Gazette, 1882), 10, as cited by Stefanco, "Pathways," 127.

37. Stefanco, "Pathways," 97, 110–129, 138–169; Marilley, *Woman Suffrage and the Origins of Liberal Feminism,* 118–119.

38. David Thomas Brundage, *The Making of Labor Radicalism: Denver's Organized Workers, 1878–1905* (Urbana and Chicago: University of Illinois

Press, 1994), 53–80. For a similar discussion of labor "domesticity" in Cripple Creek, see Elizabeth Jameson, *All That Glitters: Class, Conflict, and Community in Cripple Creek* (Urbana: University of Illinois Press, 1998), 122–133.

39. Stefanco, *Pathways*, 15–33; James Edward Wright, *The Politics of Populism: Dissent in Colorado* (New Haven and London: Yale University Press, 1974), 15–23.

40. Brundage, *The Making of Western Labor Radicalism*, 112–136.

41. *Queen Bee*, 3 Nov. 1886, 23 Nov. 1887. See also Susan Levine, "Labor's True Woman: Domesticity and Equal Rights in the Knights of Labor," *Journal of American History* 70 (Sept. 1983), 323–339.

42. Brundage, *The Making of Western Labor Radicalism*, 64–66, 134–136.

43. Anna Haskell diary, April 1886, BL.

44. Joseph R. Buchanan, *The Story of a Labor Agitator* (New York: Outlook Company, 1903), 47–52; *Labor Enquirer*, 30 July 1887.

45. Wright, *Politics of Populism*, 115–157.

46. Wright, *Politics of Populism*, 159–225, 250–265.

47. Maryjo Wagner, "Farms, Families, and Reform: Women in the Farmers' Alliance and Populist Party" (Ph.D. diss., University of Oregon, 1986), 127–129, 228–229, 254–259.

48. *Woman's Journal*, 2 Dec. 1893.

49. Wagner, "Farms, Families, and Reform," 279, 287–288; *Rocky Mountain News*, 28 July 1892.

50. *Woman's Journal*, 27 Aug. 1892, 23 Sept. 1893.

51. *Queen Bee*, 2 Oct. 1889. She was in Council Bluffs, Iowa, when she heard of the Colorado suffrage victory.

52. Stephen J. Leonard, "'Bristling for Their Rights': Colorado's Women and the Mandate of 1893," *Colorado Heritage* (Spring 1993), 11–12.

53. Stefanco, "Pathways," 130, 189–191.

54. *HWS* 4: 513.

55. Marilley, *Woman Suffrage and the Origins of Liberal Feminism*, 121–122; Stefanco, "Pathways," 191–193.

56. Wright, *The Politics of Populism*, 67–68, 106; Marilley, *Woman Suffrage and the Origins of Liberal Feminism*, 124–125.

57. Jensen, "The Woman Suffrage Movement," 64; Stefanco, "Pathways," 198–200; *HWS* 4:512–514.

58. *HWS* 4:513–514; Ellis Meredith, "Women Citizens of Colorado," *The Great Divide* (Feb. 1894), 53; Jacqueline Van Voris, *Carrie Chapman Catt: A Public Life* (New York: Feminist Press of the City University of New York, 1987), 34; Jensen, "Let the Women Vote," 15–16; William B. Faherty, "Regional Minorities," 513–514. An alternative version reports Anthony asking, "Are all those Mexicans dead yet?" See *HWS* 4:514.

59. Meredith to Anthony, 14 June 1893, Box 1.5, Meredith Collection (MSS 427), Colorado Historical Society (hereafter cited as CoHS), Denver, Colorado.

60. Anthony to Meredith, 16, 20, 25 Oct. 1893, Box 1.2, Catt to Meredith, 23 June 1893, Box 1.1, Meredith Collection, CoHS

61. Meredith to Catt, 30 June 1893, Box 1.5, Catt to Meredith, 5, 16 July 1893, Box 1.1, Meredith Collection, CoHS; Van Voris, *Carrie Chapman Catt*, 34–37; Stefanco, "Pathways," 223–225; Marilley, *Woman Suffrage and the Origins of Liberal Feminism*, 135–137.

62. Wright, *Politics of Populism*, 166–176; Stefanco, "Pathways," 203–207.

63. *Woman's Journal*, 3 June, 18 Nov. 1893, 3 March 1894.

64. Stefanco, "Pathways," 225.

65. *Woman's Journal*, 21 Oct. 1893.

66. Stefanco, "Pathways," 209–215.

67. *Woman's Journal*, 2 Sept. 1893.

68. Stefanco, "Networking," 273; *Woman's Journal*, 3 March 1894; Meredith, "Women Citizens of Colorado," 53.

69. Minnie Reynolds to Alice Stone Blackwell, 12 Dec. 1930, Reel 17, NAWSA Microfilm Collection.

70. Van Voris, *Carrie Chapman Catt*, 34–37; *Woman's Journal*, 18 Nov. 1893.

71. *Woman's Journal*, 16, 23 Sept. 1893; *Woman's Column*, 16 Sept., 23 Dec. 1893.

72. Van Voris, *Carrie Chapman Catt*, 35–36.

73. Catt to Meredith, 23 June, 16 July 1893, Box 1.1, Meredith Collection, CoHS.

74. *Woman's Journal*, 2 Dec. 1893.

75. *Woman's Journal*, 23 Dec. 1893; Marilley, *Woman Suffrage and the Origins of Liberal Feminism*, 136–145; Helen Reynolds to Emma Smith DeVoe (on NAWSA letterhead), 16 June 1896, Box 3.5, DeVoe Collection, Washington State Library, Olympia (hereafter cited as WSL).

76. *Woman's Journal*, 20 Jan. 1894.

77. *Woman's Journal*, 3 Feb. 1894.

78. *Woman's Column*, 23 Dec. 1893.

79. *Woman's Journal*, 18 Nov. 1893.

80. Meredith to Catt, 30 June 1893, Meredith to Anthony, 7 Aug. 1893, Box 1.5, Meredith Collection, CoHS; *Woman's Journal*, 18 Nov. 1893, 3 March 1894.

81. Michael Lewis Goldberg, *An Army of Women: Gender and Politics in Gilded Age Kansas* (Baltimore: Johns Hopkins University Press, 1997).

82. Jensen, "Let the Women Vote," 23; *HWS* 4:516–519.

83. *Woman's Journal,* 18 Nov. 1893, 3 March 1894; *Denver Republican,* 8 Nov. 1893, as cited by Stefanco, "Pathways," 227.

84. *Woman's Journal,* 18 Nov., 23 Dec. 1893.

85. *Woman's Journal,* 2 Dec. 1893.

86. *Spokane Spokesman-Review,* 28 Sept. 1896; Helen Reynolds to DeVoe, 4, 16 June 1896, Box 3.5, DeVoe Collection, WSL.

87. DeVoe to Minnie Reynolds, 19 March 1909, Box 3.4, DeVoe Collection, WSL.

88. Manuela Thurner, "'Better Citizens without the Ballot': American Anti-Suffrage Women and Their Rationale during the Progressive Era," *Journal of Women's History* 5:1 (Spring 1993): 43; Billie Barnes Jensen, "'In the Weird and Wooly West': Anti-Suffrage Women, Gender Issues, and Woman Suffrage in the West," *Journal of the West* 32 (July 1993), 44–49. See also Joseph F. Mahoney, "Woman Suffrage and the Urban Masses," *New Jersey History* 87 (Autumn 1969), 159–160.

89. *San Francisco Examiner,* 8 Nov. 1896; *Democrat and Chronicle* (Rochester, NY), 18 Nov. 1896.

90. Helen Sumner (Woodbury), *Equal Suffrage: The Results of an Investigation in Colorado Made for the Collegiate Equal Suffrage League of New York State* (1909; reprint, New York: Arno Press, 1972), 63–64; Lawrence Lewis, "How Woman's Suffrage Works in Colorado," *The Outlook* 82:4 (27 Jan. 1906), 170–173, 177.

91. William MacLeod Raine, "Woman Suffrage in Colorado," *Chatauquan* (Feb. 1902), 19; Lewis, "Woman's Suffrage," 174; Mary C. C. Bradford, "Equal Suffrage in Colorado," Colorado Equal Suffrage Association, n.d. (pamphlet).

92. *Woman's Tribune,* 2 Nov. 1904.

93. Sumner, *Equal Suffrage,* 57–59.

94. Sumner, *Equal Suffrage,* 31–33.

95. Sumner, *Equal Suffrage,* 66–71; *Rocky Mountain News,* 26 Aug. 1894, 1 Oct. 1900. One Pueblo resident did note the participation of seven "colored" women as delegates to the Republican county convention in 1906.

96. *Queen Bee,* 6, 20 Dec. 1893.

97. Elizabeth M. Cox, *Women State and Territorial Legislators, 1895–1995* (Jefferson, NC: McFarland, 1996), 12.

98. Helen Ring Robinson, "On Being a Woman Senator," *Independent* (April 20, 1914), 130–132.

99. Leonard, "'Bristling for Their Rights,'" 13.

100. Ignatius Donnelly to Davis Waite, 7 Dec. 1894, Waite to Donnelly, 11 Dec. 1894, Debs to Waite, 11 Dec. 1896, as cited by John R. Morris, "The Women and Governor Waite," *Colorado Magazine* 44 (Winter 1967), 11–19; *HWS* 4:520.

101. Catt to DeVoe, 9 Feb. 1895, Box 1.10, DeVoe Collection, WSL.

102. *Woman's Journal,* 7 July 1894.

103. Goldberg, *An Army of Women,* 233–242.

NOTES TO CHAPTER 5

1. *Los Angeles Times,* 17 Jan. 1888, as cited by Ralph E. Shaffer, "Letters from the People: The *Los Angeles Times* Letters Column, 1881–1889," 1999. See also http://www.intranet.csupomona.edu/~reshaffer/womenx.htm. My thanks to Professor Shaffer for this material. See also *Los Angeles Times,* 23, 30 Jan., 4 Feb. 1888.

2. On critical elections, see Walter Dean Burnham, "Periodization Schemes and 'Party Systems': The 'System of 1896' as a Case in Point," *Social Science History* 10 (Fall 1986): 263–314; and W. Lance Bennett and William Halton, "Issues, Voter Choice, and Critical Elections," *Social Science History* 4 (Fall 1980): 379–418.

3. On Populism in California, see Michael Rogin, "California Populism and the 'System of 1896,'" *Western Political Quarterly* 22 (March 1969): 179–96; Michael P. Rogin and John L. Shover, *Political Change in California: Critical Elections and Social Movements, 1890–1966* (Westport, CT: Greenwood, 1970); Alexander Saxton, "San Francisco Labor and the Populist and Progressive Insurgencies," *Pacific Historical Review* 34 (Nov. 1965): 421–438; and Donald Edgar Walters, "Populism in California, 1889–1900" (Ph.D. diss., University of California, Berkeley, 1952).

4. Mary S. Gibson, *A Record of Twenty-five Years of the California Federation of Women's Clubs, 1900–1925* (Los Angeles, 1925); Sherry Jeanne Katz, "Dual Commitments: Feminism, Socialism, and Women's Political Activism in California, 1890–1920" (Ph.D. diss., University of California, Los Angeles, 1991), 57–58.

5. J. C. (Jennie Cunningham) Croly, *The History of the Women's Club Movement in America* (New York: Henry B. Allen, 1898), 253–255; Gayle Gullett, *Becoming Citizens: The Emergence and Development of the California Women's Movement, 1880–1911* (Urbana and Chicago: University of Illinois Press, 2000); see also Gullett, "Feminism, Politics, and Voluntary Groups: Organized Womanhood in California, 1886–1896" (Ph.D. diss., University of California, Riverside, 1983).

6. "Caroline Maria Seymour Severance," in McHenry, *Famous American Women,* 377; E. G. Ruddy, ed., *The Mother of Clubs* (Los Angeles, 1906); *HWS* 4:494–495; and Joan Jensen, "After Slavery: Caroline Severance in Los Angeles," *Southern California Quarterly* 48 (July 1966), 175–186.

7. Croly, *The History of the Women's Club Movement,* 147–148; Gullett, *Becoming Citizens,* 114–119.

8. Abigail Duniway quoted Gordon in 1874 as "not in favor of the Church's

style of preaching prohibition. . . . If I think I need a glass of wine, I do not intend that any one but myself shall be allowed to say I shall or shall not take it." See Abigail Scott Duniway, *Path Breaking: An Autobiographical History of the Equal Suffrage Movement in Pacific Coast States* (reprint, 2d ed., New York: Source Book Press, 1970), 205–207.

9. Dorcas Spencer, *A History of the Woman's WCTU of Northern and Central California* (Oakland: West Coast Printing, 1912); Mary Alderman Garbutt, *Victories of Four Decades: A History of the Woman's Christian Temperance Union of Southern California, 1883–1924* (Los Angeles: WCTU, 1924); Gullett, *Becoming Citizens,* 109–112; Gilman M. Ostrander, *The Prohibition Movement in California, 1848–1933,* University of California Publications in History, vol. 57 (Berkeley: University of California Press, 1957); Women's Christian Temperance Union of California, *Annual Reports,* and *Minutes* of the state conventions, ca. 1898–1900, California WCTU papers, Modesto, California. Thanks to Rumi Yasutake for sharing this material.

10. Katz, "Dual Commitments," 47–48, and Katz, "A Politics of Coalition: Socialist Women and the California Suffrage Movement, 1900–1911," in Marjorie Spruill Wheeler, ed., *One Woman, One Vote: Rediscovering the Woman Suffrage Movement* (Troutdale, OR: New Sage Press, 1995), 245–262; Walters, "Populism in California," 18–44; Garbutt, *Victories of Four Decades,* 100–102, 105, 139–143. See also Daphne Patai, ed., *Looking Backward, 1988–1888: Essays on Edward Bellamy* (Boston: University of Massachusetts Press), especially Sylvia Strauss, "Gender, Class, and Race in Utopia," 68–90; and Mari Jo Buhle, *Women and American Socialism, 1870–1920* (Urbana: University of Illinois Press, 1981), 74–81.

11. *Los Angeles Socialist,* 13 June 1903, as cited by Katz, "Dual Commitments," 120. Aside from freeing women from housework, Bellamy's vision of women was grounded in traditional patriarchal notions, and many feminists, including Elizabeth Cady Stanton, remained unimpressed; see Strauss, "Gender, Class, and Race in Utopia," 89.

12. Charlotte Perkins Gilman, *The Living of Charlotte Perkins Gilman: An Autobiography* (New York: D. Appleton-Century, 1935), 122. See also Denise D. Knight, ed., *The Diaries of Charlotte Perkins Gilman: 1890–1935,* vol. 2 (Charlottesville: University Press of Virginia, 1994), 502–503, 506, 530; and Marian K. Towne, "Charlotte Gilman in California," *Pacific Historian* 28 (Spring 1984), 5–17.

13. Gilman, *The Living,* 130–131, 176; Towne, "Charlotte Gilman in California," 15.

14. Gilman, *The Living,* 141–145; Gullett, *Becoming Citizens,* 74–84.

15. As cited by Gail Bederman, *Manliness and Civilization: A Cultural History of Gender and Race in the United States, 1880–1917* (Chicago and London: University of Chicago Press, 1995), 134.

16. In addition to Bederman, *Manliness and Civilization,* see Louise Michele Newman, *White Women's Rights: The Racial Origins of Feminism in the United States* (New York and Oxford: Oxford University Press, 1999), 132–157; Alys Eve Weinbaum, "Writing Feminist Genealogy: Charlotte Perkins Gilman, Racial Nationalism, and the Reproduction of Maternalist Feminism," *Feminist Studies* 27:2 (Summer 2001), 271–302. Weinbaum is very critical of the tendency among Gilman scholars to overlook her racism and nativism in order to celebrate the feminist aspects of this important "foremother."

17. Gilman, *The Living,* 171–179; *San Francisco Chronicle,* 21–27 May 1895; *Woman's Journal,* 22 June 1895; Gullett, *Becoming Citizens,* 65–78. See also Robert W. Rydell, *All the World's a Fair: Visions of Empire at American International Expositions, 1876–1916* (Chicago: University of Chicago Press, 1984).

18. *San Francisco Examiner,* 1 May 1894; *Woman's Journal,* 6 June 1894. Prominent male participants included Governor James H. Budd, U.S. senator George Perkins, and Stanford University president David Starr Jordan.

19. *San Francisco Call,* 2 June 1894.

20. *San Francisco Call,* 2 June 1894.

21. *San Francisco Call,* 13 Sept. 1894. Duniway admired and sympathized with Gordon, who "was being side-tracked . . . by Eastern invaders," "professional politicians of either sex, or of both of the sexes." See Duniway, *Path Breaking,* 67. On Blinn, who died prematurely in 1909, see *San Francisco Chronicle,* 30 Sept. 1894; and *San Francisco Call,* 5 July 1909.

22. *San Francisco Call,* 12–14 Sept. 1894

23. Walters, "Populism in California."

24. *Woman's Journal,* 3 Sept. 1892.

25. Walters, "Populism in California," 156, 182.

26. *Woman's Journal,* 3 Sept., 5 Nov. 1892.

27. Walters, "Populism in California," 276.

28. *HWS* 4:485.

29. *Woman's Journal,* 4 Aug. 1894. On McComas, see Frances E. Willard and Mary A. Livermore, eds., *A Woman of the Century: Fourteen Hundred-Seventy Biographical Sketches Accompanied by Portraits of Leading American Women in All Walks of Life* (Buffalo: Charles Wells Moulton, 1893), 483–484.

30. *San Francisco Chronicle,* 25 Jan. 1895; *San Francisco Call,* 25 Jan. 1895; *Woman's Journal,* 16, 23 Feb., 4 May 1895.

31. Sarah Severance to Louise Sorbier, 9, 26 Dec. 1894, Louise Sorbier Collection, California Historical Society (hereafter cited as CHS), San Francisco, California.

32. Beaumelle Sturtevant-Peet to Sorbier, 31 Dec. 1894, Sorbier Collection, CHS.

33. Gordon to Sorbier, fragment, 10, 13 Jan. 1895, and March 1895, Sorbier Collection, CHS.

34. Severance to Sorbier, 19 March 1897, Sorbier Collection, CHS. Severance confided, "Barlow, author of the bill, told Mrs. Peet so."

35. Severance to Sorbier, 9, 26 Dec. 1894, 22 January 1895, Sorbier Collection, CHS; *Woman's Journal*, 4 May 1895.

36. Gordon to Sorbier, 10, 13 Jan. 1895, Sorbier Collection, CHS.

37. *San Francisco Call*, 8 Feb. 1895; *San Francisco Examiner*, 2 Feb. 1895

38. *San Francisco Call*, 9, 12, 20 Feb. 1895; *Woman's Journal*, 16, 23 Feb. 1895.

39. Ida Husted Harper, *The Life and Work of Susan B. Anthony*, 2 vols. (Indianapolis and Kansas City: Bowen-Merrill, 1898), 2:827–829; *San Francisco Chronicle*, 21–24 May 1895.

40. *San Francisco Chronicle*, 21, 24, 27 May 1895.

41. Harper, *Life and Work*, 2:829–838.

42. *Woman's Journal*, 15 June, 20 July, 7 Sept. 1895; Gullett, *Becoming Citizens*, 87–89.

43. Gordon to Colby, 15 July 1895, Clara Colby Collection, State Historical Society of Wisconsin, Madison.

44. Catt to Devoe, 9 July 1895, Box 1, Emma Smith DeVoe Collection, Washington State Library (WSL), Olympia.

45. Catt to Devoe, 8 Aug. 1895, DeVoe Collection, WSL; Catt to Lillie Deveraux Blake, 7 Feb. 1896, Anthony to Blake, 9 April, 15 May 1896, Blake Collection, CHS (courtesy of the Missouri Historical Society).

46. *San Francisco Call*, 11, 12, 19 Feb., 10 May 1896; *San Francisco Chronicle*, 8, 10 May 1896.

47. The standard accounts are: Harper, *Life and Work*, 2:819–893. The *History of Woman Suffrage* chapters were written by Ellen Sargent (4:478–494 [Northern California]) and Alice McComas (4:494–502 [Southern California]); Gullett, *Becoming Citizens*, 93–106; Susan Scheiber Edelman, "'A Red Hot Suffrage Campaign': The Woman Suffrage Cause in California, 1896," *California Supreme Court Historical Society Yearbook*, 2 (1995), 51–131; and Donald G. Cooper, "The California Suffrage Campaign of 1896: Its Origins, Strategies, Defeat," *Southern California Quarterly* 71:4 (Winter 1989), 311–325.

48. *Woman's Journal*, 29 Aug. 1896.

49. Stanford to Anthony, 6 Sept. 1896, Jane Stanford Collection, Special Collections Department, Stanford University; Harper, *Life and Work*, 2:820, 824. Hearst gave $1,000 anonymously; Mary Sperry and Sarah Knox-Goodrich each donated $500.

50. Harper, *Life and Work*, 2:865–876, 888–892; *Woman's Journal*, 15 Jan. 1896.

51. *Woman's Journal*, 16 May 1896; *Woman's Tribune*, 30 May 1896.

52. *Woman's Journal*, 23 May 1896; *San Francisco Call*, 3–10 May 1896; Harper, *Life and Work*, 2:869–872.

53. Harper, *Life and Work*, 2:879–880; Edelman, "'A Red Hot Suffrage Campaign,'" 65–66.

54. *San Francisco Call*, 10, 13, 14 May 1896; Anthony to Routt, 16 April 1896, Reel 35, *The Papers of Elizabeth Cady Stanton and Susan B. Anthony* (Wilmington, DE: Scholarly Resources, 1991) (microfilm). See also *Woman's Tribune*, 11 July 1896; and *Woman's Journal*, 1 Aug. 1896.

55. John Dore to Thomas Cator, 1 June 1895, Box 1.8, Thomas C. Cator Papers, Department of Special Collections, Stanford University.

56. Harper, *Life and Work*, 2:873.

57. Mary McHenry Keith, report, 16 June 1896, Carton 4, Keith Collection, Bancroft Library (BL), University of California, Berkeley.

58. *San Francisco Examiner*, 18 June 1896; *San Francisco Chronicle*, 18 June 1896. In an interview, Murray was certain that her group had "the promise of all the money we need to carry on the campaign," but she would not divulge her funding sources; *San Francisco Chronicle*, 12 June 1896.

59. Harper, *Life and Work*, 2:869–874; Edelman, "'A Red Hot Suffrage Campaign,'" 66–68.

60. *Woman's Journal*, 11 July 1896; *San Francisco Chronicle*, 27 June 1896.

61. *Woman's Tribune*, 26 Sept. 1896; *Woman's Journal*, 26 Sept. 1896; *San Francisco Call*, 11 Sept. 1896.

62. Keith report, 16 June 1896, Carton 4, Keith Collection, BL.

63. *Woman's Journal*, 15 Aug. 1896; *San Francisco Call*, 2 Aug. 1896.

64. Susan B. Anthony to Clara Colby, 26 June 1896, Colby Collection, Huntington Library (HL), San Marino, CA.

65. Anthony to Clara Colby, 11 Aug. 1896, Anthony to Jessie Anthony, 29 Aug. 1896, both in Anthony Family Collection, HL; Edelman, "'A Red Hot Suffrage Campaign,'" 110–111.

66. Harper, *Life and Work*, 2:876; *Woman's Journal,* 25 Jan. 1896; *San Francisco Call*, 29 Sept. 1896, as cited by Edelman, "'A Red Hot Suffrage Campaign,'" 84–85.

67. *HWS* 4:489; Edelman, "'A Red Hot Suffrage Campaign,'" 69–70.

68. Anna Haskell diary, 30 June–22 Oct. 1896, BL.

69. Harper, *Life and Work*, 2:866.

70. Carrie Chapman Catt and Nettie Rogers Shuler, *Woman Suffrage and Politics: The Inner Story of the Suffrage Movement* (New York: Charles Scribner's Sons, 1926), 123; *Woman's Journal*, 14 Nov. 1896; *San Francisco Call*, 5 Nov. 1896.

71. Harper, *Life and Work*, 2:867–868; Edelman, "'A Red Hot Suffrage Campaign,'" 96–101.

72. Harper, *Life and Work*, 2:870–873.

73. *Los Angeles Times*, 2 July 1895.

74. *Woman's Tribune*, 18 Aug. 1896; *Woman's Journal*, 8 Aug., 19 Dec. 1896, 20 Feb. 1897.

75. Edelman, "'A Red Hot Suffrage Campaign,'" 106.

76. *San Francisco Call*, 6 Aug. 1896.

77. *San Francisco Call*, 1 Nov. 1896; *Woman's Journal*, 2 Aug. 1896.

78. Harper, *Life and Work*, 2:867–868.

79. Englander, *Class Coalition and Class Conflict*, 43, 141, 155, citing *The Monitor*, 9 March 1895 (pro); Edelman, "'A Red Hot Suffrage Campaign,'" 80–82.

80. Michael Goldberg ascribes hostility to woman suffrage among black editors in Kansas to this annoyance as well as their close alliance with the Republican Party. He observes that these men did not necessarily speak for African American women, whose public voices were silent. See Michael Goldberg, *Army of Women: Gender Politics in Gilded Age Kansas* (Baltimore: Johns Hopkins University Press, 1997), 227–229. Goldberg mentions Anderson only as a hired WCTU organizer in 1888 (p. 63)

81. *San Francisco Chronicle*, 5 Sept. 1896.

82. *San Francisco Examiner*, 26 July 1896; *Woman's Journal*, 5 Sept. 1896; Rosalyn Terborg-Penn, "Naomi Bowman Talbert Anderson," in Darlene Clark Hine, et al., eds., *Black Women in America: An Historical Encyclopedia* (Brooklyn: Carlson, 1993), 33–34.

83. *San Francisco Call*, 1 Aug. 1896; "Colored Suffragists" [article], Carton 4, Keith Collection, BL.

84. *Woman's Journal*, 7 Nov. 1896; *Woman's Tribune*, 12 June 1897; Women's Christian Temperance Union of California, *Annual Report, 1894*, 108–109; *Annual Report, 1896*, 60–61; *Annual Report, 1897*, 51, California WCTU Collection.

85. *Woman's Journal*, 15 Feb., 2 May 1896.

86. Harper, *Life and Work*, 2:882; Anthony to Francis Willard, 17 Jan. 1895 [1896], Willard to Anthony, 18 Jan. 1896, Reel 35, *The Papers of Elizabeth Cady Stanton and Susan B. Anthony* (microfilm). See also Duniway, *Path Breaking*, 205–207.

87. Severance to Sorbier, 19 March 1897, Sorbier Collection, CHS.

88. Anthony to Sargent/Cooper, 23 Jan. 1896, Reel 35, *The Papers of Elizabeth Cady Stanton and Susan B. Anthony* (microfilm); Harper, *Life and Work*, 2:882; *San Francisco Call*, 26 March 1896; Edelman, "'A Red Hot Suffrage Campaign,'" 101–104.

89. Harper, *Life and Work*, 2:886–887.

90. *Woman's Journal*, 21 Nov. 1896.

91. *San Francisco Call*, 4 Nov. 1896. Harper later reported that hundreds of

ballots in San Francisco had only this item marked; see Harper, *Life and Work*, 2:890. See also Edelman, "'A Red Hot Suffrage Campaign,'" 70–73, 85–86; Philip J. Ethington, *The Public City: The Political Construction of Urban Life in San Francisco, 1850–1900* (Cambridge, UK: Cambridge University Press, 1994), 400–401.

92. David Burke Griffiths, "Populism in the Far West, 1890–1900" (Ph.D. diss., University of Washington, 1967), 273.

93. Harper, *Life and Work*, 2:887. See also Selina Solomons in the *Woman's Journal*, 19 Dec. 1896.

94. Anna Haskell diary, 3–4, 6 Nov. 1896, Haskell Collection, BL.

95. Catt and Shuler, *Woman Suffrage and Politics*, 115–116, 123–127.

96. *Woman's Tribune*, 12 June 1897; *Union Signal*, 28 Sept. 1911; Women's Christian Temperance Union of California, *Annual Report*, 1897, 51, California WCTU Collection.

97. *San Francisco Examiner*, 8 Nov. 1896; Philenda Spencer to Sorbier, 24 Feb. 1897, Sorbier Collection, CHS.

98. *San Francisco Examiner*, 8 Nov. 1896; *San Francisco Call*, 6 Nov. 1896; *San Francisco Chronicle*, 6, 7, Nov. 1896.

99. Harper, *Life and Work*, 2:883–885; *Woman's Tribune*, 17 Oct. 1896.

100. *Woman's Journal*, 21, 28 Nov. 1896; Edelman, "'A Red Hot Suffrage Campaign,'" 88–91.

101. Haskell diary, 3–6 Nov. 1896, Haskell Collection, BL.

102. *HWS* 4:486.

103. WCTU, *Minutes of Nineteenth Annual State Convention* [n.p., 1898], 54; *Minutes of the Twentieth Annual Convention* [n.p., 1899], 24; *Minutes of the Twenty-first Annual Convention* [n.p., 1900], 70, California WCTU Collection.

104. *HWS* 6:52.

105. Anthony to Keith, 28 Nov. 1902, Box 3, Keith Collection, BL; *HWS* 6:27–30.

106. *HWS* 6:27–40.

107. Catt to DeVoe, 9 Feb., Box 1, DeVoe Collection, WSL.

108. Beverly Beeton, *Women Vote in the West: the Woman Suffrage Movement, 1869–1896* (New York: Garland Press, 1986), 114–135.

109. Duniway, *Path Breaking*, 130, 209–212.

110. Catt to DeVoe, 20 April 1895, DeVoe Collection, WSL.

111. Catt to DeVoe, 7, 19 March, 1, 20 April 1895, Box 1, DeVoe Collection, WSL.

112. Catt to DeVoe, 9 July 1895, Box 1, DeVoe Collection, WSL.

113. Catt to DeVoe, n.d., 29 April, 8 Aug. 1895, Box 1, DeVoe Collection, WSL; *HWS* 4:590–595.

114. Frank Steunenberg, "Woman Suffrage in Idaho," *Harper's Bazaar* 33 (26 May 1900), 220–221; *HWS* 4:591–194.

115. Mary Wood Swift to Lillie Devereaux Blake, 30 March 1899, Blake Collection; Sarah Severance to Louise Sorbier, 30 March 1899, Sorbier Collection, CHS.

116. *HWS* 6:38–39.

NOTES TO CHAPTER 6

1. *Woman's Tribune*, 8 July 1905.

2. Previous studies include Marte Jo Sheeran, "The Woman Suffrage Issue in Washington, 1890–1910" (M.A. thesis, University of Washington, 1977); T. A. Larson, "The Woman Suffrage Movement in Washington," *Pacific Northwest Quarterly* 62 (April 1976), 49–62; Stella E. Pearce, "Suffrage in the Pacific Northwest: Old Oregon and Washington," *Washington Historical Quarterly* 3 (April 1912), 106–114; and John Putnam, "A 'Test of Chiffon Politics': Gender Politics in Seattle, 1897–1917," *Pacific Historical Review* 69:4 (Fall 2000), 595–616.

3. Abigail Scott Duniway, *Path Breaking: An Autobiographical History of the Equal Suffrage Movement in Pacific Coast States,* 2d ed. (Reprint, New York: Source Book Press, 1970), 111, 212–214; Karen J. Blair, *The Clubwoman as Feminist: True Womanhood Redefined, 1868–1914* (New York: Holmes and Meier, 1980), and Blair, ed., *Women in Pacific Northwest History: An Anthology* (Seattle: University of Washington Press, 1988); J. C. Croly, *The History of the Women's Club Movement in America* (New York: Henry B. Allen, 1898), 1142–1149; Sandra Haarsanger, *Organized Womanhood: Cultural Politics in the Pacific Northwest, 1840–1920* (Norman: University of Oklahoma Press, 1997); Clarence B. Bagley, *History of Seattle from the Earliest Settlement to the Present Time,* vol. 2 (Seattle: Clarke, 1916), 493.

4. John Putnam, "The Emergence of a New West: The Politics of Class and Gender in Seattle, Washington, 1880–1917" (Ph.D. diss., University of California, San Diego, 2000), 209–212; David Burke Griffiths, "Populism in the Far West, 1890–1900" (Ph.D. diss., University of Washington, 1967), 148–232; Marilyn P. Watkins, *Rural Democracy: Family Farmers and Politics in Western Washington, 1890–1925* (Ithaca, NY: Cornell University Press, 1995), 96–117; and also Watkins, "Political Activism and Community-Building among Alliance and Grange Women in Western Washington, 1892–1925," *Agricultural History* 67:2 (Spring 1993), 197–213; Jonathan Dembo, *Unions and Politics in Washington State, 1885–1935* (New York: Garland, 1983).

5. *HWS* 4:970–972; Griffiths, "Populism in the Far West," 219, citing *Seattle Post-Intelligencer, Tacoma Morning Union,* and *Tacoma Daily Ledger,* 13 Aug. 1896; *Woman's Tribune,* 3 April 1897; Barbara Cloud, "Laura Hall Peters: Pursuing the Myth of Equality," *Pacific Northwest Quarterly* 74:1 (Jan. 1983),

28–36; Sheeran, "The Woman Suffrage Issue in Washington," 26–28; *Woman's Tribune,* 3 April 1897; *Woman's Journal,* 12 Sept. 1896.

6. *Seattle Times,* 31 Oct. 1898.

7. Sheeran, "The Woman Suffrage Issue in Washington," 29–34.

8. *HWS* 4:971–973.

9. Sheeran, "The Woman Suffrage Issue in Washington," 66–67.

10. *HWS* 4:971–975.

11. *HWS* 4:974.

12. John Rogers to Mrs. Homer Hill, 14 Nov. 1898, Box 2c-2-23, John Rogers Collection, Washington State Archives, Olympia. See also A. Brisbane to Rogers, 3 Feb. 1897, Box 1, Women's Suffrage Special Collection (WSSC), Washington State Archives, Olympia.

13. Sheeran, "The Woman Suffrage Issue in Washington," 71–81.

14. Griffiths, "Populism in the Far West," 91–145.

15. HWS 4:896. This was a personal embarrassment for Duniway, since Scott was her brother. He claimed it was a misunderstanding that occurred in his absence, but there was clearly rivalry between them; see Ruth Barnes Moynihan, *Rebel for Rights: Abigail Scott Duniway* (New Haven and London: Yale University Press, 1983), 207–210.

16. *HWS* 6:538–539. Evans, the author of this section of the *History of Woman Suffrage,* was president of the Oregon State Federation of Women's Clubs, child labor commissioner, and Portland market inspector.

17. E. Claire Jerry, "Clara Bewick Colby and the *Woman's Tribune,* 1883–1909: The Free Lance Editor as Movement Leader," in Martha M. Solomon, ed., *A Voice of Their Own: The Woman Suffrage Press, 1840–1910* (Tuscaloosa: University of Alabama Press, 1991), 110–128; *HWS* 4:70–71.

18. See for example, Duniway to Catt, June 3 1916, Reel 33, Congressional Union Folder, *National American Woman Suffrage Association Records, 1850–1960,* Manuscript Division, Library of Congress, Washington, DC, 1981 (microfilm).

19. *HWS* 6:539–540; Duniway, *Path Breaking,* 218–226; Ronald W. Taber, "Sacajawea and the Suffragettes," *Pacific Northwest Quarterly* 58:1 (Jan. 1967), 7–13.

20. *HWS* 5:122–144, 6:540–541. Equi was a lesbian physician who had herself been a child worker in Massachussetts textile mills until she developed tuberculosis. She became radicalized after violent labor and free speech fights in 1913, worked with the IWW, Elizabeth Gurley Flynn, and Margaret Sanger, and was imprisoned for opposition to World War I. See Nancy Krieger, "Queen of the Bolsheviks: The Hidden History of Dr. Marie Equi," *Radical America* 17 (1983), 55–73.

21. *HWS* 5:133–134, 141–144.

22. *Woman's Tribune*, 8, 22 July 1905.

23. *Woman's Tribune*, 9 Sept., 11 Nov. 1905.

24. *Woman's Tribune*, 20 Jan., 14 April 1906.

25. *Woman's Tribune*, 12 May 1906.

26. *Woman's Tribune*, 25 Nov. 1905, 27 Oct. 1906.

27. *Woman's Tribune*, 31 March 1906, 28 April 1906; G. Thomas Edwards, *Sowing Good Seeds: The Northwest Suffrage Campaigns of Susan B. Anthony* (Portland: Oregon Historical Society Press, 1990), 247–248, 264–286.

28. *Woman's Tribune*, 24 June 1905.

29. *Woman's Tribune*, 17 Feb. 1906.

30. *Woman's Tribune*, 14, 28 April 1906.

31. *Woman's Tribune*, 28 April 1906.

32. Estimating a need for 50,000 votes, each of the 2,000 members was asked to recruit twenty-five votes: "Every retailer can get 25 votes. Besides his employees he has his grocer, his butcher, his landlord, his laundryman and every person he does business with. If every man in the business will do this we will win." *HWS* 6:543–544.

33. *Woman's Tribune* 9 June 1906.

34. *Woman's Tribune*, 10 Oct. 1906.

35. Duniway to Colby, 20 Jan. 1906, Clara Colby Collection, HL; Jerry, "Clara Bewick Colby," 112.

36. Edwards, *Sowing Good Seeds,* 294–300.

37. Laura Clay to Emma Smith DeVoe, 10 Feb. 1909, Box 1, Devoe Collection, WSL.

38. Duniway, *Path Breaking,* 179–182; *HWS* 6:544.

39. *HWS* 6:673.

40. Emma Smith (Mrs. John Henry) DeVoe, was born in Illinois in 1849, and lived there and in South Dakota before moving to Washington with her husband. See Frances E. Willard and Mary A. Livermore, eds., *A Woman of the Century: Fourteen Hundred Seventy Biographical Sketches Accompanied by Portraits of Leading Women in All Walks of Life* (Buffalo, NY: Charles Wells Moulton, 1893), 239.

41. Major sources on Hutton include Lucile F. Fargo, *Spokane Story* (Columbia University Press, 1950), 224–257; James W. Montgomery, *Liberated Woman: A Life of May Arkwright Hutton* (Fairfield, WA: Ye Galleon Press, 1974); Connie Poten, "May Arkwright Hutton: Miner to Millionaire," Wilderness Women Project, UMT, Missoula, n.d., Carton 1.4, Hutton Settlement Collection, Eastern Washington State Historical Society (hereafter cited as EWSHS); Patricia Voeller Horner, "May Arkwright Hutton: Suffragist and Politician," in Blair, ed., *Women in Pacific Northwest History,* 25–41; and Benjamin H. Kizer, "May Arkwright Hutton," *Pacific Northwest Quarterly* 57 (April 1966), 49–56.

42. Clippings, Scrapbook 3, Box 3, Hutton Collection, EWSHS.

43. Hutton to DeVoe, 25 June, 17 July 1908, Box 2, DeVoe Collection, WSL; Clippings, Scrapbooks 3 and 5, Boxes 3 and 4, Hutton Collection, EWSHS; Poten, "May Arkwright Hutton," 12–30.

44. Hutton, letter to the editor, *Spokane Spokesman Review,* 30 May 1909, and speech draft, 4 June 1909, Hutton Collection, EWSHS.

45. Hutton, "The Theory That Emancipates," Nov. 1908, Box 1, Hutton Collection, EWSHS.

46. *Spokane Spokesman-Review,* 22 Dec. 1908, *Seattle Post-Intelligencer,* 11, 30 Jan. 1909; Hutton to Harriet Taylor Upton, 8 Oct. 1908, Box 1, Hutton Collection, EWSHS; Montgomery, *Liberated Woman,* 29, 108–109; Horner, "May Arkwright Hutton," 28–29, 35; Sheeran, "The Woman Suffrage Issue in Washington," 87–88; Larson, "The Woman Suffrage Movement in Washington," 59. Larson depicts Hutton as a gross, publicity-seeking incompetent, and Sheeran misspells her name "Awkwright."

47. *Seattle Post-Intelligencer,* 11, 22 Jan. 1909. The initial delegation included DeVoe, Mrs. Homer M. Hill, Mrs. Mallott, and Mrs. Beloit, of Seattle, and Hutton and Mrs. LaReine Baker, a Spokane socialite with suffragette tendencies. There was also "an organization of self-supporting woman suffragists," probably labor activists who were in the capital to support legislation for a woman factory inspector and an eight–hour bill for women working in stores. On the eight-hour bill, see *Seattle Union Record,* 20 Feb. 1909; *Seattle Post-Intelligencer,* 27–30 Jan. 1909.

48. *Seattle Post-Intelligencer,* 4 Feb. 1909.

49. *Seattle Post-Intelligencer,* 15 Jan. 1909.

50. *Seattle Times,* 29 Jan. 1909; *Seattle Post-Intelligencer,* 4 Feb. 1909.

51. *HWS* 6:675; *Spokane Spokesman-Review,* 24 Feb. 1909; *Seattle Times,* 20–21, 29 Jan., 2–3 Feb. 1909; Sheeran, "The Woman Suffrage Issue in Washington," 93–99.

52. George Piper to Cora Eaton, 1 June 1909, Box 5, Smith to DeVoe, 19 Feb. 1909, Box 3, L. Frank Brown to DeVoe, 26 Feb. 1909, Box 1, DeVoe Collection, WSL.

53. *Seattle Times,* 23 Feb. 1909, *Seattle Post-Intelligencer,* 24 Feb. 1909; Sheeran, "The Woman Suffrage Issue in Washington," 98–108.

54. *Seattle Post-Intelligencer,* 24 Feb. 1909.

55. *HWS* 6:677–678; Robert Rydell, *All the World's a Fair: Visions of Empire at American International Expositions, 1876–1916* (Chicago: University of Chicago Press, 1984), 184–207.

56. *Seattle Daily Times,* 23 Aug. 1908.

57. Harriet Upton to DeVoe, 31 July, 31 Aug. 1908, Sapp to DeVoe, 8 Nov. 1909, all in Box 3, DeVoe Collection, WSL.

58. Moore to DeVoe, 9 June 1909, Box 2, DeVoe Collection, WSL; Hutton to Cora Mallott, 28 May 1909, Box 1, Hutton Collection, EWSHS.

59. Eaton to DeVoe, 30 May 1909, Box 2, DeVoe Collection, WSL.

60. Hutton to Leonia Browne, 28 May 1909, Hutton to Hill, 4 June 1909, and Hutton to Malott, 7 June 1909, all in Box 1, Hutton Collection, EWSHS.

61. Edith De Long Jarmuth to DeVoe, 8 June 1909, Box 2, DeVoe Collection, WSL.

62. Eaton to DeVoe, 4, 24 June 1909, Box 2, DeVoe Collection, WSL; Katherine Smith to Hutton, 26 Dec 1910, Hutton Collection, WSL.

63. Hutton to Eaton, 11 June 1909, Box 2, DeVoe Collection, WSL.

64. Eaton to Hutton, 17 June 1909, Box 2, DeVoe Collection, WSL.

65. Eaton to Catt, 24 Oct. 1909, Box 2, DeVoe Collection, WSL.

66. Hutton to Eaton, 19 June 1909 (with annotations by Eaton) Box 2, DeVoe Collection, WSL.

67. *Seattle Times,* 4 July 1909; Upton to Catt, 17 Nov. 1909, Box 3, DeVoe Collection, WSL.

68. Kate Gordon to DeVoe and Eaton, 29 March, April 19, 1909, Box 2, DeVoe Collection, WSL.

69. *Seattle Times,* 1, 4 (Coates), 5 July 1909.

70. Upton to DeVoe, 6 Aug. 1909, Box 3, DeVoe Collection, WSL.

71. DeVoe to Catt, 23, 30 Nov. 1909, Box 1, DeVoe Collection, WSL.

72. Putnam, "The Emergence of a New West," 355–356.

73. *HWS* 6:677–681; Baily, "How Washington Women Regained the Ballot," *Pacific Monthly* 26 (July 1911), 9–10; Shaw to Devoe, 4, 20 Dec. 1907, Box 3, Hester Miller to DeVoe, 2 Jan. 1908, Box 2, DeVoe Collection, WSL; *HWS* 6:679; *Washington Equal Suffrage Bulletin* (vol. 1, no. 2), 24 Jan. 1908, Miscellaneous Collection, EWSHS.

74. *Seattle Post-Intelligencer,* 13 Nov. 1910; Baily, "How Washington Women Regained the Ballot," 8–9.

75. *Spokane Chronicle,* 3, 9 Oct. 1910.

76. *Putnam,* "The Emergence of a New West," 282–286.

77. *HWS* 6:678, 682.

78. Fred W. Lewis to DeVoe, 26 June, 31 July 1909; Lewis and C. B. Kegley to DeVoe, 16 Feb. 1910; Augusta M. Kegley to DeVoe, 21 Sept., 1909, all in Box 3, DeVoe Collection, WSL.

79. *Spokane Chronicle,* 10 Nov. 1910.

80. Mrs. Frank C. Cotterill to DeVoe, 13 Aug. 1908, Box 1; Blanche H. Mason to DeVoe, 24 May 1909, Jarmuth to DeVoe, 26 July 1908, Box 2, DeVoe Collection, WSL. Frank Cotterill was a building trades union official and president of the state federation of labor. His brother George, introduced the woman suffrage bill in the Washington State Senate in 1909, and later served briefly as a reform mayor of Seattle.

81. Putnam, "The Emergence of a New West," 312–328.

82. Kathryn J. Oberdeck, "'Not Pink Teas': The Seattle Working-Class Women's Movement, 1905–1918," *Labor History* 32:2 (Spring 1991), 203–206.

83. *Seattle Union Record,* 1 Oct. 1910, also 8, 22, 29 Oct. 1910.

84. Luema Johnson to DeVoe, 11 Jan 1908, 24 Jan. 1909, Box 2, Charles C. Case to DeVoe, 13 Dec. 1909, 3 Jan. 1910, Box 3, Leaflet, 1910, Box 1, DeVoe Collection, WSL; *HWS* 6:678.

85. Johnson to Co-Workers, 11 Aug. 1910, Lucie Fulton Isaacs to DeVoe, 21 Aug. 1910, Box 2, DeVoe Collection, WSL; *Tacoma Daily Ledger,* 30 Aug., 6 Sept. 1910.

86. Johnson to Ellen Leckenby, 24 Oct. 1910, Box 2, and Charles Perry Taylor to DeVoe, 2 Aug. 1910, Box 3, DeVoe Collection, WSL.

87. *Seattle Union Record,* 30 Jan. 1909; *Spokane Chronicle,* 7 June 1910. *Report of President Charles Case before the Ninth Annual Washington State Federation of Labor at Hoquiam, Wash., Jan. 11–14, 1910* (Gray's Harbor Post, Aberdeen, WA, c. 1911), Box 2, Marion E. Hay Collection, EWSHS; Charles Perry Taylor to DeVoe, Resolution 62, Washington State Federation of Labor, Jan. 1910, Box 3, DeVoe Collection, WSL.

88. *Spokane Inland Herald,* ca. 3 Sept. 1910; *Spokane Chronicle,* 5 Nov. 1910.

89. *Seattle Union Record,* 6, 15 Nov. 1910.

90. *Spokane Spokesman-Review,* 11, 18 Sept., 1, 8 Nov. 1910. David Coates, a socialist and former publisher (*Pueblo Courier*), was head of the Colorado state labor federation in the late 1890s and was elected lieutenant governor in 1900. He moved north ca. 1906. On Coates (and a bit on Mrs. Coates), see N. W. Durham, *History of the City of Spokane and Spokane County, Washington, from Its Early Settlement to the Present Time,* vol. 2 (Seattle: Clarke, 1912), 319–322; and David Thomas Brundage, *The Making of Western Labor Radicalism: Denver's Organized Workers, 1878–1905* (Urbana: University of Illinois Press, 1994), 123–124, 134–135, 144–145,152–153.

91. Oberdeck, "'Not Pink Teas,'" 193–230.

92. *Spokane Spokesman-Review,* 14 July 1910.

93. *Spokane Spokesman-Review,* 5 Sept. 1910; *Bellingham Herald,* 29 July 1910.

94. *Spokane Spokesman-Review,* 11 Sept. 1910.

95. Clippings, Scrapbook 1, Box 3, Hutton Collection, EWSHS. On the IWW, see Melvyn Dubofsky, *We Shall Be All: A History of the Industrial Workers of the World* (Chicago: Quadrangle Books, 1969). When IWW organizer Helen Gurley Flynn, the Pacific Northwest's own "Rebel Girl," was arrested and jailed although pregnant, some Spokane clubwomen openly supported and aided her.

96. Hutton to Duniway, 13 Aug. 1909, Hutton Collection, WSL; Hutton to Leonia Browne, 23 Sept. 1909, Hutton to Hill 27 July, 13 Aug. 1909, Box 1,

Hutton Collection, EWSHS. On the Spokane College League, see *Spokane Spokesman-Review,* 13 May, 3 Oct. 1909.

97. A decade earlier Hutton had met Reynolds when she asked for advice about publishing her book. Reynolds caused a slight scandal by not using her married name, although Salvatore Scalabrino, "an Italian socialist sailor," reportedly supported his wife's work. See *Seattle Post-Intelligencer,* 23 Nov. 1910; and interview in Scrapbook 2, Box 3, Hutton Collection, EWSHS.

98. *Spokane Chronicle,* 25, 28 Oct. 1910; Sheeran, "The Woman Suffrage Issue in Washington," 137.

99. *Spokane Spokesman-Review,* 10 July, 6 Nov. 1910.

100. *HWS* 6:680–681; Clark, *The Dry Years,* 91–93, 100, 113; Sheeran, "The Woman Suffrage Issue in Washington, 1890–1910," 143.

101. *HWS* 6:681–682; *Seattle Post-Intelligencer,* 8 Nov. 1910, *Spokane Chronicle,* 3 Nov. 1910; *Western Woman Voter,* Jan.–Feb. 1911.

102. *Seattle Times,* 9 Nov. 1910; Olive Bruce to DeVoe, Nov. 1910, Box 1, DeVoe Collection, WSL.

103. *Tacoma Daily News,* 7–8 Nov. 1910; *Spokane Chronicle,* 0 Nov. 1910; *HWS* 6:682–684; *Seattle Post Intelligencer,* 9 Nov. 1910.

104. *Seattle Times,* 1, 4, 6 Nov. 1910; *Western Woman Voter,* Jan., Feb., March, Sept. 1911, Feb. 1912; Sheeran, "The Woman Suffrage Issue in Washington, 1890–1910," 144–162. Dilling later fell afoul of the reformers, and was himself replaced by George F. Cotterill.

105. Ellen Leckenby to DeVoe, 13 Feb. 1911, Box 2, DeVoe Collection, WSL.

106. *Western Woman Voter* (May 1911); Baily, "How Washington Women Regained the Ballot," 2–3, 10–11.

107. Hutton to Duniway, 13 March 1911; Hutton to R. A. Hutchinson, 27 Feb. 1911, both in Box 1, Hutton Collection, EWSHS.

108. Sapp to DeVoe, 11 Jan. 1912 [1913], Box 3, DeVoe Collection, WSL. Washington State Library, "Women in the Washington State Legislature—1913–1999." See also http://www.statelib.wa.gov:80/refdesk/databases/women.htm.

109. *Seattle Post-Intelligencer,* 10 Nov. 1910; *Western Woman Voter* (March 1911); Bernice Sapp to Berthe Knatvold Kittelsen, 18 Dec. 1911, Box 3, DeVoe Collection, WSL; *HWS* 6:684.

110. Putnam, "The Emergence of a New West," 312.

111. *Seattle Post-Intelligencer,* 9 Nov. 1910.

112. "Declaration of Principles," Pamphlet in Box 1, WSSC, Washington State Archives; Duniway, *Path Breaking,* 243–249.

113. DeVoe to Lillian Coffin, 24 Nov. 1908, Box 1, Bessie I. Savage to DeVoe, [1910?], Box 3, DeVoe Collection, WSL. As early as 1908, DeVoe appar-

ently discussed an independent "pacific states suffrage league" with Coffin, and the idea for a league of women voters with Savage.

114. Hutton to Anna Howard Shaw, 19 Feb. 1911, Box 1, and Clippings, Scrapbooks 2, Box 3, and Scrapbook 4, Box 4, Hutton Collection, EWSHS; Eaton to DeVoe, 6 Jan. 1911, Box 2, DeVoe Collection, EWSHS; "A Plain Statement of Facts: A Meeting of Protest, and Resolutions, Rev. Abbie Danforth; and Scrapbooks, Vol. 13 (Bernice Sapp), Box 8, DeVoe Collection, WSL; "Those Frozen Tears of Rage; Being the True Story of What Happened at Tacoma" by Olive M. Bruce, *The Town Crier,* and reply, Box 2, Hutton Collection, EWSHS; Smith to Hutton, 26 Dec. 1910, Hutton Collection, WSL.

115. Moynihan, *Rebel for Rights,* 216–218. See also Mary Keith to DeVoe, 22 Jan. 1912, 23 Feb. 1912, Box 2, DeVoe Collection, WSL; Cornelia Templeton Jewett to Park, 21 Feb. 1911, Box 3, and Frances W. Munds to Alice Park, 27 Jan. 1913, Box 4, Alice Park Collection, Huntington Library. Munds wrote Park, "Miss Shaw claims that those women have been very disloyal to the National. Their plan appeals to me but I could not repudiate the National."

116. Duniway, *Path Breaking,* 261–265; Moynihan, *Rebel for Rights,* 214–217.

117. Hutton to Mrs. George Smith, 19 July 1911, Hutton to Shaw, 21 Sept. 1911, and Hutton to Gov. Hay, 16 Oct. 1911, all in Box 1, Hutton Collection, EWSHS; Helen Moore (CESA) to DeVoe, 13 June [1910]; Elizabeth Lowe Watson to DeVoe, 16 March 1911, and Minerva Goodman (CESA) to DeVoe, June 1911, Box 1, Mary Sperry to Mrs. Ballard, 5 March 5 1911, Box 3, DeVoe Collection, WSL.

NOTES TO CHAPTER 7

1. Dupuy, a local French teacher, was speaking at a rally in the French quarter, as quoted in the *San Francisco Call,* 7 Sept. 1911.

2. Major works on the 1911 California campaign include College Equal Suffrage League of Northern California (CESL), *Winning Equal Suffrage in California* (San Francisco: Press of The James H. Barry Co., 1913); Selina Solomons, *How We Won the Vote in California: A True Story of the Campaign of 1911* (San Francisco: New Woman Publishing, [1912]); Ida Husted Harper, ed., *The History of Woman Suffrage,* vol. 6. Reprint ed. (Salem, NH: Ayer, 1985), 27–58; Susan Englander, *Class Coalition and Class Conflict in the California Woman Suffrage Movement, 1907–1912: The San Francisco Wage Earners' Suffrage League* (Lewiston, NY: Mellen Research University Press, 1992); Ronald Schaffer, "The Problem of Consciousness in the Woman Suffrage Movement: A California Perspective," *Pacific Historical Review* 45 (November 1976), 469–493; Donald Waller Rodes, "The California Woman Suffrage Campaign of

1911" (M.A. thesis, California State University, Hayward, 1974); Sherry Jeanne Katz, "Dual Commitments: Feminism, Socialism, and Women's Political Activism in California, 1890–1920" (Ph.D. diss., University of California, Los Angeles, 1991), 241–362, and Katz, "A Politics of Coalition: Socialist Women and the California Suffrage Movement," in Marjorie Spruill Wheeler, ed., *One Woman, One Vote: Rediscovering the Woman Suffrage Movement* (Troutdale, OR: New Sage Press, 1995), 245–262; Gayle Ann Gullett, *Becoming Citizens: The Emergence and Development of the California Women's Movement, 1880–1911* (Urbana and Chicago: University of Illinois Press, 2000), 166–192.

3. Anthony to Keith, 28 Jan. 1905, Box 5, Mary Keith, typescript chronology, Carton 3, Keith-McHenry-Pond Family Collection, BL; *HWS* 6:29–31, 39–40.

4. Mrs. Seward Adams Simons, "Equality of Opportunity," 1911, Bolerium Bookstore Collection, San Francisco, California.

5. Clara Burdette, Speech, 1902, in Program of First Convention of GFWC, Box 29.1, Clara Burdette Collection, Huntington Library (HL), San Marino, California; Mary S. Gibson, *A Record of Twenty-five Years of the California Federation of Women's Clubs, 1900–1925* (Los Angeles, 1925).

6. Gibson, *A Record of Twenty-Five Years,* 60–64; *Woman's Journal,* 3 June 1911; Jacqueline Braitman, "Katherine Philips Edson: A Progressive Feminist in California's Era of Reform" (Ph.D. diss., University of California at Los Angeles, 1988), 136–139.

7. *Los Angeles Times,* 6–7 May 1902; Gibson, *A Record of Twenty-five Years,* 21, 30–32, 34; Karen J. Blair, *The Clubwoman as Feminist: True Womanhood Redefined, 1868–1914* (New York: Holmes and Meier, 1980), 108–110; Mary I. Wood, *History of the General Federation of Women's Clubs for the First Twenty-two Years of Its Organization* (Reprint, Farmingdale, NY: Dabor Social Science Publishers), 129–131, 154–157; Gullett, *Becoming Citizens,* 120–123. On the NAWSA's southern strategy, see Rosalyn Terborg-Penn, "African American Women and the Suffrage Movement," in Wheeler, ed., *One Woman, One Vote,* 146–154, Aileen S. Kraditor, *The Ideas of the Woman Suffrage Movement, 1890–1920* (Reprint, New York: W. W. Norton, 1981), 163–218, Marjorie Julian Spruill, "Race, Reform, and Reaction at the Turn of the Century: Southern Suffragists, the NAWSA, and the 'Southern Strategy' in Context," in Jean H. Baker, ed., *Votes for Women: The Struggle for Suffrage Revisited* (Oxford and New York: Oxford University Press, 2002), 102–117, Marjorie Spruill Wheeler, *New Women of the New South: The Leaders of the Woman Suffrage Movement in the Southern States* (New York: Oxford University Press, 1993).

8. Caroline Severance, [Remarks, GFWC Biennial Convention], in Ella Giles Ruddy, ed., *The Mother of Clubs: Caroline M. Seymour Severance: An Estimate and an Appreciation* (Los Angeles: Baumgardt, 1906), 71–74. See also Joan Jensen, "After Slavery: Caroline Severance in Los Angeles," *Southern California*

Quarterly 48 (July 1966), 182–183; Booker T. Washington to Severance, 5 March 1902, Box 24, Severance Collection, HL.

9. Caroline Severance, [Remarks, Friday Morning Club], (1902), in Ruddy, *The Mother of Clubs,* 74–75.

10. *San Francisco Examiner,* 8 Nov. 1901, as cited by Rudolph M. Lapp, "Mabel Craft Deering: A Young Woman of Advanced Ideas," *California* History 66 (Sept. 1987), 166.

11. Mary Keith, untitled report, Carton 3, Keith Collection, BL. Mr. Keith died during the 1911 campaign. His sister, Eliza, was a journalist and a suffragist.

12. Alice Park to Elbert E. Porter, 30 Oct. 1918, Box 5, Park Collection, HL. For Park's unfinished autobiography and diaries, see the Alice Park Collection, Hoover Institution Archives, Stanford, California.

13. In 1919, Whitney was speaking in a church in support of African American suffrage when she was arrested. After her conviction, Whitney's privileged position protected her from prison, unlike Oregon's Dr. Marie Equi. See Lisa Rubens, "The Patrician Radical: Charlotte Anita Whitney," *California History* 65 (Sept. 1986), 158–171, 226–227fn.; C. A. Whitney, "The Alameda County Jail," *Survey* 43:13 (25 Dec. 1920), 452–453.

14. *San Francisco Call,* 8 Jan. 1908; Englander, *Class Coalition and Class Conflict,* 110–118.

15. Alice Park, "Maud Younger of S.F., Washington, D.C. and Los Gatos" (typescript), 19 May 1943, in U.S. Biographical Collection, Sophia Smith Collection, Smith College, as cited by Englander, *Class Coalition and Class Conflict,* 110–114.

16. *HWS* 6:29.

17. *San Francisco Call,* 5–6 Oct. 1907.

18. Sherry Katz, "Frances Nacke Noel and 'Sister Movements': Socialism, Feminism and Trade Unionism in Los Angeles, 1909–1916," *California History* 67 (Sept. 1988), 181–189 and 207–210fn.

19. See Ellen Carol DuBois, "Working Women, Class Relations, and Suffrage Militance: Harriot Stanton Blatch and the New York Woman Suffrage Movement, 1894–1909," *Journal of American History* 74 (June 1987), 34–58.

20. *San Francisco Call,* 23 Sept, 4 Oct. 1908.

21. Convention minutes, 29 Sept. 1909, Reel 19, pp. 24–26, National Women's Trade Union League Collection, Library of Congress, Washington, DC (hereafter cited as LC). For the streetcar strike, see Englander, *Class Conflict and Class Coalition,* 82–86.

22. *San Francisco Call,* 4 Oct. 1908.

23. *San Francisco Call,* 11 Jan. 1908; *San Francisco Examiner,* 6 Oct. 1911.

24. *San Francisco Daily News,* 22 July 1911.

25. Agnes H. Downing, "Woman Suffrage in California," *Progressive*

Woman 52 (Sept. 1911), 1; *California Social Democrat,* 2, 16 Sept. 1911; and Katz, "Dual Commitments," ix, 3, 14–16. More generally, see Mari Jo Buhle, *Women and American Socialism, 1870–1920* (Urbana: University of Illinois Press, 1981).

26. Walton Bean, *Boss Ruef's San Francisco* (Berkeley: University of California Press, 1952); for the ULP, see Jules Tygiel, "'Where Unionism Holds Undisputed Sway'—A Reappraisal of San Francisco's Union Labor Party," *California History* 62 (Fall 1983), 196–215.

27. LaRue at WTUL Convention minutes, 29 Sept. 1909, Reel 19, pp. 21–26, NWTUL Collection, LC. See also Dorothy Sue Cobble, *Dishing It Out: Waitresses and Their Unions in the Twentieth Century* (Urbana and Chicago: University of Illinois Press, 1991).

28. *San Francisco Call,* 23 Nov. 1908; Susan Englander, "Right-Minded Women: Clubwomen and the San Francisco Graft Trials," *Journal of History* (San Francisco State University) 1 (1989), 11–28, and *Class Coalition and Class Conflict,* 89–93.

29. George E. Mowry, *The California Progressives* (Berkeley: University of California Press, 1951); Spencer C. Olin, Jr., *California's Prodigal Sons: Hiram Johnson and the Progressives, 1911–1917* (Berkeley: University of California Press, 1968). More generally, see Daniel T. Rodgers, "In Search of Progressivism," *Reviews in American History* 10 (Dec. 1982), 113–132; Robert Wiebe, *The Search for Order* (New York: Hill and Wang, 1967); Richard Hofstader, *The Age of Reform: From Bryan to F.D.R.* (New York: Vintage Books, 1955); and Steven J. Diner, *A Very Different Age: Americans of the Progressive Era* (New York: Hill and Wang, 1998).

30. Anna Shaw to Mary Keith, 1 May 1906, Box 12, Keith Collection, BL.

31. *San Francisco Call,* 6 Oct. 1906; Alice Park, Memorandum (re Lillian Harris Coffin), n.d., Box 3, Park Collection, HL. See also Gullett, *Becoming Citizens,* 166–167.

32. *San Francisco Call,* 5–6 Oct. 1907; *Woman's Journal,* 19 Oct. 1907.

33. *San Francisco Call,* 3 Oct. 1909.

34. *San Francisco Call,* 6 Sept. 1911.

35. *San Francisco Call,* 3 Oct. 1909.

36. *Woman's Journal,* 8 June 1907; Henry Blackwell to Alice Park, 1 May 1907, Box 1, Park Collection, HL; *HWS* 6:53–54. Other witnesses included Mary Sperry, then state president, and the episode was recorded in the organization's minutes; see Solomons, *How We Won,* 8–9.

37. On the eight-hour-day campaign, see Rebecca J. Mead, "Trade Unionism and Political Activity among San Francisco Wage-Earning Women, 1900–1922," (M.A. thesis, San Francisco State University), 1991, 138–156. On the companion minimum wage law of 1913, see Mead, "'Let the Women Get Their Wages as

Men Do': Trade Union Women and the Legislated Minimum Wage in California," *Pacific Historical Review* 67:3 (Aug. 1998), 317–347.

38. *HWS* 6:54–55; Solomons, *How We Won,* 10. Grove Johnson was the father of future Progressive governor Hiram Johnson, but they were estranged.

39. *San Francisco Call,* 29 Aug. 1908.

40. Minutes, [1909], Carton 3, Keith Collection, BL.

41. *HWS* 6:39–41; Minutes, 10 Sept. 1910, Carton 3, and John Hyde Braly to Keith, 8 May 1920, Box 5, Keith Collection, BL; John Hyde Braly, *Memory Pictures: An Autobiography* (Los Angeles: Neuser, 1912); Marshall Stimson, "Fun, Fights, and Fiestas in Old Los Angeles" (typescript), 186, Box 4, Marshall Stimson Collection, HL; Rodes, "The California Woman Suffrage Campaign of 1911," 89–136; and Braitman, "Katherine Phillips Edson," 203–207.

42. Meyer Lissner, Speech, 30 Aug. 1912, Folder 721, and Meyer Lissner to Viola Kaufman, 20 Aug. 1908, Folder 722, Box 40, Meyer Lissner Collection, Special Collections Department, Stanford University; Lissner to Caroline Severance, 23 Dec. 1909, Box 20, Caroline Severance Collection, HL.

43. Guido Marx, "Statement on Woman Suffrage, 1911," Box 1, Folder 22, Guido Marx Collection, Special Collections Department, Stanford University.

44. Herbert Jones to Edgar E. Robinson, 23 March 1956 (quoted in finding aid), Special Collections Department, Stanford University.

45. Mary Keith, "The Political Situation," Carton 3, Keith Collection, BL. Suffragists put plenty of pressure on Johnson; see, for example, Votes for Women Club of California (Clara Foltz and Mary Foy), 29 May 1911, and the Equal Suffrage Amendment League of Oakland (Agnes Ray) to Johnson, 19 Aug. 1911, all in Box 42, Hiram Johnson Collection, BL.

46. Johnson to Meyer Lissner, 6 Nov. 1911, Johnson Collection, BL. A month later (after the Los Angeles mayoral election), Johnson commended the new women voters of California; see Johnson to Harriet Taylor Upton, 11 Dec. 1911, Johnson Collection, BL.

47. *Labor Clarion,* 8, 22 Jan. 1909. Nolan, an iron molder, was elected to the San Francisco city council in 1911, and as secretary of the SFLC in 1912. He also served as California state labor commissioner, and as a Republican member of the U.S. House of Representatives from 1913 until his death in 1922. Nolan's wife, Mae Ella, completed his term. See U.S. Congress, *Biographical Directory of the American Congress, 1774–1961* (Washington, DC, 1962).

48. Meeting minutes, n.d., Box 6, Keith Collection, BL. Park to Florence J. Hartell, 1910, Box 2, Park Collection, HL; Helen Moore to Jennie McBean, 11 Dec. 1910, Box 6, Keith Collection, BL.

49. *San Francisco Call,* 1–3 Oct. 1909. See also Elizabeth Watson to Mrs. John Snook, 17 Oct. 1909, 24 Sept. 1910, Jane Stanford Collection, Special Collections Department, Stanford University. Heney was decisively beaten by Charles Fickert.

50. *San Francisco Call,* 1 Oct. 1909. See also CESA, Program of the Annual Convention, 1909, Box 124, Franklin Hichborn Collection, Special Collections Department, University of California, Los Angeles (UCLA). See also the John Randolph Haynes Collection, UCLA.

51. Watson to McBean, 24 Sept., 14, 16, 18 Oct. 1910, 15 Jan. 1911, Box 12, Keith Collection, BL; Rodes, "The California Woman Suffrage Campaign of 1911," 44–45, 80–81.

52. Watson to McBean, 15 Jan. 1911, Box 12, Keith Collection, BL.

53. Katherine Edson to Frances Noel, 13 Jan. 1911, Box 10, Katherine Philips Edson Collection, Department of Special Collections, University of California, Los Angeles (UCLA); Braitman, "Katherine Philips Edson," 126–130.

54. Solomons, *How We Won,* 46; Rodes, "The California Woman Suffrage Campaign of 1911," 51.

55. Solomons, *How We Won,* 31; *Woman's Journal,* 16 Sept. 1911.

56. Clara Foltz to Clara Colby, 26 June 1908, 8 April, 6 June 1909, Clara Colby Collection, HL.

57. *HWS* 6:40–41; see also Dora Haynes material on the PEL, Box 228, Haynes Collection, UCLA.

58. When Alice Park asked for advice, one NAWSA official admitted that keeping "Anna Shaw away from California during the campaign . . . is too big an order for me to fill," and stated bluntly that "the real way to keep her away is to see that her expenses are not paid." See Mary Gray Peck to Alice Park, 27 July 1911, Box 2, Park Collection, HL.

59. *Woman's Journal,* 4 Nov. 1911; Ella Giles Ruddy to Caroline Severance, 17 June, 1 July 1911, Box 22, Caroline Severance Collection, HL; Gullett, *Becoming Citizens,* 182–184.

60. *California Outlook,* 11 Feb. 1911. On the *Times* bombing, see Grace Heilman Stimson, *Rise of the Labor Movement in Los Angeles* (Berkeley and Los Angeles: University of California Press, 1955), 366–406; Ira B. Cross, *A History of the Labor Movement in California* (Berkeley and Los Angeles: University of California Press, 1935), 282–283.

61. Frances Noel to Frances A. Williamson (President, Oakland Women's Union Label League), 7 March 1911, Box 11, Frances N. Noel Collection, UCLA; and Gullett, *Becoming Citizens,* 179–180; Sherry Katz, "Frances Nacke Noel and 'Sister Movements,'" 181–189 and 207–210fn.

62. *Los Angeles Herald,* 11 July 1911; *Los Angeles Tribune,* 14, 26 July, 6 Aug. 1911; *Woman's Journal,* 22 July 1911.

63. *San Francisco Examiner,* 6 Oct. 1911.

64. *San Francisco Examiner,* 18 Sept. 1911.

65. *HWS* 6:33. The first college league was formed in Boston in 1908, where the women also had early ties to the Women's Trade Union League; see Sharon Hartman Strom, "Leadership and Tactics in the American Woman Suffrage

Movement: A New Perspective from Massachusetts," *Journal of American History* 42:2 (Sept. 1975), 302–305.

66. Harriett Watson Capwell, "Votes for Woman Club," n.d., Selina Solomons Collection, BL.

67. Clara Schelingheyde to Carrie Catt, 16 Oct. 1911, Reel 4, Catt Papers, NAWSA Microfilm Collection.

68. Schelingheyde to Catt, 10 May 1911, Reel 4, Catt Papers, NAWSA Microfilm Collection.

69. CESL, *Winning,* 61–62, 106, 113–114.

70. CESL, *Winning,* 51–52; Meeting minutes, n.d. [1911]; Moore to McBean, 17 June 1911, Box 6, Keith Collection, BL; *San Francisco Call,* 7 Oct. 1911.

71. CESL, *Winning,* 62.

72. CESL, *Winning,* 61–68; Solomons, *How We Won,* 55.

73. CESL, *Winning,* 113.

74. Taylor to McBean, n.d. [1911], Box 12, Keith Collection, BL; see also Margaret Finnegan, *Selling Suffrage: Consumer Culture and Votes for Women* (New York: Columbia University Press, 1999).

75. Solomons, *How We Won,* 37–38; CESL, *Winning,* 46–48, 83–89, 129; *HWS* 6:47; *San Francisco Call,* 20 Aug. 1911.

76. CESL, *Winning,* 47; Solomons, *How We Won,* 40.

77. Watson to McBean, 24 Aug. 1911, Box 12, and Moore to McBean, 17 June 1911, Box 6; List of suffrage slides, Box 12, and Clipping, 1911, Box 4, Keith Collection, BL; CESL, *Winning,* 94–96; *Woman's Journal,* 16 Sept. 1911.

78. CESL, *Winning,* 17–24; Lapp, "Mabel Craft Deering," 162–169. Other women suffragist journalists and writers included Bessie Beatty, Vivian Pierce, Gertrude Atherton, Mary Austin, and Ina Coolbrith.

79. CESL, *Winning,* 19–20; Watson to McBean, 31 Aug. 1910, Box 12, Keith Collection, BL.

80. Clipping, 1911, Box 4, Keith Collection, BL; Solomons, *How We Won,* 37–38; CESL, *Winning,* 43–45.

81. Solomons, *How We Won,* 49; CESL, *Winning,* 76.

82. *San Francisco Call,* 28 Aug. 1911.

83. *San Francisco Call,* 5 Oct. 1911.

84. *Labor Clarion,* 11 Sept. 1908, 1, 22 Aug. 1911; *San Francisco Call,* 19, 22 Aug. 1911.

85. *San Francisco Call,* 28 Aug. 1911.

86. *San Francisco Call,* 28 Aug. 1911.

87. Frances Noel, "A Word to Socialist Voters," *Los Angeles Citizen,* 1 Sept. 1911.

88. Moore to McBean, 18 Aug. 1911, Box 12, Keith Collection, BL. Mary Keith had started this work earlier. In a 1908 article in a local French-language

paper she asked rhetorically: "Où sont les journées de travail de huit heurers pour la femme? Avec le vote, les ouvrières peuvent améliorer leur condition" (Where is the eight-hour day for women? With the vote, they can work to improve their condition"). *Le Franco-Californien, Courier de San Francisco,* 14 July 1908 [Bastille Day].

89. Younger, "Why Wage Earning Women Should Vote," and "The Wage Earners Need of the Ballot," Folders, Carton 4, Keith Collection; *San Francisco Call,* 4 July 1909; Coolidge, *Chinese Immigration,* 423–458.

90. "It would be a curious thing if when you reach China you find the Chinese women enfranchised," which indeed Catt did find in a few areas when she arrived soon thereafter. Clara Schelinghyde to Catt, 16 Oct. 1911, Reel 4, Catt Papers, NAWSA Microfilm Collection.

91. CESL, *Winning,* 87; *Woman's Journal,* 16 Sept. 1911. See also Judy Yung, *Unbound Feet: A Social History of Chinese Women in San Francisco* (Berkeley: University of California Press, 1995), 52–105.

92. *Woman's Journal,* 14 Oct. 1911.

93. Schelinghyde to Catt, 16 Oct. 1911, Reel 4, Catt Papers, NAWSA Microfilm Collection.

94. *San Francisco Call,* 14, 15 Sept. 1911; *HWS* 6:48; CESL, *Winning,* 39.

95. *Woman's Journal,* 3, 9 June 1911; *Los Angeles Tribune,* 14 July 1911, *Los Angeles Times,* 3 Oct. 1911.

96. Ann D. Gordon, et al., eds., *African American Women and the Vote, 1837–1965* (Amherst: University of Massachusetts Press, 1997); Rosalyn M. Terborg-Penn, "Afro-Americans in the Struggle for Woman Suffrage," (Ph.D diss., Howard University, 1977), 156–157, 263–265; and Terborg-Penn, *African American Women in the Struggle for the Vote, 1850–1920* (Bloomington: Indiana University Press, 1998).

97. *San Francisco Call,* 23, 24 Aug. 1911; *Woman's Journal,* 30 Sept. 1911; A. W. Hunton, "The Club Movement in California," *Crisis* (Dec. 1912), 90–92; Adella Hunt Logan, "Colored Women as Voters," *Crisis* (Sept. 1912), 242–243.

98. *Woman's Journal,* 30 Sept. 1911; Delilah L. Beasley, *The Negro Trailblazers of California* (reprint of 1919 ed.), 232–233.

99. Lawrence B. deGraaf, "Race, Sex, and Region: Black Women in the American West, 1850–1920," *Pacific Historical Review* 49 (May 1980): 309–311. One likely suffragist would have been Charlotta A. Spears [Bass], who edited the *California Eagle* (Los Angeles) with J. B. Bass, and was politically active for many years afterward; see Gerald R. Gill, "From Progressive Republican to Independent Progressive: The Political Career of Charlotta A. Bass," in Gordon, *African American Women and the Vote,* 156–171.

100. Solomons, *How We Won,* 35; *Woman's Journal,* 3 June 1911.

101. Mary Keith observed that "if women are seen talking to the A.P.A.'s, and if APA women speak before Catholic organizations . . . it's all on the bill of

fare." Keith, untitled manuscript on woman suffrage, 1911, Carton 3, Keith Collection, BL.

102. Solomons, *How We Won,* 38; *Woman's Journal,* 3, 10 June 1911; *San Francisco Examiner,* 17, 23 Sept. 1911; *HWS* 6:39; Watson to MacBean, 30 July 1911, Box 12, and Keith, untitled manuscript, 1911, Carton 3, Keith Collection, BL. Rhoda Ringrose made several country tours during the California campaign, and both women employed similar techniques later in Oregon, Nevada, and New York.

103. Catt to Schelinghyde, 13 April 1911, Reel 4, Catt Papers, NAWSA Microfilm Collection.

104. *San Francisco Call,* 14 Aug. 1911.

105. *San Francisco Daily News,* 17 Aug. 1911; *Labor Clarion,* 25 Aug. 1911; *San Francisco Call,* 18 Aug. 1911.

106. *San Francisco Examiner,* 25, 30 Sept., 8 Oct. 1911; *San Francisco Daily News,* 1 Sept. 1911; Solomons, *How We Won,* 35.

107. Schelinghyde to Catt, 10 May 1911, Reel 4, Catt Papers, NAWSA Microfilm Collection.

108. *Labor Clarion,* 6 Oct. 1911; *San Francisco Daily News,* 13 Sept. 1911.

109. *San Francisco Daily News,* 1 Nov. 1911.

110. *San Francisco Call,* 22 Aug. 1911.

111. On labor Progessivism, see Alexander Saxton, "San Francisco Labor and the Populist and Progressive Insurgencies," *Pacific Historical Review,* 34 (1965), 421–438; John L. Shover, "The Progressives and the Working-Class Vote in California," *Labor History* 10 (1969), 584–601; Michael Rogin, "Progressivism and the California Electorate," *Journal of American History* 55 (1968), 297–314; Thomas Clark, "Labor and Progressivism South of the Slot," *California History* 66 (Sept. 1987), 197–207, 234–236fn; Mary Ann Mason Burki, "The California Progressives: Labor's Point of View," *Labor History* 17 (Winter 1976), 24–37.

112. CESL, *Winning,* 96–98.

113. CESL, *Winning,* 97.

114. *San Francisco Examiner,* 5 Sept. 1911. Lillian Harris Coffin blundered early in 1911, when she actively lobbied against the women's eight-hour-day bill, perhaps motivated by her strong Republican loyalties. Coffin defended her position, supporting protective legislation in principle, but she described the proposed measure as "unreasonable and therefore unconstitutional" and proposed an alternative ten-hour-day bill. Some state senators reportedly withdrew their support for suffrage in retaliation. The labor press excoriated Coffin, noting that "it appears that suffrage does not go so far as helping the masses," and warned that "if suffrage loses at the polls it may be put down to suffragists' attack on working women's rights." The state labor federation and most California women's groups supported the bill, however, and it became law in May 1911.

See *San Francisco Daily News*, 3, 8, 10 Feb., 2, 6 March 1911; *Labor Clarion*, 24 Feb., 3, 10 March 1911.

115. CESL, *Winning*, 100–102. See also draft in Coolidge Collection, BL.

116. *San Francisco Examiner*, 11, 13 Oct. 1911.

117. CESL, *Winning*, 102.

118. *San Francisco Call*, 17 Aug. 1911.

119. Minutes (CESA Executive Board), 10 Sept. 1910, Carton 3, Watson to Keith, 16 June 1911, Box 12, Keith Collection, BL.

120. *HWS* 6:40.

121. *San Francisco Examiner*, 17 Sept. 1911.

122. Keith to Hiram Johnson, 29 May 1911 (with enclosed leaflet), Box 42, Hiram Johnson Collection, BL.

123. Jane Apostol, "'Why Women Should Not Have the Vote: Anti-Suffrage Views in the Southland in 1911," *Southern California Historical Quarterly* 70 (Spring 1988), 29–42; Manuela Thurner, "'Better Citizens without the Ballot': American Anti-Suffrage Women and Their Rationale during the Progressive Era," in Wheeler, ed., *One Woman, One Vote*, 203–220.

124. *Los Angeles Times*, 8, 10 Oct. 1911; *HWS* 6:44.

125. *California Outlook*, 22 April 1911.

126. *San Francisco Examiner*, 30 Sept., 8 Oct. 1911.

127. CESL, *Winning*, 12.

128. CESL, *Winning*, 30–31.

129. CESL, *Winning*, 36–37.

130. CESL, *Winning*, 40–41, *HWS* 6:46.

131. *HWS* 6:46; *San Francisco Call*, 6 Oct. 1911; *San Francisco Examiner*, 6 Oct. 1911.

132. CESL, *Winning*, 41–42, 54–55.

133. *San Francisco Examiner*, 10 Oct. 1911; *San Francisco Daily News*, 10 Oct. 1911; *San Francisco Call*, 10 Oct. 1911.

134. Clippings, 1911, Carton 4, Keith Collection, BL.

135. Schelinghyde to Catt, 16 Oct. 1911, Reel 4, Catt Papers, NAWSA Collection.

136. CESL, *Winning*, 105–111. Coolidge added that this woman subsequently reorganized her group into a civic club, but she does not identify her.

137. *Los Angeles Times*, 11 Oct. 1911.

138. *HWS* 6:49–50.

139. CESL, *Winning*, 106. The women could distribute leaflets as long as they stayed 100 feet away from the polls, but Alice Park later suggested that the new 100–foot rule also kept women far enough away from the polls to be "cheated out of many votes in San Francisco." See Alice Park to Editor, *Woman's Journal*, 13 Oct. 1911, Box 3, Park Collection, HL.

140. *San Francisco Examiner*, 11 Oct. 1911.

141. *San Francisco Call,* 11 Oct. 1911; CESL, *Winning,* 105.

142. *San Francisco Examiner,* 11 Oct. 1911.

143. CESL, *Winning,* 111–112; Solomons, *How We Won,* 60–62.

144. Alice Park, typescript article for the *San Francisco News,* August 1930, Box 7, Park Collection, HL.

145. *San Francisco Daily News,* 11 Oct. 1911; *San Francisco Examiner,* 11 Oct. 1911; Keith, "The Political Situation," Carton 3, Keith Collection, BL.

146. *San Francisco Examiner,* 11 Oct. 1911; *San Francisco Daily News,* 11 Oct. 1911; Rodes, "The California Woman Suffrage Campaign of 1911," 180–188.

147. Englander, *Class Coalition and Class Conflict,* 108–113.

148. Braitman, "Katherine Philips Edson," 141–142; Katz, "Dual Commitments," 297.

149. Schelinghyde to Catt, 16 Oct. 1911, Reel 4, Catt Papers, NAWSA Collection; Mabel Craft Deering, "The Women's Demonstration: How They Won and Used the Vote in California," *Collier's* 48 (6 Jan. 1912), 17–18.

150. *San Francisco Call,* 13 Oct. 1911.

151. *New York Times,* 13 Oct. 1911, as cited by DuBois, *Harriot Stanton Blatch,* 310, fn27; Rodes, "The California Woman Suffrage Campaign of 1911," 181–184.

152. Jeannette Rankin, "Why the Country Folk Did It," *Woman Voter,* Dec. 1911, 13; Solomons, *How We Won,* 64.

153. *San Francisco Examiner,* 6 Dec. 1911.

154. *Labor Clarion,* 10, 17 Nov. 1911.

155. *Los Angeles Times,* Oct. 22, Nov. 1, 1911; Deering, "The Women's Demonstration," 17.

156. *San Francisco Daily News,* 10 Nov. 1911 (with cartoon); *Labor Clarion,* 10, 17 Nov. 1911; *San Francisco Examiner,* 6 Dec. 1911; Katz, "Dual Commitments," 299–302. Harriman retained considerable support, winning 38 percent of the vote in the final general election. See James P. Kraft, "The Fall of Job Harriman's Socialist Party: Violence, Gender, and Politics in Los Angeles, 1911," *Southern California Historical Quarterly* 70 (Spring 1988), 43–68.

157. Mrs. Charles F. Edson, "The Actual Operation of Woman's Suffrage in the Pacific Coast Cities," *National Municipal Review* 1 (Oct. 1912), 620–629; and Edson, "Women's Influence on State Legislation," *California Outlook* (14 June 1913), 7–8; Braitman, "Katherine Philips Edson," 141–142.

158. In 1913 alone, women reformers instigated the passage of four new laws: a minimum wage for women, an age-of-consent bill, a health certificate for marriage bill, and the Redlight Injunction and Abatement Act. In San Francisco, they recalled a municipal judge, obtained the appointment of three policewomen, closed a municipal clinic that examined prostitutes for venereal disease, and ultimately shut down the dance halls of the Barbary Coast. See Gayle

222 | Notes to Chapter 7

Gullett, "City Mothers, City Daughters, and the Dance Hall Girls: The Limits of Female Political Power in San Francisco, 1913," in Barbara J. Harris and JoAnn K. McNamara, eds., *Women and the Structure of Society* (Durham, NC: Duke University Press, 1984), 149–159, 281–285.

159. "'Sure; they've got to treat us right now,—we're voters!' exclaimed a California working girl on hearing that the State S.C. had declared the Eighthour Law for women constitutional." In this interview, Maud Younger stated, "There was no more valuable workers for suffrage in the state than the legislative agent for the trade-unions, now Congressman-elect, John I. Nolan. 'Why do you include this bill?' inquired a puzzled legislator, who had asked him for a list of labor measures on which to vote right. 'This isn't a labor bill; it's the woman suffrage amend.' 'Woman suffrage is a labor measure,' was the reply. 'As you vote on woman suffrage, you stand or fall with labor.'" See *Woman Voter,* Jan. 1913.

160. Grace Simons, "The Actual Operation of Woman Suffrage in California," *Woman's Bulletin* 1 (June 1913), 33–36; Mary Gibson, "The Women's Legislative Council," *Woman's Bulletin* 2 (March 1914), 28–29; and a whole series by Mary Coolidge on legislative accomplishments, *Woman's Bulletin,* June–Oct. 1914. See also Grace Simons, CFWC, "A Survey of the Results of Woman Suffrage in California," 1917, Pamphlet, Huntington Library; and Katherine Edson, "Women's Influence on State Legislation," *California Outlook* (14 June 1913), 7–8.

161. Englander, *Class Coalition and Class Conflict,* 158–162; *Labor Clarion,* 29 March, 12 April 1912, 14, 21, 28 June, 5, 12, 19, 26 July, 7 Aug. 1912; *San Francisco Daily News,* 3, 10, 16, 23, 30–31 July 1912; HLL circulars, 1912, Box 1, draft report, 2 Aug. 1912, Box 10, and Noel to Mrs. Clithero, 12 Nov. 1912, Box 11, Noel Collection, UCLA. For working-class women's support for Governor Johnson, see *San Francisco Daily News,* 10–11, 16 Sept. 1914.

NOTES TO CHAPTER 8

1. As cited by Ann Warren Smith, "Anne Martin and a History of Woman Suffrage in Nevada, 1869–1914" (Ph.D. diss., University of Nevada, Reno, 1975), 191. The poem was composed in honor of Nevada millionaire and Republican political boss George Wingfield, who threatened to leave the state if the woman suffrage amendment passed. It did; he didn't. See also Anne Bail Howard, *The Long Campaign* (Reno: University of Nevada Press, 1985), 90–91.

2. On the NWP, see Christine A. Lunardini, *From Equal Suffrage to Equal Rights: Alice Paul and the National Woman's Party, 1910–1928* (New York: New York University Press, 1986); Nancy F. Cott, *The Grounding of Modern Feminism* (New Haven: Yale University Press, 1987), 53–81; and Eleanor

Flexner, *Century of Struggle* (Cambridge, MA: Belknap Press of Harvard University Press, 1975), 271–303. First-person accounts include Doris Stevens, *Jailed for Freedom* (New York: Boni and Liveright, 1920); Inez Haynes Irwin (Gillmore), *The Story of the Woman's Party* (New York: Harcourt, 1921); and Gillmore, *Up Hill with Banners Flying* (Penobscot, ME: Traversity Press, 1964).

3. The Bancroft library collected extensive oral histories from participants in these campaigns; see Sara Bard Field, "Poet and Suffragist," Mabel Vernon, "Speaker for Suffrage and Petitioner for Peace," and Jeannette Rankin, "Activist for World Peace, Women's Rights, and Democratic Government," Regional Oral History Office, University of California, Berkeley, 1972–1973 (available from the Online Archive of California). See also "Plan of Action," Martin to Mississippi Valley Suffrage Conference, 22 March 1914, Box 8, Anne Martin Collection, BL.

4. T. A. Larson, "Montana Women and the Battle for the Ballot," *Montana* 23:1 (Jan. 1973), 24–41.

5. Roeder, Richard B. "Crossing the Gender Line: Ella L. Knowles, Montana's First Woman Lawyer," *Montana* 32:3 (Summer 1982), 67.

6. Larson, "Montana Women," 26–29.

7. *HWS* 4:796–798; *Woman's Journal,* 27 July 1895, 13 July 1896.

8. Sarepta Sanders to DeVoe, Aug. 7 1895, DeVoe Collection, Box 4, WSL; *Woman's Journal,* 23 Feb. 1895; Larson, "Montana Women," 30–32; Paula Petrik, *No Step Backward: Women and Family on the Rocky Mountain Mining Frontier, Helena, Montana 1865–1900* (Helena: Montana Historical Society Press, 1987), 118–124.

9. Catt to DeVoe, 11, 22 April, 7 May, 25 June 1896, Box 1, Helen Reynolds to DeVoe, 4, 16 June 1896, Box 3, DeVoe Collection, WSL; Larson, "Montana Women," 32; Petrik, *No Step Backward,* 124–125.

10. Roeder, "Crossing the Gender Line," 64–75.

11. Roeder, "Crossing the Gender Line," 72.

12. Larson, "Montana Women," 33; Roeder, "Crossing the Gender Line," 71–75.

13. Petrik, *No Step Backward,* 128–129; *HWS* 6:360–362; Larson, "Montana Women," 34.

14. Petrik, *No Step Backward,* 130; Hannah Josephson, *Jeannette Rankin, First Lady in Congress: A Biography* (Indianapolis and New York: Bobbs-Merrill, 1974), 19–29; and Norma Smith, *Jeannette Rankin: America's Conscience* (Helena: Montana Historical Society Press, 2002), 29–56.

15. Smith, *America's Conscience,* 57–73.

16. Josephson, *Jeannette Rankin,* 30–40; Smith, *America's Conscience,* 75–81.

17. Smith, *America's Conscience,* 81; Ronald Schaffer, "The Montana Woman Suffrage Campaign, 1911–1914," *Pacific Northwest Quarterly* 55:1

(Jan. 1964), 9–15. See also Schaffer, "Jeannette Rankin, Progressive Isolationist," (Ph.D. diss., Princeton University, 1959).

18. Josephson, *Jeannette Rankin,* 40–41; *HWS* 6:360–362.

19. *HWS* 6:360–366.

20. Petrik, *No Step Backward,* 130–131; Josephson, *Jeannette Rankin,* 41–45.

21. Schaffer, "The Montana Woman Suffrage Campaign," 13.

22. Larson, "Montana Women," 37–38, citing *The Woman's Voice,* Oct. 1914.

23. Josephson, *Jeannette Rankin,* 44–45.

24. Jerry W. Calvert, *The Gibraltar: Socialism and Labor in Butte, Montana, 1895–1920* (Helena: Montana Historical Society Press, 1988), 95–99; Petrik, *No Step Backward,* 131–132; Larson, "Montana Women," 39–40.

25. Kathryn Anderson, "Steps to Political Equality: Woman Suffrage and Electoral Politics in the Lives of Emily Newell Blair, Anne Henrietta Martin, and Jeannette Rankin," *Frontiers* 18:1 (1997), 101–121.

26. Howard, *The Long Campaign,* 87–89; Jean Ford and James W. Hulse, "The First Battle for Woman Suffrage in Nevada 1869–1871—Correcting and Expanding the Record," *Nevada Historical Society Quarterly* 38:3 (Fall 1995), 174–188.

27. Ford and Hulse, "The First Battle," 180, citing *Elko Independent,* 5 Jan. 1870.

28. Ford and Hulse, "The First Battle," 185, citing *Territorial Enterprise,* 16 Feb. 1871.

29. *HWS* 3:755–756, 4:810; Smith, "Anne Martin," 8–14. Nevada-California suffragist Frances Williamson compiled the early material on Nevada in volume 4. On Williamson, see Mary Ellen Glass, *Silver and Politics in Nevada: 1892–1902* (Reno: University of Nevada Press, 1969), 95–96. Mrs. O. H. Mack, the president of the Nevada State Federation of Women's Clubs, and Bird M. Wilson, Goldfield attorney and vice-president of the state suffrage society, worked on volume 6.

30. Catt to DeVoe, 10 Dec. 1896, Box 1, DeVoe Collection, WSL.

31. *HWS* 4:810–811.

32. Catt to DeVoe, 10 Dec 1896, Box 1, DeVoe Collection, WSL; Smith, "Anne Martin," 24–33, citing *Reno Evening Gazette,* 31 Oct. 1895.

33. *HWS* 4:811–813; Smith, "Anne Martin," 33–41.

34. *HWS* 6:384–386; Smith, "Anne Martin," 54–64; Howard, *The Long Campaign,* 75. On the Mackays, see Gilman Ostrander, *Nevada: The Great Rotten Borough, 1859–1914* (New York: Alfred A. Knopf, 1966), 52–29.

35. Howard, *The Long Campaign,* 1–73; Smith, "Anne Martin," 79–87. Patricia Greenwood Harrison, *Connecting Links: The British and American*

Woman Suffrage Movements, 1900–1914 (Westport, CT, and London: Green-wood, 2000), 144–145. Martin, a college tennis champion, allegedly bashed a British bobby over the head with a racket during one mêlée; see Smith, "Anne Martin," 78.

36. *HWS* 6:386.

37. Smith, "Anne Martin," 139–143; Felice Cohn to Anne Martin, 18 Dec. 1912, 8 Jan. 1913, Box 2, Martin Collection, BL. Tasker Oddie was a Progressive Republican who made a fortune in the Tonopah gold and silver mines, but lost it in the Panic of 1907. In 1910, he won the gubernatorial race against great odds, and served in the U.S. Senate from 1920–1932, when he was succeeded by Pat McCarran; see Ostrander, *Nevada,* 150–154.

38. Minnie Bray to Martin, 16 Feb. and 4 March, 1913, Box 1, and Wilson to Martin, 4 March 1913, Box 7, Martin Collection, BL; Smith, "Anne Martin," 143–149; Howard, *The Long Campaign,* 83–84.

39. *HWS* 6:389–396; Martin to Agnes Ryan, 30 July 1914, Box 8, Martin Collection, BL; Smith, "Anne Martin," 172–186.

40. *HWS* 6:393–396.

41. Ostrander, *Nevada,* 134–140; Smith, "Anne Martin," 188–192. Visiting organizer Margaret Foley came up with the term while trying to organize in Carson City; see Margaret Foley to Martin, 18 Sept. 1914, Box 8, Martin Collection, BL.

42. Buck to Martin, 19 March 1914, Box 7, Martin Collection, BL; Smith, "Anne Martin," 243.

43. Clippings, Margaret Foley Collection, Schlesinger Library, Radcliffe College, Cambridge, Mass., as cited by Howard, *The Long Campaign,* 95–96.

44. Martin to N. L. Ricketts, *Reno Evening Gazette,* 10 April 1914, and Martin to Editor, *Ely Expositor,* 11 April 1914, Box 8, Martin Collection, BL.

45. Wilson to Martin, 5 Oct. 1914, Box 7, Martin Collection, BL, as cited by Howard, *The Long Campaign,* 95–96.

46. Martin to Bird Wilson, 10, 31 Oct. 1912, Box 1, Wilson to Martin, 11, 22 Oct., 3 Nov. 1912, Box 7, Martin Collection, BL; Howard, *The Long Campaign,* 81–82. Wilson, an attorney, produced a pamphlet entitled *Women under Nevada Laws,* based on Alice Park's earlier publication in California; see Reel 955:9585–9588, History of Women [Microform] Collection; and Bird Wilson to Alice Park, 1 March 1913, Box 4, Alice Park Collection, HL. See also Mary Austin and Anne Martin, "Suffrage and Government" (New York: NAWSA Publications, 1914), Reel 949:9096ff, History of Women Collection.

47. Cannon had already taken pains to inform Martin that she would not do clerical work; see Laura Gregg Cannon to Martin, 1 Nov. 1913, Box 2, 19 Feb. 1914, Carton 2, Martin Collection, BL.

48. Wilson to Martin, 1 Oct. 1914, Box 7, Martin Collection, BL.

49. See correspondence with Cannon (Box 2), Foley (Box 2), and Younger (Box 8), 1914, Martin Collection, BL; and Wilson to Martin, 5 Oct. 1914, Box 7, Martin Collection, BL, as cited by Howard, *The Long Campaign*, 95–96.

50. Foley to Martin, 5 March 1915, Carton 7, Shaw to Martin, 18 Sept. 1914, Box 6, Martin Collection, BL; Smith, "Anne Martin," 222–226.

51. *HWS* 6:386–387, 394; Smith, "Anne Martin," 168–173, 184; Martin to Shaw, 20 Sept. 1913, Anne Martin Suffrage Material, Nevada Historical Society (hereafter cited as NHS); Shaw to Martin, 18 Oct. 1913, Box 6, Martin Collection, BL.

52. *HWS* 6:396–399. Cotterill visited forty unions in Great Falls alone, and took the "sleepy little city" of Helena "by storm." See Bulletins, 14, 29 May, 19 June 1914, Montana Equal Suffrage Society Campaign Committee, Carton 7, Martin Collection, BL.

53. *HWS* 6:389; Smith, "Anne Martin," 172, 205–206; Howard, *The Long Campaign*, 87–89.

54. Lunardini, *From Equal Suffrage to Equal Rights*, 20–22, 36–47.

55. Lunardini, *From Equal Suffrage to Equal Rights*, 20–22, 36–47. Shaw compared the CU to "Judas Iscariot."

56. Lunardini, *From Equal Suffrage to Equal Rights*, 42; Carrie Chapman Catt and Nettie Shuler, *Woman Suffrage and Politics: The Inner Story of the Suffrage Movement* (New York: Charles Scribner's Sons, 1926), 244; *HWS* 5:380–381.

57. Lunardini, *From Equal Suffrage to Equal Rights*, 41–49, 53–54.

58. On Catt, see also Robert Booth Fowler, "Carrie Chapman Catt, Strategist," in Marjorie Spruill Wheeler, *One Woman, One Vote: Rediscovering the Woman Suffrage Movement* (Troutdale, OR: New Sage Press, 1995), 295–314; and Sara Hunter Graham, "The Suffrage Renaissance: A New Image for a New Century, 1896–1910," in Wheeler, *One Woman, One Vote*, 162–167.

59. Lunardini, *From Equal Suffrage to Equal Rights*, 73–84; Flexner, *Century of Struggle*, 281–285.

60. Organizational Reports, 1914 Campaign of the Congressional Union, NWP Papers, as cited by Lundardini, *From Equal Suffrage to Equal Rights*, 63.

61. Ethel Smith, "Testimony from Western States on Anti-Party Policy of the Congressional Union," Typescript, n.d.; Hutton to Mrs. Medill McCormic [*sic*], 1 June 1915, both Reel 33, NAWSA Collection.

62. Quote in Report, 1914 Campaign, as cited by Lunardini, *From Equal Suffrage to Equal Rights*, 49–50.

63. Vernon to Martin, 20 June 1914, Box 6, Vernon Collection, BL.

64. Ostrander described Pittman as "the one really wild man to emerge from Nevada into national and international politics." Ostrander, *Nevada*, 143. Pittman was born on a Louisiana plantation, went to Alaska during the Klondike Gold Rush, returned to the States in 1902 to the Tonopah/Goldfield

area with a reputation as a mining lawyer, and grew wealthy. Ostrander also describes him: "A skillful and tireless lawyer, Pittman was also a hopeless drunkard with homocidal tendencies" (143–144). A Progressive Wilsonian Democrat, he challenged the Wingfield machine for the U.S. Senate, unsuccessfully at first, but eventually he and Wingfield got along. See Ostrander, *Nevada,* 141–150.

65. Pittman to Martin, 10 April, 12 May 1914, Box 6, Martin to Pittman, 21 April 1914, Box 8, Martin Collection, BL; Howard, *The Long Campaign,* 92–93. The CU women, including Alice Paul, were not immune from the virulent racism of the time, and, like the NAWSA, they used their organization's single-issue focus to avoid African American women and their issues. See Cott, *Grounding,* 68–72; Rosalyn Terborg-Penn, *African American Women in the Struggle for the Vote, 1850–1920* (Bloomington: Indiana University Press, 1998), 130, 156.

66. Pittman, re-election statement, 1916, Carton 7, Martin Collection, BL.

67. Shaw to Martin, 26 June 1914, Box 6, Martin Collection, BL.

68. *Special Bulletin to the Woman's Journal,* n.d. [April 1914], p. 1, "Misc. Suffrage Material," Carton 7, Martin Collection, BL; Smith, "Anne Martin," 205.

69. Maud McCreery to Mrs. Eichelberger, n.d. [1914]; McCreery to President and Executive Committee of the Nevada Equal Franchise Society, 12 May 1914, Box 4, letter to state suffrage presidents, 26 May 1914, Carton 1, Martin Collection, BL; Smith, "Anne Martin," 204–207. Howard calls this action vindictive, but points out that since this letter was not filed with the regular correspondence, it is possible that it was never sent; see Howard, *The Long Campaign,* 195fn.

70. Smith, "Anne Martin," 172, 184–186.

71. Smith, "Anne Martin," 155–161, citing *Nevada State Journal,* 10 Oct. 1913.

72. *HWS* 6:388.

73. *HWS* 6:398; Mary E. Ringrose to Martin, 4 Oct. 1914, Box 5, Foley to Martin, 2 Oct. 1914, Carton 7, Martin Collection, BL.

74. Martin to Suffrage Presidents, 14 Oct. 1914, Box 8, Martin Collection, BL; Sara Bard Field, "The Clash in Nevada," *Outwest* (Aug. 1914), 51–66; see also Gail Laughlin, "Equal Suffrage and Nevada Prosperity," 75–76.

75. Shaw to Martin, 18 Oct. 1913, Box 6, Martin Collection, BL; Smith, "Anne Martin," 163–166; Howard, *The Long Campaign,* 97.

76. Smith, "Anne Martin," 249–254.

77. Minutes of the National Advisory Committee Meeting, March 31, 1915, and "Transcripts of Speeches Delivered at the Women Voters Convention," NWP Papers, and Vernon Interview, 144, BL, as cited by Lunardini, *From Equal Suffrage to Equal Rights,* 71, 77–78; Gillmore, *Up Hill,* 103–110.

78. Field, "Poet and Suffragist," 303.

79. Lunardini speculates that in addition to political considerations, Wilson's own daughters affected his change of mind, although one wonders how much influence they had if they had to ask Wilson's close adviser, Colonel House, for help. See Lunardini, *From Equal Suffrage to Equal Rights*, 80.

80. *HWS* 6:391–394, 399; Howard, *The Long Campaign*, 122–160; John C. Board, "Jeanette Rankin: The Lady from Montana," *Montana* 17 (Summer 1967), 2–17; Flexner, *Century of Struggle*, 293; Cott, *The Grounding*, 107–108.

81. Cott, *The Grounding*, 58.

82. Whitney to Mrs. William [Elizabeth] Kent, 26 Sept. 1915, NWP Collection; Lunardini, *From Equal Suffrage to Equal Rights*, 52; and Lisa Rubens, "The Patrician Radical: Charlotte Anita Whitney," *California History* 65 (Sept. 1986), 158–171, 226–227fn. A *friend* of Alice Paul's compared her to Vladimir I. Lenin.

83. One of her former colleagues remembered that "Anne was her own worst enemy; she loved to show off using her wealth to dominate." Private interview with Dr. Effie Mona Muck, Reno, NV, Oct. 27, 1966), as cited by Smith, "Anne Martin," 188.

84. NAWSA, *Victory: How Women Won It: A Centennial Symposium, 1840–1940* (New York: H. W. Wilson, 1940), 53, 72–73.

85. Elinor Lerner, "Immigrant and Working Class Involvement in the New York City Woman Suffrage Movement, 1905–1917: A Study in Progressive Era Politics" (Ph.D. diss., University of California, Berkeley, 1981); and Lerner, "Family Structure, Occupational Patterns, and Support for Women's Suffrage," in Judith Freidlander et al., *Women in Culture and Politics: A Century of Change* (Bloomington: Indiana University Press, 1986), 223–236; David R. Berman, "Male Support for Woman Suffrage: An Analysis of Voting Patterns in the Mountain West," *Social Science History* 11:3 (Fall 1987), 281–294; Susan Englander, *Class Coalition and Class Conflict in the California Woman Suffrage Movement, 1907–1912: The San Francisco Wage Earners' Suffrage League;* Joseph F. Mahoney, "Woman Suffrage and the Urban Masses," *New Jersey History* 87 (Autumn 1969), 151–172; James J. Kenneally, "Catholicism and Woman Suffrage," *Catholicism in America* (New York: Harper and Row, 1970), 81–91; Eileen L. McDonagh and H. Douglas Price, "Woman Suffrage in the Progressive Era: Patterns of Opposition and Support in Referenda Voting, 1910–1918," *American Political Science Review*, 79:2 (June 1985), 415–435; Philip J. Ethington, "Recasting Urban Political History: Gender, the Public, the Household, and Political Participation in Boston and San Francisco during the Progressive Era," *Social Science History* 16:2 (Summer 1992), 301–333.

86. Anna L. Harvey, "The Political Consequences of Suffrage Exclusion: Organizations, Institutions, and the Electoral Mobilization of Women," *Social Science History* 20:1 (Spring 1996), 97–132; and Harvey, *Voters without Leverage: Women in American Politics, 1920–1970* (Cambridge, UK, and New York:

Cambridge University Press, 1988); Melanie Gustrafson, Kristie Miller, and Elisabeth Israels Perry, eds., *We Have Come to Stay: American Women and Political Parties, 1880–1960* (Albuquerque: University of New Mexico Press, 1999); Kristi Anderson, *After Suffrage: Women in Partisan and Electoral Politics before the New Deal* (Chicago: University of Chicago Press, 1996).

87. Early studies often begin with the assumption that feminism was a "failure"; see William L. O'Neill, *Everyone Was Brave: The Rise and Fall of Feminism in America* (Chicago: Quadrangle Books, 1969), viii. See also William Chafe, *The American Woman: Her Changing Social, Economic and Political Roles, 1920–1970* (New York: Oxford University Press, 1972). More recently, see Kristi Andersen, *After Suffrage: Women and Partisan Electoral Politics before the New Deal* (Chicago: University of Chicago Press, 1996), 1–19; Nancy Cott, "Across the Great Divide: Women in Politics before and after 1920," in Louise A. Tilly and Patricia Gurin, eds., *Women, Politics and Change* (New York: Russell Sage Foundation, 1990); S. Sara Monoson, "The Lady and the Tiger: Women's Electoral Activism in New York City before Suffrage," *Journal of Women's History* 2 (Fall 1990), 100–135; Glenna Mathews, *The Rise of Public Woman: Woman's Power and Woman's Place in the United States, 1630–1970* (New York: Oxford University Press, 1992).

Bibliography

MANUSCRIPT COLLECTIONS

Bancroft Library, University of California, Berkeley (BL)
  Laura DeForce Gordon Collection
  Hiram Johnson Collection
  Anna Haskell Collection
  Anne Martin Collection
  Keith-McHenry-Pond Family Collection
  Hester Harland Collection
  McLean Family Collection
  Selina Solomons Collection
Bolerium Bookstore Collection, San Francisco, California
California Historical Society (CHS)
  Lillie Devereux Blake Collection
  Louise Sorbier Collection
Colorado Historical Society (CoHS)
  Ellis Meredith Collection
Eastern Washington State Historical Society (EWSHS)
  May Arkwright Hutton Collection
  Hutton Settlement Collection
  Marion E. Hay Collection
Hoover Institution Archives, Stanford, California
  Alice Park Collection
Huntington Library, San Marino, California (HL)
  Susan B. Anthony Memorial Collection
  Clara Burdette Collection
  Clara Colby Collection
  Elizabeth Boynton Harbert Collection
  Mary Emily Foy Collection
  Caroline Maria (Seymour) Severance Collection
  Tasker Oddie Collection

Alice Park Collection
Marshall Stimson Collection
Charles Erskine Scott Wood and Sara Bard Field Wood Collection
Stanford University, Department of Special Collections
  Jane Stanford Collection
  Meyer Lissner Collection
  John Powell Irish Collection
  Thomas V. Cator Collection
State Historical Society of Wisconsin, Madison
  Clara Colby Collection
University of California, Los Angeles, Department of Special Collections, Los
  Angeles, California
  Frances Noel Collection
  Katherine Philips Edson Collection
  John Randolph Haynes Collection
  Franklin Hichborn Collection
Washington State Archives, Olympia, Washington (WSA)
  John E. Rogers Collection
  Marion E. Hay Collection
  Women's Suffrage Special Collection (WSSC)
Washington State Library, Olympia, Washington (WSL)
  Emma Smith DeVoe Collection
  May Arkwright Hutton Collection
Women's Christian Temperance Union of California, Papers (WCTUC) (pri-
  vately held), Modesto, California

MICROFORM COLLECTIONS

National American Woman Suffrage Association Records, 1850–1960. Manu-
  script Division, Library of Congress, Washington, DC, 1981.
The Papers of Carrie Chapman Catt. Manuscript Division, Library of Congress,
  Washington, DC, 1978.
National Women's Trade Union League Collection. Library of Congress, Wash-
  ington, DC, 1976.
The Papers of Elizabeth Cady Stanton and Susan B. Anthony. Wilmington, DE:
  Scholarly Resources, 1991.
The Blackwell Family Papers. Manuscript Division, Library of Congress, Wash-
  ington, DC, 1975.
History of Women Microfilm Collection. New Haven, CT, Research Publica-
  tions, Inc., 1976–1979.
National Woman's Party Papers, 1913–1972. Thomas C. Pardo, ed. Glen Rock,
  NJ: Microfilming Corp. of America, 1977–1978.

ORAL HISTORIES

Bary, Helen Valeska. "Labor Administration and Social Security: A Woman's Life." Interview by Jacqueline K. Parker. Regional Oral History Office, Bancroft Library, University of California, Berkeley, 1974. Available from the Online Archive of California http://ark.cdlib.org/ark:/13030/kt6z09n8m9/.

Field, Sara Bard. "Poet and Suffragist." Regional Oral History Office, Bancroft Library, University of California, Berkeley, 1979. Available from the Online Archive of California http://ark.cdlib.org/ark:/13030/kt1p3001n1/.

Vernon, Mabel. "Speaker for Suffrage and Petitioner for Peace." Interview by Amelia R. Fry. Regional Oral History Office, Bancroft Library, University of California, Berkeley, c. 1976. Available from the Online Archive of California http://ark.cdlib.org/ark:/13030/kt2r29n5pb/.

Rankin, Jeannette. "Activist for World Peace, Women's Rights, and Democratic Government." Regional Oral History Office, University of California, Berkeley, 1972–1973. Available from the Online Archive of California http://ark.cdlib.org/ark:/13030/kt758005dx/.

PERIODICALS

California Nationalist
California Outlook
California Social-Democrat (Los Angeles)
Denver Republican
Labor Enquirer (Denver)
Los Angeles Citizen
Los Angeles Examiner
Los Angeles Express
Los Angeles Herald
Los Angeles Record
Los Angeles Times
Morning Olympian
New American Woman (Los Angeles)
New Northwest
Olympia Daily Standard
Olympia Transcript
Out West
Pioneer
Progressive Woman
Puget Sound Weekly Courier
Queen Bee
Rocky Mountain News

San Francisco Alta
San Francisco Bulletin
San Francisco Call
San Francisco Chronicle
San Francisco Daily News
San Francisco Examiner
San Francisco Labor Clarion
Seattle Post-Intelligencer
Seattle Times
Seattle Union Record
Spokane Chronicle
Spokane Spokesman-Review
Tacoma Daily News
Truth in Small Doses (San Francisco)
West Coast Magazine
Western Woman Voter
Woman Voter
Woman's Bulletin (Los Angeles)
Woman's Journal
Woman's Tribune
Yellow Ribbon (Western Woman)

GOVERNMENT DOCUMENTS

U.S. Congress. *Report of the Joint Special Committee to Investigate Chinese Immigration.* Senate Doc. 689, 44th Cong., 2d session. Washington, DC: Government Printing Office, 1877.

U.S. Department of Commerce and Labor. *Report on Condition of Women and Child Wage-Earners in the United States.* Senate Doc. 645, 61st Cong., 2d sesssion. Vol 10. John B. Andrews and W. P. D. Bliss. *History of Women in Trade Unions.* Washington, DC, 1911.

U.S. Department of Commerce and Labor. Bureau of the Census. *Special Reports: Occupations at the Twelfth Census.* Washington, DC: U.S. Government Printing Office, 1904.

U.S. Department of Commerce and Labor. Bureau of the Census. *Thirteenth Census of the United States: 1910.* Washington, DC: U.S. Government Printing Office, 1914.

U.S. Department of Commerce. Bureau of the Census. *Women in Gainful Occupations, 1870–1920.* Census Monograph 9 by Joseph Hill. Washington, DC: U.S. Government Printing Office, 1929.

U.S. Department of the Interior. Census Office. *Twelfth Census of the United*

States: 1900. Population. Part 2, Vol. 2. Washington, DC: U.S. Government Printing Office, 1902.

Colorado. Office of the Secretary of State. *To the Women of Colorado: The Record of the Parties on the Equal Suffrage Amendment.* Denver, 1893.

California. Secretary of State. *Statement of the Vote of California at the Special Election Held October 10, 1911 on Constitutional Amendments.* Sacramento, 1911.

San Francisco. Board of Supervisors. *Municipal Reports, for the Fiscal Year 1911–12.* San Francisco: Neal Publishing, 1913.

Washington. Secretary of State. *Abstract of Votes Polled in the State of Washington at the General Election held November 8, 1910.* Olympia, 1910.

Washington. Secretary of State. *Fifth Report, 1898.* Olympia, 1899.

SECONDARY SOURCES

Alexander, Thomas G. "An Experiment in Progressive Legislation: The Granting of Woman Suffrage in Utah in 1870." In Madsen, ed., *Battle for the Ballot,* 108–131.

Almaguer, Tómas. *Racial Fault Lines: The Historical Origins of White Supremacy in California.* Berkeley: University of California Press, 1994.

Anderson, Benedict. *Imagined Communities: Reflections on the Origin and Spread of Nationalism.* Rev. ed. London and New York: Verso, 1991.

Anderson, Kathryn. "Steps to Political Equality: Woman Suffrage and Electoral Politics in the Lives of Emily Newell Blair, Anne Henrietta Martin, and Jeannette Rankin." *Frontiers* 18:1 (1997), 101–121.

Andersen, Kristi. *After Suffrage: Women and Partisan Electoral Politics before the New Deal.* Chicago: University of Chicago Press, 1996.

Apostol, Jane. "'Why Women Should Not Have the Vote': Anti-Suffrage Views in the Southland in 1911." *Southern California Historical Quarterly* 70 (Spring 1988), 29–42.

Aptheker, Bettina. *Woman's Legacy: Essays on Race, Sex, and Class in American History.* Amherst: University of Massachusetts Press, 1982.

Argersinger, Peter H. *The Limits of Agrarian Radicalism: Western Populism and American Politics.* Lawrence, KS: University Press of Kansas, 1995.

Armitage, Susan H., and Deborah Gallacci Wilbert. "Black Women in the Pacific Northwest: A Survey and Research Prospectus." In Karen J. Blair, ed., *Women in Pacific Northwest History,* 136–146. Seattle: University of Washington Press, 1988.

Ault, Nelson A. "The Earnest Ladies: The Walla Wall Woman's Club and the Equal Suffrage League of 1886–1889." *Pacific Northwest Quarterly* 42 (April 1951), 123–137.

Austin, Mary, and Anne Martin. *Suffrage and Government*. New York: NAWSA Pub., 1914.

Babcock, Barbara Allen. "Clara Shortridge Foltz: Constitution-Maker." *Indiana Law Journal* 66:4 (Fall 1991), 849–940.

Babcock, Barbara. "Clara Shortridge Foltz: 'First Woman.'" *Arizona Law Review* 30 (1988), 686–695.

Bagley, Clarence B. *History of Seattle: From the Earliest Settlement to the Present Time*. Vol. 2. Seattle: Clarke Publishing, 1916.

Baily, C. H. "How Washington Women Regained the Ballot." *Pacific Monthly* 26 (July 1911), 1–11.

Baker, Jean, ed. *Votes for Women: The Struggle for Suffrage Revisited*. Oxford and New York: Oxford University Press, 2002.

Baker, Paula. "The Domestication of Politics: Women and American Political Society, 1780–1920." *American Historical Review* 89 (June 1984), 620–647.

Bakken, Gordon Morris, and Brenda Farrington. *Learning California History: Essential Skills for the Survey Course and Beyond*. Wheeling, IL: Harlan-Davidson, 1999.

Balderston, William. "The Woman's Rights Movement in Idaho." In Mary O. Douthit, ed., *The Souvenir of Western Women*, 117–118. Portland, OR: Anderson and Duniway, 1905.

Bargo, Michael. "Women's Occupations in the West in 1870." *Journal of the West* 32 (Jan. 1993), 30–45.

Barnhart, Jacqueline Baker. *The Frail but Fair: Prostitution in San Francisco, 1849–1900*. Reno: University of Nevada Press, 1986.

Basch, Norma. "Invisible Women: The Legal Fiction of Marital Unity in Nineteenth-Century America." *Feminist Studies* 5 (Summer 1979), 346–366.

Bean, Walton. *Boss Ruef's San Francisco*. Berkeley: University of California Press, 1952.

Bean, Walton, and James J. Rawls, eds. *California: An Interpretive History*. 4th ed. New York: McGraw-Hill, 1983.

Beasley, Delilah L. *The Negro Trailblazers of California*. 1919; reprint, San Francisco: R and E Associates, 1969.

Bederman, Gail. *Manliness and Civilization: A Cultural History of Gender and Race in the United States, 1880–1917*. Chicago and London: University of Chicago Press, 1995.

Beeton, Beverly. "Woman Suffrage in Territorial Utah." *Utah Historical Quarterly* 46 (Spring 1978), 100–120.

Beeton, Beverly. *Women Vote in the West: The Woman Suffrage Movement, 1869–1896*. New York: Garland Press, 1986.

Beeton, Beverly, and G. Thomas Edwards. "Susan B. Anthony's Woman Suffrage Crusade in the American West." *Journal of the West* 21 (April 1982), 5–15.

Bell, John C. *The Pilgrim and the Pioneer.* Lincoln, NE: International Publishing Assoc., 1906.

Bennett, W. Lance, and William Halton. "Issues, Voter Choice, and Critical Elections." *Social Science History* 4 (Fall 1980), 379–418.

Bennion, Sherilyn Cox. *Equal to the Occasion: Women Editors of the Nineteenth-Century West.* Reno and Las Vegas: University of Nevada Press, 1990.

Bennion, Sherilyn Cox. "*The New Northwest* and *Women's Exponent*: Early Voices for Suffrage." In Madsen, ed., *Battle for the Ballot,* 173–185.

Bennion, Sherilyn Cox. "*The Pioneer*: The First Voice for Women's Suffrage in the West." *Pacific Historian* 25:4 (Winter 1981), 15–21.

Berkhofer, Robert E. Jr. *The White Man's Indian: Images of the American Indian from Columbus to the Present.* New York: Vintage Books, 1979.

Berman, David R. "Male Support for Woman Suffrage: An Analysis of Voting Patterns in the Mountain West." *Social Science History* 11:3 (Fall 1987), 281–294.

Berwanger, Eugene H. *The West and Reconstruction.* Urbana: University of Illinois Press, 1981.

Blair, Karen J. *The Clubwoman as Feminist: True Womanhood Redefined, 1868–1914.* New York: Holmes and Meier, 1980.

Blair, Karen J., ed. *Women in Pacific Northwest History.* Seattle: University of Washington Press, 1988.

Blewett, Mary. *We Will Rise in Our Might: Workingwomen's Voices from Nineteenth-Century New England.* Ithaca, NY: Cornell University Press, 1991.

Board, John C. "Jeanette Rankin: The Lady from Montana." *Montana* 17 (Summer 1967), 2–17.

Bradford, Mary C. C. "Equal Suffrage in Colorado from 1893–1908." Colorado Equal Suffrage Association, n.d. Pamphlet in Huntington Library, #447207.

Braitman, Jacqueline. "A California Stateswoman: The Public Career of Katherine Philips Edson." *California History* LXV (1986), 82–95, 151–152fn.

Braitman, Jacqueline. "Katherine Philips Edson: A Progressive Feminist in California's Era of Reform." Ph.D. diss., University of California, Los Angeles, 1988.

Braly, John Hyde. *Memory Pictures: An Autobiography.* Los Angeles: Neuser, 1912.

Braude, Ann. *Radical Spirits: Spiritualism and Women's Rights in Nineteenth-Century America.* Boston: Beacon Press, 1989.

Bredbenner, Candice Lewis. *A Nationality of Her Own: Women, Marriage, and the Law of Citizenship.* Berkeley: University of California Press, 1998.

Brown, Joseph G. *The History of Equal Suffrage in Colorado.* Denver: News Job Printing, 1898.

Browne, J. R., ed. *Report of the Debates in the Convention of California.* Washington, DC: John T. Towers, 1850.

Brundage, David Thomas. *The Making of Western Labor Radicalism: Denver's Organized Workers, 1878–1905.* Urbana: University of Illinois Press, 1994.

Brundage, David Thomas. "The Making of Working-Class Radicalism in the Mountain West: Denver, Colorado, 1880–1903." Ph.D. diss., University of California, Los Angeles, 1982.

Buchanan, Joseph R. *The Story of a Labor Agitator.* New York: Outlook Company, 1903.

Buechler, Stephen M. "Elizabeth Boynton Harbert and the Woman Suffrage Movement, 1870–1896." *Signs* 13:1 (Autumn 1987), 78–97.

Buechler, Stephen M. *The Transformation of the Woman Suffrage Movement: The Case of Illinois, 1850–1920.* New Brunswick, NJ: Rutgers University Press, 1986.

Buhle, Mari Jo. *Women and American Socialism, 1870–1920.* Urbana: University of Illinois Press, 1981.

Buhle, Mari Jo, and Paul Buhle. *The Concise History of Woman Suffrage.* Urbana: University of Illinois Press, 1978.

Burchell, R. A. *The San Francisco Irish, 1848–1880.* Berkeley; University of California Press, 1980.

Burdette, Clara. *The Answer: Memoirs of Clara Bradley Burdette.* Pasadena, 1951.

Burki, Mary Ann Mason. "The California Progressives: Labor's Point of View." *Labor History* 17 (Winter 1976), 24–37.

Burnham, Walter Dean. "Periodization Schemes and 'Party Systems': The 'System of 1896' as a Case in Point." *Social Science History* 10 (Fall 1986), 263–314.

Calvert, Jerry W. *The Gibraltar: Socialism and Labor in Butte, Montana, 1895–1920.* Helena: Montana Historical Society Press, 1988.

Cameron, Ardis. *Radicals of the Worst Sort: Laboring Women in Lawrence, Massachusetts, 1860–1912.* Urbana: University of Illinois Press, 1993.

Carnes, Mark C., and Clyde Griffen, eds. *Meanings for Manhood: Constructions of Masculinity in Victorian America.* Chicago: University of Chicago Press, 1990.

Caswell, John E. "The Prohibition Movement in Oregon." *Oregon Historical Quarterly, pt. 1 (1836–1904):* 39 (Sept. 1938), 235–261; *pt. 2 (1904–1915):* 40 (March 1939), 65–82.

Catt, Carrie Chapman, and Nettie Rogers Shuler. *Woman Suffrage and Politics: The Inner Story of the Suffrage Movement.* New York: Charles Scribner's Sons, 1926.

Chafe, William. *The American Woman: Her Changing Social, Economic and Political Roles, 1920–1970.* New York: Oxford University Press, 1972.

Chan, Sucheng. "The Exclusion of Chinese Women, 1870–1943." In Nancy F. Cott and Elizabeth H. Pleck, eds., *A Heritage of Her Own: Toward a New*

Social History of American Women, 75–125. New York: Simon and Schuster, 1979.

Chan, Sucheng, ed. *Entry Denied: Exclusion and the Chinese Community in America, 1882–1943.* Philadelphia: Temple University Press, 1991.

Chandler, Robert J. "In the Van: Spiritualists as Catalysts for the California Women's Suffrage Movement." *California History* 73 (Fall 1994), 189–201.

Chapman, Miriam Gantz. "The Story of Woman Suffrage in Wyoming, 1869–1890." Master's thesis, University of Wyoming, 1952.

Churchill, Caroline Nichols. *Active Footsteps.* 1909; reprint, New York: Arno Press, 1980.

Clark, Norman H. *The Dry Years: Prohibition and Social Change in Washington.* Seattle: University of Washington Press, 1965.

Clark, Thomas. "Labor and Progressivism South of the Slot." *California History* 66 (Sept. 1987), 197–207.

Clifford, James. *The Predicament of Culture: Twentieth-Century Ethnography, Literature, and Art.* Cambridge, MA: Harvard University Press, 1988.

Clinch, Thomas A. *Urban Populism and Free Silver in Montana: A Narrative of Ideology in Political Action.* Missoula: University of Montana Press, 1970.

Cloud, Barbara. "Laura Hall Peters: Pursuing the Myth of Equality." *Pacific Northwest Quarterly* 74:1 (Jan. 1983), 28–36.

Cobble, Dorothy Sue. *Dishing It Out: Waitresses and Their Unions in the Twentieth Century.* Urbana and Chicago: University of Illinois Press, 1991.

Cohen, Philip N. "Nationalism and Suffrage: Gender Struggle in Nation-Building America." *Signs* 21:3 (Spring 1996), 716–718.

College Equal Suffrage League of Northern California. *Winning Equal Suffrage in California.* San Francisco: Press of the James H. Barry Co., 1913.

Cooper, Donald G. "The California Suffrage Campaign of 1896: Its Origins, Strategies, Defeat." *Southern California Quarterly* 71:4 (Winter 1989), 311–325.

Cott, Nancy. "Across the Great Divide: Women in Politics before and after 1920." In Louise A. Tilly and Patricia Gurin, eds., *Women, Politics and Change.* New York: Russell Sage Foundation, 1990.

Cott, Nancy F. *The Grounding of Modern Feminism.* New Haven: Yale University Press, 1987.

Cott, Nancy F. "Marriage and Women's Citizenship in the United States, 1830–1934." *American Historical Review* 103 (Dec. 1998), 1440–1474.

Cox, Elizabeth M. *Women State and Territorial Legislators, 1895–1995.* Jefferson, NC: McFarland, 1996.

Croly, J. C. (Jennie Cunningham). *The History of the Women's Club Movement in America.* New York: Henry B. Allen, 1898.

Cross, Ira B. *A History of the Labor Movement in California.* Berkeley and Los Angeles: University of California Press, 1935.

Daley, Caroline, and Melanie Nolan, eds. *Suffrage and Beyond: International Feminist Perspectives.* New York: New York University Press, 1994.

Dancis, Bruce. "Socialism and Women in the United States, 1900–1917." *Socialist Revolution* 6 (1976), 81–144.

Daniels, Roger. *Asian America: History of Chinese and Japanese in the United States since 1850.* Seattle: University of Washington Press, 1988.

Davis, Reda. *California Women: A Guide to Their Politics, 1885–1911.* San Francisco: California Scene, 1967.

Davis, Reda. *Woman's Republic: The Life of Marietta Stow, Cooperator.* Los Angeles: Pt. Pinos Editions, 1980.

Deering, Mabel Craft. "The Women's Demonstration: How They Won and Used the Vote in California." *Collier's* 48 (6 Jan. 1912), 17–18.

Degler, Carl N. "Charlotte Perkins Gilman on the Theory and Practice of Feminism." *American Quarterly* 8 (Spring 1956), 21–39.

de Graaf, Lawrence B. "Race, Sex, and Region: Black Women and the American West, 1850–1920." *Pacific Historical Review* 49 (May 1980), 285–313.

Dembo, Jonathan. "A History of the Washington State Labor Movement, 1885–1935." Ph.D. diss., University of Washington, 1978.

Dembo, Jonathan. *Unions and Politics in Washington State, 1885–1935.* New York: Garland, 1983.

Deutsch, Sarah. "Landscape of Enclaves: Race Relations in the West, 1865–1990." In William Cronon, George Miles, and Jay Gitlin, eds., *Under an Open Sky: Rethinking America's Western Past,* 110–131. New York: W. W. Norton, 1992.

Deverell, William, and Tom Sitton, eds. *California Progressivism Revisited.* Berkeley: University of California Press, 1994.

Dickson, Lynda F. "Lifting as We Climb: African American Women's Clubs of Denver, 1880–1925." In Elizabeth Jameson and Susan Armitage, eds., *Writing the Range: Race, Class, and Culture in the Women's West,* 372–392. Norman: University of Oklahoma Press, 1997.

Diner, Hasia R. *Erin's Daughters in America: Irish Immigrant Women in the Nineteenth Century.* Baltimore: Johns Hopkins University Press, 1983.

Diner, Steven J. *A Very Different Age: Americans of the Progressive Era.* New York: Hill and Wang, 1998.

Douthit, Mary Osborn, ed. *The Souvenir of Western Women.* Portland: Anderson and Duniway Company, 1905.

Downing, Agnes H. "Woman Suffrage in California." *Progressive Woman* 52 (Sept. 1911).

Dubofsky, Melvyn. "The Origins of Western Working Class Radicalism, 1890–1905." *Labor History* 7 (Spring 1966), 131–154.

Dubofsky, Melvyn. *We Shall Be All: A History of the Industrial Workers of the World.* Chicago: Quadrangle Books, 1969.

DuBois, Ellen Carol. *Feminism and Suffrage: The Emergence of an Independent Women's Movement in America, 1848–1869.* Ithaca, NY: Cornell University Press, 1978.

DuBois, Ellen Carol. *Harriot Stanton Blatch and the Winning of Woman Suffrage.* New Haven: Yale University Press, 1997.

DuBois, Ellen Carol. "Outgrowing the Compact of the Fathers: Equal Rights, Woman Suffrage, and the United States Constitution, 1820–1878." *Journal of American History* 74 (Dec. 1987), 836–862.

DuBois, Ellen Carol. *Woman Suffrage and Women's Rights.* New York: New York Univerity Press, 1998.

DuBois, Ellen Carol. "Working Women, Class Relations, and Suffrage Militance: Harriot Stanton Blatch and the New York Woman Suffrage Movement, 1894–1909." *Journal of American History* 74 (June 1987): 34–58.

DuBois, Ellen Carol, and Vicki L. Ruiz, eds. *Unequal Sisters: A Multicultural Reader in U.S. Women's History.* New York: Routledge, 1990.

Duniway, Abigail Scott. *Path Breaking: An Autobiographical History of the Equal Suffrage Movement in Pacific Coast States.* 2d ed., 1914; reprint, New York: Source Book Press, 1970.

Durham, N. W. *History of the City of Spokane and Spokane County Washington from Its Early Settlement to the Present Time.* Vol. 2. Seattle: S. J. Clarke, 1912.

Dye, Nancy Schrom. *As Equals and as Sisters: Feminism, the Labor Movement, and the Women's Trade Union League of New York.* Columbia: University of Missouri Press, l980.

Eaves, Lucile. *A History of California Labor Legislation, with an Introductory Sketch of the San Francisco Labor Movement.* University of California Publications in Economics, Vol. 2. Berkeley: University of California Press, 1910.

Edelman, Susan Scheiber. "'A Red Hot Suffrage Campaign': The Woman Suffrage Cause in California, 1896." *California Supreme Court Historical Society Yearbook* 2 (1995), 51–131.

Edmundson, Vera. "Feminist and Laborite." *Sunset Magazine* (June 1915), 1179–1180.

Edson, Mrs. Charles F. [Katherine Philips]. "The Actual Operation of Woman's Suffrage in the Pacific Coast Cities." *National Municipal Review* 1 (Oct. 1912), 620–629.

Edson, Katherine Phillips. "The Present Status." *Federation Courier* 2:6 (April 1911), 9.

Edson, Katherine. "Women's Influence on State Legislation." *California Outlook* (14 June 1913), 7–8.

Edwards, G. Thomas. *Sowing Good Seeds: The Northwest Suffrage Campaigns of Susan B. Anthony.* Portland: Oregon Historical Society Press, 1990.

Edwards, Rebecca. *Angels in the Machinery: Gender in American Party Politics from the Civil War to the Progressive Era.* New York: Oxford University Press, 1997.

Edwards, Rebecca. "Pioneers at the Polls: Woman Suffrage in the West." In Baker, ed. *Votes for Women,* 90–101.

Eisenstein, Sarah. *Give Us Bread, but Give Us Roses: Working Women's Consciousness in the United States, 1890 to the First World War.* London: Routledge and Kegan Paul, 1983.

Emmons, David M. *The Butte Irish: Class and Ethnicity in an American Mining Town, 1875–1925.* Urbana: University of Illinois Press, 1989.

Englander, Susan. *Class Coalition and Class Conflict in the California Woman Suffrage Movement, 1907–1912: The San Francisco Wage Earners' Suffrage League.* Lewiston, NY: Mellen Research University Press, 1992.

Englander, Susan. "Right-Minded Women: Clubwomen and the San Francisco Graft Trials." *Journal of History* 1 (1989), 11–28.

Englander, Susan L. "Maud Younger and the Eight-Hour Day." Unpublished manuscript, 1991.

Englander, Susan L. "The San Francisco Wage Earners' Suffrage League: Class Conflict and Class Coalition in the California Woman Suffrage Movement, 1907–1912." Master's thesis, San Francisco State University, 1989.

Ethington, Philip J. *The Public City: The Political Construction of Urban Life in San Francisco, 1850–1900.* Cambridge, UK: Cambridge University Press, 1994.

Ethington, Philip J. "Recasting Urban Political History: Gender, the Public, the Household, and Political Participation in Boston and San Francisco during the Progressive Era." *Social Science History* 16:2 (Summer 1992), 301–333.

Faherty, William B. "Regional Minorities and the Woman Suffrage Struggle." *Colorado Magazine* 33 (July 1956), 212–217.

Faragher, John Mack. "The Frontier Trail: Rethinking Turner and Reimagining the West." *American Historical Review* 98 (1993), 106–117.

Fargo, Lucile F. *Spokane Story.* New York: Columbia University Press, 1950.

Field, Sara Bard. "The Clash in Nevada." *Outwest* (Aug. 1914), 51–66.

Fink, Leon. *Workingmen's Democracy: The Knights of Labor and American Politics.* Urbana: University of Illinois Press, 1983.

Finnegan, Margaret. *Selling Suffrage: Consumer Culture and Votes for Women.* New York: Columbia University Press, 1999.

Fisher, James Adolphus. "A History of the Political and Social Development of the Black Community in California, 1850–1950." Ph.D. diss., State University of New York at Stony Brook, 1971.

Flexner, Eleanor. *Century of Struggle.* 1959. Rev. ed. Cambridge, MA: Belknap Press, 1975.

Flynn, Elizabeth Gurley. *The Rebel Girl: An Autobiography, My First Life (1906–1926).* Rev. ed. New York: International Publishers, 1973.

Foner, Eric. *Free Soil, Free Labor, Free Men: The Ideology of the Republican Party before the Civil War.* New York: Oxford University Press, 1970.

Ford, Jean, and James W. Hulse. "The First Battle for Woman Suffrage in Nevada, 1869–1871—Correcting and Expanding the Record." *Nevada Historical Society Quarterly* 38:3 (Fall 1995), 174–188.

Fowler, Robert Booth. "Carrie Chapman Catt, Strategist." In Marjorie Spruill Wheeler, ed., *One Woman, One Vote: Rediscovering the Woman Suffrage Movement,* 295–314. Troutdale, OR: New Sage Press, 1995.

Frankiel, Sandra Sizer. *California's Spiritual Frontiers: Religious Alternative to Anglo-Protestantism, 1850–1910.* Berkeley: University of California Press, 1988.

Garbutt, Mary Alderman. *Victories of Four Decades: A History of the Woman's Christian Temperance Union of Southern California, 1883–1924.* Los Angeles: Woman's Christian Temperance Union of Southern California, 1925.

Gibson, Mary S. *A Record of Twenty-five Years of the California Federation of Women's Clubs, 1900–1925.* Los Angeles: California Federation of Women's Clubs, 1925.

Gibson, Mary S. "The Women's Legislative Council." *Woman's Bulletin* 2 (March 1914), 28–29.

Giddings, Paula. *When and Where I Enter: The Impact of Black Women on Race and Sex in America.* New York: Bantam Books, 1984.

Gifford, Carolyn DeSwarte. "Frances Willard and the Woman's Christian Temperance Union's Conversion to Woman Suffrage." In Marjorie Spruill Wheeler, *One Woman, One Vote: Rediscovering the Woman Suffrage Movement,* 117–132. Troutdale, OR: New Sage Press, 1995.

Gill, Gerald R. "From Progressive Republican to Independent Progressive: The Political Career of Charlotta A. Bass." In Ann D. Gordon, ed., *African American Women and the Vote, 1837–1965,* 156–171. Amherst: University of Massachusetts Press, 1997.

Gillmore, Inez Haynes. "The Result in California." *Harper's Weekly* (8 May 1915), 447.

Gillmore, Inez Haynes Irwin. *The Story of the Woman's Party.* 1921; reprint, New York: Kraus Reprint, 1971.

Gillmore, Inez Haynes Irwin. *Up Hill with Banners Flying.* Penobscot, ME: Traversity Press, 1964.

Gilman, Charlotte Perkins [Stetson]. *The Living of Charlotte Perkins Gilman: An Autobiography.* New York: D. Appleton-Century, 1935.

Gilman, C. P. "A Suggestion on the Negro Problem." *American Journal of Sociology* 1 (July 1908), 78–85.

Gilman, Charlotte Perkins [Stetson]. *Women and Economics: A Study of the Economic Relation between Women and Men as a Factor in Social Evolution.* 1898; reprint, New York: Source Book Press, 1970.

Gilmore, David D. *Manhood in the Making: Cultural Concepts of Masculinity.* New Haven, CT: Yale University Press, 1990.

Glass, Mary Ellen. *Silver and Politics in Nevada, 1892–1902.* Reno: University of Nevada Press, 1969.

Goldberg, Michael L. "Non-Partisan and All-Partisan: Rethinking Woman Suffrage and Party Politics in Gilded Age Kansas." *Western Historical Quarterly* 25 (Spring 1994), 21–44.

Goldberg, Michael Lewis. *An Army of Women: Gender and Politics in Gilded Age Kansas.* Baltimore: Johns Hopkins University Press, 1997.

Goldberg, Michael Lewis. "'An Army of Women': Gender Relations and Politics in Kansas Populism, the Woman Movement, and the Republican Party, 1879–1896." Ph.D. diss., Yale University, 1992.

Goldstein, Marcia T., and Rebecca A. Hunt, "From Suffrage to Centennial: A Research Guide to Colorado and National Women's Suffrage Sources." *Colorado Heritage* (Spring 1993), 40–45.

Goodwyn, Lawrence. *Democratic Promise: The Populist Movement in America.* New York: Oxford University Press, 1976.

Gordon, Anna A. *The Beautiful Life of Frances Willard: A Memorial Volume.* Chicago: Woman's Temperance Publishing Association, 1898.

Gordon, Linda. "Black and White Visions of Welfare: Women's Welfare Activism, 1890–1945." *Journal of American History* 78 (Sept. 1991), 559–590.

Gordon, Linda, ed. *Women, the State, and Welfare.* Madison: University of Wisconsin Press, 1990.

Graham, Sara Hunter. "The Suffrage Renaissance: A New Image for a New Century, 1896–1910." In Marjorie Spruill Wheeler, *One Woman, One Vote: Rediscovering the Woman Suffrage Movement,* 162–167. Troutdale, OR: New Sage Press, 1995.

Graham, Sara Hunter. *Woman Suffrage and the New Democracy.* New Haven, CT: Yale University Press, 1996.

Gramsci, Antonio. *Selections from the Prison Notebooks of Antonio Gramsci,* ed. Quintin Hoare and Geoffrey Nowell Smith. New York: International Publishers, 1971.

Green, Elna. *Southern Strategies: Southern Women and the Woman Suffrage Question.* Chapel Hill: University of North Carolina Press, 1997.

Green, Rayna. "Native American Women: Review Essay." *Signs* 6 (Winter 1980), 248–267.

Green, Rayna. "The Pocahontas Perplex: The Image of Indian Women in Popular Culture." *Massachusetts Review* 16 (Autumn 1975), 678–714.

Griffiths, David B. "Far Western Populist Thought: A Comparative Study of John R. Rogers and Davis H. Waite." *Pacific Northwest Quarterly* 60 (Oct. 1969), 183–192.

Griffiths, David Burke. "Populism in the Far West, 1890–1900." Ph.D. diss., University of Washington, 1967.

Grimes, Alan P. *The Puritan Ethic and Woman Suffrage.* New York: Oxford University Press, 1967.

Grimshaw, Patricia. "Settler Anxieties, Indigenous Peoples, and Women's Suffrage in the Colonies of Australia, New Zealand, and Hawai'i, 1888–1902." *Pacific Historical Review* 69:4 (Nov. 2000), 553–572.

Grimshaw, Patricia. "Suffragists Representing Race and Gender in the American West: The Case of Colorado." In Patricia Grimshaw and Diane Kirkby, eds., *Dealing with Difference: Essays in Gender, Culture and History,* 79–81. Melbourne, Australia: History Department, University of Melbourne, 1997.

Grimshaw, Patricia. "Women's Suffrage in New Zealand Revisited: Writing from the Margins." In Daley and Nolan, eds., *Suffrage and Beyond,* 25–41.

Grimshaw, Patricia, and Katherine Ellinghaus. "White Women, Aboriginal Women and the Vote in Western Australia." *Studies in Western Australian History* 19 (1999), 1–19.

Gullett, Gayle. "City Mothers, City Daughters, and the Dance Hall Girls: The Limits of Female Political Power in San Francisco, 1913." In Barbara J. Harris and JoAnn K. McNamara, eds., *Women and the Structure of Society,* 149–159, 281–285. Durham, NC: Duke University Press, 1984.

Gullett, Gayle Ann. *Becoming Citizens: The Emergence and Development of the California Women's Movement, 1880–1911.* Urbana and Chicago: University of Illinois Press, 2000.

Gullett, Gayle Ann. "Feminism, Politics, and Voluntary Groups: Organized Womanhood in California, 1886–1896." Ph.D. diss., University of California, Riverside, 1983.

Gustafson, Melanie, Kristie Miller, and Elisabeth Israels Perry, eds. *We Have Come to Stay: American Women and Political Parties, 1880–1960.* Albuquerque: University of New Mexico Press, 1999.

Habermas, Jürgen. *The Habermas Reader.* William Outhwaite, ed. Cambridge, UK: Polity Press, 1996.

Hargis, Donald E. "Women's Rights: California, 1849." *Historical Society of Southern California Quarterly* 37:4 (Dec. 1955), 320–334.

Harper, Ida Husted. *The Life and Work of Susan B. Anthony.* 2 vols. Indianapolis and Kansas City: Bowen-Merrill, 1898.

Harrison, Patricia Greenwood. *Connecting Links: The British and American Woman Suffrage Movements, 1900–1914.* Westport, CT, and London: Greenwood Press, 2000.

Harvey, Anna L. "The Political Consequences of Suffrage Exclusion: Organizations, Institutions, and the Electoral Mobilization of Women." *Social Science History* 20:1 (Spring 1996), 97–132.

Harvey, Anna L. *Voters without Leverage: Women in American Politics, 1920–1970.* Cambridge and New York: Cambridge University Press, 1988.

Hauptmann, Laurence M. "Congress, Plenary Power, and the American Indian, 1870–1992." In John Mohawk and Oren Lyons, et al., *Democracy, Indian Nations, and the U.S. Constitution,* 321–326. Santa Fé, NM: Clear Light Publishers, 1992.

Hichborn, Franklin. *Story of the Session of the California Legislature of 1911.* San Francisco: Press of James H. Barry, 1911.

Hichborn, Franklin. *Story of the Session of the California Legislature of 1913.* San Francisco: Press of James H. Barry, 1913.

Hicks, John D. *The Populist Revolt: A History of the Farmers' Alliance and the People's Party.* Minneapolis: University of Minnesota Press, 1931.

Hill, Mary A. *Charlotte Perkins Gilman: The Making of a Radical Feminist, 1866–1896.* Philadelphia: Temple University Press, 1980.

Hine, Darlene Clark, et al., eds. *Black Women in America: An Historical Encyclopedia.* Brooklyn: Carlson, 1993.

Hofstader, Richard. *The Age of Reform: From Bryan to F.D.R.* New York: Vintage Books, 1955.

Hofstader, Richard. *Social Darwinism in American Thought.* Rev. ed. New York: George Braziller, 1959.

Holden, Margaret K. "Gender and Protest Ideology: Sue Ross Keenan and the Oregon Anti-Chinese Movement." *Western Legal History* 7 (Summer 1994), 223–243.

Holton, Sandra Stanley. *Feminism and Democracy: Women's Suffrage and Reform Politics in Britain, 1900–1918.* Cambridge, UK, and New York: Cambridge University Press, 1986.

Horner, Patricia Voeller. "May Arkwright Hutton: Suffragist and Politician." In Karen J. Blair, ed., *Women in Pacific Northwest History,* 25–42. Seattle: University of Washington Press, 1988.

Horsman, Reginald. *Race and Manifest Destiny: The Origins of American Racial Anglo-Saxonism.* Cambridge, MA: Harvard University Press, 1981.

Howard, Anne Bail. *The Long Campaign.* Reno: University of Nevada Press, 1985.

Hundley, Norris C., jr. "Katherine Philips Edson and the Fight for the California Minimum Wage, 1912–1913." *Pacific Historical Review* 29 (1960), 271–285.

Hunton, A. W. "The Club Movement in California." *Crisis* (Dec. 1912), 90–92.

Issel, William, and Robert W. Cherny. *San Francisco, 1865–1932: Politics, Power and Urban Development.* Berkeley: University of California Press, 1986.

Iverson, Joan. "The Mormon-Suffrage Relationship: Personal and Political Quandries." In Madsen, ed., *Battle for the Ballot,* 151–161.

Jacobs, Margaret D. "Resistance to Rescue: The Indians of Bahapki and Mrs. Annie E. K. Bidwell." In Susan Armitage and Elizabeth Jameson, eds., *Writing the Range: Race, Class, and Culture in the Women's West*, 230–251. Norman: University of Oklahoma Press, 1997.

Jameson, Elizabeth. *All That Glitters: Class, Conflict, and Community in Cripple Creek*. Urbana: University of Illinois Press, 1998.

Jameson, Elizabeth, and Susan Armitage, eds. *Writing the Range: Race, Class, and Culture in the Women's West*. Norman: University of Oklahoma Press, 1997.

Jeffrey, Julie Roy. "Women in the Southern Farmers' Alliance: A Reconsideration of the Role and Status of Women in the Late Nineteenth-Century South." *Feminist Studies* 3 (Fall 1975), 72–91.

Jensen, Billie Barnes. "Colorado Woman Suffrage Campaigns of the 1870s." *Journal of the West* 12 (April 1973), 254–271.

Jensen, Billie Barnes. "'In the Weird and Wooly West': Anti-Suffrage Women, Gender Issues, and Woman Suffrage in the West." *Journal of the West* 33 (July 1993), 41–51.

Jensen, Billie Barnes. "Let the Women Vote." *Colorado Magazine* 41 (Winter 1964), 13–25.

Jensen, Billie Barnes. "The Woman Suffrage Movement in Colorado." Master's thesis, University of Colorado, 1959.

Jensen, Joan. "After Slavery: Caroline Severance in Los Angeles." *Southern California Quarterly* 48 (July 1966), 175–186.

Jensen, Joan M. "Cloth, Butter and Boarders: Women's Household Production for the Market." *Review of Radical Political Economics* 12:2 (Summer 1980), 14–24.

Jensen, Joan M., and Gloria R. Lothrop. *California Women: A History*. San Francisco: Boyd and Fraser, 1987.

Jensen, Joan M., and Darlis A. Miller. "The Gentle Tamers Revisited: New Approaches to the History of Women in the American West." *Pacific Historical Review* 49 (May 1980), 173–213.

Jerry, E. Claire. "Clara Bewick Colby and the *Woman's Tribune*, 1883–1909: The Freelance Editor as Movement Leader." In Solomon, ed., *A Voice of Their Own*, 110–128.

Josephson, Hannah. *Jeannette Rankin: First Lady in Congress*. Indianapolis and New York: Bobbs-Merrill, 1974.

Kahn, B. Zorina. "Married Women's Property Laws and Female Commercial Activity: Evidence from United States Patent Records, 1790–1895." *Journal of Economic History* 56 (June 1996), 360–365.

Katz, Sherry. "Frances Nacke Noel and 'Sister Movements': Socialism, Feminism and Trade Unionism in Los Angeles, 1909–1916." *California History* 67 (Sept. 1988), 181–189, 207–210fn.

Katz, Sherry. "Frances Noel and the Working Class Woman: Female Solidarity and Class Consciousness in Los Angeles, 1909–1916." Seminar paper, University of California, Los Angeles, 1985.

Katz, Sherry. "Socialist Women and Progressive Reform." In William Deverell and Tom Sitton, eds., *California Progressivism Revisited*, 117–143. Berkeley: University of California Press, 1994.

Katz, Sherry J. "A Politics of Coalition: Socialist Women and the California Suffrage Movement, 1900–1911." In Marjorie Spruill Wheeler, ed., *One Woman, One Vote: Rediscovering the Woman Suffrage Movement*, 245–262. Troutdale, OR: NewSage Press, 1995.

Katz, Sherry Jeanne. "Dual Commitments: Feminism, Socialism, and Women's Political Activism in California, 1890–1920." Ph.D. diss., University of California, Los Angeles, 1991.

Kazin, Michael. "Barons of Labor: The San Francisco Building Trades, 1896–1922." Ph.D. diss., Stanford University, 1983.

Kazin, Michael. *Barons of Labor: The San Francisco Building Trades and Union Power in the Progressive Era*. Urbana and Chicago: University of Illinois Press, 1987.

Kazin, Michael. *The Populist Persuasion: An American History*. New York: Basic Books, 1995.

Kenneally, James J. "Catholicism and Woman Suffrage." In *Catholicism in America*. New York: Harper and Row, 1970.

Keneally, James J. "The Opposition to Woman Suffrage in Massachusetts, 1868–1920." Ph.D. diss., Boston College, 1963.

Keneally, James J. "Women and Trade Unions, 1870–1920: The Quandry of the Reformer." *Labor History* 4 (1973), 42–55.

Keneally, James J. *Women in American Trade Unions*. St. Albans, VT: Eden Press Women's Publications, 1978.

Kerber, Linda. *Women of the Republic: Intellect and Ideology in Revolutionary America*. Chapel Hill: University of North Carolina Press, 1980.

Kerber, Linda K. "The Meanings of Citizenship." *Journal of American History* 84 (Dec. 1997), 833–854.

Kerber, Linda K. *No Constitutional Right to Be Ladies: Women and the Obligations of Citizenship*. New York: Hill and Wang, 1998.

Kessler, Lauren. "The Fight for Woman Suffrage and the Oregon Press." In Karen J. Blair, ed., *Women in Pacific Northwest History*, 43–58. Seattle: University of Washington Press, 1988.

Kessler-Harris, Alice. *Out to Work: A History of Wage-Earning Women in the United States*. New York: Oxford University Press, 1982.

Kimmel, Michael S. "Men's Responses to Feminism at the Turn of the Century." *Gender and Society* 1 (Sept. 1987), 261–283.

Kizer, Benjamin H. "May Arkwright Hutton." *Pacific Northwest Quarterly* 57 (April 1966).

Knight, Denise D., ed. *The Diaries of Charlotte Perkins Gilman: 1890–1935.* Vol 2. Charlottesville: University Press of Virginia, 1994.

Knight, Robert. *Industrial Relations in the San Francisco Bay Area, 1900–1918.* Berkeley: University of California Press, 1960.

Kraditor, Aileen S. *The Ideas of the Woman Suffrage Movement, 1890–1920.* Reprint. New York: W. W. Norton, 1981.

Kraft, James P. "The Fall of Job Harriman's Socialist Party: Violence, Gender, and Politics in Los Angeles, 1911." *Southern California Historical Quarterly* 70 (Spring 1988), 43–68.

Krieger, Nancy. "Queen of the Bolsheviks: The Hidden History of Dr. Marie Equi." *Radical America* 17 (1983), 55–73.

Landsman, Gail H. "The 'Other' as Political Symbol: Images of Indians in the Woman Suffrage Movement." *Ethnohistory* 39:3 (Summer 1992), 247–284.

Langdon, Emma F. *The Cripple Creek Strike: A History of the Industrial Wars in Colorado, 1903-4-5.* Denver: Great Western, 1905.

Lapp, Rudolph M. "Mabel Craft Deering: A Young Woman of Advanced Ideas." *California History* 66 (Sept. 1987), 162–169, 233fn.

Larson, Robert W. *Populism in the Mountain West.* Albuquerque: University of New Mexico Press, 1986.

Larson, T. A. "Dolls, Vassals, and Drudges: Pioneer Women in the West." *Western Historical Quarterly* 3 (Jan. 1972), 5–16.

Larson, T. A. "Idaho's Role in America's Woman Suffrage Crusade." *Idaho Yesterdays* 18 (Spring 1974), 2–17.

Larson, T. A. "Montana Women and the Battle for the Ballot." *Montana* 23 (Jan. 1973), 24–41.

Larson, T. A. "Petticoats at the Polls: Woman Suffrage in Territorial Wyoming." *Pacific Northwest Quarterly* 44 (April 1953), 74–79.

Larson, T. A. "The Woman's Rights Movement in Idaho." *Idaho Yesterdays* 16 (Spring 1972), 2–19.

Larson, T. A. "Woman Suffrage in Western America." *Utah Historical Quarterly* 38 (Winter 1970), 7–19.

Larson, T. A. "Woman Suffrage in Wyoming." *Pacific Northwest Quarterly* 56 (April 1965), 57–66.

Larson, T. A. "The Woman Suffrage Movement in Washington." *Pacific Northwest Quarterly* 67 (April 1976), 49–62.

Larson, T. A. "Wyoming's Contribution to the Regional and National Women's Rights Movements." *Annals of Wyoming* 52 (Spring 1980), 2–15.

Leach, Kristine. "Common Bonds: Women's Experiences as Immigrants to the

West in the 19th and 20th Centuries." *Journal of the West* 36 (Jan. 1997), 94–103.

Leonard, Stephen J. "'Bristling for Their Rights': Colorado's Women and the Mandate of 1893." *Colorado Heritage* (Spring 1993), 7–15.

Lerner, Elinor. "Family Structure, Occupational Patterns, and Support for Women's Suffrage." In Judith Freidlander et al., *Women in Culture and Politics: A Century of Change*, 223–236. Bloomington: Indiana University Press, 1986.

Lerner, Elinor. "Immigrant and Working Class Involvement in the New York City Woman Suffrage Movement, 1905–1917: A Study in Progressive Era Politics." Ph.D. diss., University of California, Berkeley, 1981.

Lerner, Gerda. "The Lady and the Mill Girl: Changes in the Status of Women in the Age of Jackson, 1800–1840." *American Studies* 10 (Spring 1969), 5–15.

Levenson, Roger. *Women in Printing: Northern California, 1857–1890*. Santa Barbara, CA: Capra Press, 1994.

Levine, Susan. *Labor's True Woman: Carpet Weavers, Industrialization, and Labor Reform in the Gilded Age*. Philadelphia: Temple University Press, 1984.

Levine, Susan. "Labor's True Woman: Domesticity and Equal Rights in the Knights of Labor." *Journal of American History* 70 (Sept. 1983), 323–339.

Lewis, Lawrence. "How Woman Suffrage Works in Colorado." *The Outlook* 82:4 (27 Jan. 1906), 167–178.

Liddington, Jill, and Jill Norris. *One Hand Tied behind Us: The Rise of the Women's Suffrage Movement*. London: Virago Press, 1978.

Limerick, Patricia Nelson. *The Legacy of Conquest: The Unbroken Past of the American West*. New York: Norton, 1988.

Link, Arthur S., and Richard L. McCormick. *Progressivism*. Arlington Heights, IL: Harlan-Davidson, 1983.

Liu, Tessie. "Teaching the Differences among Women from a Historical Perspective: Rethinking Race and Gender as Social Categories." In Vicki Ruiz and Ellen Carol DuBois, eds., *Unequal Sisters: A Multicultural Reader in U.S. Women's History*, 2d ed., 571–583. New York: Routledge, 1994.

Locke, Mary Lou. "'Like a Machine or an Animal': Working Women of the Late Nineteenth-Century Urban Far West, in San Francisco, Portland, and Los Angeles." Ph.D. diss., University of California, San Diego, 1982.

Locke, Mary Lou. "Out of the Shadows and into the Western Sun: Working Women of the Late Nineteenth Century Urban Far West." *Journal of Urban History* 16:2 (Feb. 1990), 175–204.

Loewy, Jean. "Katherine Philips Edson and the California Suffragette Movement, 1919–1920." *California Historical Society Quarterly* 47 (Dec. 1968), 343–350.

Logan, Adella Hunt. "Colored Women as Voters." *Crisis* (Sept. 1912), 240–243.

Lukas, J. Anthony. *Big Trouble: A Murder in a Small Western Town Sets Off a Struggle for the Soul of America*. New York: Touchstone, 1997.

Lunardini, Christine A. *From Equal Suffrage to Equal Rights: Alice Paul and the National Woman's Party, 1910–1928*. New York: New York University Press, 1986.

Madsen, Carol Cornwall. "Schism in the Sisterhood: Mormon Women and Partisan Politics, 1890–1900." In Madsen, ed., *Battle for the Ballot*, 245–271. Logan: Utah State University Press, 1997.

Madsen, Carol Cornwall, ed. *Battle for the Ballot: Essays on Woman Suffrage in Utah*. Logan: Utah State University Press, 1997.

Mahoney, Joseph F. "Woman Suffrage and the Urban Masses." *New Jersey History* 87 (Autumn 1969), 151–172.

Marcell, David W. *Progress and Pragmatism: James, Dewey, Beard, and the American Idea of Progress*. Westport, CT: Greenwood Press, 1974.

Marilley, Suzanne M. *Woman Suffrage and the Origins of Liberal Feminism in the United States, 1820–1920*. Cambridge, MA: Harvard University Press, 1996.

Marshall, T. H. *Sociology at the Crossroads and Other Essays*. London: Heinemann, 1963.

Mathews, Glenna. *The Rise of Public Woman: Woman's Power and Woman's Place in the United States, 1630–1970*. New York: Oxford University Press, 1992.

Matsuda, Mari J. "The West and the Legal Status of Women: Explanations of Frontier Feminism." *Journal of the West* 14 (Jan. 1985), 47–56.

Matthews, Lillian Ruth. *Women in Trade Unions in San Francisco*. University of California Publications in Economics, vol. 3. Berkeley: University of California Press, 1913.

McCormick, Richard L. "Ethno-cultural Interpretations of Nineteenth-Century American Voting Behavior." *Political Science Quarterly* 89 (June 1974), 351–377.

McDonagh, Eileen L., and H. Douglas Price. "Woman Suffrage in the Progressive Era: Patterns of Opposition and Support in Referenda Voting, 1910–1918." *American Political Science Review* 79:2 (June 1985), 415–435.

McGerr, Michael. "Political Style and Women's Power, 1830–1930." *Journal of American History* 77 (1990), 864–885.

McHenry, Robert. *Famous American Women*. New York: Dover, 1980.

Mead, Rebecca J. "'Let the Women Get Their Wages as Me Do': Trade Union Women and the Legislated Minimum Wage in California." *Pacific Historical Review* 67:3 (Aug. 1998), 317–347.

Mead, Rebecca J. "Trade Unionism and Political Activism among San Francisco Wage-Earning Women, 1900–1922." Master's thesis, San Francisco State University, 1991.

Mei, June. "Socioeconomic Developments among the Chinese in San Francisco, 1848–1906." In Edna Bonacich and Lucie Cheng Hirata, eds., *Labor Immigration under Capitalism: Asian Immigrant Workers in the United States before World War II,* 370–401. Berkeley: University of California Press, 1984.

Meredith, Ellis. "Colorado." *Woman Voter* (Jan. 1913), 12, 18. Symposium issue.

Meredith, Ellis. "What It Means to Be an Enfranchised Woman." *Atlantic Monthly* (Aug. 1908), 196–202.

Meredith, Ellis. "Women Citizens of Colorado." *The Great Divide* (Feb. 1894), 53.

Miller, Sally M., ed. *Flawed Liberation: Socialism and Feminism.* Westport, CT: Greenwood Press, 1981.

Monoson, S. Sara. "The Lady and the Tiger: Women's Electoral Activism in New York City before Suffrage." *Journal of Women's History* 2 (Fall 1990), 100–135.

Montejano, David. *Anglos and Mexicans in the Making of Texas, 1836–1986.* Austin: University of Texas Press, 1987.

Montgomery, James W. *Liberated Women: A Life of May Arkwright Hutton.* Fairfield, WA: Ye Galleon Press, 1974.

Morris, John R. "The Women and Governor Waite." *Colorado Magazine* 44 (Winter 1967), 11–19.

Mowry, George E. *The California Progressives.* Berkeley: University of California Press, 1951.

Moynihan, Ruth Barnes. "Of Women's Rights and Freedom: Abigail Scott Duniway." In Karen J. Blair, ed., *Women in Pacific Northwest History,* 9–24. Seattle: University of Washington Press, 1988.

Moynihan, Ruth Barnes. *Rebel for Rights: Abigail Scott Duniway.* New Haven and London: Yale University Press, 1983.

Muncy, Robyn. *Creating a Female Dominion in American Reform, 1890–1935.* New York: Oxford University Press, 1991.

Murphy, John Miller. "Woman Suffrage in Washington Territory." In Mary O. Douthit, ed., *The Souvenir of Western Women,* 104–107. Portland, OR: Anderson and Duniway, 1905.

Murphy, Mary. *Mining Cultures: Men, Women, and Leisure in Butte, 1914–41.* Urbana: University of Illinois Press, 1997.

Myres, Sandra L. "Suffering for Suffrage: Western Women and the Struggle for Political, Legal, and Economic Rights." In Myres, *Westering Women and the Frontier Experience, 1800–1915,* 213–236. Albuquerque: University of New Mexico Press, 1982.

Nathan, Maud. *The Story of an Epoch-Making Movement.* Garden City, NY: Doubleday, Page, 1926.

National American Woman Suffrage Association (NAWSA). *Victory: How*

Women Won It: A Centennial Symposium, 1840–1940. New York: H. W. Wilson, 1940.

National Association of Colored Women's Clubs (NACWC). *A History of the Club Movement among the Colored Women of the United States of America.* Washington, DC: NACWA, 1902.

Nee, Victor G., and Brett de Bary. *Longtime Californ': A Documentary Study of an American Chinatown.* New York: Pantheon Books, 1972.

Newman, Louise Michele. *White Women's Rights: The Racial Origins of Feminism in the United States.* New York and Oxford: Oxford University Press, 1999.

Noun, Louise R. *Strong-minded Women.* Ames: Iowa State University Press, 1969.

Oberdeck, Kathryn J. "'Not Pink Teas': The Seattle Working-Class Movement, 1905–1918." *Labor History* 33:2 (Spring 1991), 193–230.

Oldfield, Audrey. *Woman Suffrage in Australia: A Gift or a Struggle?* Cambridge, UK: Cambridge University Press, 1992.

O'Neill, William L. *Everyone Was Brave: The Rise and Fall of Feminism in America.* Chicago: Quadrangle Books, 1969.

Ostrander, Gilman M. *Nevada: The Great Rotten Borough, 1859–1914.* New York: Alfred A. Knopf, 1966.

Ostrander, Gilman M. *The Prohibition Movement in California, 1848–1933.* University of California Publications in History, vol. 57. Berkeley: University of California Press, 1957.

Parker, Adella M. "The Woman Voter of the West: A New Force in Politics." *The Westerner* (Aug. 1912), 3–6, 37–39.

Pascoe, Peggy. "Miscegenation Law, Court Cases, and Ideologies of 'Race' in Twentieth-Century America." *Journal of American History* 83 (June 1996), 44–69.

Pascoe, Peggy. *Relations of Rescue: The Search for Female Moral Authority in the American West, 1874–1939.* New York: Oxford University Press, 1990.

Patai, Daphne, ed. *Looking Backward, 1988–1888: Essays on Edward Bellamy.* Amherst: University of Massachusetts Press, 1988.

Pateman, Carole. *The Sexual Contract.* Stanford, CA: Stanford University Press, 1988.

Payne, Elizabeth Anne. *Reform, Labor, and Feminism: Margaret Dreier Robins and the Women's Trade Union League.* Urbana: University of Illinois Press, l988.

Pearce, Roy Harvey. *Savagism and Civilization: A Study of the Indian and the American Mind.* Baltimore: Johns Hopkins University Press, 1965.

Pearce, Stella E. "Suffrage in the Pacific Northwest, Old Oregon and Washington." *Washington Historical Quarterly* 3 (April 1912), 106–110.

Peiss, Kathy. "Charity Girls and City Pleasures: Historical Notes on Working-Class Sexuality, 1880–1920." In Ellen Carol DuBois and Vicki L. Ruiz, eds., *Unequal Sisters: A Multicultural Reader in U.S. Women's History.* New York: Routledge, 1990.

Peixotto, Jessica B. "Women of California as Trade Unionists." *Publications of the Association of Collegiate Alumnae* 3 (Dec. 1908), 40–49.

Person, Stow, ed. *Evolutionary Thought in America.* New Haven: Yale University Press, 1950.

Petrik, Paula. *No Step Backward: Women and Family on the Rocky Mountain Mining Frontier, Helena, Montana 1865–1900.* Helena: Montana Historical Society Press, 1987.

Phelps, Edith M., ed. *Selected Articles on Woman Suffrage.* Debaters' Handbook Series. Minneapolis: H. W. Wilson, 1910.

Ping Chiu. *Chinese Labor in California, 1850–1880: An Economic Study.* Madison: State Historical Society of Wisconsin, 1967.

Pitt, Leonard. *The Decline of the Californios: A Social History of the Spanish-Speaking Californians, 1846–1890.* Berkeley: University of California Press, 1966.

Ploeger, Louise M. "Trade Unionism among the Women of San Francisco, 1920." Master's thesis, University of California, Berkeley, 1920.

Poll, Richard. "The Political Reconstruction of Utah Territory, 1866–1890." *Pacific Historical Review* 27 (May 1958), 111–126.

Poten, Connie. "May Arkwright Hutton: Miner to Millionaire." Wilderness Women Project, UMT, Missoula, n.d., Carton 1.4, Hutton Settlement Collection, Eastern Washington State Historical Society.

Putnam, John. "The Emergence of a New West: The Politics of Class and Gender in Seattle, Washington, 1880–1917." Ph.D. diss., University of California, San Diego, 2000.

Putnam, John. "A 'Test of Chiffon Politics': Gender Politics in Seattle, 1897–1917." *Pacific Historical Review* 69:4 (Fall 2000), 595–616.

Raftery, Judith. "Los Angeles Clubwomen and Progressive Reform." In William Deverell and Tom Sitton, eds., *California Progressivism Revisited,* 144–174. Berkeley: University of California Press, 1994.

Raine, William MacLeod. "Woman Suffrage in Colorado." *Chatauquan* 34 (Feb. 1902), 482–284. Reprinted in Edith M. Phelps, ed., *Selected Articles on Woman Suffrage,* 19–23. Minneapolis: H. W. Wilson, 1910.

Rankin, Jeannette. "Why the Coutnry Folk Did It." *Woman Voter* (Dec. 1911), 13.

Rastall, Benjamin M. *The Labor History of the Cripple Creek District: A Study in Industrial Evolution.* Bulletin of the University of Wisconsin, no. 198. Madison, 1908.

Reiff, Janice L. "Urbanization and the Social Structure: Seattle, Washington, 1852–1910." Ph.D. diss., University of Washington, 1981.

Robinson, Helen Ring. "On Being a Woman Senator." *The Independent* 78 (20 April 1914), 131–132.

Robinson, Helen Ring. *Preparing Women for Citizenship*. New York: Macmillan, 1918.

Rodes, Donald Waller. "The California Woman Suffrage Campaign of 1911." Master's thesis, California State University, Hayward, 1974.

Rodgers, Daniel T. "In Search of Progressivism." *Reviews in American History* 10 (Dec. 1982), 113–132.

Roeder, Richard B. "Crossing the Gender Line: Ella L. Knowles, Montana's First Woman Lawyer." *Montana* 32:3 (Summer 1982), 64–75.

Roediger, David. *The Wages of Whiteness: Race and the Making of the American Working Class*. London: Verso, 1991.

Rogin, Michael. "California Populism and the 'System of 1896.'" *Western Political Quarterly* 22 (March 1969), 179–196.

Rogin, Michael. "Progressivism and the California Electorate." *Journal of American History* 55 (1968), 197–314.

Rogin, Michael P., and John L. Shover. *Political Change in California: Critical Elections and Social Movements, 1890–1966*. Westport, CT: Greenwood, 1970.

Rosen, Ruth. *The Lost Sisterhood: Prostitution in America, 1900–1918*. Baltimore: Johns Hopkins University Press, 1982.

Rosenberg, Charles. "Sexuality, Class and Role in Nineteenth-Century America." *American Quarterly* 35 (May 1973), 131–153.

Rosenow, Beverly Paulik, ed. *The Journal of the Washington State Constitutional Convention, 1889*. Seattle: Book Publishing Company, 1961.

Rotundo, E. Anthony. *American Manhood: Tranformations in Masculinty from the Revolution to the Modern Era*. New York: Basic Books, 1993.

Rubens, Lisa. "The Patrician Radical: Charlotte Anita Whitney." *California History* 65 (Sept. 1986), 158–171, 226–227fn.

Ruddy, E. G., ed. *The Mother of Clubs: Caroline M. Seymour Severance*. Los Angeles: Baumgardt, 1906.

Ruiz, Vicki L. "A Promise Fulfilled: Mexican Cannery Workers in Southern California." In Ellen Carol DuBois and Vicki L. Ruiz, eds., *Unequal Sisters: A Multicultural Reader in U.S. Women's History*, 264–274. New York: Routledge, 1990.

Ryan, Mary P. *Cradle of the Middle Class: The Family in Oneida County, New York, 1790–1865*. Cambridge, UK: Cambridge University Press, 1981.

Ryan, Mary P. "Gender and Public Access: Women's Politics in Nineteenth-

Century America." In Craig Calhoun, ed., *Habermas and the Public Sphere*, 259–288. Cambridge, MA: MIT Press, 1996.

Ryan, Mary P. *Women in Public: Between Banners and Ballots, 1825–1880*. Baltimore: Johns Hopkins University Press, 1990.

Rydell, Robert W. *All the World's a Fair: Visions of Empire at American International Expositions, 1876–1916*. Chicago: University of Chicago Press, 1984.

Saltvig, Robert D. "The Progressive Movement in Washington." Ph.D. diss., University of Washington, 1966.

Salyer, Lucy E. *Laws Harsh as Tigers: Chinese Immigrants and the Shaping of Modern Immigration Law*. Chapel Hill: University of North Carolina Press, 1995.

Sandmeyer, Elmer Clarence. *The Anti-Chinese Movement in California*. 1939. Reprint, Urbana: University of Illinois Press, 1991.

Saxton, Alexander. *The Indispensable Enemy: Labor and the Anti-Chinese Movement in California*. Berkeley: University of California Press, 1971.

Saxton, Alexander. *The Rise and Fall of the White Republic: Class Politics and Mass Culture in Nineteenth-Century America*. London: Verso, 1990.

Saxton, Alexander. "San Francisco Labor and the Populist and Progressive Insurgencies." *Pacific Historical Review* 34 (Nov. 1965), 421–438.

Schaffer, Ronald. "The Montana Woman Suffrage Campaign, 1911–1914." *Pacific Northwest Quarterly* 55 (Jan. 1964), 9–15.

Schaffer, Ronald. "The Problem of Consciousness in the Woman Suffrage Movement: A California Perspective." *Pacific Historical Review* 45 (Nov. 1976), 469–493.

Scharnhorst, Gary. *Charlotte Perkins Gilman: A Bibliography*. Metuchen, NJ: Scarecrow Press, 1985.

Scharnhorst, Gary. "Making Her Fame: Charlotte Perkins Gilman in California." *Califonria History* 64 (Summer 1985), 192–201.

Schofield, Ann. "Rebel Girls and Union Maids: The Woman Question in the Journals of the AFL and IWW, 1905–1920." *Feminist Studies* 9 (Summer 1983), 335–358.

Schuele, Donna. "'A Robbery to the Wife': Culture, Gender and Marital Property in California Law and Politics, 1850–1890." Ph.D. diss., University of California, Berkeley, 1999.

Schuele, Donna C. "Community Property Law and the Politics of Married Women's Rights in California." *Western Legal History* 7:2 (Summer 1994), 245–281.

Schwantes, Carlos. *Radical Heritage: Labor, Socialism and Reform in Washington and British Columbia, 1885–1917*. Seattle: University of Washington Press, 1979.

Schwantes, Carlos A. "Protest in a Promised Land: Unemployment, Disinheritance, and the Origin of Labor Militancy in the Pacific Northwest, 1885–1886." *Western Historical Quarterly* 13 (1982), 373–390.

Shaffer, Ralph E. "Letters from the People: The *Los Angeles Times* Letters Column, 1881–1889," 1999. http://www.intranet.csupomona.edu/~reshaffer/womenx.htm.

Shaffer, Ralph Edward. "Radicalism in California, 1869–1929." Ph.D. diss., University of California, Berkeley, 1962.

Shammas, Carole. "Re-assessing the Married Women's Property Acts." *Journal of Women's History* 6 (Spring 1994), 9–30.

Sheeran, Marte Jo. "The Woman Suffrage Issue in Washington, 1890–1910." Master's thesis, University of Washington, 1977.

Shinn, Milicent W. "Women on School Boards." *Overland Monthly* 12 (Nov. 1888), 547–554.

Shklar, Judith N. *American Citizenship: The Quest for Inclusion.* Cambridge, MA: Harvard University Press, 1991.

Shover, John L. "The Progressives and the Working-Class Vote in California." *Labor History* 10 (1969), 584–601.

Shover, Michele. "Chico Women: Nemesis of a Rural Town's Anti-Chinese Campaigns, 1876–1888." *California History* 67 (Dec. 1988), 228–243, 289–291fn.

Shover, Michele. "Fighting Back: The Chinese Influence on Chico Law and Politics, 1880–1886." *California History* 74 (Winter 1995–96), 409–421, 449–450fn.

Siegel, Reva B. "The Modernization of Martial Status Law: Adjudicating Wives' Rights to Earnings, 1860–1930." *Georgetown Law Journal* 82 (Sept. 1994), 2127–2211.

Silver, Mae, and Sue Cazaly. *The Sixth Star: Images and Memorabilia of California Women's Political History, 1868–1915.* San Francisco: Ord Street Press, 2000.

Simons, Grace. "The Actual Operation of Woman Suffrage in California." *Woman's Bulletin* 1 (June 1913), 33–36.

Simpson, Anna Pratt. *Problems Women Solved: Being the Story of the Woman's Board of the Panama-Pacific International Exposition.* San Francisco: The Woman's Board, 1915.

Sklar, Kathryn Kish. *Florence Kelley and the Nation's Work: The Rise of Women's Political Culture, 1830–1900.* New Haven and London: Yale University Press, 1995.

Skocpol, Theda. *Protecting Soldiers and Mothers: The Political Origins of Social Policy in the United States.* Cambridge, MA: Belknap Press of Harvard University Press, 1992.

Smith, Ann Warren. "Anne Martin and a History of Woman Suffrage in Nevada, 1869–1914." Ph.D. diss., University of Nevada, Reno, 1975.

Smith, Norma. *Jeannette Rankin: America's Conscience.* Helena: Montana Historical Society Press, 2002.

Snapp, Meredith A. "Defeat the Democrats: Union for Woman Suffrage in Arizona, 1914–1916." *Journal of the West* 14 (Oct. 1975), 131–159.

Sneider, Allison. "Reconstruction, Expansion, and Empire: The U.S. Woman Suffrage Movement and the Re-Making of National Political Community, 1870–1900." Ph.D. diss., University of California, Los Angeles, 1999.

Sneider, Allison. "Woman Suffrage in Congress: American Expansion and the Politics of Federalism, 1870–1890." In Jean H. Baker, ed., *Votes for Women: The Struggle for Suffrage Revisited,* 77–89. Oxford and New York: Oxford University Press, 2002.

Solomon, Martha M., ed. *A Voice of Their Own: The Woman Suffrage Press, 1840–1910.* Tuscaloosa: University of Alabama Press, 1991.

Solomons, Selina. *How We Won the Vote in California: A True Story of the Campaign of 1911.* San Francisco: New Woman Publishing, [1912].

Spencer, Dorcas. *A History of the Woman's WCTU of Northern and Central California.* Oakland: West Coast Printing, 1912.

Spruill, Marjorie Julian. "Race, Reform, and Reaction at the Turn of the Century. Southern Suffragists, the NAWSA, and the 'Southern Strategy' in Context." In Baker, ed., *Votes for Women,* 102–117.

Stanley, Amy Dru. "Conjugal Bonds and Wage Labor: Rights of Contract in the Age of Emancipation." *Journal of American History* 75 (Sept. 1988), 471–500.

Stansell, Christine. *City of Women: Sex and Class in New York, 1789–1860.* Urbana: University of Illinois Press, 1982.

Stanton, Elizabeth Cady, Susan B. Anthony, Matilda Josyln Gage, and Ida Husted Harper, eds. *The History of Woman Suffrage.* 6 vols. Reprint ed., Salem, NH: Ayer, 1985.

Stefanco, Carolyn. "Networking on the Frontier: The Colorado Women's Suffrage Movement, 1876–1893." In Susan Armitage and Elizabeth Jameson, eds., *The Women's West,* 265–276. Norman and London: University of Oklahoma Press, 1987.

Stefanco, Carolyn J. "Harvest of Discontent: The Depression of 1893 and the Women's Vote." *Colorado Heritage* (Spring 1993), 16–21.

Stefanco, Carolyn J. "Pathways to Power: Women and Voluntary Associations in Denver, Colorado, 1876–1893." Ph.D. diss., Duke University, 1987.

Stepan, Nancy Leys. "Race, Gender, Science and Citizenship." *Gender and History* 10 (April 1998), 26–52.

Stern, Madeline, et al. *Georgiana: Feminist Reformer of the West.* Santa Cruz, CA: Santa Cruz Historical Trust, 1987.

Steunenberg, Frank. "Woman Suffrage in Idaho." *Harper's Bazaar* 33 (26 May 1900), 220–221.

Stevens, Doris. *Jailed for Freedom.* New York: Boni and Liveright, 1920.

Stimson, Grace Heilman. *Rise of the Labor Movement in Los Angeles.* Berkeley: University of California Press, 1955.

Stocking, George. *Victorian Anthropology.* New York: Free Press, 1987.

Strauss, Sylvia. "Gender, Class, and Race in Utopia." In Daphne Patai, ed., *Looking Backward, 1988–1888: Essays on Edward Bellamy,* 68–90. Amherst: University of Massachusetts Press, 1988.

Strom, Sharon Hartman. "Leadership and Tactics in the American Woman Suffrage Movement: A New Perspective from Massachusetts." *Journal of American History* 62:2 (Sept. 1975), 296–315.

Strom, Sharon Hartman. *Politcal Woman: Florence Luscomb and the Legacy of Radical Reform.* Philadelphia: Temple University Press, 2001.

Suggs, George G., Jr. "Catalyst for Industrial Change: The WFM, 1893–1903." *Colorado Magazine* 45 (Fall 1968), 322–339.

Sumner (Woodbury), Helen L. *Equal Suffrage: The Results of an Investigation in Colorado Made for the Collegiate Equal Suffrage League of New York State.* 1909. Reprint, New York: Arno Press, 1972.

Swift, Carolyn, and Judith Steen, eds. *Georgiana: Feminist Reformer of the West.* Santa Cruz, CA: Santa Cruz County Historical Trust, 1987.

Taber, Richard W. "Sacajawea and the Suffragettes." *Pacific Northwest Quarterly* 58 (Jan. 1967), 7–13.

Taft, Philip. *Labor Politics American Style: The California Federation of Labor.* Cambridge, MA: Harvard University Press, 1968.

Taggart, Harold F. "California and the Silver Question in 1895." *Pacific Historical Review* 6:3 (Sept. 1937), 249–269.

Tax, Meredith. *The Rising of the Women: Feminist Solidarity and Class Conflict, 1880–1917.* New York: Monthly Review Press, 1980.

Taylor, Quintard. *In Search of the Racial Frontier: African Americans in the American West, 1528–1990.* New York: W. W. Norton, 1998.

Tentler, Leslie Woodcock. *Wage-Earning Women: Industrial Work and Family Life in the United States, 1900–1930.* New York: Oxford University Press, 1979.

Terborg-Penn, Rosalyn. *African American Women in the Struggle for the Vote, 1850–1920.* Bloomington: Indiana University Press, 1998.

Terborg-Penn, Rosalyn. "Naomi Bowman Talbert Anderson." In Darlene Clark Hine et al., eds., *Black Women in America: An Historical Encyclopedia,* 33–34. Brooklyn: Carlson, 1993.

Terborg-Penn, Rosalyn M. "Afro-Americans in the Struggle for Woman Suffrage." Ph.D. diss., Howard University, 1977.

Thurner, Manuela. "'Better Citizens without the Ballot': American Anti-Suffrage Women and Their Rationale during the Progressive Era." *Journal of Women's History* 5:1 (Spring 1993), 33–60.

Tilly, Louise A., and Patricia Gurin, eds. *Women, Politics and Change.* New York: Russell Sage Foundation, 1990.

Towne, Marian K. "Charlotte Gilman in California." *Pacific Historian* 28 (Spring 1984), 5–17.

Turner, Frederick Jackson. *The Frontier in American History.* New York: Holt, Rinehart, and Winston, 1920.

Turner, Frederick Jackson. "The Significance of the Frontier in American Historiography." In Turner, *Rereading Frederick Jackson Turner: "The Significance of the Frontier in American History" and Other Essays,* 225–241. New York: H. Holt, 1994.

Turner, James. "Understanding the Populists." *Journal of American History* 67 (Sept. 1980), 354–373.

Tygiel, Jules. "'Where Unionism Holds Undisputed Sway'—A Reappraisal of San Francisco's Union Labor Party." *California History* 62 (Fall 1983), 196–215.

Tygiel, Jules. "Workingmen in San Francisco, 1880–1901." Ph.D. diss., University of California, Los Angeles, 1977.

Van den Berghe, Pierre. *The Ethnic Phenomenon.* New York: Elsevier Science, 1981.

Van den Berghe, Pierre. *Race and Ethnicity.* New York: Basic Books, 1970.

Van Nuys, Frank. "Rose Bower: The Bugler Suffragist." *South Dakota Magazine* 8:5 (Jan–Feb. 1993), 26–31.

Van Voris, Jacqueline. *Carrie Chapman Catt: A Public Life.* New York: Feminist Press of the City University of New York, 1987.

Vigil, Maurilio E. "The Political Development of New Mexico's Hispanas." *Latin Studies Journal* 7:2 (Spring 1996), 3–29.

Wagner, Maryjo. "Farms, Families, and Reform: Women in the Farmers' Alliance and Populist Party." Ph.D. diss., University of Oregon, 1986.

Waite, Davis H., and Lorenzo Crounse. "Woman Suffrage in Practice." *North American Review* 158 (June 1894), 737–744.

Wall, Wendy. "Gender and the 'Citizen Indian.'" In Elizabeth Jameson and Susan Armitage, eds., *Writing the Range: Race, Class, and Culture in the Women's West,* 202–229. Norman: University of Oklahoma Press, 1997.

Walters, Donald Edgar. "Populism in California, 1889–1900." Ph.D. diss., University of California, Berkeley, 1952.

Ward, Doris Buck. "The Winning of Woman Suffrage in Montana." Master's thesis, Montana State University, 1974.

Watkins, Marilyn P. "Political Activism and Community-Building among Alliance and Grange Women in Western Washington, 1892–1925." *Agricultural History* 67:2 (Spring 1993), 197–213.

Watkins, Marilyn P. *Rural Democracy: Family Farmers and Politics in Western Washington, 1890–1925.* Ithaca, NY: Cornell University Press, 1995.

Weinbaum, Alys Eve. Writing Feminist Genealogy: Charlotte Perkins Gilman,

Racial Nationalism, and the Reproduction of Maternalist Feminism." *Feminist Studies* 27:2 (Summer 2001), 271–302.

Wertheimer, Barbara Mayer. *We Were There: The Story of Working Women in America.* New York: Pantheon Books, 1977.

West Coast Magazine. "Six Months of Woman Suffrage in California." *Symposium* 12 (July 1912), 419–435.

Wheeler, Marjorie Spruill. *New Women of the New South: The Leaders of the Woman Suffrage Movement in the Southern States.* New York: Oxford University Press, 1993.

Wheeler, Marjorie Spruill, ed., *One Woman, One Vote: Rediscovering the Woman Suffrage Movement.* Troutdale, OR: New Sage Press, 1995.

White, Jean B. "Woman's Place Is in the Constitution: The Struggle for Equal Rights in Utah in 1895." In Madsen, ed., *Battle for the Ballot,* 221–243.

Whitney, C. A. "The Alameda County Jail." *Survey* 43:13 (25 Dec. 1920), 452–453.

Wiebe, Robert. *The Search for Order.* New York: Hill and Wang, 1967.

Wilentz, Sean. *Chants Democratic: New York City and the Rise of the American Working Class, 1788–1850.* New York: Oxford University Press, 1984.

Willard, Frances E., and Mary A. Livermore, eds. *A Woman of the Century: Fourteen Hundred-Seventy Biographical Sketches Accompanied by Portraits of Leading American Women in All Walks of Life.* Buffalo, NY: Charles Wells Moulton, 1893.

Williams, Mattie L. "History of Woman Suffrage in Arizona and the Nation." *Arizona Historical Review* 1 (Jan. 1929), 69–73.

Williams, R. Hal. *The Democratic Party and California Politics, 1880–1896.* Stanford, CA: Stanford University Press, 1973.

Williams, R. Hal. *Years of Decision.* New York: John Wiley and Sons, 1978.

Willis, E. B., and P. K. Stockton. *Debates and Proceedings of the Constitutional Convention of the State of California [1878].* Sacramento, 1880.

Wood, Mary I. *History of the General Federation of Women's Clubs for the First Twenty-two Years of Its Organization.* Reprint, Farmingdale, NY: Dabor Social Science Publishers.

Wright, Harriet G. R. "Colorado Women in Politics." *Woman Voter* (Jan. 1913), 11–12. Symposium issue.

Wright, James Edward. *The Politics of Populism: Dissent in Colorado.* New Haven and London: Yale University Press, 1974.

Wright, James R., Jr. "The Assiduous Wedge: Woman Suffrage and the Oklahoma Constitutional Convention." *Chronicles of Oklahoma* 51:4 (Winter 1973–1974), 421–443.

Yamane, Nan. "Women, Power, and the Press: The Case of San Francisco, 1868 to 1896." Ph.D. diss., University of California, Los Angeles, 1995.

Yasutake, Rumi. "Transnational Women's Activism: The Woman's Christian

Temperance Movement in Japan and Beyond, 1858–1920." Ph.D. diss., University of California, Los Angeles, 1998.

Yellin, Jean Fagan. "DuBois' *Crisis* and Woman's Suffrage." *The Massachusetts Review* 14:2 (Spring 1973), 365–375.

Younger, Maud. "Taking Orders." *Sunset Magazine* (Oct. 1908), 518–522.

Yung, Judy. *Unbound Feet: A Social History of Chinese Women in San Francisco.* Berkeley: University of California Press, 1995.

Zanjani, Sally Springmeyer. "A Theory of Critical Realignment: The Nevada Example, 1892–1908." *Pacific Historical Review* 48:2 (May 1979), 259–280.

Index

About the Author

Rebecca J. Mead is Assistant Professor of History at Northern Michigan University.